*ADDRESSING RACIAL DISPROPORTIONALITY
AND DISPARITIES IN HUMAN SERVICES*

Addressing Racial Disproportionality and Disparities in Human Services

MULTISYSTEMIC APPROACHES

Edited by Rowena Fong, Alan Dettlaff, Joyce James, and Carolyne Rodriguez

 COLUMBIA UNIVERSITY PRESS   NEW YORK

COLUMBIA UNIVERSITY PRESS
Publishers Since 1893
New York   Chichester, West Sussex

cup.columbia.edu

Library of Congress Cataloging-in-Publication Data
Addressing racial disproportionality and disparities in human services :
multisystemic approaches / edited by Rowena Fong, Alan Dettlaff, Joyce James,
and Carolyne Rodriguez.
     pages   cm
  ISBN 978-0-231-16080-3 (cloth) — ISBN 978-0-231-16081-0 (pbk.) — ISBN
978-0-231-53707-0 (ebook)
   1. United States—Race relations—History. 2. Minorities—United States—History.
I. Fong, Rowena, editor of compilation.
  E184.A1R32297 2014
  362.7089'00973—dc23

2014011304

Cover design: James Perales
Cover image: © Getty

TO VULNERABLE CHILDREN, FAMILIES,
AND COMMUNITIES WHO HAVE EXPERIENCED
DISPROPORTIONALITY AND DISPARITIES.

CONTENTS

▶ *TERRY L. CROSS*

RACE, CULTURE, ETHNICITY, CLASS, NATIONALITY, faith, gender, sexual orientation, and generation are each in their own way complex classifications of people among which we as human beings play out the dynamics of difference, power, and privilege. These are the arenas in which we, as individuals, act out a range of behaviors—from unintentional bias to genocide. We are not individuals in isolation, however, but rather beings in relationship with each other. Systems are, in reality, people in relationship to one another. If our individual dynamics regarding how we relate to difference are complex, then the systems we create reflect the same complexity.

One basic human dilemma is how to be with one another in an increasingly diverse world. Even those of us who value diversity and strive for social justice and equity must grapple with the reality that awareness of our unintentional biases, along with learned strategies to mitigate the negative impacts of our most basic human tendencies with regard to those who are different, may be the best we can hope for. Nowhere is this a more poignant reality than in social work, where our primary tool is relationship and where we see the consequences of bias playing out before us in the form of poverty, discrimination, social inequities, disparities, and disproportionality. All of which are, at least in part, reflections of the inadequacies of our field's strategies to change them. Something much larger is at play here.

If we as individuals are inherently wired to react to difference with an "us versus them" self-preserving response, it is no wonder that the dynamics that are meant to protect "us" are the very dynamics that threaten to cripple the larger society. Like the human immune system that attacks that which it perceives as different to defend the body, the responses intended to protect us as members of social groups can, as in the case of arthritis, do painful and lasting damage. Played out on the human services stage, this phenomenon contributes to systems that risk perpetuating inequity, trauma, and injustice rather than mitigating them. If we are to change this, we must act on it as certainly and as powerfully as it acts on us in ways that frustrate our aspirations for a better world.

Fong, Dettlaff, James, and Rodriguez's new book faces these issues head-on with a challenging inquiry about systems and their role in achieving greater capacity in social work to work effectively in the context of diversity and, with intention and action, change the way that we address the most pressing social work issues of our time. This book is an opportunity for the reader to get into the balcony, to get a different perspective on the field and its challenges in diversity, and to think about our role in the systems through which we practice our craft. In 50 years, when the field looks back on today's practices, will it view disproportionality in the same way that we today view the boarding school era, orphanages, and institutionalization? This work will help the reader examine that question sooner rather than later.

A GROWING PROBLEM AND A national concern, disproportionality is the overrepresentation of an ethnic population in a system of care, referring to the "racial difference of children in a service population when compared to their representation in a general population" (Wells, 2011, p. 4). For example, the number of African American children in the public child welfare system has been of concern for four decades, with research raising concerns about racial bias (Dettlaff et al., 2011; James, Green, Rodriguez, & Fong, 2011), disparate treatment (Billingsley & Giovanni, 1972), and racial inequities in systems (Gatowski & Dobbin, 2011). However, the concerns do not limit themselves to the African American community. Latino, Native American, Asian American, and Pacific Islander populations also experience social injustices, a situation that raises concerns related to safety and well-being (Cross, 2011; Dettlaff, 2011; Godinet, Arnsberger, Li, & Kreif, 2011). Other systems besides child welfare have been identified as needing to reduce racial disproportionality and disparities in their assessment practices and intervention planning and in implementation when offering services to children and families of color. To achieve this, more information is needed about the problems facing children and families of color when they interact with the child welfare system, juvenile justice system, mental health system, the schools, and health care systems. This textbook, *Addressing Racial Disproportionality and Disparities in Human Services: Multisystemic Approaches,* fills this gap and gives students, educators, policymakers, practitioners, and administrators new knowledge in providing culturally competent services that address disproportionality and disparities affecting children and families of color.

IMPORTANCE AND SIGNIFICANCE

There has been sufficient concern about disproportionality and disparities as they are manifested in other systems besides child welfare (Bullard, 2011; Gatowski & Dobbin, 2011) that the literature should include more books that focus on the courts, schools, counseling centers, and hospitals serving children and families of color. This book will address disproportionality as it relates to all four ethnic groups in each of these systems (child welfare, juvenile courts, schools, mental health, and health care).

CONTENTS AND ORGANIZATION

Addressing Racial Disproportionality and Disparities in Human Services: Multisystemic Approaches is divided into four parts, totaling 13 chapters. Part One has two chapters: Chapter 1 is an introduction to the book offering definitions, ethnic population issues, cross-systems challenges, and a systems theoretical framework. Chapter 2 addresses cross-systems approaches to racial disproportionality and disparities in the child welfare system, and in the juvenile justice, educational, mental health, and health-care systems.

Part Two has four chapters, which discuss the individual and family issues of the four major ethnic populations: African American children and families (Chapter 3), Latino children and families (Chapter 4), Asian American and Pacific Islander children and families (Chapter 5), and American Indian/Alaska Native children and families (Chapter 6).

Part Three has five chapters describing disproportionality and disparities as they are manifested in systems: child welfare (Chapter 7), juvenile justice and the courts (Chapter 8), education (Chapter 9), mental health (Chapter 10), and health care (Chapter 11).

Part Four includes the final two chapters, which present a case study based on efforts to eliminate disproportionality and disparities across systems in Texas (Chapter 12) and concludes with future directions for eliminating racial disproportionality and disparities (Chapter 13).

REFERENCES

Billingsley, A., & Giovanni, J. (1972). *Children of the storm: Black children and American child welfare.* New York: Harcourt Brace Jovanovich.

Bullard, L. (2011). Mitigating racial disproportionality in residential care. In D. Green, K. Belanger, R. McRoy, & L. Bullard (Eds.), *Challenging racial disproportionality in child welfare: Research, policy, and practice* (pp. 211–218). Washington, DC: CWLA Press.

Cross, T. (2011). Disproportionality in child welfare: An American Indian perspective. In D. Green, K. Belanger, R. McRoy, & L. Bullard (Eds.), *Challenging racial disproportionality in child welfare: Research, policy, and practice* (pp. 111–118). Washington, DC: CWLA Press.

Dettlaff, A. J. (2011). Disproportionality of Latino children in child welfare. In D. Green, K. Belanger, R. McRoy, & L. Bullard (Eds.), *Challenging racial disproportionality in child welfare: Research, policy, and practice* (pp. 119–129). Washington, DC: CWLA Press.

Dettlaff, A. J., Rivaux, S. R., Baumann, D. J., Fluke, J. D., Rycraft, J. R., & James, J. (2011). Disentangling substantiation: The influence of race, income, and risk on the substantiation decision in child welfare. *Children and Youth Services Review, 33*, 1630–1637.

Gatowski, S. I, & Dobbin, S. A. (2011). National judicial initiatives to reduce racial disproportionality and disparities in the dependency court system. In D. Green, K. Belanger, R. McRoy, & L. Bullard (Eds.), *Challenging racial disproportionality in child welfare: Research, policy, and practice* (pp. 319–326). Washington, DC: CWLA Press.

Godinet, M. T., Arnsberger, P., Li, F., & Kreif, T. (2010). Disproportionality, Ohana conferencing, and the Hawai'i child welfare system. *Journal of Public Child Welfare, 4*, 387–405.

James, J., Green, D. K., Rodriguez, C., & Fong, R. (2011). Innovations in Texas: Undoing racism, developing leaders, and engaging communities. In D. Green, K, Belanger, R., McRoy, & L. Bullard (Eds.), *Challenging racial disproportionality in child welfare: Research, policy, and practice* (pp. 285–296). Washington, DC: CWLA Press.

Wells, S. (2011). Disproportionality and disparities of outcomes in child welfare: An overview of definitions and methods of measurement. In D. Green, K. Belanger, R. McRoy, & L. Bullard (Eds.), *Challenging racial disproportionality in child welfare: Research, policy, and practice* (pp. 3–12). Washington, DC: CWLA Press.

*ADDRESSING RACIAL DISPROPORTIONALITY
AND DISPARITIES IN HUMAN SERVICES*

PART **1**

Introduction

1

Introduction to Racial Disproportionality and Disparities

▸ *ROWENA FONG, ALAN DETTLAFF,*
AND TIANCA CROCKER

INTRODUCTION TO RACIAL DISPROPORTIONALITY AND DISPARITIES

RACIAL DISPROPORTIONALITY AND DISPARITIES ARE a growing concern as the population of ethnic minorities increases in the United States. As of 2010, the U.S. Census Bureau reported that Latinos represented the largest and fastest growing minority group, with 50.5 million people representing 16.3% of the U.S. population. Between 2000 and 2010, the Latino population grew by 43%, increasing from 35.3 million in 2000 (Humes, Jones, & Ramirez, 2011). African Americans, with 39 million people, represented the second largest minority group in the United States, at 12.6% of the total U.S. population (Humes et al., 2011). In contrast, African Americans represent 26% of juvenile arrests, 44% of youth detained, 46% of youth judicially waived to criminal court, and 58% of youth admitted to state prisons (National Association for the Advancement of Colored People, 2012). Within the public child welfare system, African American children represented 24.1% of new entries into foster care in 2010 and 28.8% of all children in foster care (Summers, Wood, & Russell, 2012).

Although African American youth are disproportionately overrepresented in the juvenile justice and child welfare systems (McRoy, 2012; Models for Change, 2011), they and Latino youth are also overrepresented among those receiving disciplinary actions in public schools in the educational system, including suspensions and expulsions (U.S. Department of Education, 2012). Disproportionality and disparities challenge Asian/Pacific Islander and American Indian/Alaska Native populations as well. With the mandate to provide culturally relevant services, the child welfare, juvenile justice, education, health, and mental health systems each face the burden of examining the overrepresentation of ethnic minority children and families in their processes of service delivery. This chapter will begin by defining disproportionality and disparities and then begin to examine how they manifest across systems, a theme that will be expanded upon in later chapters. The chapter will then present a theoretical framework for examining disproportionality and disparities across systems in order to further an understanding of how and why disproportionality and disparities exist and to begin a dialogue on how they can be addressed using a cross-systems perspective.

DEFINING DISPROPORTIONALITY AND DISPARITIES

The terms used to describe disproportionality and disparities vary across systems, yet they describe similar phenomena. However, the meaning of these terms has evolved over time, and it is only recently that a common understanding of these terms has reached consensus. For example, within the child welfare system, the terms disproportionality and disparities have held numerous definitions in the literature devoted to this topic over the past two decades. The concept of disproportionality in child welfare initially grew from efforts in the juvenile justice system and arose from a growing recognition that children of different races were represented in the child welfare system at different rates (Derezotes & Poertner, 2005). The initial identification and use of the term disproportionality was intended to document this phenomenon and to acknowledge the need to better understand why it was occurring (Derezotes & Poertner, 2005). However, as the use of the terms disproportionality and disparities evolved over time, the words have taken on connotations that denote a problem resulting from either racial bias or from differential treatment of children of color. Understanding these terms and what they mean for health and other service systems is an important component in developing an appropriate response for addressing them.

Disproportionality

The term disproportionality refers to the state of being out of proportion. It describes a condition that exists when the proportion of people of a certain race or ethnicity in a target population differs from the proportion of people of the same group in a reference population. For example, in the context of the child welfare system, disproportionality is most commonly used to describe a condition when the proportion of one group in the child welfare population (i.e., children in foster care) is either proportionately larger (overrepresented) or smaller (underrepresented) than the proportion of the same group in the general child population. This phenomenon has most significantly affected African American children, with data from 2010 indicating that African American children represented 29% of children in foster care, although they represented only 14.5% of children in the general population (U.S. Census Bureau, 2012; U.S. Department of Health and Human Services, 2011). In and of itself, overrepresentation in the child welfare system may not be indicative of a problem because representation in this system should be based on need. This can be true for any system that provides services based on need within the population. However, when disproportionality results from racial biases or stereotypes that negatively impact ethnic minority populations, there is clearly a need to understand and address this issue to avoid the harmful effects that may result from this overrepresentation.

Disparity

Although disproportionality refers to the state of being out of proportion, disparity refers to a state of being unequal. Within systems, disparity is typically used to describe unequal outcomes experienced by one racial or ethnic group when compared to *another* racial or ethnic group (in contrast, disproportionality compares the proportion of one racial/ethnic group in the child welfare system to the *same* racial/ethnic group in the population). Continuing with the example of the child welfare system, disparities can occur at every decision-making point in this system, including the initial report that brings children to the attention of the system, acceptance of reports for investigation, substantiation of maltreatment, entries into substitute care, and exits from substitute care. For example, if the rate of African American children being reported to the child welfare system in a state differed considerably when compared to the rate of White children being reported to the same system, this would denote a disparity. Ultimately, disparities that occur in entries to and exits from the system produce disproportionality. Thus, understanding where disparities exist and why they are occurring is essential to understanding disproportionality. However, similar to disproportionality, the presence of a disparity at a given decision-making point is not an indicator of bias or of disparate treatment in the absence of data that identifies the explanatory factors contributing to the disparity. Efforts to understand these explanatory factors have received considerable attention over the past two decades.

A number of studies have identified disparities at various decision-making points along the child welfare service delivery pathway. These include the initial report of alleged maltreatment (Fluke, Yuan, Hedderson, & Curtis, 2003; Lu et al., 2004), acceptance for investigation (Gryzlak, Wells, & Johnson, 2005; Zuravin, Orme, & Hegar, 1995), substantiation of alleged maltreatment (Ards, Myers, Malkis, Sugrue, & Zhou, 2003; Rolock & Testa, 2005), placement into out-of-home care (Rivaux et al., 2008; Wulczyn & Lery, 2007), and exits from care (Hill, 2005; Lu et al., 2004). Several studies have examined factors that may explain these disparities, and findings have been mixed regarding the role of race. Some studies have found that race is a significant factor at various decision-making points (e.g., Hill, 2005; Lu et al., 2004; Rivaux et al., 2008), while others have found no significant effect for race when controlling for other factors (e.g., Goerge & Lee, 2005; Harris, Tittle, & Poertner, 2005). Still others have found that it is a combination of race with other factors that results in observed disparities (e.g., type of abuse by race—Gryzlak, Wells, & Johnson, 2005; severity of injury by race—Sedlak & Schultz, 2005; family structure by race—Harris & Courtney, 2003).

Although the existence of racial disproportionality and disparities in the child welfare system has been well-established, of concern to the field are the explanatory factors that underlie them because these are the issues that must be understood in order to develop appropriate responses as well as to shape policy. In addition to the child welfare system, relevant discussions have occurred in the juvenile justice, education, mental health, and health systems about the definitions and existence of disproportionality and disparities among ethnic minority populations. Yet although the identification of the explanatory factors that underlie disproportionality and disparities is an essential step in addressing those phenomena, it is a complex undertaking due to the multiple and intersecting factors that are likely contributors.

At issue within most systems when attempting to identify the factors that contribute to disproportionality and disparities is whether observed levels of overrepresentation result from racial biases within those systems or from differing levels of need among children and families of color. Continuing with the example of the child welfare system, much of the research over the past two decades that has identified the existence of disproportionality and disparities has consistently cited racial bias as a primary cause. This conclusion was based on findings from the federally funded National Incidence Studies of Child Abuse and Neglect (NIS) conducted in 1980 (NIS–1), 1986 (NIS–2), and 1993 (NIS–3), which had consistently shown no significant differences in the actual incidence of maltreatment across children of different racial groups (Sedlak, 1991; Sedlak & Broadhurst, 1996; Sedlak & Schultz, 2005). This led to many researchers concluding that in the absence of differences in the incidence of maltreatment, any observed overrepresentation among children of color must be the result of some form of bias within the system.

Yet this prevailing view was called into question upon publication of a paper by Elizabeth Bartholet (2009) entitled, *The Racial Disproportionality Movement in Child Welfare: False Facts and Dangerous Directions.* In her paper, Bartholet contended that the observed differences in the representation of African American children in the child welfare system occur because African American children are in fact maltreated at higher rates than children of other races and thus should be placed into foster care at higher rates than other children. She contended that higher rates of maltreatment in African American families are to be expected because African American children are more likely to be exposed to many of the risk factors associated with maltreatment, including poverty, substance abuse, and single parenting.

These claims were initially met with resistance because of the findings of the prior National Incidence Studies. However, in 2010, just a few months after the publication of Bartholet's paper, the latest version of the NIS (NIS–4) was released, which found for the first time that rates of maltreatment for African American children were significantly higher than those for White or Hispanic children (Sedlak et al., 2010). In supplemental analyses of these race differences, the authors concluded that these observed differences were the result of greater precision of the NIS–4 estimates as well as an increased disparity in income between African American and White families since the NIS–3 (Sedlak, McPherson, & Das, 2010). These findings and the subsequent discussions that arose regarding their implications have led many child welfare systems to reevaluate their efforts to address disproportionality, particularly those efforts that focused solely on reducing bias within child welfare systems. Today most researchers and policymakers acknowledge that disproportionality and disparities are complex phenomena that are likely caused by multiple factors and each warrant attention and consideration by child welfare systems. Although current evidence indicates that poverty and associated risk factors are significant contributors to the disproportionality and disparities that exist in child welfare, other studies have continued to find evidence of racial bias even after controlling for poverty and risk (e.g., Dettlaff et al., 2011; Rivaux et al., 2008). Thus, rather than debating which factors contribute *most* to disproportionality and disparities, a more useful response would be to acknowledge the contribution of each and to support the continued exploration and understanding of these phenomena. This is true not only in child welfare but also in other health and social service systems.

The Impact of Disproportionality and Disparities

Although there remains some debate concerning how and why disproportionality and disparities exist in certain systems, the negative effects of disproportionality and disparities to children and families of color are clear. Within the child welfare system, multiple studies have documented that children who are removed from their homes experience not only significant trauma but also are more likely than other children to experience negative outcomes as adults, including low educational attainment, homelessness, poverty, unemployment, unplanned pregnancies, mental health disorders, and involvement in the criminal justice system (Courtney, Dworsky, Lee, & Rapp, 2010; Courtney, Piliavin, Grogan-Kaylor, & Nesmith, 2001; Pecora et al., 2003). For African American families, overrepresentation in the child welfare system not only separates parents from children but also can serve to perpetuate many of the oppressive conditions and negative ste-reotypes that have historically affected African Americans (Roberts, 2002). Similarly, increased involvement with the juvenile justice system by youth of color leads to lasting harmful effects, including diminished educational outcomes due to school interruption, stigma, and social isolation. Research shows that youth with a history of detention are less likely to graduate from high school, are more likely to be unemployed as adults, and are more likely to be arrested and imprisoned as adults (Holman & Zeidenberg, 2006). Within the education system, disproportionate rates of suspensions, expul-sions, and school-based arrests among youth of color lead not only to poor educational outcomes but also to referrals to the juvenile justice system, often referred to as the school to prison pipeline (Christle, Jolivette, & Nelson, 2005). And within health and mental health systems, disparities that limit access to needed services perpetuate poor health and mental health outcomes among youth and families of color. These unmet needs among youth and families of color contribute not only to poor health out-comes but also to risk of involvement in other systems.

Cross-System Concerns

Multiple studies have been devoted to identifying and understanding the factors contributing to disproportionality and disparities in various sys-tems, and these will be discussed in later chapters. Yet by using a systems framework, although there are some system-specific differences, the factors contributing to disproportionality and disparities can be organized into the following schema: (1) individual and family factors, (2) community fac-tors, and (3) agency and systemic factors.

Individual and family factors include those factors within an individual or family system that either increase the likelihood of contact with certain systems (e.g., child welfare, juvenile justice, disciplinary actions in the edu-cation system) or limit access to services from other systems (e.g., health or mental health). For example, in the context of the child welfare system, this is sometimes referred to as *disproportionate need,* an idea that suggests that certain individual or family risk factors place children and youth of color at greater need for intervention from this system. Primary among these risk factors is the disproportionate number of youth and families of color who live in poverty. Census data from 2010 indicate that African

American, Latino, and Native American children are more than twice as likely as White children to be living in poverty (Annie E. Casey Foundation, 2012). Poverty can increase risk of involvement in certain systems as well as limit access to other systems. For example, children in low-income households experience some form of maltreatment at a rate more than five times the rate of other children (Sedlak et al., 2010), which may increase the risk of involvement with the child welfare system. Conversely, children living in poverty are less likely than other children to be covered by health insurance, which may limit their access to health or mental health services (DeNavas-Walt, Proctor, & Smith, 2012).

Community factors include those factors associated with the neighborhood context in which an individual resides. This body of literature focuses primarily on the social and structural characteristics of neighborhoods that are associated with poor health and well-being outcomes. This literature suggests that neighborhoods characterized by structural deficits, primary among these being poverty, increase the likelihood of poor outcomes for youth and families. For example, this research has consistently found that when compared with more affluent areas, neighborhoods with high rates of poverty are more likely to have higher rates of violence, greater unemployment, more visible displays of crime, cultural norms that promote crime, increased access to alcohol and tobacco, and lower quality schools (e.g., Novak, Reardon, Raudenbush, & Buka, 2006; Tobler, Livingston, & Komro, 2011). In turn, residence in these communities is associated with several poor outcomes for youth, including juvenile delinquency, substance abuse, and violent behavior (Molnar, Cerda, Roberts, & Buka, 2008; Tobler et al., 2011). Because ethnic minority youth are more likely than White youth to live in disadvantaged neighborhoods, these factors may increase their risk for involvement in juvenile justice and child welfare systems, increase their risk for disciplinary referrals in educational settings, and may limit their access to needed resources from health and mental health systems.

Agency and systemic factors include those factors within an agency and among agency staff that may contribute to disproportionality and disparities. Although these factors are many and will be elaborated upon in later chapters, they include racial biases in decision making that negatively impact children and youth of color, a lack of culturally appropriate resources for children and youth of color, a lack of culturally competent staff, and a lack of meaningful engagement between health and social service systems and communities of color. Each of these factors are well-documented within health and social service systems and contribute not only to disproportionality and disparities, but also serve to perpetuate the general lack of mistrust between these systems and communities of color. This mistrust acts as a further barrier to needed services, which facilitates the existence of disproportionality and disparities.

As indicated previously, there is a growing consensus that disproportionality and disparities are complex phenomena that likely result from a combination of all of these factors across system levels. Although there remains some debate about the *relative contribution* of each, it is clear that research has identified the presence of each of these factors across health and social service systems. Thus, although greater need may exist for some of the most vulnerable populations of children and youth of color, it is clear that the disproportionality and disparities that exist across systems are unjust, harmful, and need to be addressed by these systems, singularly and collectively. Efforts to address disproportionality and disparities should acknowledge the underlying social conditions that contribute to their existence as well as the agency and systemic problems that perpetuate them.

Cross-System Solutions

Because the factors contributing to disproportionality and disparities share cross-system commonalities, so do many of the strategies designed to address them. These will be elaborated upon in later chapters that address each system, but in this chapter, we will review the main themes across systems that are found in these strategies. These include culturally competent practices, cross-systems collaborations, and community engagement.

Culturally competent practices. Definitions of *cultural competence* vary greatly and have evolved considerably over the years. In early uses of the term, the emphasis tended to focus on knowledge of other cultures, whereas current understanding of the meaning of cultural competence focuses more on an attitude of openness and humility and on honoring and respecting others' values and beliefs. This transition came from a growing recognition that the notion of cultural competence was often misinterpreted to imply that an individual must know everything there is to know about a particular culture to be competent in that culture. This interpretation of cultural competence is largely impractical because it is not possible to be perfectly competent in every culture for which one might be involved, even when an individual is of the same culture (Dettlaff & Fong, 2011). *Cultural appropriateness* is a related term that was intended to steer away from some of these misinterpretations by acknowledging that people may never by fully knowledgeable or sensitive of another culture (or even of their own), but service providers strive to provide services that are culturally appropriate and culturally relevant to each of the diverse populations served by their respective systems. Thus, *culturally competent practices* are those practices designed to most fully integrate aspects of an individual or family's unique culture into all aspects of service provision and are consistent with the communication styles, meanings, and social networks of program participants (Fong, 2004; Fong & Furuto, 2001; Fong, McRoy, & Hendricks, 2006).

Cross-systems collaborations build from the acknowledgment that many children and youth who receive services from one agency or system may also be receiving services from others. Thus, eliminating disproportionality and disparities requires cross-systems reforms that examine and address the factors that contribute to disproportionality across these systems. The chapters that follow will spotlight emerging and evidence-based cross-systems collaborations designed to reduce disproportionality and disparities across systems and to expand the availability of resources to children and youth of color to reduce some of the underlying conditions that contribute to their overrepresentation in these systems.

Community engagement extends from the acknowledgment that service systems can only address disproportionality and disparities through the development of community partnerships that meaningfully involve stakeholders from those communities most significantly affected by disproportionality and disparities (Dettlaff & Fong, 2011; Fong, 2004; Rycraft & Dettlaff, 2009). Community engagement activities acknowledge that health and social service systems must learn from their respective clients in order to provide services that adequately meet their needs and reduce the barriers that exist to accessing these services. Thus, community engagement integrates culturally competent practices and cross-systems collaborations in ways that are intended to facilitate access, reduce barriers to service provision, and to strengthen the cultural appropriateness of service delivery. In doing this, health and social service agencies need to recognize the barriers that exist to community engagement. These include fear, distrust, and a perception of these agencies as harmful within many communities of color. Overcoming these barriers requires a longstanding commitment that begins with efforts to promote a change in those perceptions. The chapters that follow will discuss the various ways in which these systems are participating in community engagement activities, within and across systems.

Disproportionality and Disparities Across Systems

As an example of cross-systems involvement, we can examine outcomes for African American youth that integrate both the factors that contribute to disproportionality and disparities and how they manifest within systems:

- African American children are three times as likely to be poor as White children and are more than three times as likely as White children to live in extreme poverty.
- African American children are seven times as likely as White children to be persistently poor.
- African American babies are more than twice as likely as White babies to be born to a teen mother.
- African American babies are more than twice as likely to die before their first birthday as are White babies.
- African American children are 63% more likely than are White children to be uninsured.
- Less than 40% of African American children live with two parents, compared to 75% of White children.
- African American children are seven times as likely as White children to have a parent in prison.
- African American children are four times as likely as are White children to be in foster care.
- Youth in foster care frequently experience school changes and score lower on standardized tests than their peers.
- African American children are 2.5 times as likely as are White children to be held back or retained in school.
- African American children are more than 1.5 times as likely as are White children to be placed in a class for students with emotional disturbances.
- African American students are 3.5 times as likely to be suspended or expelled from school as are their White peers.

- Youth who are suspended from school are at greater risk of juvenile justice involvement.
- The arrest rate among African American youth is twice the rate of their White peers.
- White youth are twice as likely to be defended by private attorneys as are African American youth.
- African American youth are more than four times as likely as are White youth to be detained in a juvenile correction facility. (Compiled primarily from Children's Defense Fund, 2011, with additional statistics from Casey Family Programs, 2011, and Annie E. Casey Foundation, n.d.)

Although these statistics are most alarming for African American youth, similar patterns exist for other racial and ethnic minorities across service systems. These patterns clearly indicate the overlapping and interlocking relationship among systems because deficits or poor outcomes in one system facilitate poor outcomes in others. Thus, there is a clear need to advance the understanding of not only the ways in which systems intersect to produce disproportionality and disparities but also the ways in which systems can work together to reduce these phenomena. Systems biases need to be examined, and more attention needs to be paid to evidence-based, culturally competent services, within and across systems. Although there is an emerging body of literature on practices designed to reduce disproportionality and disparities within single systems, much less attention has been given to efforts that link multiple systems to facilitate positive outcomes for children and youth of color. Thus, a systems approach that ties the individual and family to the child welfare, juvenile justice, education, mental health, and health systems could facilitate the advanced understanding that is necessary to address the issues related to disproportionality and disparities across these systems.

Theoretical Framework

As laid out in this chapter, the causes of disproportionality and the potential solutions for eliminating disproportionality are embedded within and across the systems in which children and families reside and interact. Systems-related theories, specifically ecological systems theory, provide useful perspectives for understanding how social work researchers and practitioners can pursue positive social change for vulnerable populations and can advance evidence-based practices, policies, and legislative mandates related to disproportionality and disparities. Blending an ecological framework with general systems theory provides social workers with a direct service perspective of the clients' needs as understood within social systems (Zastrow & Kirst-Ashman, 2004), including individuals, families, communities, and organizations. Ecological systems theory gives social workers tools for tapping into stakeholder networks needed to influence their practice and policy processes.

Before systems are changed, a societal impetus must arise that drives the problem identification and subsequent definition. The driving force may stem from a variety of sources, such as a single noteworthy event highlighting a long-standing problem (for example, revisions to child protection laws due to a particular case that draws attention to a systemic gap) or by contractions in the economy that lead to cuts in social service programs. The reflexive nature of the systems change process means that social workers are often some of the first professionals to observe an identified problem in the environment through either social service practice or research. This process of problem identification, definition, and subsequent efforts to promote systems change to address racial disproportionality and disparities using a systems perspective will be examined throughout this text.

The systems framework, in essence, advocates for a holistic consideration of a problem, starting with the needs of the micro or macro subsystem before placing the need within the larger societal context. This approach is often in opposition to the symptomatology and assumed rationality that permeates many of the proposed solutions to societal problems that seek to curb specific behaviors rather than create structural change by shifting societal norms (Stewart & Ayres, 2001).

Thus, with its holistic approach, a systems framework allows social work practitioners, system administrators, and policymakers to better understand the issues of disproportionality and disparities faced by historically underrepresented groups in the child welfare, juvenile justice, educational, mental health, and healthcare systems. The remainder of this text will explore these issues from a systems perspective, integrating the themes of culturally competent practice, cross-systems collaborations, and community engagement throughout. Using the systems perspective, we will examine the individual, family, community, and organizational factors that contribute to disproportionality and disparities as they manifest within and across systems, as well as the strategies within and across systems that can be engaged to address and eliminate them.

REFERENCES

Annie E. Casey Foundation. (n.d.). *Race matters: Unequal opportunities for juvenile justice.* Baltimore, MD: Author. Retrieved from http://www.aecf.org/upload/publicationfiles/fact_sheet12.pdf

Annie E. Casey Foundation. (2012). *Kids count data book: State trends in child well-being.* Baltimore, MD: Author.

Ards, S. D., Myers, S. L., Malkis, A., Sugrue, E., & Zhou, L. (2003). Racial disproportionality in reported and substantiated child abuse and neglect: An examination of systemic bias. *Children and Youth Services Review, 25,* 375–392.

Bartholet, E. (2009). The racial disproportionality movement in child welfare: False facts and dangerous directions. *Arizona Law Review, 51,* 871–932.

Casey Family Programs. (2011). *Education is the lifeline for youth in foster care.* Seattle, WA: Author. Retrieved from http://jimcaseyyouth.org/sites/default/files/documents/nationalWorkingGroup_ResearchHighlights_2.pdf

Children's Defense Fund. (2011). *Portrait of inequality 2011: Black children in America.* Washington, DC: Children's Defense Fund. Retrieved from: http://www.childrensdefense.org/programs-campaigns/black-community-crusade-for-children-II/bccc-assets/portrait-of-inequality.pdf

Christle, C. A., Jolivette, K., & Nelson, C. M. (2005). Breaking the school to prison pipeline: Identifying school risk and protective factors for youth delinquency. *Exceptionality: The Official Journal of the Division for Research of the Council for Exceptional Children, 13*(2), 69–88.

Courtney, M., Piliavin, I., Grogan-Kaylor, A., & Nesmith, A. (2001). Foster care transitions to adulthood: A longitudinal view of youth leaving care. *Child Welfare, 80,* 685–717.

Courtney, M. E., Dworsky, A., Lee, J. S., & Rapp, M. (2010). *Midwest evaluation of the adult functioning of former foster youth: Outcomes at ages 23 and 24.* Chicago, IL: Chapin Hall at the University of Chicago.

DeNavas-Walt, C., Proctor, B. D., & Smith, J. C. (2012). *Income, poverty, and health insurance coverage in the United States: 2011* (U.S. Census Bureau, Current

Population Reports, P60–243). Washington, DC: U.S. Government Printing Office.

Derezotes, D., & Poertner, J. (2005). Factors contributing to the overrepresentation of Black children in the child welfare system. In D. Derezotes et al. (Eds.), *Race matters in child welfare: The overrepresentation of African American children in the system* (pp. 1–23). Washington, DC: CWLA Press.

Dettlaff, A. J., & Fong, R. (2011). Conducting culturally competent evaluations of child welfare programs and practices. *Child Welfare, 90*(2), 49–68.

Dettlaff, A. J., Rivaux, S. R., Baumann, D. J., Fluke, J. D., Rycraft, J. R., & James, J. (2011). Disentangling substantiation: The influence of race, income, and risk on the substantiation decision in child welfare. *Children and Youth Services Review, 33,* 1630–1637.

Fluke, J. D., Yuan, Y. T., Hedderson, J., & Curtis, P. A. (2003). Disproportionate representation of race and ethnicity in child maltreatment: Investigation and victimization. *Children and Youth Services Review, 25,* 359–373.

Fong, R. (Ed.). (2004). *Culturally competent practice with immigrant and refugee children and families.* New York: Guilford Press.

Fong, R., & Furuto, S. (2001). *Culturally competent practices: Skills, interventions, and evaluations.* Boston, MA: Allyn and Bacon.

Fong, R., McRoy, R., & Hendricks, C. (Eds.). (2006). *Intersecting child welfare, substance abuse, and family violence: Culturally competent approaches.* Alexandria, VA: Council on Social Work Education.

Goerge, R. M., & Lee, B. J. (2005). The entry of children from the welfare system into foster care: Differences by race. In D. Derezotes, J. Poertner, & M. Testa (Eds.), *Race matters in child welfare: The overrepresentation of African American children in the system* (pp. 173–185). Washington, DC: CWLA Press.

Gryzlak, B. M., Wells, S. J., & Johnson, M. A. (2005). The role of race in child protective services screening decisions. In D. Derezotes, J. Poertner, & M. Testa (Eds.), *Race matters in child welfare: The overrepresentation of African American children in the system* (pp. 63–96). Washington, DC: CWLA Press.

Harris, G., Tittle, G., & Poertner, J. (2005). Factors that predict the decision to place a child in substitute care. In D. Derezotes, J. Poertner, & M. Testa (Eds.), *Race matters in child welfare: The overrepresentation of African American children in the system* (pp. 163–172). Washington, DC: CWLA Press.

Harris, M. S., & Courtney, M. E. (2003). The interaction of race, ethnicity, and family structure with respect to the timing of family reunification. *Children and Youth Services Review, 25,* 409–429.

Hill, R. B. (2005). The role of race in parental reunification. In D. Derezotes, J. Poertner, & M. Testa (Eds.), *Race matters in child welfare: The overrepresentation of African American children in the system* (pp. 215–230). Washington, DC: CWLA Press.

Holman, B., & Zeidenberg, J. (2006). *The dangers of detention: The impact of incarcerating youth in detention and other secure facilities.* Washington, DC: Justice Policy Institute.

Humes, K. R., Jones, N. A., & Ramirez, R. R. (2011). *Overview of race and Hispanic origin: 2010 census briefs.* Washington, DC: United States Census Bureau.

Lu, Y., Landsverk, J., Ellis-MacLeod, E., Newton, R., Ganger, W., & Johnson, I. (2004). Race, ethnicity, and case outcomes in child protective services. *Children and Youth Services Review, 26,* 447–461.

McRoy, R.G. (2012). Overrepresentation of children and youth of color in foster care. In Mallon, G. P., & Hess, P. M. (Eds.), *Child welfare for the twenty-first century: A handbook of practices, policies, and programs.* New York, NY: Columbia University Press.

Models for Change. (2011). *Knowledge brief: Are minority youths treated differently in juvenile probation?* Retrieved from http://www.modelsforchange.net/publications/314

Molnar, B. E., Cerda, M., Roberts, A. L., & Buka, S. L. (2008). Effects of neighborhood resources on aggressive and delinquent behaviors among urban youths. *American Journal of Public Health, 98,* 1086–1093.

National Association for the Advancement of Colored People. (2012). *Criminal justice fact sheet.* Baltimore, MD: National Association for the Advancement of Colored People. Retrieved from www.naacp.org/pages/criminal-justice-fact-sheet

Novak, S. P., Reardon, S. F., Raudenbush, S. W., & Buka, S. L. (2006). Retail tobacco outlet density and youth cigarette smoking: A propensity-modeling approach. *American Journal of Public Health, 96,* 670–676.

Pecora, P., Williams, J., Kessler, R., Downs, C., O'Brien, K., Hiripi, E., & Morello, S. (2003). *Assessing the effects of foster care: Early results from the Casey National Alumni Study.* Seattle, WA: Casey Family Programs.

Rivaux, S. L., James, J., Wittenstrom, K., Baumann, D., Sheets, J., Henry, J., & Jeffries, V. (2008). The intersection of race, poverty, and risk: Understanding the decision to provide services to clients and to remove children. *Child Welfare, 87,* 151–168.

Roberts, D. (2002). *Shattered bonds: The color of child welfare.* New York, NY: Basic Civitas Books.

Rolock, N., & Testa, M. (2005). Indicated child abuse and neglect reports: Is the investigation process racially biased? In D. Derezotes et al. (Eds.), *Race matters in child welfare: The overrepresentation of African American children in the system* (pp. 119–130). Washington, DC: CWLA Press.

Rycraft, J. R., & Dettlaff, A. J. (2009). Hurdling the artificial fence between child welfare and the community: Engaging community partners to address disproportionality. *Journal of Community Practice, 17,* 464–482.

Sedlak, A. (1991). *National incidence and prevalence of child abuse and neglect 1988: Revised report.* Washington, DC: U.S. Department of Health and Human Services.

Sedlak, A. J., & Broadhurst, D. (1996). *Third national incidence study of child abuse and neglect: Final report.* Washington, DC: U.S. Department of Health and Human Services.

Sedlak, A. J., McPherson, K., & Das, B. (2010). *Supplementary analyses of race differences in child maltreatment rates in the NIS-4.* Washington, DC: U.S. Department of Health and Human Services, Administration for Children and Families.

Sedlak, A. J., Mettenburg, J., Basena, M., Petta, I., McPherson, K., Greene, A., & Li, S. (2010). *Fourth national incidence study of child abuse and neglect (NIS–4): Report to Congress.* Washington, DC: U.S. Department of Health and Human Services, Administration for Children and Families.

Sedlak, A. J., & Schultz, D. (2005). Racial differences in child protective services investigation of abused and neglected children. In D. Derezotes et al. (Eds.), *Race matters in child welfare: The overrepresentation of African American children in the system* (pp. 97–118). Washington, DC: CWLA Press.

Stewart, J., & Ayres, R. (2001). Systems theory and policy practice: An exploration. *Policy Sciences, 34,* 79–94.

Summers, A., Wood, S., & Russell, J. (2012). *Disproportionality rates for children of color in foster care.* Reno, NV: National Council of Juvenile and Family Court Judges.

Tobler, A. L., Livingston, M. D., & Komro, K. A. (2011). Racial/ethnic differences in the etiology of alcohol use among urban adolescents. *Journal of Studies on Alcohol and Drugs, 72,* 799–810.

U.S. Census Bureau. (2012). *2010 census data* [Data file]. Retrieved from http://www.census.gov/2010census/data/

U.S. Department of Education, Office of Civil Rights. (2012). *The transformed civil rights data collection—March 2012 data summary.* Retrieved from http://www2.ed.gov/about/offices/list/ocr/data.html

U.S. Department of Health and Human Services, Administration for Children and Families, Administration on Children, Youth, and Families, Children's Bureau. (2011). *The AFCARS report: Preliminary FY 2010 estimates as of June 2011.* Retrieved from http://www.acf.hhs.gov/programs/cb/stats_research/afcars/tar/report18.pdf

Wulczyn, F., & Lery, B. (2007). *Racial disparity in foster care admissions.* Chicago: Chapin Hall Center for Children, University of Chicago.

Zastrow, C. H., & Kirst-Ashman, K. K. (2004). *Understanding human behavior and the social environment* (6th ed.). Belmont, CA: Thomson Learning.

Zuravin, S., Orme, J., & Hegar, R. (1995). Disposition of child physical abuse reports: Review of the literature and test of a predictive model. *Children and Youth Services Review, 17,* 547–566.

2

A Cross-Systems Approach to Racial Disproportionality and Disparities

▸ CAROLYNE RODRIGUEZ, JOYCE JAMES,
RATONIA C. RUNNELS, AND ROWENA FONG

A CROSS-SYSTEMS APPROACH TO RACIAL DISPROPORTIONALITY AND DISPARITIES

DISPROPORTIONALITY REFERS TO THE REPRESENTATION of a particular racial or ethnic group of children in a system at a higher or lower percentage than their representation in the general population. Within the context of the child welfare system, researchers have found family risk factors, community risk factors, and systemic factors as causes for disproportionality and that the disparity exists at several stages throughout African American families' encounters with Child Protective Services (CPS), including decision points, treatment, services, and resource availability (Fluke, Harden, Jenkins, & Ruehrdanz, 2011). There is a noted differential response to children and families of color by professionals in the child welfare system at critical decision points. These responses have been traced back to explicit and implicit racial bias. These biases have been shown to impact decision making among caseworkers employed by state agencies responsible for investigating and monitoring reports of abuse and neglect. Cultural misunderstandings at various levels, including among juvenile and family court judges, also play a role in the disproportionate number of African American children entering foster care (U.S. Government Accountability Office [GAO], 2007). As a result, structural or institutional racism pervades the system and maintains the racial and socioeconomic inequalities that exist in our communities. The term "institutional racism" describes societal patterns that have the net effect of imposing oppressive or otherwise negative conditions against identifiable groups on the basis of race or ethnicity.

Several states (California, Iowa, Michigan, Illinois, Washington, Texas, North Carolina, Minnesota, Tennessee, and Connecticut) have researched disproportionality in the child welfare system and have offered insight into the causes for increased numbers of children of color entering state custody. Through legislative action, seven states (Florida, Illinois, Iowa, Michigan, Minnesota, Texas, and Washington) have created commissions or separate departments to secure funding for research and to generate recommendations from research to address African American disproportionality in the child welfare system (Dixon, 2008). *Places to Watch*, a publication from the Center for the Study of Social Policy's Alliance for Racial Equity (2006), highlights the work of 10 jurisdictions that are committed to reducing racial disproportionality and disparity in their child welfare systems. The report documents strategies, activities, and trends emerging in the cities, states, and counties represented. Although there are unique aspects to each jurisdiction's work, there are also several common themes, which suggest a trajectory for how child welfare agencies are choosing to address the issue of racial equity.

Many of these sites are affiliated with the Annie E. Casey Foundation's Family to Family Initiative or the Casey Family Programs' Breakthrough Series Collaborative and are implementing the strategies of the Family to Family Initiative. First, sites began by highlighting the problem of racial inequity in their child welfare system and prioritizing the need to address it. Sites gathered data and included communities in the discussion to allow for the development of more comprehensive action plans and for strategies aimed at reducing disproportionality in their systems. Access to support services is being expanded for families and communities experiencing the highest levels of disproportionate intervention by the child welfare system. Policy changes have been made by some jurisdictions to reinforce the child welfare system reforms, and ongoing evaluation strategies have been instituted to ensure continued tracking of progress. Additionally, all sites are seeking external funding to support their work.

In 2005, the Texas Legislature passed Senate Bill 6, requiring the state to take specific actions to address disproportionality. Senate Bill 6 mandated the provision of cultural competency training and development for all service delivery staff; targeted recruitment efforts to ensure diversity among state department staff; increased targeted recruitment for foster and adoptive parents to meet the needs of children waiting for homes; required an analysis to determine if and why disproportionality and disparities exist; required the development and implementation of a remediation plan; and provided funding for evidence-based programs in the community to prevent child abuse. To combat the pervasive disproportionality identified within the Texas child welfare system, the Texas Department of Family Protective Services (TDFPS) and Casey Family Programs (CFP) implemented a statewide strategic plan utilizing community building strategies that include *Undoing Racism* training from the People's Institute for Survival and Beyond, values-based leadership, and community engagement (James, Green, Rodriguez, & Fong, 2008). The goals of the initiative are to encourage and emphasize community engagement, to employ a values-based leadership philosophy and framework within and throughout the system, and to spark attitudinal changes through the *Undoing Racism* trainings, which discuss institutional racism and its impact on vulnerable populations and communities.

Over the last decade, greater coordination and integration of human service programs have been addressed in many states through legislation, local innovations made possible by changes in welfare administration, and through significant research studies. Many of the states have formed collaborations between the private and public sectors and data collecting mechanisms including universities to document the progress of the strategies. However, although progress is being made in these areas, true integration of policies into key organizational structures has remained elusive.

Federal program instruction and planning tools emphasize community and grassroots participation and application of the technical expertise of strategic planning. Guidelines urging programs to actively engage stakeholders in planning to ensure that they have all of the information and support they need to be full participants often fall short because they focus on administration, budgeting, and similar issues, rather than on interpreting program information and research data in a way that galvanizes and mobilizes a community. Lloyd (1997) suggests combining participation with high-level expertise, skills, and knowledge in the area of planning as a potential antidote to the dilemmas introduced by multiple stakeholders. Expertise in human service activity and the principles, patterns, and strategies of family preservation and support is essential. Knowledge of program design, service innovation, and collaborative strategies has the potential to benefit and inform cross-systems human service approaches.

More competency-based approaches to training have been criticized lately due to their grounding in analysis of what is currently being done rather than in providing coaching toward innovative program planning and design. Application of a significant paradigm shift across systems requires major changes in the values, desires, and behavior of decision makers, employees, and stakeholders of each system, and changes across systems must occur at the policy, administrative, and service levels of all agencies serving children and families. These systems include health, juvenile justice, mental health, and developmental disabilities. The success of each state plan can be determined by how responsive the leadership of each system can be to the emerging needs for expertise, leadership, and participation. Formulating a cross-systems approach requires the development of instruments and curricula for cross-systems application, caseload management, and implementation of funding strategies for managed care, as well as requiring increased training and technical assistance (Gatowski, Maze, & Miller, 2008).

Research suggests that the frontline worker and agency staff in human service organizations have developed patterns and structures that they feel may have greater legitimacy than new management initiatives or plans for reform resulting in structural impediments that can hamper the kind of collaboration that policymakers intended. The collective beliefs of frontline staff become critical to service delivery when organizations are mandated to collaborate. Staff interactions require appropriate navigation of differing views and points of contention, making negotiation especially challenging. Therefore, the framework of beliefs that frontline staff collectively generate about organizations in their environment can significantly impede collaboration. There must be recognition of the social structures that guide people's actions, that help them to develop appropriate routines, and that justify inaction, in order for them to intentionally evolve within the organization itself. In frontline welfare offices, these underlying social structural processes emerge in large part from the nature of daily street-level practice (Sandfort, 2004).

THE TEXAS COMMUNITY ENGAGEMENT MODEL

Texas has developed a framework for institutional and community transformation to reduce disproportionality and disparities within the Texas child welfare system that will ideally transcend individual views of workers within the organizational and systemic context. This work has laid the foundation for expansion and continued system improvement by addressing and eliminating disparities across systems. The Texas Community Engagement Model (TCEM) is a four-stage process that has helped to reduce disproportionality in child welfare and to ensure equity in child welfare services.

Stage 1: Community Awareness and Engagement

This is the foundational stage of the model, defined by key concepts that must be introduced in the earliest stage of engagement in addressing disproportionality and disparities. It involves the following processes:

- Making the problem and issue visible in communities as well as within systems
- Sharing the data with the community and within organizational systems by:
  o Making the facts known
  o Ensuring that the facts are communicated in real numbers and percentages
  o Augmenting the data with anecdotal stories about how the conditions of disproportionality and disparities have impacted people through their day-to-day interactions with human services systems
- Telling the story—through media, through voices of constituents who have experienced the effects of disproportionality and disparities firsthand, through their own experiences
- Engaging community leaders who can commit resources and who can make internal systems changes once informed about the disproportionality and disparities experienced by those directly impacted
- Building local and systems allies who can join in championing change, bringing prolific voice and advocacy to the issues and the need for sustainable change

Stage 2: Community Leadership

Stage 2 involves building and sharing leadership in communities for systems improvement. In the Texas child welfare system, community advisory committees have provided leadership in partnership with systems and organizations. This stage emphasizes that there are key concepts that work to inform community members and leaders about disproportionality and disparities so that they can be the best advocates for change and systems improvement. This includes:

- Leadership needs to expand beyond organizations and institutions to the level where real change can occur—at the community level.
- Communities ought to claim responsibility for what needs to happen to address the issues out of their knowledge of community strengths and resilience.
- The belief that the community, in partnership with systems, will lead the systems changes through a facilitative leadership process as a comprehensive systems improvement effort.
- The work is done through a shared leadership model—systems leadership and community leadership—involving community partnerships, technical assistance from partners, and systems leaders.
- Community advisory committees, with a wide range of membership representing the systems with which families interact, do work at the community level through written charters that define their vision for change, desired outcomes for improvement, membership, roles, leadership/operational structure, decision-making processes, and so on.
- Charters also articulate assumptions and beliefs about the condition of disproportionality and disparities, suggested strategic work efforts, and how the work is sponsored and to whom the committees are accountable.
- At this stage, community investment and ownership in systems improvements to impact disproportionality are directly linked to community assets and strengths, to constituency voice, and to needs identified by the community—its members and its leaders.
- Importantly, the work reveals community leaders/members who appear to be resistant but who can and often do become the best allies in the work/ the best advocates for needed change.

This means that systems leaders must be willing to be vulnerable; be able to listen to areas of practice that have been less than supportive of families and youth; be willing to change based on stakeholder information, experiences, and proposed solutions; and be willing to operate in nontraditional ways to meet children's and families' needs.

Stage 3: Community Organization

Stage 3 involves a process that elevates the importance of collaborative efforts where community and systems leaders guide the work. The role of community members in this process must be legitimized and the value of their contributions applied in the selection and analysis of strategies for sustainable change. This stage emphasizes:

- Going to the community, being guided by it to learn what the strengths are, what the needs are, hearing from residents impacted by interventions coming from outside the community to interpret its needs and what will work best
- Bringing community members "to the table" as key informants
- Legitimizing the process—selecting practices to be applied in the community *from the community's perspectives*
- Ensuring that the community is given the opportunity for meaningful contribution in selecting and applying strategies for change
- Using town hall meetings, focus groups, and community forums to hear from the community as well as providing them with information

This stage has the following areas of emphasis:

- Work is guided by antiracist principles (People's Institute for Survival and Beyond [PISAB], 2007).
- Principles of community organizing are embedded throughout the work.
- The premise of "the community knows best" is a leading mantra.
- Communities are resilient as are their residents/their members.
- The *Undoing Racism* (PISAB, 2007) principles form a lens through which the work is guided and approached:
  - Analyzing power
  - Defining racism—a belief that racism was done and can be undone
  - Understanding the manifestations of racism
  - Learning from history

○ Cultural sharing

○ Organizing, internally and externally, to undo racism within systems, institutions, and in the community

Stage 4: Community Accountability

Stage 4 involves mutual and reciprocal accountability and a full investment by community and systems leaders in identifying, developing, and achieving desired and measurable outcomes. This stage emphasizes:

- It is important to work to achieve desired, measurable outcomes—short- and long-term outcomes that can be tracked to ensure that milestones reflect progress toward meeting desired results.
- Everyone is contributing to what the outcomes should be, how they are defined, and how they will be measured.
- Sustainability is the ultimate condition—lasting change in systems and leaving communities in a better place once issues are known and strategies are applied.
- It is important to not approach this work by implementing new programs or projects and then leaving the community without a way to continue implementation and promote sustainability. Instead, the goal is an established presence of services and resources that are often site-specific in a community or as a network of services on which community members can depend.
- A guiding belief is that communities are the owners of their solutions—building on what they know they need to be successful.
- Community leaders are speaking out and not staying silent—they advocate and create a "call to action" climate.
- There is reciprocal/mutual accountability at this stage—*to* the community and *back from* the community.
- Replication of evidence-based, best, and promising practices occurs at this stage—spreading successful models, for example, the Port Arthur Helping Our People Excel (HOPE) approach.
- Accountability is visible at this stage through formal agreements among partners such as memorandums of understanding (MOUs), letters of agreement, state level agreements, and so on.

Community engagement initiated through child welfare can be leveraged to help lead to improvements in other areas. The TCEM helps engage and empower affected communities in innovative ways to support individual and community efforts. It emphasizes that (CFP, 2010, p. 10):

- Community partnerships are essential to address disproportionality.
- Child welfare organizations cannot do this work in isolation.
- Parents and young people who have experienced the child welfare system, as well as other constituents, must actively participate.
- The existence of institutional racism must be acknowledged.

The fundamental principles and beliefs about the work to impact—and ultimately eliminate—disproportionality and disparities are:

- Community partnerships form the cornerstone for addressing disproportionality and disparities.
- Disproportionality and disparities are not solely CPS problems—they involve many systems with which families and youth interact and through which they are impacted.
- The work addresses disparate outcomes as well as the disproportionate representation of African American children in the Texas child welfare system.
- There is an understanding that a community response is imperative.
- The community must lead the work in partnership with CPS and must invest in success over time to ensure sustainability of efforts.
- Communities have strengths, and community members/residents know best what they need to maximize these strengths and to successfully function in their communities.
- Success depends on a systemic, organizational cultural change within the child welfare system and other systems.
- Internal cultural change must be directed to family-centered practices across every stage of service.
- Constituents—families, youth in care, alumni of foster care, kinship caregivers, foster and adoptive families, and families who have experienced the child welfare system—must be "at the table" to inform this work from their perspectives and from their own experiences.

- Challenges and barriers as well as opportunities are "givens" in this work.
- There will be community resistance and debate that questions why this work is being done.
- Raising the bar for those populations who have the least favorable outcomes means better results for *all* children and families.
- Understanding the history of disproportionality and how it came to be is imperative in order to have a successful response to the issue.
- Successful efforts must acknowledge the existence of institutional/systemic racism—that racism was done and can be undone—and that the work must be grounded in antiracist principles (PISAB, 2007).

As stated earlier, the TCEM has four stages; the model is very specific in the descriptions but the stages are very interdependent and do not occur in a solely linear way. The stages will sometimes be happening simultaneously or independently but more often are interdependent throughout the implementation of the work. Community engagement involves:

- Making the problem visible in communities as well as within systems that serve families and youth; it is about describing the facts regarding the disproportionality and disparities that exist.
- Exposing the data to the community and within systems—making the undisputable facts known so that the problem is grounded in real numbers/ real percentages and is augmented with real anecdotal stories from families/ youth who have experienced the systems in which the disproportionality/ disparities exist.
- Telling the story—through media and through the voices of constituents— alumni of foster care, birth parents, kinship caregivers, foster and adoptive parents—who know firsthand, from their own experiences, what disproportionality and disparities are and their effects and impact, long- and short-term.
- Being open about the way people are invited to join in and recognizing the historical disappointment people have experienced as they have interacted with systems.
- Engaging/"enrolling" community leaders/natural leaders/people in power in communities who can commit resources linked to sustainable change strategies, and who can be informed advocates for the link to community strengths and needs.

SYSTEMS IMPROVEMENT

Systems improvement efforts require an approach that is based on various principles that begin with applying certain criteria to ensure that the selected work and methods are those that can lead to the most sustainable change. The criteria are utilized to determine what parts of the system need to be adjusted and how strategies should be implemented. When approaching a system that is in need of and ready for change, questions are asked about sustainability, replication, measurability, level of impact, evidence-based practice, permanency, involvement of constituents, cost efficiency, and timeliness.

SUSTAINABILITY

The first question to ask is: Will this work be sustainable in the broader system? For instance, can it be applied across different geographic regions? Can it be incorporated in all rural and urban areas? Is it something that can be applied in different units of varying professional disciplines and backgrounds? Are there needed resources to ensure long-term implementation? Is there leadership commitment to the systems change? These are important questions to ask in order to know if the changes we are making will apply across different populations and demographic groups.

REPLICATION

Another factor to consider is how well this change might be replicated in other parts of the state or in other jurisdictions. Some areas may have fewer resources. Others may have very different needs and populations. It is important to look at whether the plan of action can be easily and consistently replicated by others wishing to apply this change.

MEASURABILITY

When deciding how best to improve systems, it is vital that the work is *measurable*. This means that the practices being implemented can be evaluated with precise measures to determine success and whether desired outcomes have been realized. The measurability criterion leads to another related concept that must be considered—whether this systems improvement effort can be documented. The ability to document a broad system change is essential so that it can be made visible to other similar organizations and can be implemented on a wider scale and across systems. If a change is made in the child welfare system (CWS), documentation can serve as a guide and resource to other similar systems and communities who are looking to make comparable changes.

LEVEL OF IMPACT

The degree to which the changes leave a large impact on the system should be considered before making the changes. Additionally, the length of time it will take before impact occurs should be taken into account. Ideally, the time before impact takes place should be minimal, although recognizably, some systems change efforts can take multiple years before the full scope of expected impact occurs. The scope of the proposed systemic change should also be examined. There should be maximum impact in scope, geographically and with regard to resources. In terms of strategic impact, will there be maximum strategic impact? These are all important factors to consider before making any system improvement efforts.

EVIDENCE-BASED PRACTICE

Evidence-based practice (EBP) is defined as "the conscientious, explicit, and judicious use of current best evidence in making decisions about the care of individual patients," (Mullen, Bledsoe, & Bellamy, 2008, p. 326). EBP was originally designed for health-care professionals working with individuals. However, it has now broadened its scope and is being applied to other realms and fields. In looking at big systems and how to improve them, it is critical that the practices being implemented be evidence-based when possible. Sometimes it is not possible to implement an evidence-based practice because there is not enough research or data on the practice. If it is not evidence-based, questions we might want to ask are: Is it then a best or promising practice? Have others tried to implement it and realized success?

PERMANENCY

Questions about permanency include: Will the permanency of change be maximized? Can the work lead to change that can be embedded in specific areas of the system so that staff implementing the change are held accountable to the systems change, such as in staff training, in program policy, in quality assurance processes, and in the organization's personnel procedures, including employee evaluation?

INVOLVEMENT OF CONSTITUENTS

Perspectives of the constituents are important. One question to ask is: Will the change involve—and maximize the involvement of—constituents (e.g., parents, youth, community partners, etc.)?

COST EFFICIENCY

Cost and resources are critical in systems improvement. It is important to know: Is the cost of the effort such that long-term implementation and possible replication can be successful with reasonably available financial resources?

TIMELINESS

Because timeliness plays a key role, it is important to find out if the work is building on a window of opportunity for change. For example, is systems improvement taking advantage of legislation that has been enacted or of a new federal regulation that must be applied in organizational practice?

LEADERSHIP VISION AND COMMITMENT

In considering the systems change that occurred in Texas in addressing disproportionality and disparities, the vision for the changes and initiatives that took place between 2004 and 2009 was the result of a leader's willingness to examine the systems response and to elevate the accountability for improving outcomes. Systems change requires willingness on the part of leadership to be vulnerable and to examine at a deeper level the root causes of disproportionality. Leadership partnering with stakeholders requires a shared vision as well as a willingness to commit resources that support the vision and the desired outcomes and improvements. Some examples that demonstrate the collaborative work between Casey Family Programs and CPS in Texas follow.

WORKFORCE DEVELOPMENT

An example of workforce development has been Casey Family Programs' support of extensive training and coaching of Family Group Decision Making staff, impacting front-end and back-end CPS stages of services through Family Team Meetings, Family Group Conferences, and Circles of Support.

LEADERSHIP DEVELOPMENT

One example of leadership development has been Casey Family Programs' collaborative, multiyear continuous quality improvement (CQI) effort with the American Public Human Services Association (APHSA), which embedded a CQI methodology within TDFPS and CPS that has been used to address a variety of issues, including the cultural shift to an inclusive family focus practice as well as issues related to staff turnover and retention.

PRACTICE AND POLICY DEVELOPMENT

Practice and policy improvements have been supported by Casey Family Programs through methodologies to develop and strengthen policies and procedures in a number of CPS program areas, including the kinship program, transition services, residential contracts, and the foster/adoptive program. Methods such as business process mapping, compression planning, and peer technical assistance have been successfully applied.

PUBLIC POLICY AND RESEARCH

Public policy and research have included Casey Family Programs' steady education of policymakers, providing best practice information to inform legislative committees, and invited testimony during legislative sessions in support of child welfare initiatives. Research capacity has been provided for such efforts as a multiyear foster care alumni study focused on outcomes of young adults who aged out of foster care and the state disproportionality evaluation.

DISPROPORTIONALITY

Disproportionality work has been a broad systems improvement effort incorporating *Undoing Racism* workshops, community engagement strategies, leadership development of systems managers centered on vision and values and family-centered practices, data-driven efforts at the community level, advisory committee development, and implementation support for the Casey Family Programs' *Knowing Who You Are* cultural identity formation training, now adopted across all of TDFPS.

AREAS OF FOCUS IN SYSTEMS CHANGE

Strategies to make organizational systems change will typically focus on the following areas: workforce development, leadership development, practice and policy development, public policy and research, and disproportionality efforts. Although there needs to be criteria when making broad system changes, the different criteria will not all be weighted equally. Work efforts will always need to meet some specific criteria, but criteria relating to scope, timing, and measurability, for example, may or may not apply based on the strategic objective for the work effort. There is no rigid formula for applying the criteria. The selection of work efforts may be systematic, but it is not formulaic—it is as much an art as a science.

Typically, work efforts are undertaken in which resources can be leveraged or reinvested; ideally, there would be collaborative effort and investment in resourcing change efforts. For example, it could be that there is partnering with foundations that would assist in resourcing the work or with community-based groups that would add to the resourcing.

Finally, taking on a work effort in order to build strategic partnerships is important. Although these work efforts may have a small impact, they can play an important role in future work opportunities.

LESSONS LEARNED WORKING WITH A STATE SYSTEM

When assessing opportunities to partner with a state agency, it is important to acknowledge the many factors that contribute to the often challenging nature of state systems, including:

- The overall political climate
- Federal requirements
- State legislative mandates
- State executive mandates
- Program funding streams
- Agency staff turnover rate
- State bureaucracy
- Public awareness/opinion, including media scrutiny
- Rules and regulations related to state operations

Early on in Texas, it was helpful to formalize engagement through a written agreement. Agreements outline the strategies to be carried out for mutually determined work efforts. Charters have been used to delineate desired outcomes, outline the decision-making process, clarify roles and responsibilities, define a communication plan, and to create a steering committee or leadership team that would have the role of overseeing and guiding the work. This process has typically been used at the local or regional level.

Child welfare has found value in technical assistance that is implementation-focused. Technical assistance (TA) that brings clarity to implementation can strongly position work efforts for success. Providing TA that uses facilitative methodologies to help with planning and implementation of practice improvements has been important throughout most large systems' improvement efforts. Some examples of TA and specific methodologies utilized are:

- Peer learning opportunities
- Breakthrough series collaborative (BSC)
- Business process mapping (BPM)
- Compression planning
- Shared learning opportunities
- Facilitated site visits
- Short-term and long-term project management

- Facilitation/facilitative leadership
- Strategic planning
- Convening of partners, subject matter experts (SMEs), constituents
- Leadership development
- Program evaluation
- Sustainability planning
- Documentation/chronicling of work efforts/practice models

In general, imposing a rigid practice framework with inflexible procedures on a state system is not an acceptable approach, given the system's own inertia and internal and external pressures. Supporting the implementation of practice into the existing organizational structure can often have good results. Sometimes state systems will not explicitly solicit consultation, although they may find such consultation useful. It has been important to be physically present at meetings where decisions are made in order to suggest ways of providing supportive TA so that opportunities can be identified and acted on.

As a part of the ongoing collaboration process, joint business planning with state partners can be a way to ensure a transparent and open process. In reviewing potential work efforts, applying the explicit set of criteria outlined earlier can work well. Chronicling and publicizing collaborative efforts is important to the state system and for the external audience receiving the information. This is particularly true when the focus is on the state system and its efforts to improve practices.

REFERENCES

Alliance for Racial Equity. (2006). *Places to watch: Promising practices to address racial disproportionality in child welfare.* Washington, DC: Center for the Study of Social Policy.

Casey Family Programs. (2010). *Processes, activities, and methods to impact disproportionality in the Texas child welfare system.* Austin, TX: Author.

Dixon, J. (2008). The African-American Child Welfare Act: A legal redress for African-American disproportionality in child protection cases. *Berkeley Journal of African American Law and Policy, 10,* 109–145.

Fluke, J. D., Harden, B. J., Jenkins, M., & Ruehrdanz, A. (2011). A research synthesis on child welfare disproportionality and disparities. In *Disparities and disproportionality in child welfare: Analysis of the research* (pp. 1–93). Washington, DC: Center for the Study of Social Policy.

Gatowski, S., Maze, C., & Miller, N. (2008). Courts catalyzing change: Achieving equity and fairness in foster care—transforming examination into action. *Juvenile and Family Justice Today, 17,* 16–20.

James, J., Green, D., Rodriguez, C. & Fong, R. (2008). Addressing disproportionality through Undoing Racism, leadership development, and community engagement. *Child Welfare, 87,* 279–296.

Lloyd, J. (1997). Conceptual bases of the planning process in family preservation/ family support state plans. *Journal of Family Strengths, 2,* 7.

Mullen, E. J., Bledsoe, S. E., & Bellamy, J. L. (2008). Implementing evidence-based social work practice. *Research on Social Work Practice, 18,* 325–338.

People's Institute for Survival and Beyond. (2007). *Training information.* Retrieved from http://www.pisab.org

Sandfort, J. (2004). Why is human service integration so difficult to achieve? *Focus, 23,* 5–8.

U.S. Government Accountability Office. (2007). *Black children in foster care: Additional HHS assistance needed to help states reduce the proportion in care* (GAO Publication No. GAO-07-816). Washington, DC: Author.

PART 2

Ethnic Minority Populations

3

African American Children and Families

▸ *RUTH G. MCROY AND RATONIA C. RUNNELS*

POPULATION OF ETHNICALLY DIVERSE CLIENTS IN SYSTEMS

DESPITE THE FACT THAT FOR the first time in the history of the United States, a Black man, Barack Obama, was not only elected president in 2008 but was reelected four years later in 2012, we still know that race continues to make a difference in terms of outcomes, justice, and life experiences. For example, as the National Association of Black Social Workers President Joe Benton stated as he reflected on the egregious killing of Trayvon Martin in Sanford, Florida, in 2012, "We are still in a time in which Black men, regardless of age, bring immediate fear to everyone, and the only way to control them is through violence toward them" (Benton, 2012, p. 1).

Clearly, race continues to play a major role in the lives of African Americans. Despite the stereotypic belief that "all Blacks are alike," there are numerous within and between group differences. For example, terms such as Afro- or Africentricism, culture, and racial identity are used to define and categorize inherent differences between Africans and African Americans, Blacks and other ethnic minorities, Blacks and Whites, and among African Americans themselves. Race, as a socially constructed concept, has provided a phenotypical classification of persons of African descent that has great consequence in life opportunities and experience in the United States. Sellers, Smith, Shelton, Rowley, & Chavous (1998) make a distinction between the terms Black and African American, referring to Black as a category that may or may not be inclusive of all persons of African descent. This category may include African Americans only or could include anyone of African descent within the African diaspora, depending on the point of view. The term African American is often reserved for those individuals of African descent who have received a significant portion of their socialization in the United States and, therefore, making the term African American exclusive to those whose culture is formed within the context of American society.

There continue to be disparities in earnings and poverty rates by race and significant achievement gaps between Blacks and other racial groups of students in the nation's schools. According to the Children's Defense Fund, in 2011, "Black children are two and a half times as likely as White children to be held back or retained in school" (Aud, Fox, & KewalRamani, 2010, p. 92). Also, there are gender differences in these disparate educational outcomes. The Council on Great City Schools (an advocacy group for urban public schools) reported that only 12% of Black fourth grade boys as compared to 38% of White fourth grade boys are proficient in reading and only 12% of Black eighth-grade boys are proficient in math as compared to 44% of White boys (Gabriel, 2010). The study also considered economic differences and found that Black males who are not eligible for free or reduced price meals are doing no better than White males who are economically poor.

Disparities are also apparent in the school-to-prison pipeline. In 2003, according to Snyder (2005), "Although African Americans represented about 16% of the nation's overall juvenile population, they accounted for 45% of juvenile arrests" (p. 9). In addition to enrollment in underperforming schools, problematic child welfare and juvenile justice systems, and a youth culture that glorifies violence, Edelman (2007) identified access to health care as another factor that can impact whether a child enters the prison pipeline. She noted that lack of health insurance, attendance in a school environment without the resources to recognize and diagnose mental and physical developmental delays, as well as other health issues such as hyperactivity disorder, attention deficit disorder, and post-traumatic stress, can all lead to children's behavior being viewed as insubordinate or disruptive and to expulsion and sometimes even an arrest (Edelman, 2007).

African American males experience major disparities in overall physical health in comparison to Whites. For example, "African American males have higher risks of hypertension, diabetes, heart attack, stroke, higher incidence rate and mortality rate for cancer than White males and the African American male life expectancy rate is 69.7 compared to 77.7 years for all U.S. population groups" (Miller & Bennett, 2011, p. 265). In fact, the Centers for Disease Control and Prevention (CDC, 2008) reported that, according to the 2008 National Health Interview Survey, 30.4% of Hispanics, 17% of Blacks, and 9.9% of Whites did not have health insurance.

Just as disparities exist in the educational system, health care, criminal justice system, and in poverty rates, the child welfare system also is characterized by disproportionately high numbers of African American children being removed from their families and placed in foster care (McRoy, 2011a). As mentioned earlier, African American children are much more likely to be living in families who are at or below the poverty line, and African American children are far more likely than White children to be residing in foster care. For example, according to the U.S. Children's Bureau's Preliminary Adoption and Foster Care Analysis and Reporting System (AFCARS) estimates for FY 2012, 397,122 children were in foster care and 26% (approximately 101,915) of these children were African American (U.S. Department of Health and Human Services [USDHHS], Administration for Children and Families, 2013). Of the 101,666 children waiting for adoptive placements in 2012, 26% (approximately 26,135) of these children were African American. However, as the representation of African American children in the U.S. population was 14% (2011 Census estimates), African American children were significantly overrepresented in care (USDHHS, 2013).

This chapter provides a glimpse of these conflicting experiences and disparate outcomes, as well as the challenges and issues confronting African American children, families, men, and women today. It includes an overview of the demographic characteristics of African Americans in the United States, as well as data on current disparate outcomes for African American children and families. Programs and practices that seem to be working well to improve outcomes and reduce and/or eliminate these disparities will be discussed and suggestions will be given for additional strategies to address many of these ongoing inequities. Clearly, the experiences of African Americans in the United States are very different from other ethnic groups. This chapter is designed to explore historical and contemporary factors that have led to some of these disparate outcomes as well as to provide a much needed overview of strengths, culture, and other survival strategies. Values, norms, and within group ethnic diversity will be presented, and promising culturally competent practice approaches with African Americans will be highlighted.

DEMOGRAPHIC OVERVIEW

In 2012, the U.S. Census Bureau released updated population estimates from 2011, and reported that African Americans, with 43.9 million persons, represented the second largest U.S. minority population, and that Hispanics, with 52 million persons, represented the largest and fastest growing minority group (U.S. Census Bureau, 2012). In 2011, although 15.1% of all Americans were living below the poverty level, which was the highest level since 1993, the African American poverty rate was 27% (which represented a 2% jump from 2009) and the Hispanic poverty rate was 26% (up from 25% in 2009). The Asian poverty rate was 12.1% (unchanged from 2009) and the White poverty rate was 9.9% (up from 9.4% in 2009) (Tavernise, 2011, p. 2).

Similarly, in 2010, the African American unemployment rate was 16.5%, almost twice the White unemployment rate, with almost one in five African American men between the ages of 20 and 24 unemployed (Morial, 2010). A closer look at income differences among Blacks, Hispanics, and Whites reveals further disparities. In 2010, the median Black household earnings were $34,218, compared to the Hispanic median household income of $37,913 and that of Whites, $55,530. In terms of home ownership, about 75% of White families own homes, whereas only about 47.4% of Blacks and about 49.1% of Hispanics own homes (Wilson, 2010).

Economically challenged circumstances of parents have a major impact on children within these families. Recent statistics reveal that 39% of Black, non-Hispanic children; 35% of Hispanic children; and 12% of White, non-Hispanic children lived in poverty in 2010. This rate was even higher for children living in female-headed households. According to the Federal Interagency Forum on Child and Family Statistics (2012):

> The poverty rate was 57% for Hispanic children in female-headed households, 53% for Black, non-Hispanic children and 36% for White, non-Hispanic children. Also, it should be noted that only about 61% of Hispanic children, 53% of Black, non-Hispanic children as compared to 79% of White, non-Hispanic children lived in families considered to have secure parental employment in 2010.

The following facts provided in a recent report by the Children's Defense Fund (2011) highlight ongoing African American inequality and disparities in the United States today:

- Black children are three times as likely to be poor than White children, and Black children are seven times more likely than White children to be persistently poor.
- Fifty percent of Black children live with only their mother.
- Black children are four times as likely as White children to be residing in foster care.
- Black children are seven times as likely as White children to have a parent in prison.
- Infants born to Black mothers are almost twice as likely to be born at low birth weight as infants born to White mothers, and a child born at low birth weight is more likely to have health, behavioral, and learning problems down the road.

CONTEXT OF CULTURAL VALUES AND NORMS

African Americans have faced unique forms of oppression and discrimination in the United States not experienced by other ethnic groups. The U.S. Constitution denied Africans human freedom upon entry into American society. Against the backdrop of slavery, African Americans were legally defined as property by the U.S. government for nearly a century. Structurally and systematically, laws were enacted to criminalize contact between Blacks and Whites, and they perpetually define a race of people as second-class citizens. As slaves, African Americans were systematically prohibited from retaining their indigenous culture and were forced to adopt the European culture of their captors and masters. Although much cultural context has been lost for Americans of African descent, several traditions and values have been forged to reintroduce and honor that which remains. African values transmitted from generation to generation include but are not limited to affiliation, collectivity, sharing, obedience to authority, and spirituality. This collectivism is referred to in the literature as Afrocentricity.

Afrocentricity is seen as a tool for community development, as opposed to personal enrichment, which has been associated with a more Eurocentric perspective. The Afrocentric perspective is built on the assumptions that human identity is a collective identity—an individual cannot be understood outside of his or her social context; and the spiritual or nonmaterial aspects of human life are as important as the material components (Schiele, 1996). The unique historical struggle of Africans in the United States has resulted in significant deficits in the environment, while highlighting numerous individual strengths within the ethnic group. An example of group strength is immediate and extended familial support to complete various developmental and social tasks related to survival. Similarly, African Americans' identification with the larger African American community has been found to enhance self-esteem. African American culture generally encourages an emphasis on sharing, cooperation, and social responsibility—important cultural values in the African American community (Adeleke, 2005; Cokley, 2005; Patton, 2006; Prather et al., 2006; Schiele, 1996; Stewart, 2004). Social responsibility emphasizes the importance of communal relationships rather than individuality and is manifested through cooperation, concern for others, family security, and respect for traditions and elders (Nobles, 1991; Schiele, 1996).

African Americans tend to attach significant importance to family values, regular kinship connections, extended family households, and to shared family practices (Sellers et al., 1998). Through collective responsibility, African Americans minimize their alienation and isolation and support each other when overwhelmed by the oppressive and racist environment. Collective responsibility means taking care of each other and sharing the trauma of painful experiences. These practices have helped many African Americans survive and deal with prejudice, racism, and oppression.

EXPLANATION OF WITHIN GROUP ETHNIC DIVERSITY

According to the 2010 Census, 38.9 million people (13% of the population) identified as Black alone (U.S. Census Bureau, 2012). An additional 3.1 million people (1%) reported Black in combination with one or more other races. The majority of the "Black alone" population identified as non-Hispanic (97%), and 3% identified as Hispanic. Hispanic-Blacks accounted for 5% of all people who reported multiple races in 2000, and this increased to 7% in 2010. Among those people reporting Black and one or more additional races, the majority identified as both Black and White (59%), followed by Black and some other race (10%), Black and American Indian and Alaska Native (9%), and Black and White and American Indian and Alaska Native (7%). The 2010 Census reports that nearly 60% of all Blacks in the United States live in ten states: New York (3.3 million), Florida (3.2 million), Texas (3.2 million), Georgia (3.1 million), California (2.7 million), North Carolina (2.2 million), Illinois (2.0 million), Maryland (1.8 million), Virginia (1.7 million), and Ohio (1.5 million). More than 50% of all African Americans in the United States live in southern states (U.S. Census Bureau, 2012).

In 1979, the National Survey of Black Americans (NSBA) was conducted by an all-Black professional staff who interviewed 2000 African Americans. The most notable finding from that survey was that all Blacks are not alike (Jackson, 2008). The National Survey of American Life (NSAL) (Jackson et al., 2004) extended the work of the NSBA and was the first national sample of Blacks (African Americans and Afro-Caribbeans), with more than 80% of the adult face-to-face interviews involving persons of African descent. Today, there are approximately 1.7 million Caribbean-born Black immigrants in the United States. Most come from Jamaica, Haiti, Trinidad and Tobago, and the Dominican Republic (Thomas, 2012). NSAL researchers found that when compared to African Americans, Caribbeans were more likely to be employed, had more education on average than African Americans, and Caribbeans' family income exceeded that of African Americans—and nearly exceeded that of White American households. Socioeconomic status was found to be the deciding factor for most differences found among African Americans. Family histories related to immigration and ancestry contributed greatly to social class heterogeneity. Although heterogeneity exists in terms of ethnicity, class, gender, immigration, socioeconomic status (SES), education, and health, and although U.S.-born Afro-Caribbeans tended to have higher incomes, race still superseded ethnicity when respondents among all Black groups were asked about racialized experiences (Jackson, 2008).

Terrazas (2009) reported that the number of African immigrants in the United States has grown from 35,355 to 1.4 million over the last 50 years. A majority of the African immigrants in the United States come from Nigeria, Egypt, and Ethiopia and are concentrated in New York, California, Texas, Maryland, and Virginia (Terrazas, 2009). African-born immigrants tend to be highly educated and speak English well, to work in higher-level occupations, and to have higher earnings, but they are less likely to be naturalized U.S. citizens when compared to other immigrants. Interestingly, research on the children of immigrants finds that they experience greater socioeconomic disadvantages than their counterparts with U.S.-born parents. There are documented differences in educational attainment that are conditional on race and that may also have implications for racial disparities in child poverty. Black immigrants generally have lower levels of education compared with non-Black immigrants. Furthermore, the racial and ethnic identities of Black immigrants have an influence on assimilation patterns. With increasing exposure to the United States, Black immigrants with visible minority characteristics are expected to be more likely than White immigrants without visible minority characteristics to experience downward assimilation patterns (Thomas, 2011). Due to the social construction of race in the United States, Black immigrants are more likely to face structural barriers to their social mobility than are their White counterparts.

Children of Black immigrants are more likely to live in two-parent families than children of U.S.-born Blacks. Additionally, Black children are less likely than non-Black children to live in families with married parents (Brandon, 2002). The children of U.S.-born Blacks are also twice as likely to live in single-parent families as other Black immigrant groups. Although the children of Black Africans are the least likely to live in single-parent families, this family structure is most common among the children of non-Hispanic Blacks from the Caribbean. Further, young children in U.S.-born Black families are more likely to live in poverty than are their counterparts in immigrant families. Children with parents from the non-Hispanic Black immigrant groups (i.e., African, non-Hispanic Caribbean, and other Blacks) have poverty levels that are about 50% lower than are those among the children of U.S.-born Blacks (Thomas, 2011). Skin color has been consistently shown to be a barrier to social mobility for immigrants with phenotypical similarities to U.S.-born Blacks.

BRIEF HISTORY RELATED TO SOCIAL AND ECONOMIC JUSTICE

In order to further contextualize the ongoing disparate outcomes experienced in the United States by African Americans, it is important to review their history. Between 1654 and 1865, West Africans were forcibly removed from their homeland and transported to the Americas. They were separated from their communal history, traditions, and lives and were enslaved on plantations as a source of cheap labor to support the American agricultural economy. This period was characterized by the dehumanization and "thingification" of Blacks, "justified by theories of inferiority and subhuman status, which laid the groundwork for the economic, political, and social discrimination and oppression that characterized the post slavery era" (McRoy & Lombe, 2011, p. 283). It took slave rebellions, abolitionist movements, the secession of southern states from the Union, and the Civil War to lead to the signing of the Emancipation Proclamation on January 1, 1863, and then the 1865 ratification of the Thirteenth Amendment, which officially abolished slavery. However, the end of slavery was followed by the implementation of Black Codes, which restricted the movement of freed Blacks and enforced legal segregation of schools, restaurants, water fountains, restrooms, schools, and all public facilities until 1954, when the Supreme Court declared the policy of "separate but equal" unconstitutional. More than a decade later, with the passage of the Civil Rights Act of 1964 and the Voting Rights Act of 1965, African Americans were slowly provided equal access to jobs, housing, and educational opportunities (McRoy & Lombe, 2011). However, despite these changes, outcomes for African Americans often remained unequal.

PROBLEMS/ISSUES FACING CLIENTS RELATED TO DISPROPORTIONALITY AND DISPARITIES

Educational Disparities

Disparities exist between African American and White students in high school graduation rates. In 2003, the graduation rate for White students was 78% compared to 55% for African American students. Gender disparities also existed, with approximately 5% fewer White males graduated than White females; among African American females, 59% graduated compared to only 48% of African American males (Greene & Winters, 2006; Miller & Bennett, 2011).

Also, according to the American Civil Liberties Union (ACLU), students of color are more likely than their peers to be suspended or expelled, may not have legal representation, and if placed in a juvenile detention facility, they are less likely to reenter traditional schools and many never graduate (ACLU, n.d.a).

A recent study noted that although only about 8.6% of public school students have been identified as having disabilities that impact their ability to learn, four times that number of students with disabilities are represented in correctional facilities (Quinn, Rutherford, & Leone, 2001). This may occur because children with special learning or emotional needs are punished more severely for problematic behaviors and may be more likely to end up in the juvenile justice system (ACLU, n.d.b). This often results from schools having inadequate resources, lacking funding for counselors, having overcrowded classrooms, and from schools instituting harsh disciplinary and zero-tolerance policies that often lead to student disengagement, dropouts, and a greater likelihood of police and court involvement. In fact, African American children with disabilities are "three times more likely to receive short-term suspensions than their White counterparts, and are more than four times as likely to end up in correctional facilities" (ACLU, n.d.b; Wald & Losen, 2003).

Criminal Justice Disparities

According to the National Association for the Advancement of Colored People (NAACP) (2012), African Americans represent 26% of juvenile arrests, 44% of youth who are detained, 46% of youth who are judicially waived to criminal court, and 58% of the youth admitted to state prisons. Referring to this as the school-to-prison pipeline, the ACLU noted that, nationally, we are focused on criminalizing through zero-tolerance policies rather than on educating our children. Through the use of secured detention facilities and the employment and utilization of full-time police officers to patrol schools, there are increases in the number of arrested youth. Many of these arrests are actually for nonviolent acts such as disruptive contact or disturbance of the peace. Also due to schools being pressured through the No Child Left Behind Act to boost student performance on tests, there is some evidence that schools are increasing expulsions, suspensions, and school-based arrests to decrease the likelihood of low-performing students being present during the period of standardized test taking (ACLU, n.d.b) and thereby increasing overall test scores of students and the rating of the school.

According to a recent report by the Southern Poverty Law Center (2012), schools are only one entry point into the juvenile justice system. As a result of some of their experiences in failing foster care systems or

mental health systems, youth may be unfairly targeted for arrest and confinement and end up in the juvenile justice system. Once arrested, they may
experience abuse and neglect in overcrowded, squalid detention facilities
and often do not get their educational, medical, or mental health needs
met while in these facilities (Southern Poverty Law Center, 2012).

The U.S. Bureau of Justice estimated that in 2008, although African
Americans made up 13.6% of the U.S. population, Black men represented
40.2% of prison inmates (Alexander, 2011). In fact, Alexander (2011) has
noted that there are more African American men in prisons and jails or
on probation or parole than there were slaves before the beginning of the
Civil War. Differential sentencing for drug offenses has also been identified as a cause of the disproportionate imprisonment of African Americans.
According the NAACP, although five times as many Whites use drugs as
compared to African Americans, African Americans are sent to prison for
drug offenses at a rate 10 times higher than that of Whites. This report also
noted that African Americans serve about 58.7 months for a drug offense
compared to Whites serving a similar number of months (61.7 months) for
a violent offense (NAACP, 2012). A number of factors have been identified
as contributing to these criminal justice disparities including the mandatory minimum sentencing for crack cocaine versus powder cocaine as well
as some of the new zero-tolerance policies and the "get tough on crime"
and "war on drugs" policies (NAACP, 2012).

Health Disparities

Health disparities can be defined as differences in morbidity, mortality, and
access to health care among population groups categorized by factors such
as socioeconomic status, gender, residence, and race or ethnicity (Dressler,
Oths, & Gravlee, 2005). A recent congressionally mandated study by the
Institute of Medicine on racial and ethnic disparities in health care reported
"African Americans have the highest rates of morbidity and mortality of
any other U.S. racial and ethnic group" (Smedley, Stith, & Nelson, 2003,
p. 82). It also found that "African Americans are less likely to possess private or employment-based health insurance relative to White Americans,
and are almost twice as likely as non-Hispanic Whites to be uninsured"
(Smedley et al., 2003, p. 85). One of the reasons for this disparity is that a
disproportionate percentage of African Americans work in jobs in which

no health insurance is provided (Duckett & Artiga, 2013). According to a recent report from the CDC (2013), in 2010, the top leading causes of death for African Americans were heart disease, cancer, stroke, diabetes, unintentional injuries, nephritis, chronic lower respiratory disease, homicide, septicemia, and Alzheimer's disease. The CDC has reported additional African American health disparities including:

- Among females 20 to 39 years of age, the prevalence of obesity was largest among African Americans than other groups.
- In 2008, the HIV infection rate was highest among African Americans, compared to other groups.
- In 2006, infants born to African American women had death rates twice as high as infants of White American women.
- In 2007, adolescent and adult African Americans between the ages of 15 and 59 had the highest death rates from homicide, as compared with other racial and ethnic populations of the same ages.
- Between 2005 and 2008, persons with the greatest prevalence of hypertension were African American adults 65 years and older, U.S. born adults, adults with less than a college education, and those with public health insurance (64 years and younger), diabetes, obesity, or a disability.
- In 2009, more African American adults lived in inadequate and unhealthy housing than did White adults.

Finally, the CDC report concluded that a number of factors contribute to these disparate health outcomes for African Americans, including discrimination, cultural barriers, and lack of access to health care. Additional variables that have been used to explain the disparate health status of African Americans are genetics, behavior, socioeconomic status, and psychosocial stress. Using these variables, researchers have found that, compared to Whites, Blacks suffer more in nearly every indicator of morbidity and mortality (Dressler, Oths, & Gravlee, 2005).

Child Welfare Disparities

Data suggest that "African American children not only are more likely to be in out-of-home care, they remain in care longer, are less likely to return home to their families of origin, are less likely to be adopted, and are more likely to be emancipated from the child welfare system without permanent connections with at least one adult" (McRoy, 2005, p. 624.). These inequities in service delivery and outcomes have been noted for a number of years. In 2008, the U.S. Government Accountability Office issued a report noting that, in 2006, African American children were more likely to be placed in foster care than White or Hispanic children, and at each decision point in the child welfare process, the disproportionality of African American children grows (Baynes-Dunning, 2012; Brown, 2008). A number of factors—including disproportionate poverty in African American communities, disproportionately high rates of single parenthood, disproportionately high numbers of African American men incarcerated, and disproportionate stress—are of major concern as potential reasons for these disparities. However, much recent attention has also been placed on the potential impact of cultural misunderstandings and racially biased decision making within many systems (including child welfare, mental health, education, criminal justice, and the judicial system) on disparate outcomes for African American children and families (McRoy, 2011b). All of these factors must be considered in developing strategies to eliminate these disparities. It is essential to bring together representatives from these multiple systems to acknowledge the issue and to develop culturally appropriate interventions to better serve African American children and families.

CULTURALLY COMPETENT ASSESSMENTS AND INTERVENTIONS

Tools for Assessing Disproportionality

Before implementing interventions to address disproportionality, agencies need baseline data about the existence of disproportionality in their particular jurisdiction. For example, in the field of child welfare, agencies need to collect and monitor accurate data trends on children involved in the system to assess factors that may contribute to disproportionality. To meet this need, the National Association of Public Child Welfare Administrators (NAPCWA) developed the Disproportionality Diagnostic Tool

(American Public Human Services Association [APHSA], 2008) to help agencies examine societal, system, and individual factors that may be contributing to disparate treatment of minority children. The design of the tool is two-dimensional. The first dimension has 11 domains: (1) Strategy, (2) Culture, (3) Policy, (4) Legal System, (5) Training and Education, (6) Communication, (7) Resources, (8) Practices, (9) Economic Issues, (10) Data Collection, and (11) Personnel and Community (APHSA, 2008). The second dimension examines spheres of influence (society, system, and individual) as interconnected layers directly influencing child welfare service delivery. The Diagnostic Tool provides a framework for a systemic view of the issue of disproportionality and enables organizations to identify their areas of relevant strength and their weaknesses (Fabella, Slappey, Richardson, Light, & Christie, 2007).

In addition, the Equality Scorecard,™ developed by the Casey Foundation/Center for the Study of Social Policy Alliance on Racial Equity, has been used to provide a framework for organizing and analyzing data on disproportionality and disparities in child welfare (Richardson & Derezotes, 2010). The scorecard measures involvement with the child welfare system by race at six key points (Children's Bureau Express, 2008): (1) acceptance of a hotline report for investigation; (2) assessment or investigation; (3) in-home service provision or out-of-home placement; (4) type of placement; (5) permanency goal; and (6) time to permanency. Data collected at each of these points highlight where improvements are needed most. Once problem areas are identified using the scorecard, communities are then able to develop strategies for addressing and eliminating disparities in those areas. Assessment tools are needed to measure change and to monitor and provide feedback on issues related to disproportionality in the child welfare system, a key starting point for implementation of effective interventions.

Culturally Competent Interventions

Effective interventions for African Americans should include activities that strengthen the self-concept and emotional and psychological development. By developing a more positive and realistic sense of self, the African American client is able to make better decisions about life, significant relationships, and about relationships in general. Cokley (2005) explores the relationship between ethnicity and mental health by defining internalized racialism as identifying with and internalizing negative and positive stereotypes about one's racial group. This internalization can have a two-pronged effect based on whether the stereotypes are negative (such as all Blacks are criminals) or positive (for example, Blacks are better athletes). A central theme of multicultural counseling and psychological literature has focused on the psychological importance of developing and maintaining a positive group identity. Proponents of the Afrocentric perspective argue that Afrocentricity is a tool for improving self-esteem.

Manning, Cornelius, and Okundaye (2004) suggest empowerment theory as a framework for developing interventions that target African Americans. Empowerment theory asserts that on the individual and interpersonal level, African Americans are encouraged to reduce the self-blame and take responsibility for solving their problems. Using an Afrocentric perspective, effective interventions should include assessment of a client's spiritual belief and orientation. It is important to assess how these beliefs have positively influenced and impacted the African American client's cultural development and to determine how to build on this foundation. Furthermore, empowerment groups for African Americans should be led by African Americans who can act as role models and offer emotional support in identifying and responding to racism.

Borum (2007) indicates that it is essential for practitioners to have an understanding of the history of African Americans and the need for an Afrocentric approach for service delivery to African Americans in this country. They should know and understand that, given their history, African Americans are often "wary of services delivered by professionals, especially those from different ethnic backgrounds, due to past instances of racism and neglect by service providers" (Borum, 2007, p. 123). Also, Borum (2007) notes that often African Americans may view certain parenting and disciplinary styles as showing warmth and love, while others view the same behaviors as "harsh" and "over-controlling" (p. 124). Understanding these differences and the importance of the role of spirituality as well as how history, culture, language, power, and knowledge impact the coping behaviors of many African Americans is essential for culturally relevant service delivery.

Community Engagement Models

Using a systems theory framework, it is possible to see that a community is a living breathing organism, consisting of individual components that function to meet community needs. Interdependence and collaboration are necessary for the community to function well. Promoting public participation and engagement of diverse communities is a recommended strategy to eliminate disparities. To assess structural and nonstructural barriers at the community, programmatic, and individual levels, Strickland and Strickland (1996) conducted household interviews and focus groups with community leaders. Reminder/recall interventions for families requiring follow-up, such as door-to-door interviews and multiple phone calls, were also cited as being instrumental in reducing racial/ethnic disparities in childhood immunization rates (Szilagyi et al., 2002). An example of a promising community engagement model to address educational disparities in inner-city Chicago is After School Matters (ASM). ASM offers Chicago high school teens after school activities in science, technology, sports, and other disciplines. The program uses field experts and providers from community organizations, has donors for financial support, and collaborates with the Chicago Public Schools, Chicago Public Library, and the Chicago Park District to access neighborhood resources. The program provides knowledge, experience, and job skills for the teens as well as services to the city of Chicago (After School Matters, 2011).

In 2011, the Clinical and Translational Science Award (CTSA) Community Engagement Key Function Committee updated the 1997 Principles of Community Engagement to provide public health professionals, health-care providers, researchers, and community-based leaders and organizations with guidance for engaging community partners (National Institutes of Health, 2011). These principles, various protocols, and guidelines have served to assist government agencies and research teams in developing efficient process and evaluative techniques for the community engagement process. The ecomap is one assessment tool that has been used to illustrate the strength of positive and negative relationships among agencies in the community (Richardson & Derezotes, 2010). By identifying the nature and direction of community relationships, collaborators are better equipped to outline strategies and to establish goals for the future.

NINE PRINCIPLES OF COMMUNITY ENGAGEMENT

Be clear about the purposes or goals of the engagement effort and the populations and/or communities you want to engage.

Become knowledgeable about the community's culture, economic conditions, social networks, political and power structures, norms and values, demographic trends, history, and experience with efforts by outside groups to engage it in various programs. Learn about the community's perceptions of those initiating the engagement activities.

Go to the community, establish relationships, build trust, work with the formal and informal leadership, and seek commitment from community organizations and leaders to create processes for mobilizing the community.

Remember and accept that collective self-determination is the responsibility and right of all people in a community. No external entity should assume it can bestow on a community the power to act in its own self-interest.

Partnering with the community is necessary to create change and improve health.

All aspects of community engagement must recognize and respect the diversity of the community. Awareness of the various cultures of a community and other factors affecting diversity must be paramount in planning, designing, and implementing approaches to engaging a community.

Community engagement can only be sustained by identifying and mobilizing community assets and strengths and by developing the community's capacity and resources to make decisions and take action.

Organizations that wish to engage a community as well as individuals seeking to effect change must be prepared to release control of actions or interventions to the community and be flexible enough to meet its changing needs.

Community collaboration requires long-term commitment by the engaging organization and its partners.

Educational Supports and Interventions

According to the Southern Poverty Law Center (2012), some schools are utilizing a program called Positive Behavior Interventions and Supports (PBIS) that has demonstrated promising results in improving overall school climates and academic performance, as well as in improving student retention

SPOTLIGHT: PROMISING PRACTICE INVOLVING COMMUNITY ENGAGEMENT

Point of Engagement, Compton, California

Point of Engagement (POE) was developed in Compton, CA (part of Los Angeles County) , as a collaborative family- and community-centered practice approach that has led to reduced child removals, increased family reunifications within one year, and increased numbers of children achieving legal permanency (Marts, Lee, McRoy, & McCroskey, 2011). This "multidisciplinary, family-centered approach enlists the support of community from both providers and citizens to prevent and address child abuse issues. One of the most promising practices in this model included the referral of children and families to multidisciplinary assessment teams (MATS) to assess children for developmental, educational, and mental health issues within 30-45 days post-placement. Through the identification of treatment needs, stabilizing the relevant relationships, addressing the issues for placement, assessing biological parents for mental health issues, evaluating current caregivers for suitability and for permanency if children needed a permanent family, and by developing back-up family members who could step up if needed," this model proved to be very successful (Marts, Lee, McRoy, & McCroskey, 2011, p. 172). The key elements in this model include initial assessments for substance abuse, domestic violence and mental health issues, assignment of an intensive services worker, relationship building with families, as well as empowering families by giving them a voice in the process and team decision making, which includes social workers, families, faith-based partners, community partners, and age appropriate children. Utilizing this model since 2004, Compton has experienced a reduction in child removals, an increase in children returned to their families with 12 months, an increase in adoptions, a reduction in length of stay in the system, a reduction of African American cases, as well as reduced substantiations.

in the classroom and reducing out of school suspension rates. To address some of the education inequities, in 2010, President Obama called for a major change in the No Child Left Behind Law, which called for schools to increase the number of students who graduate from high school prepared for college and a career. In addition, under the new proposals, schools would be assessed on how well they reduce the achievement gap between poor and affluent students (Dillon, 2010).

Another example of programming designed to lessen the educational disparities among low-income students is the Cristo Rey work-study initiative in Chicago, which began at the Cristo Rey School. More than 1,500 partner businesses provide the internships for Cristo Rey that expose students to the workplace and that generate revenue for the school (Callahan, 2013).

Cross-Systems Collaboration

Efforts are being made to address disparities in the child welfare system. For example, in 2000, Children's Rights in New York City filed a class action lawsuit against the state of Tennessee and the Department of Children's Services noting that Tennessee made fewer efforts to secure placements, services, and permanent homes for African American children in care than for White children (Baynes-Dunning, 2012). Such class action lawsuits represent one tool that can be used to call legal attention to the inequities and to recognize such disparities as a violation of Title VI of the Civil Rights Act. It is clear that states must be held legally accountable for their inequitable results, and close attention must be paid to race equity issues in all child welfare reform initiatives.

In 2005, Senate Bill 6 was passed in Texas, which called for comprehensive reform of that state's Child Protective Services (CPS) system. This reform included a focus on the development of programs to remedy disparities as well as a variety of systemic and practice changes in service delivery, such as hiring a statewide disproportionality director and disproportionality specialists in each region of the state, training CPS staff on disproportionality and requiring participation in *Undoing Racism* training, increasing the proportion of African American and Hispanic staff relative to Anglo staff, developing partnerships with community organizations, increasing kinship placements, and utilizing the Family Group Decision-Making model as a means of increasing the engagement of youth and families (Texas Department of Family and Protective Services, 2010, p. 5). A recent study of the impact of these systemic and practice changes revealed that "some progress has been made in reducing the disproportionate number of African American and Native American children entering substitute care while keeping children safe" (Texas DFPS, 2010, p. 6).

Another example of a proactive attempt to legislatively address disproportionality is Dixon's (2008) proposed African-American Child Welfare
Act, which calls for a radical change in institutional policies and subjective
decision making to address the disproportionality of African-American
children in the child welfare system. Noting that disproportionality has
not only occurred in the child welfare system for a number of decades
(Hill, 2006) but has occurred in all fifty states, and race impacts decision
making at almost every point in the process, Dixon (2008) further stated
that children of color and their families "have less access to services and
their outcomes are poorer" (Dixon, 2008, p. 110). Her proposed federal
legislation would address the disparities identified at each decision point
for children who come into the child welfare system. Her hope is that
through legal action it will be possible to reduce the number of children
that enter the system and, at the same time, place children who are in
foster care back with their families or in an adoptive home. Specifically,
through her proposed African-American Child Welfare Act, disparate
treatment at each decision point—reporting, investigations, substantiation,
provision of remedial services, placement in foster care, and exits from
care (p. 142)—would be acknowledged and addressed through a variety
of remedies. Dixon called for: "required cultural competence training in
university settings for professionals in public and private sectors and mandated reporters on the issue of race, culture, and social policies." The state
would be required to provide "clear and convincing evidence of mistreat-
ment to reduce the number of unwarranted removals, and [to] increase
the likelihood of services being offered which will keep African American
children and parents together" (p. 143).

Dixon (2008) also called for: "(1) the use of risk assessment tools that
caseworkers must respond to about the possible risks the child will encounter if he or she stays in the home; (2) early identification of fathers and
paternal relatives for temporary or permanent placements; and (3) better
services and funding for the provision of wraparound services by culturally
competent service providers to reduce removals and time in care" (p. 144).
These very specific recommendations are clearly based on the issues that
lead African American children to enter care and to remain in care. They
address the decision makers and the decision-making process in order to
provide "race-based relief" and equal protection for African American children and families (p. 145). Such aggressive and legal mandates for changes

SPOTLIGHT: PROMISING PRACTICE ACROSS SYSTEMS

Project Hope, Port Arthur, Texas

Project Hope (Helping Our People Excel) was founded by Joyce James (Former Associate Deputy Executive Commissioner of the Center for the Elimination of Disproportionality and Disparities) and the Texas Community Engagement Model in partnership with Casey Family Programs. It was designed to improve educational and employment outcomes in Port Arthur, a community characterized by high poverty rates, few community resources, and high overrepresentation of African American children in the child welfare system. This model involved partnerships and referrals across systems and community sectors including child welfare, juvenile courts, mental health providers, local businesses, colleges, and schools. Interventions and services included General Educational Development (GED) preparation services, a parenting program, youth anger management, and case management with clients from CPS and other agencies to help families having difficulty with accessing services. Through service coordination and culturally appropriate in-home and agency-based services, Project Hope is building on community assets and strengthening partnerships. Outcomes measured include decreased child welfare referrals and increased birth family reunifications, as well as application of child development knowledge and reduction of parental stress (Casey Family Programs, 2011).

in service delivery to remediate and hopefully eliminate the longstanding racial disparities in child welfare are drastically needed and, hopefully, will receive congressional support in the near future.

FUTURE DIRECTIONS

January 2013 marked the 150th anniversary of the signing of the Emancipation Proclamation, which freed Blacks from slavery and which was intended to lead to economic, political, educational, and social equality and economic empowerment. However, this chapter has provided evidence of ongoing disparities and inequities that still exist 150 years later. The question remains, how long does it take to ensure that African Americans children and families are truly free and have equal access and equal outcomes?

Much still needs to be done to eliminate these ongoing inequities that still differentially impact outcomes for African American children today. As Marsiglia and Kulis (2009, p. 14) have noted, the field of social work needs to adopt a culturally grounded approach that involves social workers acquiring sensitivity and awareness of the diversity among clients and communities, but they must also have an understanding of the "dynamics of oppression and [work] to promote social justice." Through this awareness as well as an understanding of power and injustice, we can begin work to eliminate and overcome the disparities identified in this chapter and throughout this book. Understanding the present issues and historical injustices faced by minority populations will help build awareness and lead to empowerment strategies for overcoming stereotypes and oppressive policies that lead to disproportionate outcomes.

Intersystemic reform (i.e., education, child welfare, juvenile justice, corrections, etc.) is needed to eliminate the growing problem of disproportionality. Just as civil rights legislation was passed in the 1960s to end unequal rights for African Americans, judicial and legislative intervention is needed today to eliminate ongoing inequities in outcomes for African Americans in multiple systems throughout the United States. It is time for resources to be shifted from supporting residual services and institutions (such as prisons, residential settings, etc.) to promoting prevention programs, which support and protect families and communities and lead to improved outcomes for all. The following strategies should be under way now and in the future.

STRATEGIES FOR ADDRESSING AND ELIMINATING DISPROPORTIONALITY AND DISPARITIES

States must prioritize identifying factors leading to disproportionate outcomes across systems and develop strategies to track and eliminate the disproportionality and disparate outcomes of individuals who move from one system to another.

Culturally based model programs need to be developed and evaluated for effectiveness in providing prevention, family support, resources for educational attainment, job skills training, and other services that will improve overall outcomes for African American families.

Programs utilizing the strengths of African American families to cope, to survive, and to thrive through strong religious beliefs should be developed to provide ongoing family support and prevent child removals.

Staff in various service systems must be required to receive training on service delivery to African American families and communities and to be regularly evaluated to assess effectiveness.

Family group or team decision-making practice models need to be widely implemented in order to enhance service delivery to African American families.

Service systems (mental health, education, child welfare, etc.) that demonstrate differential outcomes for specific population groups must be held accountable for inequitable outcomes, and funding should be tied to equitable and successful outcomes for all populations.

States should be given financial rewards for providing evidence of an increase in the number of family reunifications and of improved educational outcomes for children.

States should be rewarded for improvement in the number of African American children passing achievement tests, reducing the number of African American men in prison, reducing the number of child removals, shortening the time African American children remain in out-of-home care, and for increasing the number of African Americans graduating from college.

REFERENCES

Adeleke, T. (2005). Historical problematic of Afrocentric consciousness. *Western Journal of Black Studies, 29*(1), 547–557.

After School Matters. (2011). Retrieved from http://www.afterschoolmatters.org/index.php

Alexander, M. (2011, October 13). More black men are in prison today than were enslaved in 1850. *The Huffington Post*. Retrieved from http://www.huffingtonpost.com/2011/10/12/michelle-alexander-more-black-men-in-prison-slaves-1850_n_1007368.html

American Civil Liberties Union. (n.d.a). *Locating the school-to-prison pipeline.* Retrieved from https://www.aclu.org/files/images/asset_upload_file966_35553.pdf

American Civil Liberties Union. (n.d.b). *Talking points: The school-to-prison pipeline*. Retrieved from https://www.aclu.org/files/assets/stpp_talkingpoints.pdf

American Public Human Services Association. (2008). National Association of Public Child Welfare Administrators Disproportionality Diagnostic Tool. Retrieved from: http://www.aphsa.org/content/dam/NAPCWA/PDF%20DOC/Resources/Disproportionality%20Diagnostic%20Tool/Disproportionality ToolInstructions.pdf

Aud, S., Fox, M. A., & KewalRamani, A. (2010). *Status and trends in the education of racial and ethnic groups*. Washington, DC: U.S. Department of Education, Institute of Education Statistics.

Baynes-Dunning, K. (2012). Is child welfare class action litigation a viable tool to achieve race equity? In J. Meltzer, R. M. Joseph, & A. Shookhoff (Eds.), *For the welfare of children: Lessons learned from class action litigation* (pp. 85–95). Washington, DC: Center for the Study for Social Policy. Retrieved from http://www.cssp.org/publications/child-welfare/class-action-reform/For-the-Welfare-of-Children_Lessons-Learned-from-Class-Action-Litigation_January-2012.pdf

Benton, J. (2012). *NABSW asks where is the justice?* National Association of Black Social Workers 44th Annual Conference. Retrieved from http://NABSW.org

Borum, V. (2007). Why we can't wait: An Afrocentric approach in working with African American families. *Journal of Human Behavior in the Social Environment, 15*(2–3), 115–135.

Brandon, P. (2002). The living arrangements of children in immigrant families in the United States. *International Migration Review, 36*(2), 416–436.

Brown, K. (2008). *African American children in foster care: HHS and congressional actions could help reduce proportion in care (GAO-08-1064T)*. Washington, DC: U.S Government Accounting Office. Retrieved from http://www.gao.gov/products/GAO-08-1064T

Callahan, S. (2013). *Cristo Rey: Schools that work*. Retrieved from http://www.faithandleadership.com/features/articles/cristo-rey-schools-work?page=0%2c1

Casey Family Programs. (2011). *Port Arthur HOPE: Helping our people excel by building community strengths and assets*. Retrieved from: http://www.casey.org/resources/publications/hopechronicle.htm

Centers for Disease Control and Prevention. (2008). *People without health insurance coverage, by race and ethnicity*. Atlanta, GA: Centers for Disease Control and Prevention. Retrieved from http://www.cdc.gov/Features/dsHealthInsurance/index.html

Centers for Disease Control and Prevention (2013). *Black or African American populations*. Retrieved from http://www.cdc.gov/minorityhealth/populations/REMP/black.html

Children's Bureau Express. (2008). *Strategies and tools for practice*. Retrieved from https://cbexpress.acf.hhs.gov/index.cfm?event=website.viewPrinterFriendlyArticle&articleID=2458

Children's Defense Fund. (2011). *Portrait of inequality 2011: Black children in America*. Washington, DC: Children's Defense Fund. Retrieved from http://www.childrensdefense.org

Cokley, K. (2005). Racial(ized) identity, ethnic identity, and Afrocentric values: Conceptual and methodological challenges in understanding African American identity. *Journal of Counseling Psychology, 52*(4), 517–526.

Dillon, S. (2010, May 13). Obama calls for major change in education law. *The New York Times*. Retrieved from http://www.nytimes.com/2010/03/14/education/14child.html

Dixon, J. (2008). The African-American child welfare act: A legal redress for African-American disproportionality in child protection cases, 10 *Berkeley J. Afr.-AM.L. & Pol'y 109 (2008). Available at: http://scholarship.law.berkeley.edu/bjalp/vol10/iss2/3*

Dressler, W., Oths, K., & Gravlee, C. (2005). Race and ethnicity in public health research: Models to explain health disparities. *Annual Review of Anthropology, 34*, 231–252.

Duckett, P. & Artiga, S. (2013). Health coverage for the Black population today and under the Affordable Care Act. Henry J. Kaiser Family Foundation. Retrieved from http://kff.org/disparities-policy/fact-sheet/health-coverage-for-the-black-population-today-and-under-the-affordable-care-act/

Edelman, M.W. (2007). *The cradle to prison pipeline: An American health crisis*. Atlanta, GA: Centers for Disease Control and Prevention. Retrieved from http://www.cdc.gov/pcd/issues/2007/jul/07_0038.htm

Fabella, D., Slappey, S., Richardson, B., Light, A., & Christie, S. (2007). Disproportionality: Developing a public agency strategy. National Association of Public Child Welfare Administrators. Retrieved from www.napcwa.org/content/dam/NAPCWA/PDF DOC/Resources/DisproportionalityDiagnosticTool/DisproportionalityArticle.pdf

Federal Interagency Forum on Child and Family Statistics. (2012). *America's children in brief: Key national indicators of well-being 2012*. Washington, DC: U.S. Government Printing Office. Retrieved from www.ChildStats.gov/americaschildren/eco.asp

Gabriel, T. (2010, November 9). Proficiency of black students is found to be far lower than expected. *The New York Times.* Retrieved from http://www.nytimes.com/2010/11/09/education/09gap.html

Greene, J. P. & Winters, M. (2006). *Leaving boys behind: Public high school graduation rates. Civic Report No. 48.* New York, NY: Manhattan Institute for Policy Research.

Hill, R. (2006). *Synthesis of research on disproportionality in child welfare: An update.* Washington, DC: The Casey-CSSP Alliance for Racial Equity in the Child Welfare System.

Jackson, J. (2008, August 18–19). Growing black diversity in America: Economic, social and political implications. AACORN 5th Annual Meeting, Diversity within African American communities: Implications for advancing research on weight issues and related disparities, Philadelphia. Retrieved from http://www.aacorn.org/uploads/files/3rdInvitedWorkshopCompendium Final09WW.pdf

Jackson, J., Torres, M., Caldwell, C., Neighbors, H., Nesse, R., Taylor, R., & Williams, D.R. (2004). The national survey of American life: A study of racial, ethnic, and cultural influences on mental disorders and mental health. *International Journal of Methods in Psychiatric Research, 13*(4), 196–207.

Manning, M., Cornelius, L. G., & Okundaye, J. N. (2004). Empowering African Americans through social work practice: Integrating an Afrocentric perspective, ego psychology, and spirituality. *Families in Society: The Journal of Contemporary Social Sciences 85*(2), 229–235.

Marsiglia, F., & Kulis, S. (2009). *Diversity, oppression and change.* Chicago, IL: Lyceum.

Marts, E., Lee, E.-K. O., McRoy, R., & McCroskey, J. (2011). Point of engagement: Reducing disproportionality and improving outcomes. In D. Greene, K. Belanger, R. McRoy, & L. Bullard (Eds.), *Challenging racial disproportionality in child welfare: Research, policy, and practice* (pp. 167–187). Washington, DC: Child Welfare League of America.

McRoy, R. G. (2005). Overrepresentation of children and youth of color in foster care. In Mallon, G. P., & Hess, P. M. (Eds.), *Child Welfare for the Twenty-First Century: A Handbook of Practices, Policies and Programs* (pp. 623–634). New York: Columbia University Press.

McRoy, R. G. (2011a). Contextualizing disproportionality. In D. Greene, K. Belanger, R. McRoy, & L. Bullard (Eds.), *Challenging racial disproportionality in child welfare: Research, policy, and practice* (pp. 67–72). Washington, DC: Child Welfare League of America.

McRoy, R. G. (2011b). Selected resources for addressing African American adoption disproportionality. In D. Greene, K. Belanger, R. McRoy, & L. Bullard (Eds.), *Challenging racial disproportionality in child welfare: Research, policy, and practice* (pp. 331–340). Washington, DC: Child Welfare League of America.

McRoy, R. G., & Lombe, M. (2011). Cultural competence with African Americans. In D. Lum (Ed.), *Culturally competent practice: A framework for understanding diverse groups and justice issues* (4th ed.), (pp. 273–301). New York: Brooks-Cole.

Miller, D., & Bennett, D. (2011). Challenges, disparities, and experiences of African American males. *Research on Social Work Practice, 21*(3), 265–268.

Morial, M. (2010). From the president's desk. In Jones, S. J. (Ed.), *The state of black America 2010 jobs: Responding to the crisis* (pp. 6–7). New York: National Urban League.

National Association for the Advancement of Colored People. (2012). *Criminal justice fact sheet.* Baltimore, MD: National Association for the Advancement of Colored People. Retrieved from www.naacp.org/pages/criminal-justice-fact-sheet

National Institutes of Health. (2011). *Principles of community engagement* (2nd ed.). Washington, DC: U.S. Department of Health and Human Services. Retrieved from http://www.atsdr.cdc.gov/communityengagement/pdf/PCE_Report_508_FINAL.pdf

Nobles, W. (1991). African philosophy: Foundations for black psychology. In R. L. Jones (Ed.), *Black psychology* (3rd ed.) (pp. 47–63). Berkeley, CA: Cobb and Henry.

Patton, T. (2006). Hey girl, am I more than my hair? African American women and their struggles with beauty, body image, and hair. *NWSA Journal 18*(2), 24–51.

Prather, C., Fuller, T. R., King, W., Brown, M., Moering, M., Little, S., & Phillips, K. (2006). Diffusing an HIV prevention intervention for African American women: Integrating Afrocentric components into the SISTA diffusion strategy. *AIDS Education & Prevention 18*(4), 149–160.

Quinn, M. Rutherford, R., & Leone, P. (2001). Students with disabilities in correctional facilities. *ERIC Digest* (Pub. No. ED461958). Retrieved from http://eric.ed.gov/?id=ED461958

Richardson, B., & Derezotes, D. (2010). Measuring change in disproportionality and disparities: Three diagnostic tools. *Journal of Health and Human Services Administration, 33*(3), 323–352.

Schiele, J. (1996). Afrocentricity: An emerging paradigm in social work practice. *Social Work 41*(3), 284–294.

Sellers, R., Smith, M., Shelton, N., Rowley, S., & Chavous, T. (1998). Multidimensional model of racial identity: A reconceptualization of African American racial identity. *Personality and Social Psychology Review, 2*(1), 18–39.

Smedley, B., Stith, A., & Nelson, A. (2003). *Unequal treatment: Confronting racial and ethnic disparities in health care.* Washington, DC: National Academies Press.

Snyder, H. (2005). *Juvenile arrests 2003.* OJJDP Juvenile Justice Bulletin. Washington, DC: U.S. Department of Justice.

Southern Poverty Law Center. (2012). *Children at risk.* Montgomery, AL: Southern Poverty Law Center. Retrieved from http://www.splcenter.org/what-we-do/children-at-risk

Stewart, P. (2004). Afrocentric approaches to working with African American families. *Families in Society, 85*(2), 221–228.

Strickland, J., & Strickland, D. L. (1996). Barriers to preventive health services for minority households in the rural south. *The Journal of Rural Health, 12*(3), 206–217.

Szilagyi, P., Schaffer, S., Shone, L., Barth, R., Humiston, S., Sandler, M., & Rodewald, L. (2002). Reducing geographic, racial, and ethnic disparities in childhood immunization rates by using reminder/recall interventions in urban primary care practices. *Pediatrics, 110*(5), e.58.

Tavernise, S. (2011, September 8). Soaring poverty casts spotlight on "lost decade." *The New York Times.* Retrieved from http://www.nytimes.com/2011/09/14/us/14census.html

Terrazas, A. (2009). *African immigrants in the United States.* Washington, DC: Migration Policy Institute. Retrieved from http://www.migrationpolicy.org/article/african-immigrants-united-states-0

Texas Department of Family and Protective Services. (2010). *Disproportionality in child protective services: The preliminary results of statewide reform efforts in Texas.* Austin, TX: Texas Health and Human Services Commission. Retrieved from http://www.hhsc.state.tx.us/hhsc_projects/cedd/publications.shtml

Thomas, K. (2011). Familial influences on poverty among young children in black immigrant, U.S.-born black, and non-black immigrant families. *Demography 48*(2), 437–460.

Thomas, K. (2012). *A demographic profile of black Caribbean immigrants in the United States.* Washington, DC: Migration Policy Institute. Retrieved from http://www.migrationpolicy.org/research/CBI-demographic-profile-black-caribbean-immigrants

U.S. Census Bureau. (2012). *The black population: 2010, 2010 census briefs*. Census Bureau Reports. Washington, DC: U.S. Census Bureau. Retrieved from http://www.migrationpolicy.org/pubs/CBI-CaribbeanMigration.pdf

U.S. Department of Health and Human Services, Administration for Children and Families. (2013). *The AFCARS report, preliminary estimates for FY 2012 as of November 2013*. Washington, DC: U.S. Department of Health and Human Services, Administration for Children and Families. Retrieved from https://www.acf.hhs.gov/sites/default/files/cb/afcarsreport20.pdf

Wald, J., & Losen, D. (2003). Defining and re-directing a school-to-prison pipeline. *New Directions for Youth Development*, *99*, 9–15.

Wilson, V. (2010). Introduction to the 2010 equality index. In Jones, S. J. (Ed.), *The state of black America 2010 jobs: Responding to the crisis* (pp. 10–16). New York: National Urban League.

4

Latino Children and Families

▸ *ALAN DETTLAFF, MICHELLE JOHNSON-MOTOYAMA,*
AND E. SUSANA MARISCAL

POPULATION OF ETHNICALLY DIVERSE CLIENTS IN SYSTEMS

CONSISTENT WITH OTHER HISTORICALLY MARGINALIZED populations, Latino children and families are at disproportionate risk of experiencing a number of psychosocial problems, primary among these being poverty. As of 2010, more than one in four (26.6%) U.S. Latinos lived in poverty, the highest this rate has been since 1993 and an increase of more than 5% since 2007 (DeNavas-Walt, Proctor, & Smith, 2011). Among racial groups, only African Americans slightly exceeded that percentage, with a poverty rate of 27.4%, while just one in ten (9.9%) White Americans lived in poverty (DeNavas-Walt et al., 2011). However, among children in the United States, more Latino children are living in poverty than any other racial or ethnic group. In 2010, Latino children represented 37.3% of all poor children, while 30.5% were White and 26.6% were African American (Lopez & Velasco, 2011). This marked the first time in history that the largest proportion of poor children in the United States was not White. In addition to poverty, studies have documented that Latinos experience a disproportionate number of other poor psychosocial outcomes, including low educational attainment (Fry, 2010; Pew Research Center, 2009), mental health concerns (Canino & Roberts, 2001; Vega & Amaro, 1998), poor health (Finch, Hummer, Kolody, & Vega, 2001; Finch & Vega, 2003), substance abuse (Vega, Alderete, Kolody, & Aguilar-Gaxiola, 1998), and exposure to violence (Aldarondo, Kaufman, & Jasinski, 2002).

Consistent with these poor outcomes, Latinos are disproportionately overrepresented in a number of systems. For example, Latino youth represent approximately 19% of all youth ages 10 to 17, yet they represent 25% of youth who are incarcerated (Saavedra, 2010). Of further concern, the share of Latino youth under 18 who were held in adult prisons increased from 12% to 20% from 2000 to 2008, while during the same period, the share of White and African American youth in adult facilities decreased (Saavedra, 2010). In the child welfare system, Latino children are slightly underrepresented at the national level. As of 2010, they represented 18.3% of children in foster care compared to 20.1% of children in the general population (Summers, Wood, & Russell, 2012). However, significant variation exists at the state level, where Latino children are considerably overrepresented in certain states, while underrepresented in others. In 2010, Latino children were overrepresented in six states, with the greatest overrepresentation occurring in Maine, where they were represented in foster care at a proportion more than double their share of the general population. Further, even in states that have proportional representation, there can be overrepresentation at the regional level. For example, in California, Latino children are slightly underrepresented at the state level. Yet in Santa Clara County, one of the largest counties in the state, they are considerably overrepresented, with Latino children comprising 64.5% of children in care, although they represent only 39% of the child population (Needell et al., 2012). Within the educational system, although Latino children are proportionately represented among children identified with a learning disability and in need of special education services, they are underrepresented among children participating in gifted and talented programs, and Latino males are overrepresented among youth receiving disciplinary actions including suspensions and expulsions (U.S. Department of Education, Office of Civil Rights, 2012).

In addition to being overrepresented among certain systems, significant disparities exist that affect Latinos' access to other systems and receipt of services, particularly as they concern their health and mental health. For example, health care utilization among Latinos is low, with only 70% of Latino adults reporting they had seen a doctor in the past year, compared to 83% of White adults (Schiller, Lucas, Ward, & Peregoy, 2012). Similarly, 27% of Latinos report not having a regular health care provider, compared to only 15% of their White counterparts (Schiller et al., 2012). This may in part be related to disparities that exist in health insurance coverage. Among racial and ethnic groups, Latinos are the least likely to have health insurance coverage. Nationally, the uninsured rate among Latinos is 31%, compared to 12% for Whites and 20.5% for African Americans (National Council of La Raza, 2012). Although uninsured rates are generally lower among children than among adults, Latino children are still more than twice as likely to be uninsured than White children (National Council of La Raza, 2012). Additional barriers to health care access include cultural differences, availability of bilingual health professionals, and generational status (Brotanek, Halterman, Auinger, & Weitzman, 2005; Burgos, Schetzina, Dixon, & Mendoza, 2005), as well as perceived discrimination within the health care system (Friedman et al., 2005; Smedley, Stith, & Nelson, 2003).

Similarly, although research has consistently found no significant differences in the need for mental health services between Latino youth and youth of other races (e.g., Briggs-Gowan, Horwitz, Schwab-Stone, Leventhal, & Leaf, 2000; Costello et al., 1996), a number of studies have found that Latino youth are significantly less likely to receive needed mental health services than White and African American youth (Hough et al., 2002; Kataoka, Zhang, & Wells, 2002). Research has suggested that barriers to the receipt of mental health services among Latino youth may include differing cultural values and beliefs concerning mental health treatment (Ho, Yeh, McCabe, & Hough, 2007), cultural differences in the interpretation of children's behaviors (Roberts, Alegría, Roberts, & Chen, 2005; Zimmerman, Khoury, Vega, Gil, & Warheit, 1995), or a lack of culturally appropriate services available to Latino families (Gudiño, Lau, & Hough, 2008; Lopez, Bergren, & Painter, 2008).

DEMOGRAPHIC OVERVIEW

Latinos are the largest ethnic minority group in the United States and the fastest-growing segment of the U.S. population. As of 2010, Latinos represented 16.3% of the total U.S. population, an increase of 15.2 million people since 2000. Between 2000 and 2010, the Latino population increased by 43%, which was more than four times the growth of the total U.S. population (Ennis, Rios-Vargas, & Albert, 2011). As of 2010, Latino children represented nearly one-fourth of all children in the United States, comprising

24% of all children under the age of 18 (U.S. Census Bureau, 2012). By 2050, the Latino population's share of the total population is expected to nearly double, reaching 30% of the total population. Thus, nearly one in three U.S. residents would be Latino (U.S. Census Bureau, 2008).

Among Latino adults, 52% are foreign-born immigrants who migrated to the United States (Pew Research Center, 2012). However, among Latino children, only 8% are foreign-born (Pew Research Center, 2012). Yet it is important to note that although the large majority of Latino children are born in the United States, more than half (52%) of Latino children have at least one immigrant parent (Fry & Passel, 2009). Overall, the Latino population is relatively youthful compared to other racial and ethnic groups in the United States: the median age of Latinos in the United States in 2010 was 27, compared to 42 for Whites, 32 for Blacks, and 35 for Asians (Pew Research Center, 2012). Important differences also exist between native and foreign-born children with regard to population size and distribution. Whereas children comprise 49.5% of the native-born Latino population, only 7.4% of foreign-born Latinos are children (Pew Research Center, 2012). The age distributions of native and foreign-born children also differ. The age distribution of U.S.-born Latino children is shaped like a pyramid, with younger children represented among the largest age groupings. The pyramid is inverted for immigrant children; older children form the largest age groupings while younger children represent a very small proportion of the total foreign-born Latino child population (Pew Research Center, 2010). Older immigrant children tend to be disproportionally male, reflecting the gendered nature of migration patterns from Latin American countries to the United States (Pew Research Center, 2010).

Geographically, more than three-quarters of the Latino population live in the South (36%) and the West (41%), with more than half of the Latino population in the United States residing in just three states—California, Texas, and Florida (Ennis et al., 2011). A similar pattern exists among foreign-born Latinos. However, recent trends in migration patterns suggest that immigrants who once settled in large urban centers are now moving to destinations in suburban and rural communities with little history or experience with immigrants. As a result, over the past ten years, states in the Midwest, Rocky Mountains, and Southeast have experienced more than a 200% increase in their immigrant population (Fortuny, Capps, Simms, & Chaudry, 2009).

CONTEXT OF CULTURAL VALUES AND NORMS

Although Latinos are a highly diverse group, they share a similarity of certain values resulting from their shared history of Spanish colonization and influence from the Catholic Church (Gonzalez, 2000). Particularly relevant to the context of practice with children and families, *familismo* is considered one of the most important cultural values across Latino populations. This value involves a strong identification and attachment with nuclear and extended family along with a deep sense of family commitment, involvement, and responsibility. The family offers emotional security and a sense of belonging to its members and is the unit to which individuals turn for help in stressful or difficult situations. When family members are in need, others will help, particularly those in stable situations. Similarly, when parents are experiencing challenges that affect their ability to adequately parent their children, it is expected that extended family will provide assistance. For immigrant families, a strong sense of family responsibility and parents' desires for a better life for their children often underlies many families' reasons for immigration. Although the challenges associated with immigration may cause strain within families at times, the family may draw considerable strength and pride resulting from their accomplishments, particularly among parents who are able to meet the needs of their children in the midst of ongoing challenges.

Many Latinos also share a common faith, with Catholicism being the predominant religion among most Latinos (Sanchez & Jones, 2010). This faith is deeply rooted in Latino culture, and although it may be expressed differently and with different levels of participation in organized activities, the values and practices of the Catholic Church have important cultural significance for many Latinos. Similar to their sense of family responsibility, faith can be an important source of strength for many Latino families.

Among some Latino families, views concerning gender and gender roles may also be present and impact families' interactions with certain systems. Latino families are commonly associated with traditional gender roles in which wives assume a more submissive role to their husbands. Although there is some research that suggests these views are increasingly less common, other research indicates that these traditional views have an influence over certain behaviors and interactions among Latinos (e.g., Flores, Eyre, & Millstein, 1998; Raffaelli & Ontai, 2004). However, research also suggests that traditional notions of gender may be considerably challenged upon families' immigration to the United States, due to differing cultural norms and to economic considerations that may require women entering the workforce and men needing to accept additional responsibilities for child care and housework (Coltrane, Parke, & Adams, 2004). However, although immigrant women who are employed in the United States generally experience greater autonomy and independence, men often experience the opposite (Pessar, 1999). This situation is further compounded when men struggle with unemployment because this may increase the risk for relationship conflict (Aldarondo et al., 2002; Cunradi, Caetano, & Schafer, 2002).

Yet, although Latinos share a colonial past, a common language, and similarity of certain values, Latinos are a highly diverse group, representing more than 20 countries of origin with distinct cultural values, traditions, and worldviews. Added to this variation are differences in social class, education, age, gender, sexual orientation, acculturation, migration history, and other individual and family differences. As a result, it is important to be aware that although one may know generalities about a particular culture, assumptions cannot be made about an individual or family. Rather, knowledge of a particular culture represents a hypothesis about a particular member of that culture that needs to be individually assessed and explored, including when a client is a member of one's own cultural group (Dalton, 2005). Ultimately, helping professionals need to be aware of cultural issues, although at the same time avoiding stereotypes and generalizations that take away from their clients' individuality.

EXPLANATION OF WITHIN GROUP ETHNIC DIVERSITY

Although many factors contribute to the heterogeneity that exists among Latinos, there are several factors that may be particularly relevant to the disparities that affect Latino families. These include country of origin, generation in the United States, and immigration status.

Country of Origin

A recent national survey revealed that most Latinos identify themselves first based on country of origin and then as either Hispanic or Latino

(Taylor, Lopez, Martinez, & Velasco, 2012). This preference is defined as ethnic identity, the ethnic component within the self-concept, which influences psychosocial adjustment and coexists and evolves together with other identities and roles. Information about the countries of origin of Latinos in the United States comes from self-described family ancestry or from place of birth in the 2010 Census (Table 4.1). According to this data, Latinos of Mexican (63%), Puerto Rican (9.2%), and Cuban (3.5%) origin or descent represent the nation's three largest Hispanic groups. Over the past decade, the population size of several smaller groups has grown considerably. For example, Latinos of Salvadoran origin, the fourth largest group, grew by 152% from 2000 to 2010. Similarly, the Dominican population grew by 85%, Guatemalans by 180%, and Colombians by 93% (Ennis et al. 2011).

This diversity is further reflected in the states and communities in which Latinos reside. In many metropolitan areas, Mexican-origin Latinos are by far the dominant group. For example, in the San Antonio, Texas, metropolitan area, Mexicans comprise 91.3% of all Latinos. In Chicago, nearly eight in ten (79.2%) of the area's Latinos are of Mexican origin, and in Atlanta, more than half (58.1%) of Latinos are of Mexican origin. However, in other metropolitan areas, other groups are dominant. For example, Puerto Ricans are the largest Latino group in the New York area (29.4%), Cubans are the largest group in the Miami area (50.9%), and Salvadorans are the largest group in the nation's capital (33.7%) (Lopez & Dockterman, 2011). As these figures suggest, it is not uncommon for multiple Latino country-of-origin groups to reside in the same communities. For example, though Puerto Ricans are the largest Latino group (28.0%) in the Boston area, Dominicans comprise nearly one-quarter of the Latino population (23.2%), followed by Salvadorans (10.8%), Guatemalans (7.9%), Mexicans (6.9%), and Cubans (2.1%), with a large population (21.0%) comprising "other" backgrounds (Lopez & Dockterman, 2011).

Generation in the United States

The family histories of some Latinos extend back as many as 16 generations, although others may be newcomers who are crossing the U.S. border today (Camarillo, 2007). In 2000, 40% of Latinos were immigrants of the first generation. More than one-quarter (28%) of Latinos were of the second

TABLE 4.1   U.S. Hispanic Population by Country of Origin, 2010

ORIGIN GROUP	POPULATION (IN THOUSANDS)	SHARE (%)
Mexican	31,798	63.0
Puerto Rican	4,624	9.2
All other Hispanic	3,452	6.8
Cuban	1,786	3.5
Salvadoran	1,649	3.3
Dominican	1,415	2.8
Guatemalan	1,044	2.1
Colombian	909	1.8
Spaniard	635	1.3
Honduran	633	1.3
Ecuadorian	565	1.1
Peruvian	531	1.1
Nicaraguan	348	0.7
Argentinean	225	0.4
Venezuelan	215	0.4
Panamanian	165	0.3
Chilean	127	0.3
Costa Rican	126	0.3
Bolivian	99	0.2
Uruguayan	57	0.1
Other Central American	32	0.1
Other South American	22	< 0.1
Paraguayan	20	< 0.1

Note. From *U.S. Hispanic Country-of-Origin Counts for Nation, Top 30 Metropolitan Areas,* by M. H. Lopez and D. Dockterman, 2011, Washington, DC: Pew Research Center. With permission.

generation (U.S. born with at least one foreign-born parent) and another third (32%) were third generation or higher (U.S. born with U.S.-born parents) (Suro & Passel, 2003). However, the Latino population has been changing dramatically over the past decade as births have outpaced immigration as a key source of growth. Today, three in five Latinos are U.S. born (Morin, 2009).

Most Latinos in the United States speak Spanish (82%), which facilitates connections of Latinos with their cultures of origin as well as among different Latino communities (Taylor et al., 2012). However, generation in the United States may be associated with changes in cultural orientation and social location as reflected in language use and preference, educational attainment, intermarriage, and household income level. For example, first-generation or immigrant Latinos account for most of the Spanish-speakers in the United States. The second generation is fundamentally bilingual, while the third or higher generations speak predominately English (Suro & Passel, 2003). First-generation Latinos tend to have lower levels of education when compared to other generations: less than half of Latino immigrants had a high school diploma in 2000, compared to more than three-quarters of their U.S-born counterparts. Similarly, household income levels are greater for U.S.-born Latinos when compared to immigrants. For example, in 2003, the mean weekly earnings among Latinos were $457 for the first generation, $535 for the second generation, and $550 for the third generation (Suro & Passel, 2003). First-generation Latinos also tend to marry within their ethnic group, which occurs less often among U.S.-born Latinos across generations in the United States. When compared to Latino immigrants, who intermarry at a relatively low rate of 8%, intermarriage is much more common among the second (32%) and the third or higher (57%) generations.

Immigration Status

Among Latinos, immigration to the United States is predominately economically driven. Other reasons for migration include political instability, war-related hardship and persecution, as well as family conflict and persecution related to sexual orientation (Organista, 2007). For Latino immigrants, the process of immigration to the United States is often characterized by loss, trauma, fear, and isolation. These experiences vary depending on country of origin, type of migration, and individual motivations (Glick, 2010; Rumbaut, 1994). Since 1959, Cuban Americans have migrated to the United States as refugees, a status that provides financial and housing assistance, and in most cases, a pathway to citizenship. Puerto Ricans are U.S. citizens by birth as a result of the 1917 Jones Act, which distinguishes them from most other Latin Americans, who are required to enter the country as immigrants with alien status and apply for citizenship.

Immigration status and citizenship are tied to legal rights, access to services, and entitlements to benefits. Of the 40.2 million foreign-born individuals who were in the United States in 2010, nearly three-quarters were legal immigrants (72%) including naturalized citizens, permanent residents, and legal temporary migrants, and more than one-quarter (28%) were unauthorized or without documentation. Mexicans (58%) and other Latin Americans (23%) account for the majority of the immigrant population without documentation in the United States (Passel & Cohn, 2011). Nearly two-thirds of these immigrants have lived in this country for at least 10 years, and nearly half are parents of minor children (Taylor, Lopez, Passel, & Motel, 2011). Immigrants without legal documentation represent a particularly vulnerable population given risks of deportation and exploitation, restricted access to health and social services, and the experience of discrimination (Hancock, 2005; Padilla & Perez, 2003; Smart & Smart, 1995; Solis, 2003).

At least nine million people are part of "mixed status" families that include at least one unauthorized adult and at least one U.S.-born child (Taylor et al., 2011). Policies that impact immigrants without documentation are likely to have "spillover" effects on U.S.-born family members. For example, restricted access to means-tested programs such as food stamps may contribute to food insecurity among children in mixed status families (Fix & Passel 1999, 2002; Fix & Zimmerman, 2001; Van Hook & Balisteri, 2006). Additionally, children in mixed status families may have less access to health insurance and experience other barriers to access to health care when compared to families with two U.S.-born parents (Capps, Fix, Ost, Reardon-Anderson, & Passel, 2004; Douglas-Hall & Koball, 2004; Granados, Puvvula, Berman, & Dowling, 2001; Ku & Matani, 2001).

As families endure contextual stresses in the migration and settlement process, they tend to develop coping skills through the dynamic balance of change and continuity. Meaning and hopefulness are essential for the development of resilience among these families. Falicov (2002) states, "Immigrant families attempt to restore meaning and purpose in life in the midst of multiple ambiguous losses through family connectedness, family rituals, awareness of social marginalization, and belief of spiritual systems" (p. 278). Nonetheless, most immigrants are aware of the prejudice, inequalities, and structural exclusion that surround them. The awareness of social marginalization and injustice may debilitate sense of self as marginalization is internalized. Yet, it may also be empowering and a source of resilience when it inspires activism for social justice (Falicov, 2002). Long-held beliefs and spiritual systems can inform a family's meaning making and their ability to deal with adversity. Cultural values contribute to Latinos' acceptance of suffering and adversities as part of life (*cargar la cruz*—bear the cross). By believing that little in life is in their hands, "mastery of the possible" (Falicov, 2002, p. 281), what can be solved is solved and what cannot is accepted.

BRIEF HISTORY RELATED TO SOCIAL AND ECONOMIC JUSTICE

The history of Latinos as an ethnic minority in the United States was forged primarily through American colonization and the annexation of formerly Mexican lands in the U.S. Southwest during the 19th century (Camarillo, 2007). Basic socioeconomic and political structures were transformed in the 1900s through the rapid influx of Whites, the commercialization of land, and shifts from a pastoral system to a wage-based economy (Telles & Ortiz, 2008). The failure of the Mexican economy in 1907, followed by the decade-long Mexican Revolution that began in 1910, sparked a period of mass authorized immigration to the United States, which continued until the Great Depression of 1929. Over time, the U.S. economy has grown increasingly intertwined with the Mexican economy and has become reliant upon workers from Mexico. At the same time, the United States continues to impose more legal limits on immigration from Mexico, particularly in the wake of the Great Recession of 2007–2009.

The Mexican-origin population is more likely to be of low socioeconomic status when compared to other Latino subgroups. This is largely due to the diverse political and economic legacies of Latino country of origin groups but is also shaped by historical racist practices and discriminatory immigration policies. For example, whereas Mexican immigrants in the United States are often poor and in search of better economic opportunities, Cubans who came to the United States were members of a prosperous middle class who feared the consequences of a takeover by Fidel Castro, and who were later able to use their skills, networks, and U.S. political support to integrate into the middle class.

Today more Latino children are living in poverty than any other racial/ ethnic group, a product of high birthrates to Latina immigrants and declining economic opportunities for families (Lopez & Velasco, 2011). In 2010, poverty rates were highest for Latino children with single mothers (57.3%) followed by families with parents who had a high school diploma or less (48.3%). Census data reveal that only 67.6% of Latinos graduate from high school, while only 13% earn a bachelor's degree, and 3.6% attain a graduate degree (U.S. Census Bureau, 2013). Latinos also have the highest high school drop-out rate in the nation at 29%, twice that of African Americans (13%) and four times that of Whites (7%) (Morin, 2009). Although Latinos are more likely than other parents to seek work, they often remain in jobs that are low skill and low paying (Ortega, Grogan-Kaylor, Ruffolo, Clarke, & Karb, 2010). Considering that higher levels of education are associated with higher levels of earnings, these trends reveal a vicious cycle (U.S. Department of Labor, 2006).

Recent policies targeting immigration have exacerbated these patterns by restricting immigrants' access to services and programs while limiting their rights. For example, California Proposition 187 was a 1994 ballot initiative that sought to prohibit undocumented residents from receiving health care, public education, and other social services in the state (Gibbs & Bankhead, 2001). This initiative was later overturned by a district court decision in 1995, just before the passage of the Personal Responsibility and Work Opportunity Reconciliation Act of 1996 (PRWORA), which restricted eligibility of undocumented immigrants as well as many legal immigrants for a variety of public programs. For example, most legal permanent residents became ineligible for (a) means-tested public-benefit programs for five years after receiving permanent residence and (b) Medicare and Social Security for ten years after receiving permanent residence. National and local evaluations suggest that the restrictions embedded in these initiatives successfully reduced immigrant families' participation in public programs along with the participation of refugees, citizen children, and other populations whose eligibility was not restricted (Borjas, 2011; Fix & Passel, 2002; Zimmerman & Fix, 1998). For example, decreases in the utilization of prenatal care among foreign-born women were recorded, as were a number of preventable deaths to individuals who avoided medical treatment for fear of immigration authorities (Mizoguchi, 1999). Immigrants have also been found to avoid social services and other public programs for fear of becoming a "public charge," a consideration in determining inadmissibility or adjustment in immigration status (Fix & Passel, 1999).

In 1996, the Illegal Immigration Reform and Immigrant Responsibility Act expanded the definition of what constitutes an "aggravated felony" and created a new process to speed the deportation of immigrants without a formal hearing (Ewing, 2012). That same year, the Antiterrorism and Effective Death Penalty Act was passed to allow for the detention and deportation of non-U.S. citizens on the basis of "secret evidence." In the wake of the terrorist attacks of 9/11, the federal government has instituted a number of measures that conflate antiterrorism concerns with renewed attempts to control unauthorized immigration at the federal and local levels (Ewing, 2012). The enforcement of federal immigration laws to control undocumented immigration has played a crucial role in the significant increase in the number of incarcerated Latino federal offenders. The number of Latinos sentenced in federal courts quadrupled between 1991 and 2007, and immigration offenses accounted for 48% of these sentences. In 2007, Latinos represented 40% of all sentenced federal offenders, and nearly one in three of the federal incarcerated inmates (Lopez & Light, 2009).

On the one hand, Latinos have been "relegated to virtual invisibility" (Morin, 2009, p. 6) given that their history in the United States is largely absent from the public eye. On the other hand, more than 66% of news stories about Latinos focus on crime, illegal immigration, and terrorism (Morin, 2009), adding to public misperceptions while fueling prejudice, discrimination, and social injustice.

PROBLEMS/ISSUES FACING CLIENTS RELATED TO DISPROPORTIONALITY AND DISPARITIES

Despite adversity, multiple empirical studies have documented health outcomes that are better among Latino immigrants when compared to non-Latino racial/ethnic groups and U.S.-born Latinos (Franzini, Ribble, & Keddie, 2001; Hayes-Bautista, 2002; Jasso, Massey, Rosenzweig, & Smith, 2004; Palloni & Arias, 2004; Palloni & Morenoff, 2001). These trends in the health of Latinos have been described as *epidemiologic* or *health paradoxes* (Acevedo-Garcia & Bates, 2008). For example, two important measures of infant health include infant mortality and infant low birth weight (< 2,500 g or < 5.5 lb) and are considered significant health indicators given their association with a range of physical and cognitive disabilities across the life span. In general, the prevalence of infant mortality and low birth weight among

Latinos is lower than African American and White infants (MacDorman & Mathews, 2008). What is considered "paradoxical" is that many Latinos have socioeconomic profiles that place other racial/ethnic groups at risk for poor infant health due to factors such as low household income, limited access to medical care, and low rates of prenatal care utilization. Moreover, groups that tend to be the most socioeconomically disadvantaged within the Latino population, such as immigrants, often have healthier infants than their U.S.-born counterparts (Johnson & Marchi, 2009).

Despite these paradoxes in infant health, the initial advantages observed in Latino children have been found to erode for certain indicators. For example, when compared to African Americans and Whites, Latino children are less likely to be fully immunized and more likely to have tuberculosis (Zambrana & Logie, 2000). With regard to oral health, Mexican American children are more likely to have dental cavities in their primary and permanent teeth and are less likely to have dental cavities treated or filled when compared to other racial/ethnic groups (Flores et al., 2002). Although Latino youth face a smaller risk of developing diabetes in adolescence than African American youth (Lipton, Drum, Li, & Choi, 1999), they bear a disproportionate burden of risks for diabetes and obesity in adulthood (Acevedo-Garcia & Bates, 2008). Among adolescents, Latinos have the highest rate of teen pregnancy and adolescent birthrate with 82.2 births per 1,000 women age 15 to 19 years, compared to 64.8 for African Americans and 27.5 for Whites (Ryan, Franzetta, & Manlove, 2005). Of the three ethnic groups, Latino youth are the least likely to report using condoms when compared to African Americans and Whites, placing them at greatest risk of teenage pregnancy, sexually transmitted diseases, and adult HIV/AIDS (Cubbin, Santelli, Brindis, & Braveman, 2005). With regard to substance use, Latino youth have been found to engage in heavy drinking, illicit drug use, and cigarette smoking to a lesser extent than Whites but to a greater extent than African Americans (Zambrana & Logie, 2000). Studies have found that Mexican American adolescents report significantly higher levels of depression and distress when compared to Whites (Choi, Meininger, & Roberts, 2006). When compared to Whites and African Americans, Latino girls are the most likely to report attempted suicide (Flores et al., 2002).

Health conditions also exist for which some Latino subgroups show a disadvantage, although others show an advantage. For example, although

Puerto Ricans are the U.S. racial/ethnic group with the highest adult asthma rates, Mexicans have the lowest rates (Lara, Akinbami, Flores, & Morgenstern, 2006; Rose, Mannino, & Leaderer, 2006). Studies also suggest that Latino immigrants have more positive health behaviors, particularly related to substance use and mental health outcomes, when compared to their U.S.-born counterparts (Alegría, 2007; Grant et al., 2004; Vega et al., 1998).

At least three arguments have been made to explain Latino paradoxes in the health literature: the presence of cultural and/or social protective factors, immigrant selection, and artifacts of data. Cultural and/or social protective arguments highlight the social support grounded in social networks, strong cultural ties, religiosity, *familismo*, and salutary health behaviors (Hayes-Bautista, 2002). The protective factors argument is often presented in association with an acculturation hypothesis that predicts the erosion of such protective factors with time spent in the United States and across generations. The theory of immigrant selection suggests that so-called paradoxes are simply the result of processes that bring Latino immigrants to the United States who are healthier than their counterparts who stay behind (Palloni & Morenoff, 2001). Finally, some researchers suggest that paradoxical patterns might be due to data artifacts such as undercounts of morbidity and mortality, inconsistent ways of defining Latino identity, and the underreporting of health problems among Latinos (Franzini, Ribble, & Keddie, 2001; Jasso et al., 2004; Palloni & Morenoff, 2001). Given the limited ability of most studies to account for all of these possible explanations, the question of Latino health paradoxes is far from settled. As such, the paradoxes observed in some areas of Latino health should not lead professionals to overlook the considerable barriers that face the Latino population.

Ultimately, disparities in the health and well-being of Latinos are influenced by numerous factors at the individual, family, and neighborhood levels. Individual factors include genetics, biology, temperament, developmental stage, and level of acculturation. Family factors include family structure, parenting beliefs and practices, physical and mental health of family members, household socioeconomic conditions, generation in the United States, cultural orientation, and immigration status of family members. Neighborhoods also influence disparities and disproportionality through four interrelated pathways: social, economic, physical, and institutional.

Social Influences

Individuals are influenced positively and negatively through involvement and participation in *social networks*. Social networks typically include peers, family members, and other neighborhood acquaintances. The collective resources that are available to youth from their social networks are known as forms of *social capital* (Portes, 1998). Forms of social capital include the psychological and economic resources that are provided to individuals through the support of their families. Social capital that may be present within Latino neighborhoods include the psychosocial resources that support newcomers in their adaptation to the host culture and buffer them from discrimination. Social capital also includes benefits that are provided by people outside of the immediate family, such as a community's political power and influence to bring health resources into a neighborhood. Social control, another type of social capital, represents values that discourage or promote health behaviors among residents. For example, studies show that close-knit Latino communities characterized by strong cultural values tend to have lower teen pregnancy rates when compared to more diffuse communities. Shared norms regarding early childbearing contribute to social control in these communities through the close monitoring and protection of girls (Denner, Kirby, Coyle, & Brindis, 2003).

Economic Effects

The economic dimensions of neighborhood life include the quality and quantity of employment opportunities available to residents, and commercial services such as grocery stores, banks, and restaurants. Whereas vibrant commercial services attract investment and increase property values, neighborhood disinvestment can lead to a loss of jobs and businesses such as grocery stores that provide healthy food options. Access to ethnic-specific markets in thriving Latino neighborhoods may allow residents to maintain the diets and health practices of their culture of origin. Ethnic neighborhoods may also offer employment to immigrants who may be undocumented or who lack the language skills of the host culture. Enclaves can also provide access to credit, employment information, and "on-the-job" training in lieu of specific educational requirements. Conversely, a lack of documentation, language skill, and educational background can lead to exploitation in enclave settings such as low wages, poor benefits, and hazardous labor conditions (Johnson, 2012).

Physical Effects

The quality of the air, water, and land as well as housing, parks, and recreation facilities influences disparities. The geographic access that families have to economic opportunities throughout the larger region also has important implications for the economic well-being of residents. The way in which a neighborhood is designed can also influence exercise opportunities for children and their families such as walking outdoors, running, and bicycling.

Neighborhood Institutions

As mentioned, the disparities that have been observed in the health of Latinos are due in part to limited access and utilization of health care and mental health services (Morales, Lara, Kington, Valdez, & Escarce, 2002). Immigrant Latinos are particularly vulnerable given the decreased access to health care and diminished use of social services when compared to U.S.-born Latinos (Flores et al., 2002). A neighborhood's institutions may influence the accessibility, affordability, quality, and acceptability of health care for Latino children and families. Mainstream organizations such as hospitals and clinics may tailor their services to serve specific immigrant populations within Latino neighborhoods, while barriers to access within mainstream services may give rise to private and/or self-help organizations that are formed and led by community members. In general, the more institutionally complete the enclave setting, the more likely immigrants will be able to meet their health-related needs despite limited knowledge of the host culture and language barriers (Johnson, 2012).

CULTURALLY COMPETENT ASSESSMENTS AND INTERVENTIONS

Culturally competent assessment of Latino children and families is critical given the diversity within the Latino population and the range of factors that may be contributing to their involvement with service systems.

Culturally competent practice with Latino families requires that practitioners clearly assess the history, values, and traditions of Latino families and how these values and traditions influence their thoughts and behaviors. Cultural values shape the ways in which families view their problems, accept responsibility, and respond to interventions. Thus, considerable effort should be spent learning about the cultural background, values, and traditions of each family in order to understand the dynamics of the family system and their concerns through the cultural lens of the family. These cultural factors should be understood prior to any discussion concerning possible interventions.

Assessment of immigrant Latino families requires particular attention because immigrant families are the least acculturated and therefore among the most difficult to assess. When working with unfamiliar cultures, professionals may make assessments by filtering information through their own cultural lens, resulting in inaccurate assessments of the family dynamics and underlying issues and making families vulnerable to bias. Cultural bias can affect Latino families when personal values, cultural differences, and professional judgments influence decision making, resulting in misinterpretation or misdiagnosis of the presenting issues. Thus, when conducting assessments of immigrant Latino families, providers should be aware of the probable influence of their own cultural values and biases, and effort should be spent attempting to understand the dynamics of the situation through the cultural lens of the immigrant family.

Careful assessment of immigrant Latino families is also important due to the likely impact of acculturative stress within families. Although acculturation refers to the internal process of change experienced by immigrants upon exposure to a new culture (Padilla & Perez, 2003), acculturative stress refers to the stress that directly results from the acculturative process (Berry, Kim, Minde, & Mok, 1987). Upon migration, individuals are faced with a multitude of challenges as they attempt to navigate the new culture. Acculturative stress results when individuals lack the necessary skills or means to interact and be successful in the new environment (Berry et al., 1987). For many immigrants, the acculturative stress experienced following immigration is lifelong, pervasive, and intense. Language barriers, lack of employment, loss of social support, inadequate financial resources, and discrimination experienced in the new culture are all factors associated with acculturative stress (Berry, 2005).

Although acculturative stress is supported in the literature among all immigrants, this literature suggests that acculturation is more difficult for those immigrants who are more distinct from the host culture (Leon & Dziegielewski, 1999; Padilla & Perez, 2003). When significant differences exist between the country of origin and the host culture, the process of acculturation becomes more challenging as a result of the cultural negotiation that must occur because these immigrants must cope with the societal standards and traditions of the new culture while making decisions about the level to which they will integrate into the host culture. Accented speech, unfamiliar customs, and differences in skin color are all factors that identify immigrants as outsiders to those in the dominant culture. These immigrants may experience additional stress because members of the host culture may question their motives and limit their opportunity for involvement in the host culture (Padilla & Perez, 2003). Given these issues, several researchers have suggested that the acculturative stress experienced by Latinos is different from that of other immigrant populations (Fontes, 2002; Hancock, 2005; Padilla & Perez, 2003). Additionally, the process of moving from ethnic majority in their country of origin to a minority in the United States can be disorienting for many Latino immigrants (Espin, 1987). This transition to minority status combined with the anti-immigrant sentiment that exists in many parts of the United States may result in feelings of stigmatization and isolation for Latino families. This can lead to feelings of powerlessness and low self-esteem as immigrants become aware that judgments are made against them based on assumptions of their ethnicity rather than on their actual abilities (Casas, Ponterotto, & Sweeney, 1987).

Following assessment, it is important to remember that families' experiences with immigration and acculturation will continue to affect service delivery. In general, families who experience greater amounts of acculturative stress will be less likely to be able to engage in the development of new skills or resources that are necessary for addressing the issues they are facing. It is also less likely that these families will be able to draw on existing strengths and coping abilities to effectively address these issues due to the stress they are experiencing. As a result, issues of acculturative stress and the associated anxiety experienced by immigrant families must be addressed first in order for long-term change to result. Thus, literature on intervention with Latino immigrant families stresses the importance of interventions that increase social support and reduce isolation (Denner et al., 2003; Fontes, 2002). Social support has been shown to reduce stress and provide the protective factors that are necessary to minimize the negative effects of acculturative stress (Denner et al., 2003).

Culturally Competent Interventions

In developing and implementing interventions with Latino children and families, the importance of cultural competence or cultural sensitivity has been widely emphasized (e.g., Dettlaff & Rycraft, 2010; Hall, 2001; Hodge, Jackson, & Vaughn, 2010; Uttal, 2006). Despite this, surprisingly little research has been conducted on the effectiveness of culturally competent interventions with Latino populations. Additionally, the notion of what makes an intervention culturally competent has varied widely across studies. However, an emerging body of research has begun to identify a number of factors that may facilitate positive outcomes among this population. These factors typically involve some form of cultural adaptation that seeks to incorporate aspects of the target population's culture into a given intervention. This can occur either in the structure and process of service delivery or in the content of the intervention itself.

Structure and Process of Service Delivery

Adaptations concerning the structure and process of service delivery can involve either aspects associated with the service provider or aspects associated with the space and/or location in which the intervention is delivered. At the service provider level, perhaps of primary importance to practice with Latino children and families is the provision of services in their preferred language. It is well established in the research literature that language barriers between patients and providers contribute to health disparities (e.g., Jacobs, Agger-Gupta, Chen, Piotrowski, & Hardt, 2003). Specific concerns include delay or denial of services, decreased likelihood of follow-up care, problems with medication management, underutilization of preventative services, and misdiagnosis of symptoms (Brach & Fraser, 2000; Gandhi et al., 2000; Jacobs, Shepard, Suaya, & Stone, 2004; Karliner, Perez-Stable, & Gildengorin, 2004). In contrast, language concordance has been shown to increase patient satisfaction, self-reported health status, and adherence with medication and follow-up care (Freeman et al., 2002; Perez-Stable, Napoles-Springer, & Miramontes, 1997). Even for families that may speak English, it is important to recognize that they may prefer to receive services in their native language, particularly when the information or service provided concerns their health and well-being or that of their children. And while it may not always be possible for direct service providers to provide services in a family's native language, the use of professional interpreters has consistently been associated with improved outcomes in health settings (Karliner, Jacobs, Chen, & Mutha, 2007).

Ethnic matching between providers and service recipients may also contribute to positive outcomes (e.g., Casas, Vasquez, & Ruiz de Esparza, 2002; Vasquez, 2007). Providers of the same ethnicity may be more likely to understand the culture-specific values or norms of the client, resulting in a more effective assessment and intervention plan. Service recipients may also have increased trust in discussing or disclosing certain issues when working with providers of the same ethnicity. Research concerning the effectiveness of ethnic matching has primarily shown little to no effect of ethnic matching on outcomes (e.g., Cabral & Smith, 2011; Maramba & Hall, 2002). However, a recent randomized clinical trial examining the role of ethnic matching on the effectiveness of brief alcohol interventions with Latino adults found improved outcomes among individuals who received services from a Latino provider compared to those who received services from providers of other races/ethnicities (Field & Caetano, 2010).

Consideration may also be given to the space and/or location in which interventions are provided to facilitate cultural competence. For example, provision of services within the community of the service recipient is a common intervention strategy that is done to facilitate access as well as to maintain connections to recipients' communities and cultural norms, both of which may facilitate positive outcomes. However, little research has been conducted to examine the effectiveness of this strategy, particularly in isolation of other intervention components that may contribute to differences in outcomes. Yet as a means to address barriers to access, the location of service delivery remains an important consideration in culturally competent service delivery.

SPOTLIGHT: PROMISING PRACTICE USING COMMUNITY-BASED
STRATEGIES

Poder Latino

Poder Latino is a community-based HIV/AIDS prevention program for inner-city
Latino youth (Sellers, McGraw, & McKinlay, 1994). This multifaceted intervention
targets Latino youth, ages 14 to 20, who are at elevated risk for HIV/AIDS. One facet
of the intervention involves raising awareness of HIV/AIDS within predominantly
Latino communities through public services announcements that broadcast risk
reduction messages. The program also aims to reduce HIV/AIDS infections through
the responsible use of condoms. Ongoing activities are held within communities
by trained peer leaders, including workshops in schools and health centers, group
discussions in teens' homes, presentations at large community centers, and door-
to-door canvassing. Results have indicated that the intervention appears to reduce
the incidence of multiple sexual partners and delay the onset of sexual activity.

Intervention Content

In developing or adapting the content of interventions to facilitate cultural competence, Resnicow, Braithwaite, Ahluwalia, and Baranowski
(1999) distinguish between *surface structure* and *deep structure*. The former
involves tailoring the materials and messages of an intervention to observ-
able social and behavioral characteristics of the population, while the latter
integrates the cultural, psychological, social, and historical factors of the
target population that influence behaviors into the content of the intervention. For example, surface structure tailoring may involve using photo-
graphs of people or places with which the target population can identify
or integrating language, music, or foods specific to the target population
into the intervention. In contrast, deep structure tailoring would involve
integrating unique cultural values that promote well-being into the content
of the intervention.

Surface structure tailoring is necessary to facilitate receptivity, com-
prehension, and acceptance of the message involved in the intervention

(Resnicow et al., 1999). Although research is limited with Latinos, a small number of studies have documented improved outcomes associated with surface structure tailoring. For example, in an intervention to prevent smoking among Latino adolescents, Johnson et al. (2005) integrated Latino cultural referents throughout the curriculum, including scenarios and activities that were culturally relevant (e.g., an activity about a girl's *quinceañera* and a role play acted out in the style of a telenovela) as well as images of Latinos in print materials. Results found that use of this curriculum was more effective in preventing smoking among Latino students in predominantly Latino schools as compared to a standard intervention without these cultural referents. Similarly, Gans et al. (2009) tailored a print and video intervention to improve nutrition among Latino adults by substituting pictures, graphics, and food choices that were identified as culturally relevant to Latinos in the development of the intervention. Results showed that the tailored intervention was more effective than a nontailored version in improving dietary behaviors.

Deep structure tailoring is necessary to convey salience and to determine program impact (Resnicow et al., 1999). This level of tailoring involves understanding how members of the target population perceive and understand the causes or issues associated with the concern as well as their perceptions regarding the determinants of specific behaviors. Thus, the intervention demonstrates an appreciation for how cultural values, religion, family, and historical experiences shape the ways in which individuals behave and respond to interventions. For example, Gloria and Peregoy (1996) discuss the importance of integrating values such as *simpatia* (sympathy), *personalismo* (personalism), *familismo* (familial ties), *hembrismo* (brotherhood), *verguenze* (pride), and *espiritismo* (spiritualism) into prevention programs. Although research is similarly limited, Mausbach et al. (2008) adapted an intervention to improve functional skills of Latino adults with schizophrenia by basing the format, content, and treatment goals around a number of these values, and they found improved outcomes for participants who received the culturally tailored intervention compared to those who received a standard intervention.

Deep level tailoring may also require an understanding of child-rearing norms, which have been found to be influenced by and vary across cultures (Jambunathan, Burts, & Pierce, 2000; Roer-Strier, 2001). For example, a number of studies have identified differences in the parenting styles and

SPOTLIGHT: PROMISING PRACTICE INVOLVING CULTURAL ADAPTATIONS

Culturally Competent Systems of Care for Latino Children and Families

As a result of the rapidly growing Latino population in Texas, and growing recognition of the need for culturally responsive practice models, the state's child welfare system, in collaboration with several university partners, developed and pilot tested an adaptation of the Systems of Care practice model that was designed to respond to the unique cultural and service needs of Latino children and families (Dettlaff & Rycraft, 2009). Systems of Care is an evidence-based practice framework that was originally developed in response to the needs of children with serious emotional and mental health disorders. In addition to adapting the model for practice in the child welfare system, the model was adapted to frame Systems of Care within the context of Latino cultural values and the strategies of the Systems of Care model were adapted to emphasize Latino cultural values and other cultural issues in the processes of engagement, assessment, and intervention to facilitate positive outcomes with Latino children and families. Child welfare caseworkers across the state were trained to use the model with Latino families. Using this model, caseworkers reported that they spent more time with families and that families were more engaged in the process of service planning. Caseworkers also reported that by using this model families felt more engaged and more empowered to take control of identifying their own needs and developing their problem-solving skills.

expectations of children among immigrant Latino parents (e.g., Earner, 2007; Mendez, 2006). Studies have also identified differences in the values concerning discipline among immigrant Latino parents, who are likely to use an authoritarian style of parenting and view corporal punishment as a strategy to correct behavior (Fontes, 2002; Frias-Armenta & McCloskey, 1998). These values and norms need to be understood in the development of prevention and intervention programs in order to be relevant to this population. The lack of understanding of the influence of culture has been cited as the primary barrier to adequate assessment and effective intervention in cases of child maltreatment among immigrant families (Shor, 1999).

FUTURE DIRECTIONS

Although the Latino population is diverse in culture and country of origin, Latinos in the United States are affected by many of the same issues that contribute to disproportionality and disparities in health and social service systems. Although Latinos experience positive health outcomes in some indicators and are not overrepresented in certain systems, strategies are needed that address those areas where disproportionality and disparities are present, particularly as they negatively affect the health and well-being of vulnerable children and families. Specifically, we propose the following strategies to advance efforts to eliminate disproportionality and disparities as they affect Latino children and families:

STRATEGIES FOR ADDRESSING AND ELIMINATING DISPROPORTIONALITY AND DISPARITIES

Further research is needed that addresses differences within the Latino population according to generation and citizenship status. Issues of country of origin and citizenship contribute to the diversity of the Latino population but also may considerably impact Latinos' access to and receipt of health and social services. Although some data is available concerning the differential involvement of Latinos in certain systems based on these factors, much additional data is needed to fully understand issues of over- and/or underrepresentation in service systems and how generation and citizenship status affect this.

Further research is needed that examines the effectiveness of culturally competent interventions with Latino children and families. Although there is a body of literature on interventions that may be effective with Latinos, much of this literature is limited by designs that fail to use appropriate comparison groups or that fail to isolate the cultural components of the intervention to determine their effectiveness. As a result, little is known about how to adapt or develop interventions to improve cultural competence with Latino children and families.

Cross-systems collaborations are needed that address the pipelines that exist among systems that negatively impact Latino children, youth, and families. These collaborations should engage in efforts that enhance our understanding of the factors that contribute to cross-systems involvement and in the development of

policies and programs designed to address the needs of cross-system youth to reduce their representation across systems.

Strategies to address disproportionality and disparities lie not only within systems but also within Latino communities affected by those phenomena. Systems
need to engage with community partners to understand the factors that contribute
to disproportionality and disparities and to develop programs that provide support
for families in need. This includes community members, community service providers, law enforcement, the courts, schools, local government, and other community
stakeholders. To be successful, a strategic plan for community engagement must
be developed through a coalition of service providers and community stakeholders
that emphasizes developing and utilizing support systems within the community to
ensure access to needed services. Where resources do not exist, service systems
need to work with community leaders to develop them. In doing so, systems need
to recognize the barriers that may exist to community engagement. These include
fear, distrust, and a perception of some systems as harmful within many communities of color. Overcoming these barriers will require a longstanding commitment
that begins with efforts to promote healing and a change in those perceptions.

REFERENCES

Acevedo-Garcia, D., & Bates, L. M. (2008). Latino health paradoxes: Empirical
evidence, explanations, future research, and implications. In H. Rodriguez, R.
Saenz, & C. Menjivar (Eds.), *Latino/as in the United States: Changing the face
of America* (pp. 101–113). New York: Springer.

Aldarondo, E., Kaufman, G. K., & Jasinski, J. (2002). A risk marker analysis of wife
assault in Latino families. *Violence Against Women, 8,* 429–454.

Alegría, M. (2007). Prevalence of psychiatric disorders across Latino subgroups in
the United States. *American Journal of Public Health, 97,* 68–75.

Berry, J. W. (2005). Acculturation: Living successfully in two cultures. *International Journal of Intercultural Relations, 29,* 697–712.

Berry, J. W., Kim, U., Minde, T., & Mok, D. (1987). Comparative studies of acculturative stress. *International Migration Review, 21,* 491–511.

Borjas, G. J. (2011). Poverty and program participation among immigrant children.
The Future of Children, 21, 247–266.

Brach, C., & Fraser, I. (2000). Can cultural competency reduce racial and ethnic disparities? A review and conceptual model. *Medical Care Research Review, 57,* 181–217.

Briggs-Gowan, M. J., Horwitz, S. M., Schwab-Stone, M. E., Leventhal, J. M., & Leaf, P. J. (2000). Mental health in pediatric settings: Distribution of disorders and factors related to service use. *Journal of the American Academy of Child & Adolescent Psychiatry, 39,* 841–849.

Brotanek, J. M., Halterman, J., Auinger, P., & Weitzman, M. (2005). Inadequate access to care among children with asthma from Spanish-speaking families. *Journal of Health Care for the Poor and Underserved, 16,* 63–73.

Burgos, A. E., Schetzina, K. E., Dixon, L. B., & Mendoza, F. S. (2005). Importance of generational status in examining access to and utilization of health care services by Mexican American children. *Pediatrics, 115,* 322–330.

Cabral, R. R., & Smith, T. B. (2011). Racial/ethnic matching of clients and therapists in mental health services: A meta-analytic review of preferences, perceptions, and outcomes. *Journal of Counseling Psychology, 58,* 537–554.

Camarillo, A. M. (2007). Mexico. In M. Waters, & R. Ueda (Eds.), *The new Americans: A guide to immigration since 1965* (pp. 504–517). Cambridge, MA: Harvard University Press.

Canino, G., & Roberts, R. E. (2001). Suicidal behavior among Latino youth. *Suicide and Life-Threatening Behavior, 31,* 122–131.

Capps, R., Fix, M., Ost, J., Reardon-Anderson, J., & Passel, J. (2004). *The health and well-being of young children of immigrants.* Washington, DC: Urban Institute.

Casas, J. M., Ponterotto, J. G., & Sweeney, M. (1987). Stereotyping the stereotyper: A Mexican-American perspective. *Journal of Cross-Cultural Psychology, 18,* 45–57.

Casas, J. M., Vasquez, M., & Ruiz de Esparza, C. A. (2002). Counseling the Latina/o: A guiding framework for a diverse population. In P. B. Pederson, J. G. Draguns, W. J. Lonner, & J. E. Trimble (Eds.), *Counseling across cultures* (pp. 133–160). Thousand Oaks, CA: Sage.

Choi, H., Meininger, J. C., & Roberts, R. E. (2006). Ethnic differences in adolescents' mental distress, social stress, and resources. *Adolescence, 41,* 263–283.

Coltrane, S., Parke, R. D., & Adams, M. (2004). Complexity of father involvement in low-income Mexican American families. *Family Relations, 53,* 179–189.

Costello, E. J., Angold, A., Burns, B. J., Stangl, D. K., Tweed, D. L., Erkanli, A., & Worthman, C. M. (1996). The Great Smoky Mountains Study of Youth:

Goals, design, methods, and the prevalence of DSM-III-R disorders. *Archives of General Psychiatry, 53,* 1129–1136.

Cubbin, C., Santelli, J., Brindis, C. D., & Braveman, P. (2005). Neighborhood context and sexual behaviors among adolescents: Findings from the national longitudinal study of adolescent health. *Perspectives on Sexual Reproduction and Health, 37*(3), 125–134.

Cunradi, C. B., Caetano, R., & Schafer, J. (2002). Socioeconomic predictors of intimate partner violence among white, black, and Hispanic couples in the United States. *Journal of Family Violence, 17,* 377–389.

Dalton, B. (2005). Teaching cultural assessment. *Journal of Teaching in Social Work, 25,* 45–61.

DeNavas-Walt, C., Proctor, B. D., & Smith, J. C. (2011). *U.S. Census Bureau, current population reports (P60-239), income, poverty, and health insurance coverage in the United States: 2010.* Washington, DC: U.S. Government Printing Office.

Denner, J., Kirby, D., Coyle, K., & Brindis, C. (2003). The protective role of social capital and cultural norms in Latino communities: A study of adolescent births. In M. Aguirre-Molina & C. M. Molina (Eds.), *Latina health in the United States: A public health reader.* San Francisco: Jossey-Bass.

Dettlaff, A. J., & Rycraft, J. R. (2009). Culturally competent systems of care with Latino children and families. *Child Welfare, 88*(6), 109–126.

Dettlaff, A. J., & Rycraft, J. R. (2010). Adapting systems of care for child welfare practice with immigrant Latino children and families. *Evaluation and Program Planning, 33,* 303–310.

Douglas-Hall, A., & Koball, H. (2004). *Children of recent immigrants: National and regional trends.* New York: National Center for Children in Poverty, Columbia University.

Earner, I. (2007). Immigrant families and public child welfare: Barriers to services and approaches to change. *Child Welfare, 86*(4), 63–91.

Ennis, S. R., Ríos-Vargas, M., & Albert, N. G. (2011). *The Hispanic population: 2010.* Washington, DC: U.S. Census Bureau.

Espin, O. M. (1987). Psychological impact of migration on Latinas. *Psychology of Women Quarterly, 11,* 489–503.

Ewing, W. A. (2012). *Opportunity and exclusion: A brief history of U.S. immigration policy.* Washington, DC: Immigration Policy Center, American Immigration Council.

Falicov, C. (2002). Ambiguous loss: Risk and resilience in Latino immigrant families. In M. Suarez-Orozco & M. Paez (Eds.), *Latinos remaking America.* Los Angeles: University of California Press.

Field, C., & Caetano, R. (2010). The role of ethnic matching between patient and provider on the effectiveness of brief alcohol interventions with Hispanics. *Alcoholism: Clinical and Experimental Research, 34,* 262–271.

Finch, B. K., Hummer, R. A., Kolody, B., & Vega, W. A. (2001). The role of discrimination and acculturative stress in the physical health of Mexican-origin adults. *Hispanic Journal of Behavioral Sciences, 23,* 399–429.

Finch, B. K., & Vega, W. A. (2003). Acculturation stress, social support, and self-rated health among Latinos in California. *Journal of Immigrant Health, 5*(3), 109–117.

Fix, M., & Passel, J. (1999). *Trends in non-citizens' and citizens' use of public benefits following welfare reform: 1994-1997.* Washington, DC: The Urban Institute.

Fix, M., & Passel, J. (2002). *The scope and impact of welfare reform's immigrant provisions.* Washington, DC: The Urban Institute.

Fix, M., & Zimmermann, W. (2001). All under one roof: Mixed status families in an era of reform. *International Migration Review, 35*(134), 397–419.

Flores, E., Eyre, S., & Millstein, S. G. (1998). Sociocultural beliefs related to sex among Mexican American adolescents. *Hispanic Journal of Behavioral Sciences, 20,* 60–82.

Flores, G., Fuentes-Afflick, E., Barbot, O., Carter-Pokras, O., Claudio, L., Lara, M., et al. (2002). The health of Latino children: Urgent priorities, unanswered questions, and a research agenda. *The Journal of the American Medical Association, 288*(1), 82–90.

Fontes, L. A. (2002). Child discipline and physical abuse in immigrant Latino families: Reducing violence and misunderstanding. *Journal of Counseling and Development, 80,* 31–40.

Fortuny, K., Capps, R., Simms, M., & Chaudry, A. (2009). *Children of immigrants: National and state characteristics.* Retrieved from http://www.urban.org/publications/411939.html

Franzini, L., Ribble, J. C., & Keddie, A. M. (2001). Understanding the Hispanic paradox. *Ethnicity and Disease, 11*(3), 496–518.

Freeman, G. K., Rai, H., Walker, J. J., Howie, J. G., Heaney, D. J., & Maxwell, M. (2002). Non-English speakers consulting with the GP in their own language: A cross-sectional survey. *British Journal of General Practice, 52,* 36–38.

Frias-Armenta, M., & McCloskey, L. A. (1998). Determinants of harsh parenting in Mexico. *Journal of Abnormal Child Psychology, 26*, 129–139.

Friedman, J. Y., Anstrom, K. J., Weinfurt, K. P., McIntosh, M. Bosworth, H. B., Oddone, E. Z., et al. (2005). Perceived racial/ethnic bias in healthcare in Durham County, North Carolina: A comparison of community and national samples. *North Carolina Medical Journal, 66*, 267–275.

Fry, R. (2010). *Hispanics, high school dropouts and the GED.* Washington, DC: Pew Research Center.

Fry, R., & Passell, J. S. (2009). *Latino children: A majority are U.S.-born offspring of immigrants.* Washington, DC: Pew Hispanic Center.

Gandhi, T. K., Burstin, H. R., Cook, E. F., Puopolo, A. L., Haas, J. S., Brennan, T. A., et al. (2000). Drug complications in outpatients. *Journal of General Internal Medicine, 15*, 149–154.

Gans, K. M., Risica, P. M., Strolla, L. O., Fournier, L., Kirtania, U., Upegui, D., et al. (2009). Effectiveness of different methods for delivering tailored nutrition education to low income, ethnically diverse adults. *International Journal of Behavioral Nutrition and Physical Activity, 6*, 24.

Gibbs, J. T., & Bankhead, T. (2001). *Preserving privilege: California politics, propositions, and people of color.* Westport, CT: Praeger.

Glick, J. E. (2010). Connecting complex processes: A decade of research on immigrant families. *Journal of Marriage and Family, 72*(3), 498–515.

Gloria, A. M., & Peregoy, J. J. (1996). Counseling Latino alcohol and other substance users/abusers: Cultural considerations for counselors. *Journal of Substance Abuse Treatment, 13*, 119–126.

Gonzalez, J. (2000). *Harvest of empire: A history of Latinos in America.* New York: Penguin.

Granados G., Puvvula, J., Berman, N., & Dowling, P. T. (2001). Health care for Latino children: Impact of child and parental birthplace on insurance status and access to health services. *American Journal of Public Health, 91*(11), 1806–1807.

Grant, B., Stinson, F., Hasin, D., Dawson, D., Chou, S., & Anderson, K. (2004). Immigration and lifetime prevalence of DSM-IV psychiatric disorders among Mexican Americans and non-Hispanic whites in the United States: Results from the National Epidemiologic Survey on Alcohol and Related Conditions. *Archives of General Psychiatry, 61*(12), 1226–1233.

Gudiño, O. G., Lau, A. S., & Hough, R. L. (2008). Immigrant status, mental health need, and mental health service utilization among high-risk Hispanic and Asian Pacific Islander youth. *Child Youth Care Forum, 37*, 139–153.

Hall, G. C. N. (2001). Psychotherapy research with ethnic minorities: Empirical, ethical, and conceptual issues. *Journal of Consulting and Clinical Psychology, 69,* 502–510.

Hancock, T. (2005). Cultural competence in the assessment of poor Mexican families in the rural southeastern United States. *Child Welfare, 84,* 689–711.

Hayes-Bautista, D. E. (2002). The Latino health research agenda for the twenty-first century. In M. M. Suarez-Orozco & M. Paez (Eds.), *Latinos remaking America* (pp. 215–235). Berkeley: University of California Press; David Rockefeller Center for Latin American Studies.

Ho, J., Yeh, M., McCabe, K., & Hough, R. L. (2007). Parental cultural affiliation and youth mental health service use. *Journal of Youth and Adolescence, 36,* 529–542.

Hodge, D. R., Jackson, K. F., & Vaughn, M. G. (2010). Culturally sensitive interventions for health behaviors among Latino youth: A meta-analytic review. *Children and Youth Services Review, 32,* 1331–1337.

Hough, R. L., Hazen, A. L., Soriano, F. I., Wood, P. A., McCabe, K., & Yeh, M. (2002). Mental health services for Latino adolescents with psychiatric disorders. *Psychiatric Services, 53,* 1556–1562.

Jacobs, E. A., Agger-Gupta, N., Chen, A. H., Piotrowski, A., & Hardt, E. J. (2003). *Language barriers in healthcare settings: An annotated bibliography of the research literature.* Woodland Hills, CA: The California Endowment.

Jacobs, E. A., Shepard, D. S., Suaya, J. A., & Stone, E. (2004). Overcoming language barriers in health care: Costs and benefits of interpreter services. *American Journal of Public Health, 94,* 866–869.

Jambunathan, S., Burts, D. C., & Pierce, S. (2000). Comparisons of parenting attitudes among five ethnic groups in the United States. *Journal of Comparative Family Studies, 31,* 395–406.

Jasso, G., Massey, D. S., Rosenzweig, M. R., & Smith, J. P. (2004). Immigrant health selectivity and acculturation. In N. B. Anderson, R. A. Bulatao, & B. Cohen (Eds.), *Critical perspectives on racial and ethnic differences in health in late life* (pp. 227–266). Washington, DC: The National Academies Press.

Johnson, C. A., Unger, J. B., Ritt-Olson, A., Palmer, P. H., Cen, S. Y., Gallaher, P., et al. (2005). Smoking prevention for ethnically diverse adolescents: 2-year outcomes of a multicultural, school-based smoking prevention curriculum in Southern California. *Preventive Medicine, 40,* 842–852.

Johnson, M. A. (2012). Ethnic enclaves. In S. Loue & M. Sajatovic (Eds.) *Encyclopedia of Immigrant Health.* New York: Springer Publishing.

Johnson, M. A., & Marchi, K. S. (2009). Segmented assimilation theory and peri-
natal health disparities among women of Mexican descent. *Social Science &
Medicine, 69*(1), 101–109.

Karliner, L. S., Jacobs, E. A., Chen, A. H., & Mutha, S. (2007). Do professional
interpreters improve clinical care for patients with limited English proficiency?
A systematic review of the literature. *Health Services Research, 42,* 727–754.

Karliner, L. S., Perez-Stable, E., & Gildengorin, V. (2004). The language divide:
The importance of training in the use of interpreters for outpatient practice.
Journal of General Internal Medicine, 19, 175–183.

Kataoka, S. H., Zhang, L., & Wells, K. B. (2002). Unmet need for mental health
care among U.S. children: Variation by ethnicity and insurance status. *American
Journal of Psychiatry, 159,* 1548–1555.

Ku, L., & Matani, S. (2001). Left out: Immigrants' access to health care and insurance. *Health Affairs, 20*(1), 247–256.

Lara, M., Akinbami, L., Flores, G., & Morgenstern, H. (2006). Heterogeneity of
childhood asthma among Hispanic children: Puerto Rican children bear a disproportionate burden. *Pediatrics, 117,* 43–53.

Leon, A. M., & Dziegielewski, S. F. (1999). The psychological impact of migration:
Practice considerations in working with Hispanic women. *Journal of Social
Work Practice, 13*(1), 69–82.

Lipton, R. B., Drum, M., Li, S., & Choi, H. (1999). Social environment and year of
birth influence type 1 diabetes risk for African-American and Latino children.
Diabetes Care, 22(1), 78–85.

Lopez, C., Bergren, M. D., & Painter, S. G. (2008). Latino disparities in child
mental health services. *Journal of Child and Adolescent Psychiatric Nursing, 21,*
137–145.

Lopez, M. H., & Dockterman, D. (2011). *U.S. Hispanic country-of-origin counts for
nation, top 30 metropolitan areas.* Washington, DC: Pew Research Center.

Lopez, M. H., & Light, M. T. (2009). *A rising share: Hispanics and federal crime.*
Washington, DC: Pew Research Center.

Lopez, M. H. & Velasco, G. (2011). *Childhood poverty among Hispanics sets record,
leads nation.* Washington, DC: Pew Research Center.

MacDorman, M. F., & Mathews, T. J. (2008). Recent trends in infant mortality in
the United States. *NCHS Data Brief,* 1–8.

Maramba, G. G., & Hall, G. C. (2002). Meta-analyses of ethnic match as a predictor of dropout, utilization, and level of functioning. *Cultural Diversity and
Ethnic Minority Psychology, 8,* 290–297.

Mausbach, B. T., Bucardo, J., McKibbin, C. L., Goldman, S. R., Jeste, D. V., Patterson, T. L., et al. (2008). Evaluation of a culturally tailored skills intervention for Latinos with persistent psychotic disorders. *American Journal of Psychiatric Rehabilitation, 11*, 61–75.

Mendez, J. A. O. (2006). Latino parenting expectations and styles: A literature review. *Protecting Children, 21*(2), 53–61.

Mizoguchi, N. (1999). Proposition 187: California's anti-immigrant statute. In E. J. Kramer, S. L. Ivey, & Y. Ying (Eds.). *Immigrant women's health: Problems and solutions*. San Francisco: Jossey-Bass.

Morales, L. S., Lara, M., Kington, R. S., Valdez, R. O., & Escarce, J. J. (2002). Socioeconomic, cultural, and behavioral factors affecting Hispanic health outcomes. *Journal of Health Care for the Poor and Underserved, 13*(4), 477–503.

Morin, J. L. (2009). *Latino/a rights and justice in the United States*. Durham, NC: North Carolina Academic Press.

National Council of La Raza. (2012). *Fast facts: Latinos and health care*. Retrieved from http://www.nclr.org/images/uploads/publications/FastFacts_Latinosand HealthCare2012.pdf

Needell, B., Webster, D., Armijo, M., Lee, S., Dawson, W., Magruder, J., et al. (2012). *Child welfare services reports for California*. Retrieved from http://cssr. berkeley.edu/ucb_childwelfare/

Organista, K. (2007). *Solving Latino psychosocial and health problems: Theory, practice, and populations*. Hoboken, NJ: John Wiley & Sons.

Ortega, R. M., Grogan-Kaylor, A., Ruffolo, M. C., Clarke, J., & Karb, R. (2010). Racial and ethnic diversity in the initial child welfare experience. In M. B. Webb, K. L. Dowd, B. J. Harden, J. Landsverk, & M. F. Testa (Eds.), *Child welfare & child well-being* (pp. 236–272). New York: Oxford University Press.

Padilla, A., & Perez, W. (2003). Acculturation, social identity, and social cognition: A new perspective. *Hispanic Journal of Behavioral Sciences, 25*(1), 35–55.

Palloni, A., & Arias, E. (2004). Paradox lost: Explaining the Hispanic adult mortality advantage. *Demography, 41*(3), 385–415.

Palloni, A., & Morenoff, J. D. (2001). Interpreting the paradoxical in the Hispanic paradox: Demographic and epidemiologic approaches. *Annals of the New York Academy of Sciences, 954*, 140–174.

Passel, J. S., & Cohn, D. (2011). *Unauthorized immigrant population: National and state trends, 2010*. Washington, DC: Pew Research Center.

Perez-Stable, E. J., Napoles-Springer, A., & Miramontes, J. M. (1997). The effects of ethnicity and language on medical outcomes of patients with hypertension or diabetes. *Medical Care, 35,* 1212–1219.

Pessar, P. R. (1999). Engendering migration studies: The case of new immigrants in the United States. *American Behavioral Scientist, 42,* 577–600.

Pew Research Center. (2009). *Between two worlds: How young Latinos come of age in America.* Washington, DC: Author.

Pew Research Center. (2010). *Statistical profiles of the Hispanic and foreign-born populations in the U.S.* Washington, DC: Author.

Pew Research Center. (2012). *Statistical portrait of Hispanics in the United States, 2010.* Washington, DC: Author.

Portes, A. (1998). Social capital: Its origins and applications in modern sociology. *Annual Review of Sociology, 24,* 1–24.

Raffaelli, M., & Ontai, L. L. (2004). Gender socialization in Latino/a families: Results from two retrospective studies. *Sex Roles, 50,* 287–299.

Resnicow, K., Braithwaite, R., Ahluwalia, J., & Baranowski, T. (1999). Cultural sensitivity in public health: Defined and demystified. *Ethnicity and Disease, 9,* 10–21.

Roberts, R. E., Alegría, M., Roberts, C. R., & Chen, I. G. (2005). Mental health problems of adolescents as reported by their caregivers: A comparison of European, African, and Latino Americans. *Journal of Behavioral Health Services & Research, 32,* 1–13.

Roer-Strier, D. (2001). Reducing risk for children in changing cultural contexts: Recommendations for intervention and training. *Child Abuse & Neglect, 25,* 231–248.

Rose, D., Mannino, D., & Leaderer, B. (2006). Asthma prevalence among U.S. Adults, 1998–2000: Role of Puerto Rican ethnicity and behavioral and geographic factors. *American Journal of Public Health, 96*(5), 880–888.

Rumbaut, R. G. (1994). Origins and destinies: Immigration to the United States since World War II. *Sociological Forum, 9,* 583–621.

Ryan, S., Franzetta, K., & Manlove, J. (2005). *Hispanic teen pregnancy and birth rates: A look behind the numbers.* Washington, DC: Pew Research Center.

Saavedra, J. D. (2010). *Just the facts: A snapshot of incarcerated Hispanic youth* [fact sheet]. Washington, DC: National Council of La Raza.

Sanchez, T. W., & Jones, S. (2010). The diversity and commonalities of Latinos in the United States. In R. Furman & N. Negi (Eds.), *Social work practice with Latinos: Key issues and emerging themes* (pp. 31–44). Chicago: Lyceum.

Schiller, J. S., Lucas, J. W., Ward, B. W., & Peregoy, J. A. (2012). *Summary health statistics for U.S. adults: National Health Interview Survey, 2010.* Washington, DC: National Center for Health Statistics.

Sellers, D. E., McGraw, S. A., & McKinlay, J. B. (1994). Does the promotion and distribution of condoms increase teen sexual activity? Evidence from an HIV prevention program for Latino youth. *American Journal of Public Health, 84,* 1952–1959.

Shor, R. (1999). Inappropriate child rearing practices as perceived by Jewish immigrant parents from the former Soviet Union. *Child Abuse & Neglect, 23,* 487–499.

Smart, J., & Smart, D. (1995). Acculturative stress of Hispanics: Loss and challenge. *Journal of Counseling and Development, 73,* 390–396.

Smedley, B., Stith, A. Y., & Nelson, A. R. (Eds.). (2003). *Unequal treatment: Confronting racial and ethnic disparities in health care.* Washington, DC: Institute of Medicine.

Solis, J. (2003). Re-thinking illegality as a violence against, not by Mexican immigrants, children, and youth. *Journal of Social Sciences, 59,* 15–31.

Summers, A., Wood, S., & Russell, J. (2012). *Disproportionality rates for children of color in foster care.* Reno, NV: National Council of Juvenile and Family Court Judges.

Suro, R., & Passel, J. S. (2003). *The rise of the second generation: Changing patterns in Hispanic population growth.* Washington, DC: Pew Research Center.

Taylor, P., Lopez, M. H., Passel, J. S., & Motel, S. (2011). *Unauthorized immigrants: Length of residency, patterns of parenthood.* Washington, DC: Pew Research Center.

Taylor, P., Lopez, M. H., Martinez, J. H., & Velasco, G. (2012). *When labels don't fit: Hispanics and their views of identity.* Washington, DC: Pew Research Center.

Telles, E. E., & Ortiz, V. (2008). *Generations of exclusion: Mexican Americans, assimilation and race.* New York: Russell Sage Foundation.

United States Census Bureau. (2008). *An older and more diverse nation by midcentury.* Retrieved from http://www.census.gov/newsroom/releases/archives/population/cb08-123.html

United States Census Bureau. (2012). *2010 census data* [Data file]. Retrieved from http://www.census.gov/2010census/data/

United States Census Bureau. (2013). *Educational Attainment in the United States: 2013.* Retrieved from http://www.census.gov/hhes/socdemo/education/data/cps/2013/tables.html

United States Department of Education, Office of Civil Rights. (2012). *The transformed civil rights data collection—March 2012 data summary.* Retrieved from http://www2.ed.gov/about/offices/list/ocr/data.html

United States Department of Labor. (2006). Education and income: More learning is key to higher earnings. *Occupational Outlook Quarterly, 50*(3), 60. Retrieved from http://www.bls.gov/opub/ooq/2006/fall/oochart.pdf

Uttal, L. (2006). Organizational cultural competency: Shifting programs for Latino immigrants from a client-centered to a community-based orientation. *American Journal of Community Psychology, 38,* 251–262.

Van Hook, J., & Balisteri, K. S. (2006). Ineligible parents, eligible children: Food stamps receipt, allotments, and food insecurity among children of immigrants. *Social Science Research, 35*(1), 228–251.

Vasquez, M. J. (2007). Cultural differences and the therapeutic alliance: An evidence-based analysis. *American Psychologist, 62,* 878–885.

Vega, W.A., Alderete, E., Kolody, B., & Aguilar-Gaxiola, S. (1998). Illicit drug use among Mexicans and Mexican Americans in California: The effects of gender and acculturation. *Addiction, 93,* 1839–1850.

Vega, W. A., & Amaro, H. (1998). Lifetime prevalence of DSM III-R psychiatric disorders among rural and urban Mexican Americans in California. *Archives of General Psychiatry, 55,* 771–782.

Zambrana, R. E., & Logie, L. A. (2000). Latino child health: Need for inclusion in the U.S. national discourse. *American Journal of Public Health, 90*(12), 1827–1833.

Zimmerman, R. S., Khoury, E. L., Vega, W. A., Gil, A. G., & Warheit, G. J. (1995). Teacher and parent perceptions of behavior problems among a sample of African American, Hispanic, and non-Hispanic white students. *American Journal of Community Psychology, 23,* 181–197.

Zimmerman, W., & Fix, M. E. (1998). *Declining immigrant applications for Medi-Cal and welfare benefits in Los Angeles County.* Washington DC: The Urban Institute.

5

Asian American and Pacific Islander Children and Families

▸ MERIPA GODINET, ROWENA FONG, AND BRITT URBAN

POPULATION OF ETHNICALLY DIVERSE CLIENTS IN SYSTEMS

THE U.S. OFFICE OF MANAGEMENT and Budget (OMB) defines "Asians" as those persons "having origins in any of the original peoples of the Far East, Southeast Asia, or the Indian subcontinent, including, for example, Cambodia, China, India, Japan, Korea, Malaysia, Pakistan, the Philippine Islands, Thailand, and Vietnam," (U.S. Census Bureau, 2012a, p.2). The U.S. Census Bureau uses this definition in its collecting and categorizing of race data in the United States.

However, this broad label of "Asian" does not accurately depict the diversity of culture, language, socioeconomic status, and education levels that exist among the various Asian groups in the United States. Despite the large variability in these characteristics, there is still often a generalized view of what being Asian means. This definition includes the idea of the "model minority," which portrays Asians as highly intelligent, well-educated, and of a higher socioeconomic category. This stereotype overlooks the within-group diversity that exists and the disproportional overrepresentation of some Asian groups in certain U.S. institutions.

Prior to the 2000 U.S. Census, the Pacific Islander ethnic groups were subsumed under the Asian and Pacific Islander racial group. In 1997, a directive by the OMB separated this racial group into Asian or Pacific Islander racial categories (U.S. Census Bureau, 2010). To better illustrate the profile of each racial group, it was necessary to separate the two groups because they vary greatly in profile indicators such as social economic status. Factors such as median income and high educational achievement showed Asians to be above the national rate, although earnings and educational attainment for Pacific Islanders generated lower numbers in higher education and earnings. Therefore, smaller groups such as Pacific Islanders were misrepresented because they are the smallest ethnic/racial group in the United States (U.S. Census Bureau, 2010; Vakalahi, Godinet, & Fong, 2006). Thus, any misreporting will have a large impact on the profile of Pacific Islanders.

DEMOGRAPHIC OVERVIEW

The Asian Population

In 2010, there were 308.7 million people living in the United States (U.S. Census Bureau, 2012a). The "Asian alone" (the term used by the U.S. Census Bureau for those who report being of only the Asian race) population makes up 4.8% of the total population, at 14.7 million people. In addition to the "Asian alone" population, there were another 2.6 million people who identify as being of partial Asian descent "in combination with one or more other races" (U.S. Census Bureau, 2012a, p. 3). Therefore, the total population of Asians in the United States is 17.3 million people, 5.6% of the population.

The Asian population in the United States has increased rapidly over the last decade. In comparison to U.S. population growth overall, the "Asian alone" population has grown at a rate four times as fast (U.S. Census Bureau, 2012a). Additionally, this same group has grown "at a faster rate than all other race groups in the country" (U.S. Census Bureau, 2012a, pp. 3–4). The U.S. Asian population also varies by region. Nearly half (46%) of all people of Asian descent live on the West Coast. The South and Northeast regions are also home to large numbers of Asians, with 22% and 20%, respectively, of the U.S. Asian population living in those locations (U.S. Census Bureau, 2012a).

The Pacific Islander Population

Native Hawaiians and Pacific Islanders (NHPIs) are a rapidly growing racial group in the United States. According to the 2010 Census, Pacific Islanders make up 1.2 million (0.4%) of the total U.S. population, which constitutes a 40% growth from 2000 to 2010. Although more than half of the total NHPI population (52%) reside in the states of Hawaii and California (U.S. Census Bureau, 2010), other southern and western states have also shown a fast increase, such as Texas, Delaware, Washington, North and South Dakotas, Kansas, and Ohio, as well as the District of Columbia, to name a few. Although the growth is worth noting, challenges emerge for a diverse race of people living in a dominant culture that is often times counter to their own.

CONTEXT OF CULTURAL VALUES AND NORMS

The Asian Population

Because Asians are a highly diverse group, they may share traditional cultural values but norms may be slightly different for East Asians, South Asians, and Southeast Asians. Asian cultures value family/kin responsibilities, obligations, filial piety, respect, loyalty, and righteousness (Ross-Sheriff & Husain, 2001). Saving face, a traditional cultural value, prevents behaviors that will shame the family but also limits individual choice and initiative.

The Pacific Islander Population

E sao mai i le Amouta 'ae tali le Amotai, fai fo'i o lea, a o le toe aso i Moamoa.
We have overcome some difficulties, but there are more ahead (Schultz, 1950, p. 46).

As noted in this Samoan proverb, regardless of what seem to be insurmountable challenges encountered by Pacific Islanders, difficulties are seen as a part of life. Thus, knowing that there are still hurdles to overcome, it helps to reflect on how previous challenges were successfully addressed and can be used to address current and future obstacles. Focusing therefore on the values, practices, and key social systems embedded within the array of cultures under the NHPI umbrella can help to refocus from limitations to strengths. Relevant to the Hawaiian worldview is the emphasis on self in relation to various entities (*akua*—deity; *kanaka*—mankind; ☐*aina*—land/environment) (see Figure 5.1).

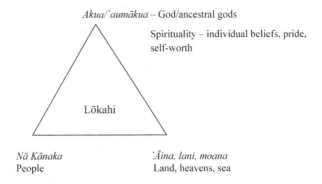

- Apex: *Akua/`aumākua* (God/Ancestral gods)
- Bottom left: *nā kānaka* (People)
- Bottom right: *`Āina, lani, and moana* (Environment)
- Within these boundaries there exists *Lōkahi* (Unity, harmony, and balance).

FIGURE 5.1 Hawaiian Worldview—Macro Level

When harmony and balance are established among the three entities, *lōkahi* (unity) is achieved. Conversely, when a state of lōkahi is not realized, it can mean negative consequences for the individual, the community, and for the environment (Duponte, Martin, Mokuau, & Paglinawan, 2010; McCubbin & Marsella, 2009). Also relevant to other Pacific Islander cultures are spirituality, family, and land—a sense of place. The goal of harmony and balance also extends to the family and community systems because it is a vital component in the fabric of their cultural systems. Interdependency among family members is a way of life for Pacific Islanders. They are expected to be responsible for each other and to learn the values of respect, reciprocity, integrity, filial piety, and honor (Vakalahi, Godinet, & Fong, 2006). When one understands the value of family to Pacific Islanders, one would have a context in which an individual sacrifices something important for the family—a practice and a value that at times are in conflict with Western values. An example would be an adult male son who decides to withdraw from college because he is expected to carry on the responsibilities of his father, a chief, upon the father's death. Although the situation may be seen from a Western perspective as sacrificing one's future, from a cultural perspective this would be seen as honorable and necessary for the survival of a legacy and the passing on of indigenous cultural knowledge. Placing communal and/or family needs above individualism can lead to issues in a Western educational system that defines success as achieving self-reliance (Ratliffe, 2011).

Contrary to the stigma and stereotypes brought about by the high numbers of NHPIs in the child welfare systems, Pacific Islander cultures value and love children, as expressed in a Samoan saying, *o le au o matua o fanau*, "the pinnacle of parents' affection are their children" (Tamasese, 2006, p. 4). Although methods of child rearing and bonding differ than those of the Western world, children are valued and have definite responsibilities within a family when they reach a certain age. Raising a child is a crucial responsibility shared not only by parents but also the adults in an *aiga* (nuclear and extended family), which includes grandparents, elders, and the *matai* (chief) to ensure proper nurturing. That is, the child is taught moral standards and obligations so that he or she will develop a good character and thus become a contributing member of the family. Because children are nurtured and taught by the elders of the family, they are also part of the reciprocity process. Young sons and daughters are expected to assist the family by means of caring for their younger siblings and by helping with daily household needs and family or community functions/activities. In this way, the children play a crucial part in the family's reputation in the larger community (Lowe, 2003). With regard to discipline methods, although physical punishment is condoned as a means of discipline or correcting bad behavior within Samoan families, no Samoan proverbs, customs, or traditions support or promote excessive physical abuse (Tamasese, 2006).

Because devotion and commitment to family (extended and nuclear) are important factors in many Pacific Island cultures and can be positive ways of expanding social support, these qualities can also be their downfall. Such is the case when a member of the family is in trouble; other members will get involved to help out their own. Although the act of chivalry stems from good intentions, these behaviors at times result in individuals being arrested for assault. As shown in a study of Hawaii's juvenile justice system, Samoan adolescents are overrepresented in personal offenses (Godinet & Li, 2012). Thus, the intersection of protectiveness of the family and poverty places Pacific Islanders at high risk for involvement in the criminal justice system.

EXPLANATION OF WITHIN-GROUP ETHNIC DIVERSITY

The Asian Population

Within the U.S. Asian population, there is a great deal of diversity in ancestral heritage and culture. Those of Chinese descent account for the most populous Asian subgroup in the United States, with 3.3 million people. The number increases to 4 million when people with at least mixed-Chinese heritage are taken into account (U.S. Census Bureau, 2012a).

After people of Chinese descent, Filipinos and Asian Indians are the second and third largest Asian subgroups in the United States, with 3.4 million people of at least partial Filipino heritage, and 3.2 million people of at least partial Asian Indian heritage. Other substantial Asian subgroups include people of Japanese, Korean, and Vietnamese backgrounds. There are 1.8 million Vietnamese, 1.7 million Koreans, and 1.3 million Japanese people (single-race and/or partial-race) in the United States (U.S. Census Bureau, 2012a).

The Pacific Islander Population

Pacific Islanders are grouped into one of the three geographical categories: Polynesians (Native Hawaiian, Samoan, Tongan, Tahitian, Maori, Fijian, Tokelauan), Micronesians (Chamorro or Gumanian/Guahanian, Marian Islander, Saipanese, Palauan, Carolinian, Kosraean, Pohnpeian, Chuukese, Yapese, Marshallese, I-Kiribati), and Melanesians (i.e., Papua New Guinean, Solomon Islander, Ni-Vanuatu). Per the 2010 census, the median age is 28.9, which is lower than that of the national population. Similar to the 2000 U.S. Census, the largest NHPI group in the United States is Native Hawaiians (NHs). Samoans were the second largest, followed by Chamorros. A group that has shown to be the fastest growing within the NHPIs is the Chuukese. Their population is six times larger than what was reported in 2000.

BRIEF HISTORY RELATED TO SOCIAL
AND ECONOMIC JUSTICE

The Asian Population

There is a long history of racism and injustice toward Asian and Pacific Islander populations in the United States. The largest group of Asians in the United States—the Chinese—have endured a great deal of oppression since first arriving as immigrants. In 1848, gold was discovered in California, which sparked the California Gold Rush and a mass influx of people from around the world seeking opportunity and riches. This is when Chinese immigrants began to flock to the United States. Quickly, between 1850 and 1860, the Chinese population exploded from just 758 to more than 35,000 (Gibson & Lennon, 1999). It continued to grow during the post-Civil War era because more laborers were needed in the rebuilding efforts.

Due to this new labor source, Central Pacific Railroad began recruiting Chinese workers in 1865 to help construct the Transcontinental Railroad, which was completed three years later. The labor utilized for this project was 90% Chinese (Pegler-Gordon, 2006). It is at this time that an anti-Chinese sentiment began to emerge and grow, as it often does in the United States when there is a flood of immigrant workers. In many U.S. cities, particularly in California, violence began to break out in the early 1870s, in objection to Chinese immigrants and citizens. This hostility spread and, as Lee (2002) highlighted, is well illustrated by the declaration of H. N. Clement (an attorney in San Francisco) to a California Senate committee in 1876: "The Chinese are upon us. How can we get rid of them? The Chinese are coming. How can we stop them?" (Lee, 2002, p. 36). Finally, in 1882, a law was passed that indelibly changed U.S. immigration policy—the Chinese Exclusion Act (CEA) of 1882. This legislation made all immigration by Chinese workers illegal, "for a period of ten years and barred all Chinese immigrants from naturalized citizenship" (Lee, 2002, p. 36). It eventually came to include all Chinese people, with a few exceptions made for diplomats and other individuals of the Chinese upper class.

Despite the dominant argument of the era that this policy was enacted because of the United States' need to protect its borders and from any perceived threats (Lee, 2002), it was actually the first time that immigration policy had been determined based on race and class (Pegler-Gordon, 2006). Additionally, the Federal Immigration Bureau at that time began to photograph Chinese women and children, "then all Chinese immigrants, and finally U.S. citizens of Chinese descent" (Pegler-Gordon, 2006, p. 53) as a way to document and regulate the Chinese community and to enforce this policy of exclusion. The systematic exclusion of the Chinese continued for more than 60 years until China became a U.S. ally during World War II.

In 1943, the Exclusion Act was at last repealed. Despite the repeal, its legacy cannot be erased. It encouraged viewing foreigners through a racist lens and as "others." This discrimination toward Asians in the United States persists even today.

This oppression, although creating barriers and challenges for Chinese immigrants and their American descendants, has actually created opportunities and benefits for many others in the United States. When Chinese immigrants were first permitted to enter the United States to help build the Transcontinental Railroad, to work on early infrastructure projects, and to rebuild our nation after a destructive civil war, U.S. leaders profited from this cheap labor. When exclusion began, this White, privileged class was the only one that benefitted from all the hard work of the Chinese laborers, allowing for more accumulation of wealth by Whites, and helping to perpetuate the unequal socioeconomic structure based on race. Additionally, the exclusion policy encouraged further racial profiling and discrimination, and it perpetuated the belief in White superiority in the United States. By "racializing Chinese immigrants as permanently alien, threatening, and inferior on the basis of their race, culture, [and] labor," (Lee, 2002, p. 38), Whites in power were able to validate their argument and rationalize their behavior, which would in the end benefit them economically, socially, and politically.

Another Asian group that has suffered oppression and discrimination in the United States is the Japanese. During World War II, Japan infamously bombed Pearl Harbor, a U.S. naval base in Hawaii. This generated an onslaught of distrust and discrimination toward Japanese and Japanese-Americans living in the United States. It eventually led to the internment of 120,000 people of Japanese descent in camps established for that sole purpose. The internment camps "were surrounded by barbed wire and armed guard towers, yet two-thirds of those incarcerated were American citizens born in this country (second generation, or Nisei, Japanese Americans)" (Nagata, 1990, p. 48). Similar to the CEA, this action was taken to supposedly protect the United States—in this case, from espionage and sabotage during the war. However, "neither German nor Italian Americans were subjected to massive incarceration, despite the fact that the United States was at war with Germany and Italy as well" (Nagata, 1990, p. 48). This relatively recent event in U.S. history highlights how racism and fear took precedence over basic civil rights.

The Pacific Islander Population

Although each Pacific Islander nation within the NHPI group has a unique historical, cultural, socioeconomic, and political context, they share similar challenges as a result of colonization, oppression, marginalization, immigration, and racial discrimination (Blaisdell & Mokuau, 1991; Godinet, Arnsberger, & Garlock, 2011; Pobutsky, Buenconsejo-Lum, Chow, Palafox, & Maskarinec, 2005; Vakalahi, Godinet, & Fong, 2006). As for Native Hawaiians, the impact of colonization continues to resonate deeply in their lives. As described by the Aboriginal Healing Foundation, unresolved grief and loss experienced through the generations are passed on within a culture. Historical trauma not resolved will continue to affect "individuals, families, and communities until the trauma has been addressed mentally, emotionally, physically, and spiritually" (Wesley-Esquimaux, & Smolewski, 2004, p. 3). For Native Hawaiians, the additive impact of the loss of land, language, and religion, in addition to the illegal overthrow of the Hawaiian monarchy has been connected to historical trauma. The impact of such severe trauma continues as reflected in disproportionate numbers of Kanaka Maoli (Native Hawaiians) experiencing a variety of health, social, psychological, and economic problems (Duponte et al., 2010; McCubbin & Marsella, 2009). Early on, the devastating impact of colonization contributed to the glaring decline of the Native Hawaiian population from one million in 1778 to 40,000 in the late 1800s. This was due to diseases and distress from the loss of cultural values and traditions along with numerous other troubling conditions. Currently, issues related to the loss of land and their kingdom continue to plague Native Hawaiians; they are over-represented in homelessness in Hawaii compared to other ethnic groups (Yuan, Kole, & Yuen, 2008). In addition, Native Hawaiians have one of the highest mortality rates in Hawaii, as well as high rates of alcohol and substance abuse and high rates of incarceration and recidivism in the criminal justice system—phenomena that were rare before colonization (Else, Andrade, & Nahulu, 2007). Thus, to better understand the circumstances that are related to the current predicament of Pacific Islanders, understanding the contribution of colonization and historical and generational trauma is imperative.

Migration for Pacific Islanders is not a new phenomenon. The literature tells us that, given the expanse of numerous islands that spans nearly

33% of the world (Smith, 2008) and their remote locations in the Pacific Ocean, Pacific Islanders were skilled seafarers who journeyed to these locations and were possibly the original settlers. Whatever the reasons for their initial migration in historical times, Pacific Islanders managed to build communities, thrive in the face of challenges, and establish their respective nations, society, and roots (Joakim, 2000). As more and more of their countries are impacted by the era of industrialization, and the presence and influence of Western society, migration continues as a means to seek out resources that will provide opportunities for employment, health care, and education. Unfortunately as immigrants, Pacific Islanders have encountered a slew of hardships in adjusting to their new environments. These challenges are a result of language barriers, lack of adequate health care, lack of job skills, lower paying jobs, lack of education, discrimination, and involvement in stigmatizing systems such as child welfare and the criminal justice systems. Due to cultural and language differences, and unfamiliarity with their new environments, Pacific Islanders are faced with the reality of being at high risk for poverty. As with Hawaiians, suicide is also a concern among the younger generations in other nations of the Pacific Islands, which have some of the highest rates of completed suicides in the world (Booth, 1999; Pinhey & Millman, 2004). This epidemic started in the 1960s during the post-war era and has impacted the lives of villagers (Else et al., 2007).

PROBLEMS/ISSUES FACING CLIENTS RELATED TO DISPROPORTIONALITY AND DISPARITIES

The Asian Population

Past discrimination that many Asians in the United States have faced has lasting effects on the life circumstances and overall treatment of these groups today. Although the overall stereotype of the Asian population is that of the "model minority," distanced from poverty, crime and other social ills, the reality for many Asians in the United States is very different. This includes disparities in opportunities and disproportional overrepresentation in many systems. However, because there are so many Asian subgroups, it is hard to examine the Asian population in the United States as a homogenous unit. There are similar cultural values that many Asian subgroups share, but the socioeconomic and political power of the subgroups

varies greatly based on each subgroup's particular history. The tendency
to categorize ethnicity in broad terms "discounts the diversity of cultures
within these categories and obscures potentially important intra-group differences" (Elliott & Urquiza, 2006, p. 797). This overgeneralization of an
ethnic group can lead not only to discrimination by workers in a system
(e.g., child welfare) but also to poor outcomes for the ethnic group because
the nuances of cultural values are ignored. For this reason, it is imperative
to examine disparities for the U.S. Asian population overall, as well as the
different Asian subgroups.

The U.S. Child Welfare System (CWS) is a prime example of how people of color are often disproportionately and unfairly represented in large
systems. The CWS often receives a great deal of attention when it comes
to racial disproportionality. However, the focus is often on the overrepresentation of African American children and families, compared to other
racial and ethnic groups. There is not a great deal of research on Asians
in the CWS, but there is some data that suggests that Asians do, in fact,
experience racial discrimination in the CWS. Hines, Lee, Osterling, and
Drabble's (2007) study of disproportionality in the CWS indicates, for
example, that Asian groups have lower rates of family reunification than
do Whites and Latinos. This means that Asian children who are removed
from their families by child welfare agencies are less often reunited with
their birth families than are White and Latino children. This same study
did point out that because of the broad ethnic categorization of Asians,
there was no acknowledgement of the varied length of time that different
subgroups had been in the United States or of these subgroups' very different educational, socioeconomic, and cultural backgrounds, which all have
an effect on the experience these groups might have in the CWS. Southeast
Asian families, for example, tend to face more barriers than other Asians,
due to language barriers, refugee status, and lower socioeconomic class
(Hines et al., 2007). This again demonstrates how overgeneralizing can lead
to inaccurate assumptions and outcomes.

One way in which a lack of knowledge about cultural and socioeconomic differences can manifest itself is when child welfare workers unintentionally discriminate. This discrimination comes in the form of "interpreter
services falling short, placement needs not being met, context of families
not being addressed . . . [with] an overall experience of oppression for these

families and . . . negative outcomes for children and families" (Maiter & Stalker, 2011, p. 140).

Apart from disproportionality in the CWS, there are also disparities in utilization of and access to mental health care services by Asian populations in the United States. There is a great deal of research that has focused on the mental health care needs of Asian Americans and Asian immigrants. Time and time again, the research has shown that Asian Americans are "less likely to seek help for mental health problems than other racial demographic groups, and less than their representation in the U.S. population," (Chu & Sue, 2011, p. 3). Although there is some evidence that the prevalence of mental health issues for Asian Americans is lower than that of other racial and ethnic groups, the data on this varies widely because it is difficult to assess with precision. Reporting bias, methodology variance, cultural issues, and many other factors play a part in the challenges of accurately calculating mental health prevalence among Asian Americans (Sue, Yan Cheng, Saad, & Chu, 2012). However, significantly lower utilization rates still exist for Asian Americans, even when factors such as gender, age, education level, ethnic subgroup, and prevalence are taken into account (Chu & Sue, 2011). The underutilization of mental health services by Asians in the United States thus still begs an explanation.

There are several key factors that impact these mental health utilization rates by U.S. Asians. To begin with, Asian culture conceptualizes mental health treatment in a very different way than that of the West. Although the Western perspective follows a medical model, with clearly defined diagnoses, prescription medication, and professional treatment, Asians often first look at informal remedies to their problems including relying on help from family, friends, and their community (Chu & Sue, 2011). Additionally, distress is often exhibited through somatic symptoms in Asian cultures so the Diagnostic and Statistical Manual of Mental Disorders (DSM-IV) diagnostic criteria, which mainly focus on psychological symptoms, may not be an appropriate measure of mental disorders for all ethnic groups.

In Japan, for example, "*taijin-kyofusho* is defined as a fear of offending others because of socially awkward behavior or an imagined physical offense (e.g., body odor)" (Juckett & Rudolph-Watson, 2010, p. 210). So, symptoms of distress for a Japanese person in the United States may not manifest themselves in the same way that an American might express their social phobia. This can become problematic when trying to treat symptoms based on a Western model without consideration of cultural factors in treatment options.

Another illustration is from Korean culture, where women may experience a culture-bound syndrome called *hwa-byung* (Juckett & Rudolph-Watson, 2010). This syndrome might be defined as depression in the Western model, but in Korean culture, it manifests itself as stomach pain. This abdominal pain is somatic and often not substantiated as a medical condition but is understood as having to do with a person's emotional distress. The Western idea of a formal mental health diagnosis is foreign to many Asian cultures. This leads to one of the other factors that marginalize Asian groups from mental health care in the United States—lack of cultural competence and accommodation by service providers.

Due to the very different cultural conceptualizations of mental illness by different ethnic groups, there are sure to be challenges in providing appropriate services to such a diverse population as in the United States. Yet if equality in service provision is to be a goal in our society, as is purported, it is essential that service providers begin to understand the various cultures within their communities. Typically, mental health services in the United States are provided in an individual or group setting, often with an emphasis on sharing personal experiences and processing through these. In addition to individual and group therapy, psychotropic medications are frequently a part of mental health treatment. These treatment modalities have proven to be effective with the general population. However, as discussed earlier, many Asian groups may not benefit from or may not feel culturally comfortable with these types of treatment.

In general, there is a stigma regarding mental illness in Asian cultures. This stigma can lead to shame for an individual and their family if the information were to become public. This is a deterrent to seeking mental health services for many people in Asian communities. Additionally, if services are finally sought, an Asian American patient who holds certain traditional Asian beliefs, including that of not shaming one's family, may be less likely to engage fully in therapy in the same way that a White patient might (Kim, Atkinson, & Umemoto, 2001).

Asians in the United States face numerous barriers to accessing mental health services. This obviously contributes to the underutilization of services discussed earlier. It also points to an overall disparity in access to health care by people of color. For many Asian immigrants, the language barrier presents one of the biggest challenges. The importance of language becomes exceedingly clear when a person's health is at stake. Poor communication can lead to major errors in diagnoses and inappropriate treatment planning by providers, as well as to a lack of understanding by patients. The most vulnerable groups to face language barriers are often newly arrived immigrants and refugees, who may already be disoriented by the U.S. health care system, the Western medical model, and American culture, making it that much more difficult to advocate for their health needs. Many recent studies have begun to examine the impact of limited English proficiency (LEP) on utilization of and access to mental health services. It has been found that "LEP Asians are . . . much less likely than those who are English proficient to seek and continue to receive services," (Snowden, Masland, Peng, Lou, & Wallace, 2011, p. 231). English language proficiency, again, varies by subgroup: "The percentage of persons five years or older who do not speak English at home varies among Asian American groups: 55% of Vietnamese, 46% of Chinese, 22% of Filipinos, and 22% of Asian Indians are not fluent in English" (U.S. Office of Minority Health, 2011), putting these subgroups in a more vulnerable position in terms of health-care access.

In addition to language and cultural barriers, there are also economic barriers that make it difficult for some Asian subgroups in the United States to obtain mental health services. Although the average Asian household has the highest median income of all race groups, this does not acknowledge the wide variance among subgroups. Asian subgroups that have arrived more recently, such as the Hmong, are generally poor. Additionally, Asians as a group have a higher overall rate of poverty than do Whites (U.S. Census Bureau, 2012b).

Finally, a person's economic status is often directly related to whether that person has health insurance (U.S. Census Bureau, 2012b). In 2011, the uninsured rate for the general population was 15.7%. The number was lower for Whites (11.1%) than the national average. For Asians, however, the rate of uninsured (16.8%) was higher than that of the general population and that of Whites (U.S. Census Bureau, 2012b). Again, when examined more closely, it becomes clear that insurance coverage rates also differ greatly by Asian subgroup. In 2010, for example, the "uninsured status [was] 20% for Vietnamese, 11% for Filipino, [and] 13% for Chinese"

(U.S. Office of Minority Health, 2011). These low levels of insurance rates for certain subgroups makes it much more challenging for those people to get needed mental health services because people without insurance often have to search for greater lengths of time for sliding scale services, may be put on waiting lists, or may not be able to afford any out-of-pocket costs.

The Pacific Islander Population

Although small in numbers relative to other racial groups in the United States, the glaring overrepresentation of NHPIs in various welfare, health, and social systems has been well noted in the literature. Reports and studies from the state of Hawaii have shown that percentages of Native Hawaiian (47%) and Samoan (3.2%) children and families involved in the CWS (Department of Human Services, State of Hawaii, 2013) foster care system were markedly higher compared to their respective proportion in the population (21.32% and 2.37%, respectively) (EPIC, 2014; Office of Hawaiian Affairs, 2010; U.S. Census Bureau, 2010). Such an alarming disparity has existed over the course of many years and continues to the current period. Findings from another study suggested that a similar phenomenon exists in the state of Washington (Pelczarski & Kemp, 2006)—a state that has the third largest NHPI population in the United States (U.S. Census, 2010). Further examination of the disproportionality suggests concerns over the inconsistency in the treatment of Pacific Islanders within the CWS. As indicated in a study of Hawaii's CWS, "being Native Hawaiian predicted greater length of time in the system, a greater chance of not being re-unified with their family, and a greater risk of re-entering the system," controlling for type of abuse (Godinet et al., 2011, p. 41). The justice system is no exception with regard to the high rate of NHPI adults and youth. Native Hawaiians are also overrepresented in all phases of Hawaii's criminal justice system—from arrest (27%), detention (33%), probation (29%), prison admission (36%), incarceration (39%), and parole (39%), to parole revocation (41%). Further examination of the data found that, in the adult criminal system, NHs are more likely to be imprisoned, have longer prison sentences and longer probation terms controlling for charge severity, have the highest percentage incarcerated in prisons outside of the state, have the highest number of women in prison, and have a high percentage of parole revocations

(Office of Hawaiian Affairs, Justice Policy Institute, University of Hawaii and Georgetown University, 2010). The juvenile justice system follows the same disproportionality trend with the NHPI adolescents. A crime analysis study done of Hawaii's juvenile justice data from 2009 to 2011 found that Native Hawaiians, mixed Pacific Islanders, and Samoans were generally overrepresented at each decision point: arrest, referral, diversion, petition, detention, adjudication, probation, correctional facility, and waiver to adult court (Godinet & Li, 2012). Furthermore, other study findings suggest that Samoans and Native Hawaiian youth were treated differently compared to White youth and were likely to receive more severe court outcomes (MacDonald, 2003).

CULTURALLY COMPETENT ASSESSMENTS AND INTERVENTIONS

The Asian Population

The importance of cultural competency in mental health service provision and other large systems is clear, based on the significant challenges Asians in the United States face, as described earlier. Without culturally sensitive interventions, the degree of client satisfaction, utilization of services, and length of treatment all diminish. Additionally, the likelihood of effective and successful outcomes decreases.

In order to be culturally competent when working with Asians with mental health issues, for example, it is important to be aware of Asian cultural norms and attitudes. First, because of the stigma associated with mental illness in Asian culture, it is vital that informal subsystems are involved in the process of treating mental health issues in this community. This means involving community members, traditional healers, and Asian providers. Often times, minority ethnic groups feel more comfortable seeking services from those of their own ethnicity, and this should be taken into consideration by social service providers. Another important adaptation is incorporation of language interpreters, allowing Asian clients to understand their providers and to communicate their mental health care needs and problems. Of course, this means additional resources must by found and utilized, which is often a challenge.

It is common in many Asian cultures to use folk medicine for minor physical ailments. For example, historically in Chinese culture, herbal medicine is a vital part of the health care system. Wherever they settled, Chinese immigrants used herbal medicine as a transitional object while moving from one cultural tradition to another and forming a hybrid identity. Chinese medicine represents a link to the homeland and to continuous lifestyles, even though overseas. If a major illness occurred, Chinese herbal medicine usually supplemented Western medicine. Whatever the clashes between Chinese health beliefs and practices and those of mainstream Western medicine, the traditions were used side by side.

Other practices that might be incorporated in treatment and services for Asian Americans include those that align with traditional Asian values and beliefs. An example might be Buddhist practices, or those based on Buddhism, such as mindfulness. Additionally, including Asian community providers and leaders as a way to bridge gaps and limitations in Western service provision is another potential mode to increase cultural competency. On the macro level, for example, increasing cultural awareness of practitioners, through training, is another possibility. Finally, policy and legislative changes are other vital tools for addressing issues of the uninsured and overall access to care.

The Pacific Islander Population

Factors contributing to challenges facing NHPIs are numerous, including varying perspectives that are at times seen as blaming the victim. To better understand the existence of issues such as child abuse and neglect and delinquency, one needs to examine them from a micro- to macroterrain with a multifaceted approach (Godinet, 2013). That is, a bi/multicultural approach that incorporates the varying levels of influence from outside (etic) and inside (emic) perspectives. For example, literature on the overrepresentation of minority youth in the juvenile justice system has found that discriminatory and biased practices that are based on preconceived stereotypes of a group (i.e., Samoans as naturally violent) have been documented in assessment records thus impacting further involved in the juvenile justice system for minority youths (Bridges & Steen, 1998). Although the issue of overrepresentation of minority youth in the juvenile justice system can be explained from a structural/macro view, this issue is limited in its ability to explain why an adolescent becomes involved in the act of delinquency. Literature that focuses on the ecology of the individual purports that family, peer, and community relationships are associated with involvement in delinquency activities. Findings of these studies indicate that poor supervision and communication, parental conflict, low attachment with parents, and involvement with delinquent peers (to name a few) are associated with delinquency. Other factors that are also relevant at the micro level in understanding delinquency are the presence of substance abuse and a mental health diagnosis related to personality disorder (Shader, n.d.). Additionally, social structures within society such as discrimination and social economic status have been linked to delinquency. However, a community that showed "strong informal social networks, strong social bonds, and high social integration has been suggested to mediate the impact of negative social economic disadvantage" on delinquency (Godinet, 1998, p. 24; Elliott, Wilson, Huizinga, Sampson, & Rankin, 1996; Figueria-McDonough, 1992). Nonetheless, for Pacific Islanders, integrating into a larger community has been a challenge because they are often seen as adding to existing problems rather than as individuals who have potential as contributing members. In addition, language barriers and cultural differences steer one to seek out those within the same or similar ethnicity as a means of support and survival in a new environment. Transcultural adaptation is an important issue for Pacific Islanders because they are tasked with adjusting and negotiating with a host culture that is at times in conflict with their culture of origin. Acculturative stress in significant amounts—a key component to understanding adjustment issues of immigrants—can result in maladaptive behaviors impacting immigrants' physical and mental health, when not addressed (Berry, 1997).

Similar to the overrepresentation of NHPIs in the juvenile justice system, the child welfare system has also been linked to discriminatory systemic practices (Godinet et al., 2011) and lack of cultural sensitivity and awareness (Children's Bureau Express, 2004), in addition to ineffective child welfare policies (Hines et al., 2007). Specifically for NHPIs, a study by Godinet and Garlock-Tuialii (2007) of the Hawaii state child welfare system "suggests that of those who re-entered the child welfare system, 25.8% were Hawai'ian versus 17.3% of all other races (P <. 001); Hawai'ians on average spend more time in the system than non-Hawai'ians (P < 0.01). Of those cases where children were removed as part of a court ordered mandate, 28.6% were Hawai'ians as opposed to 17.9% of all other ethnicities (P < 0.001)" (Godinet, Arnsberger, Li, & Kreif, 2010, p. 390). Negative outcomes such as increased removals and reentry are also issues for NHPIs once they are in the system. Poverty as a strong predictor of re-referral to child welfare services is a great concern for NHPIs because it is connected to single-headed households as well as to being at risk of living in neighborhoods that are in a state of social disorganization (Shaw & McKay, 1942). As shown in the U.S. Census (2010), poverty and single-headed household rates for NHPIs are higher than that of the general population. Factors that are also present in NHPI communities associated with child abuse and neglect include parental history of abuse, domestic violence, social isolation, marital conflict, harsh and punitive parenting, and lack of supervision (Goldman, Salus, Wolcott, & Kennedy, 2003).

As mentioned earlier, to better understand the plight of NHPIs, their current condition, and the social ills they face requires an approach that is multifaceted, one that does not ignore the relevance of historical and cultural factors. The view must be through a comprehensive lens that includes cultural perspectives and worldviews, including issues such as historical factors (i.e., colonization, loss of land, culture, and/or language), cultural dissonance (host vs. origin), intergenerational disconnect due to acculturation differences of family members (Else et al., 2007), and migration. The inclusion of such factors will not only guide us toward the discovery of the what, how, and why of these challenges but more importantly how NHPI groups endured and persevered through the trauma, loss, and significant adversity. It is all the more important to recognize and acknowledge the contribution of indigenous knowledge to "conflict resolution, interpersonal problem-solving, family relationships, community building, spiritual healing, and general well-being" (McCubbin & Marsella, 2009, p. 386; Smith, 1999) and toward healing and resolution.

An Integrative Approach

The theory of social disorganization (Shaw & McKay, 1942) posits that structural challenges (lack of resources and opportunities) are linked to conditions that create disarray within a community or neighborhood resulting in hopelessness and avoidance of the host culture's values and beliefs. Feelings of apathy about a situation foster alienation and isolation, and/or become the catalyst for nonconventional means to cope with current living situations (Godinet, 1998). Through the lens of the lōkahi model (Duponte et al., 2010) from the Hawaiian worldview, disorganization stems from relevant forces (see Figure 5.1) being out of balance. That is, when one is not connected to their spiritual source, people (family, friends), and their sense of place, they are more likely to experience challenges. The longer the entities in their lives are not in harmony, the higher the risk of exhibiting maladaptive behaviors as a coping mechanism.

A suggested integrative approach is one that takes into account various perspectives and crosses various domains to examine relevant social structural variables as well as mezzo and micro level factors simultaneously (Godinet, 2013). For instance, social structures such as social and economic disadvantages, cultural values and beliefs, historical and generational trauma, and discrimination, have varying impacts that permeate into the family, community, and individual systems thus contributing to disharmony and imbalance. Families that are not in harmony will find it difficult to resolve conflicts effectively and subsequently will learn similar ineffective ways to resolve problems. Thus, important to the social work model of culturally competent practice is an awareness of existing culturally sensitive tools that will help develop comprehensive assessments of Pacific Islanders that are culturally and contextually relevant, while concurrently engaging them in a meaningful and helpful working relationship.

Culturally Relevant Tools

Lōkahi Wheel

The Lōkahi Wheel (see Figure 5.2) was developed by the Kamehameha Schools Bishop Estate Extension Education Division for their Health and Wellness and Family Education Program (Martin, 2009). This tool was adapted by the University of Hawaii Myron B. Thompson School of Social Work Child Welfare Training academy for assisting clients and social workers in assessing situations and circumstances occurring within various domains from the viewpoint of the client—a practice utilized in the social work field that resonates with a strength perspective (Saleeby, 1992) of starting where the client is at. Although the tool was adapted for child welfare, it is also relevant for use in various helping systems.

There are six domains within the Lōkahi Wheel: (1) thinking/mind, (2) spiritual/soul, (3) friends/family, (4) feelings/emotions, (5) work/school, and (6) physical/body. Traditionally, Native Hawaiians value the use of cultural imagery and metaphors to express themselves (Ho`omanawanui,

FIGURE 5.2   Lōkahi Wheel

2004). As shown in Figure 5.2, each domain shows a visual image. Domains were selected based on the Native Hawaiian worldview, which can be adapted to other ethnic groups to reflect domains that are important in their cultural perspective. As indicated in the literature, spirituality among NHs and other Pacific Islanders is an essential part of their social structure as a means of obtaining overall balance with themselves and in their lives (Blaisdell & Mokuau, 1991; Mokuau, Reid, Napalapalai, 2002). Although, in an initial meeting, some clients may find that spirituality is an omission in their lives, with the Lōkahi Wheel they are able to get a visual of this domain. As the working relationship progresses, they are able to revisit the domains to assess for themselves those areas that need more attention or that are receiving too much attention if balance is to be established. The thinking/mind domain provides an avenue for clients to contemplate particular situations in their lives or their current circumstances.

The next set is friends/family, which is an essential domain for Pacific Islanders. Although family and friends can be seen as a system in which love, care, and trust are shared, for some it can also be a domain that evokes feelings of distress. Hence, the feelings/emotions domain is directly across the wheel. The image of people paddling in the canoe can also be a point of discussion for hope that comes when working together. "Child welfare workers can use this image as a metaphor to depict the importance of working collaboratively towards the well-being of the family. With the client, CW workers, and other service team members paddling together in the canoe, they can arrive and achieve the goal that is in the best interest of the child" (Martin, 2009, p. 8). The emotions domain is depicted by a volcano, which may assist one in speaking openly about underlying issues of anger and frustration and about regrets. It can mean that a crisis within the family is a sign to reexamine existing relationships. It can be a time to address concerns so that the pathway to healing can start. As one progresses with services, it can mean a time of new growth—for whatever was destroyed or damaged in the crisis now can be repaired through the healing process.

The final pair of domains is work/school and physical/body. The work/school domain offers opportunities for clients to discuss and share what they value in terms of employment or education. The metaphor of the *o'o* (digging) stick can be used by the social worker to help families understand the rationale for asking questions that can be perceived as intrusive. Like the *o'o*, there will be "digging" that will occur during "assessment in which knowledge beneath the surface can be brought to the surface to be cleared. Once cleared, there can be a new beginning and solid foundation can be rebuilt" (Martin, 2009, p. 9). Again, a comprehensive and in-depth assessment will provide many pathways to best support the family to work toward balance. The image of the *wailele* (waterfall) can be interpreted as resources that flow to families through work and school to support health and well-being. The area of physical/body shows people climbing a hill and symbolizes a journey that is not easy but also by working together they can achieve their goal. This highlights the value of the family (*Ohana*) and systems working together. Although challenging, this unity can bring about physical well-being to accomplish all that is in their service plan (Godinet & Martin, 2010). Having a visual tool allows workers and clients to see for themselves areas that may be "balanced" or "imbalanced," to reflect on what they may be willing to change, and to prioritize goals that will support the restoration of balance (Martin, 2009).

The Lōkahi Wheel is a tool that can be utilized on its own or to supplement an assessment instrument. It takes more of a story telling approach that is culturally relevant for Pacific Islanders. It invites the client to talk about their situation by using symbols and culturally appropriate visual aids that resonate with their worldview. Particularly in involuntary situations, clients are reluctant to disclose because of the mandatory nature of their contact with service systems. The use of the Lōkahi Wheel creates a conversational type of interview that can facilitate a less intimidating nonjudgmental environment. Additional picture cards can be utilized for clients to place in the different domains to initiate the assessment, particularly with clients who are less vocal. Social workers can then ask questions regarding the cards selected and the reasons for a card being placed in a particular domain. For example, they may ask about what the picture represent for them (e.g., "What does the volcano represent for you in the family domain?" rather than interpreting the clients' selections by saying, "Does the volcano represent anger for your family?"). This strategy of not interpreting the cards on behalf of the client is key to the engagement with NHPI families because they are able to share their story from their point of view in a natural conversational manner rather than a standardized assessment (Martin & Godinet, n.d). When clients are given a choice as to how and how much they disclose, it offers clients freedom to choose what they share, which communicates the message that their "story" matters and they feel validated rather than judged.

Family Group Conferencing

Most Pacific Island cultures strive for harmony and balance within and among systems. Thus, in times of crisis, the need to "make things right" or to reestablish harmony is accomplished by employing cultural protocols and practices. Conflict resolutions such as *Ho'oponopono* from the Native

Hawaiian culture (Mokuau, 2002); *Fa'aleleiga*, a Samoan practice (Mulitalo-Lauta, 2000); and *Afamaolek* with Chamorro (Furuto, San Nicolas, Kim, & Fiaui, 2001) are culturally relevant ways of knowing and doing that help to restore and foster peace, goodwill, justice, and interdependence. The head of household, elders, and/or chiefs of families of the victim and the offender usually encourage these cultural practices. Impelled by the overrepresentation of indigenous Maori children in the child welfare and juvenile justice system in New Zealand, a similar indigenous practice of "making things right" known as Family Group Conferencing (FGC) was implemented as a culturally based practice that was intended to help address the disproportionality rates of indigenous children and their families in these systems (Pakura, 2003). This family-centered approach re-empowers families to involve their support network (i.e., extended family, community members, friends, pastors) in the decision-making process involving the case of their child. In addition, cultural resources and perspectives are taken into consideration as understood by family members (Godinet et al., 2010). The role of the family in FGC was summarized into the following key premises (Pakura, 2003):

- Families knew their own members better than anyone else, thus they are the best source to resolve their own issues.
- Families are the best caretakers of their own children. Extended family would be the next option in the event that parents are not able.
- Extended families would provide a more "therapeutic" environment in which a child is helped to rebuild and flourish until the family is able to resume their parenting duties.
- Family members take the responsibility in negotiating an agreement for reparation with the intent of helping both the victim and the offender to achieve positive outcomes.
- A people (originally the Maoris) "would reclaim the responsibility for their children" (Pakura, 2003, p. 4) as major players in the future of their children and families.

Adopted by the state of Hawaii in 1996 to address concerns of the child welfare system that was overrepresented by Native Hawaiian and Samoan children and families, FGC was met with optimism because it was one of the few culturally sensitive practices that resonated with a Pacific Island cultural practice. The FGC model in Hawaii, known as *Ohana* (Family) Conferencing, is offered by Effective Planning and Innovative Communication (EPIC), Inc., a nonprofit organization. The core values are: "(1) family-centeredness, (2) strength focused, (3) community-based, and (4) culturally relevant" (Godinet et al., 2010, p. 393).

Keeping to the intentions of the conference, family members relevant to the child are invited to the meeting by the family and/or the child welfare worker. Invited participants may also include service providers (e.g., pastors, school counselors, teachers) working with the family. Two trained staff members of the EPIC organization facilitate the meetings.

Although Family Group Conferencing gained recognition throughout the world because it was a culturally promising practice that was inclusive and empowering, implementation of the model varied from place to place and region to region. As a result, studies of the FGC model received mixed reviews on its efficacy (Crampton, 2007; Lemon, D'Andrade, & Austin, 2005; Sundell & Vinnerljung, 2004; Vesneski & Kemp, 2000; Walker, 2005). However, there is still a glimmer of hope. An exploratory study that was done on *Ohana* Conferencing showed that the number of removals and reentry rates were statistically significantly lower for those who received *Ohana* Conferencing compared to those who did not (Godinet et al., 2010). Although the findings are not generalizable due to sampling limitations, FGC still remains a viable option for the NHPI population.

FUTURE DIRECTIONS

The Asian Population

Awareness of the diversity within the different groups is critical because it will allow for the request and upholding of traditional values and norms without stigmatizing "all Asians as model minorities." Caution needs to be taken to avoid overgeneralizing so that inaccurate assessments and outcomes can be prevented.

In treatment, cross-systems issues will be to address the stigma of having mental health or other problems. Language barriers will need to be addressed because of the immigrant family members living in native-born households, which at times can cause multigenerational tensions. Asian populations are very family-oriented when living in communities, so the inclusion of family members, traditional healers, and Asian social service providers would be critical in cross-systems treatments for this population.

SPOTLIGHT: SUMMARY OF PROMISING PRACTICES

Lōkahi Wheel

Encourages engagement from a strength perspective by utilizing visual symbolism, which is important for PI families.

Visual tool that invites clients to share their stories or situation within the six domains: (1) thinking/mind, (2) spiritual/soul, (3) friends/family, (4) feelings/ emotions, (5) work/school, and (6) physical/body.

Inviting clients to share their situation in the various domains will help them see the balance or imbalance in their lives.

May be utilized in conjunction with existing assessment tools used by various systems (child welfare, juvenile justice, education, health) as a means to help engage clients who are not only voluntary but are also mandated for services.

Promotes collaboration between client and social worker.

Family Group Conferencing

Implemented as a culturally based practice that was intended to help address the disproportionate rates of indigenous children and their families in the child welfare and juvenile justice systems.

Core values are: (1) family-centeredness, (2) strength focused, (3) community-based, and (4) culturally relevant (Godinet et al., 2010).

Family members relevant to the child are invited to the meeting by the family and/ or the social worker. Invited participants may also include service providers (e.g., pastors, school counselors, teachers) working with the family.

The Pacific Islander Population

The discussion on cultural ways of knowing and doing, indigenous knowledge, and cultural practices remains a discourse that needs to continue— as articulated in the *Olelo No'eau* (Hawaiian proverb): *'A'ohe pau ka 'ike i ka halau ho'okah,* (All knowledge is not taught in one school; one learns from many sources.) (Pukui, 1983). Native Hawaiians and Pacific Islanders have a wealth of knowledge to share within communities and with the rest of the world. Like the Lōkahi Wheel and Family Group Conferencing, indigenous knowledge can contribute to our understanding and improvement of the human condition.

In summary, we propose the following strategies to advance efforts to eliminate disproportionality and disparities as they affect Asian and Pacific Islander children and families.

STRATEGIES FOR ADDRESSING AND ELIMINATING DISPROPORTIONALITY AND DISPARITIES

The discussion on cultural ways of knowing and doing, indigenous knowledge, and cultural practices is a discourse that needs to continue. Asian and Pacific Islanders focus on cultural values as a means of knowing and behaving, which cannot be ignored in culturally competent practices. The traditional value of "saving face" needs to be respected when serving this population but not used as a justification for not providing the necessary social services needed.

Like the Lōkahi Wheel and Family Group Conferencing, indigenous knowledge can contribute to the understanding and improvement of the human condition. Indigenous knowledge requires a biculturalization of interventions, blending Western and indigenous approaches to addressing disproportionality and disparities.

Promising practices such as Family Group Conferencing facilitate opportunities for cross-systems work as the family system and the helping systems are able to dialogue in a conference setting that honors various perspectives and contributions to the solution.

The model minority myth is detrimental for Asians and Pacific Islanders who experience disproportionality and disparities in child welfare, mental health, and health systems of care. The stereotype undermines the welfare, mental health, and health needs of this population.

Community involvement is important in cross-systems treatment to show respect for traditional cultural values and norms, to facilitate language interpretation for immigrant family members, and to monitor overgeneralizations that could be made leading to inaccurate assessments, inappropriate interventions, and to social services that are not culturally competent.

Particularly for Pacific Islanders, historical factors (i.e., colonization, loss of land, culture, and/or language), cultural dissonance, intergenerational disconnect, and context of migration are important factors to be cognizant of when assessing and engaging NHPI families in various cross systems because they will guide the practitioner toward more culturally relevant services for clients.

REFERENCES

Berry, J. W. (1997). Immigration, acculturation, and adaptation. *Applied Psychology: An International Review, 46* (1), 5–68.

Blaisdell, K., & Mokuau, N. (1991). Kānaka maoli: Indigenous Hawaiians. In N. Mokuau (Ed.), *Handbook of social services for Asian and Pacific Islanders* (pp. 131–154). Westport, CT: Greenwood.

Booth, H. (1999). Pacific Island suicide in comparative perspective. *Journal of Biosocial Science, 31,* 433–448.

Bridges, G. S., & Steen, S. (1998). Racial disparities in official assessments of juvenile offenders: Attributional stereotypes as mediating mechanisms. *American Sociological Review, 63*(4), 554–570.

Children's Bureau Express. (2004, July/August). Overrepresentation of minority children: How the child welfare system is responding. Retrieved from https://cbexpress.acf.hhs.gov/index.cfm?event=website.viewArticles&issueid=55&sectionid=1&articleid=836

Chu, J., & Sue, S. (2011, June). Asian American mental health: What we know and what we don't know. *Online Readings in Psychology and Culture, Unit 3.* Retrieved from http://scholarworks.gvsu.edu/orpc/vol3/iss1/4

Crampton, D. (2007). Research Review: Family group decision-making: a promising in need of more programme theory and research. *Child & Family Social Work, 12*(2), 202–209.

Department of Business, Economic Development & Tourism (n.d.). Retrieved on February 12, 2012 from http://hawaii.gov/dbedt/info/census/Census_2010/demographic

Department of Human Services, State of Hawaii. (2013). *Child abuse and neglect in Hawaii.* Retrieved on June 26, 2012 from http://hawaii.gov/dhs/protection/social_services/child_welfare/ChildAbuse/

Duponte, K., Martin, T., Mokuau, N., & Paglinawan, L. (2010). Ike Hawai'i— A training program for working with Native Hawaiians. *Journal of Indigenous Voices in Social Work, 1*(1), 1–24.

Elliott, D. S., Wilson, W. J., Huizinga, D., Sampson, R. J., & Rankin, B. (1996). The effects of neighborhood disadvantage on adolescent development. *Journal of Research in Crime and Delinquency, 33*(4), 389–426.

Elliott, K., & Urquiza, A. (2006). Ethnicity, culture & child maltreatment. *Journal of Social Issues, 62*(4), 787–809.

Else, I. R., Andrade, N. N., & Nahulu, L. B. (2007). Suicide and suicidal-related behaviors among indigenous Pacific Islanders in the United States. *Death Studies, 31,* 479–501.

EPIC, Inc. (2007). Ohana conferencing brochure. Retrieved from http://epicohana. info/images/stories/files/epic_family_brochure.pdf

EPIC, Inc., & AAAJ (2014). Native Hawaiians Pacific Islanders and a community of contrasts in the United States. Retrieved from http://empoweredpi.org/ wp-content/uploads/2014/06/A_Community_of_Contrasts_NHPI_ US_2014-1.pdf

Figueira-McDonough, J. (1992). Community context and dropout rates. *Children and Youth Services Review, 14,* 273–288.

Furuto, S. B. C. L, San Nicolas, R. J., Kim, G. E., & Fiaui, L. M. (2001). Interventions with Kanaka Maoli, Chamorro, and Samoan communities. In R. Fong & S. Furuto (Eds.), *Culturally competent practice* (pp. 372–342). Boston: Allyn and Bacon.

Gibson, C. & Lennon, E. (1999). *Historical census statistics on the foreign-born population of the United States: 1850-1990.* U.S. Census Bureau, Population Division. Retrieved on December 3, 2012 from http://www.census.gov/population/ www/documentation/twps0029/twps0029.html

Godinet, M. T. (1998). *Exploring a theoretical model of delinquency with Samoan adolescents.* Unpublished doctoral dissertation. University of Washington.

Godinet, M. T. (2013). Testing a model of delinquency with Samoan adolescents. *Journal of Social Work, 13*(1), 54–74.

Godinet, M. T., Arnsberger, P., & Garlock, J. (2011). Native Hawaiian families: Systemic disparities in Hawaii's child welfare system. *Asia Pacific Journal of Social Development, 21*(2), 34–45.

Godinet, M. T., Arnsberger, P., Li, F., & Kreif, T. (2010). Disproportionality, Ohana Conferencing, and the Hawai'i child welfare system. *Journal of Public Child Welfare, 4,* 387–405.

Godinet, M. T., & Garlock-Tuialii, J. (2007, June). *Overrepresentation of Hawaiians in the child welfare system.* Paper presented at the Indigenous Conference. Honolulu, HI.

Godinet, M. T., & Li, F. (2012). *Crime analysis 2009–2011.* Report for the Office of Youth Services, Department of Human Services, State of Hawaii. Honolulu, HI.

Godinet, M. T., & Martin, T. (2010, September*). A cultural approach to engagement for child welfare service professionals.* International Society for the Prevention of Child Abuse and Neglect (IPSCAN) XVIIIth International Congress on Child Abuse and Neglect. Honolulu, HI.

Goldman, J., Salus, M. K., Wolcott, D., & Kennedy, K. Y. (2003). *A coordinated response to child abuse and neglect: The foundation for practice.* Office on Child Abuse and Neglect.

Hines, A., Lee, P., Osterling, K., & Drabble, L. (2007). Factors predicting family reunification for African-American, Latino, Asian, and White families in the child welfare system. *Journal of Children and Family Studies, 16,* 275–289.

Ho'omanawanui, K. (2004). Hä, mana, leo (breath, spirit, voice). Kanaka Maoli empowerment through literature. *American Indian Quarterly, 28*(1&2), 86–91.

Joakim, P. (2000). Chuukese travelers and the idea of horizon. *Asia Pacific Viewpoint, 41*(3), 253–267.

Juckett, G., & Rudolph-Watson, L. (2010). Recognizing mental illness in culture-bound syndromes. *American Family Physician, 81*(2), 206–210.

Kim, B. S. K., Atkinson, D. R., & Umemoto, D. (2001). Asian cultural values and the counseling process: Current knowledge and directions for future research. *The Counseling Psychologist, 29*(4), 570–603.

Lee, E. (2002). The Chinese exclusion example: Race, immigration, and American gatekeeping, 1882–1924. *Journal of American Ethnic History, 21*(3), 36–62.

Lemon, K., D'Andrade, A., & Austin, M. J. (2005, July). *Understanding and addressing disproportionality in the front end of the child welfare system.* Berkeley, CA: The Center for Social Sciences Research. Retrieved June 1, 2012, from http://cssr.berkeley.edu/bassc/public/EvidenceForPractice3_Disproportionality_FullReport.pdf

Lowe, E. (2003). Identity, activity, and the well-being of adolescents. *Culture, Medicine, & Psychiatry, 27,* 187–219.

MacDonald, J. M. (2003). The effect of ethnicity on juvenile court decision making in Hawaii. *Youth & Society, 35*(2), 243–263.

Maiter, S., & Stalker, C. (2011). South Asian immigrants' experience of child protection services: Are we recognizing strengths and resilience? *Child & Family Social Work, 16,* 138–148.

Martin, T. (2009). *Engaging families using a strengths-based, solution-focused approach,* A curriculum for University of Hawaii, Myron B. Thompson School of Social Work Child Welfare Training Academy.

Martin, T., & Godinet, M. (n.d). *A cultural approach to engagement with child welfare workers.* University of Hawaii School of Social Work Child Welfare Training Academy, Manoa, HI.

McCubbin, L. D., & Marsella, A. (2009). Native Hawaiians and psychology: The cultural and historical context of indigenous ways of knowing. *Cultural Diversity & Ethnicity Minority Psychology, 15*(4), 374–387.

Mokuau, N. (2002). Culturally based interventions for substance use and child abuse among Native Hawaiians. *Public Health Reports*, Supplement 1, *117*(3), S82–S87.

Mokuau, N., Reid, N., & Napalapalai, N. (2002). *Ho'omana (Spirituality): Views of Native Hawaiian women.* Honolulu, HI: University of Hawai'i School of Social Work and the State Department of Health, Office of Equity.

Mulitalo-Lauta, P. T. I. M. T. (2000). *Fa'aSamoa and social work within the New Zealand context.* Palmerston North, N.Z.: Dunmore.

Nagata, D. (1990). The Japanese American internment: Exploring the transgenerational consequences of traumatic stress. *Journal of Traumatic Stress, 3*(1), 47–69.

Office of Hawaiian Affairs. (2010). *Databook 2010.* Retrieved on June 29, 2012 from http://www.ohadatabook.com/QT-P9_United%20States.pdf

Office of Hawaiian Affairs, Justice Policy Institute, University of Hawai'i and Georgetown University. (2010). *The disparate treatment of Native Hawaiians in the criminal justice system.* Washington, DC: Justice Policy Institute (JPI), University of Hawai'i, and Georgetown University.

Pakura, S. (2003). A review of the family group conference 13 years on. *Social Work Review, 15*(3), 3–7.

Pegler-Gordon, A. (2006). Chinese exclusion, photography, and the development of U.S. immigration policy. *American Quarterly, 58*(1), 51–77.

Pelczarski, Y., & Kemp., S. P. (2006). Patterns of child maltreatment referrals among Asian and Pacific Islander families. *Child Welfare, 85*(1), 5–31.

Pinhey, T. K., & Millman, S. R. (2004). Asia/Pacific Islander adolescent sexual orientation and suicide risk in Guam. *American Journal of Public Health, 94*(7), 1204–1206.

Pobutsky, A. M., Buenconsejo-Lum, L., Chow, C., Palafox, N., & Maskarinec, G. G. (2005). Micronesian migrants in Hawaii: Health issues and culturally appropriate, community-based solutions. *Californian Journal of Health Promotion, 3*(4), 59–72.

Pukui, M. K. (1983). *'Ōlelo No'eau, Hawaiian proverbs and poetical sayings.* Honolulu, HI: Bishop Museum.

Ratliffe, K. T. (2011). Micronesian voices: Culture and school conflict. *Race, Ethnicity, and Education, 14*(2), 233–252.

Ross-Sheriff, F., & Husain, A. (2001). Ethics and values in social work practice with Asian Americans: A South Asian Muslim case example. In R. Fong & S. Furuto (Eds.), *Culturally competent practice: Skills, interventions, and evaluations* (pp. 75–88). Boston: Allyn & Bacon.

Saleeby, D. (1992). *The strengths perspective in social work practice.* New York: Longman.

Schultz, E. (1950). Proverbial expressions of the Samoans. *The Journal of the Polynesian Society, 59*(1), 35–62.

Shader, M. (n.d.). *Risk factors for delinquency: An overview.* U.S. Department of Justice, Office of Justice Programs, OJJDP. Retrieved July 1, 2012 from https://www.ncjrs.gov/pdffiles1/ojjdp/frd030127.pdf

Shaw, C. R., & McKay, H. D. (1942). *Juvenile delinquency in urban areas.* Chicago: University of Chicago Press.

Smith, L. T. (1999). *Decolonizing methodologies: Research and indigenous peoples.* London: Zed.

Smith, R. (2008). Beyond the blue horizon. *National Geographic, 213*(3), 106–123.

Snowden, L., Masland, M., Peng, C., Lou, C., & Wallace, N. (2011). Limited English-proficient Asian Americans: Threshold language policy and access to mental health treatment. *Social Science & Medicine, 72,* 230–237.

Sue, S., Yan Cheng, J. K., Saad, C. S., & Chu, J. P. (2012). Asian American mental health: A call to action. *American Psychologist, 67*(7), 532–544.

Sundell, K., & Vinnerljung, B. (2004). Outcomes of family group conferencing in Sweden: A 3-year follow-up. *Child Abuse & Neglect, 28,* 267–287.

Tamasese, F. (2006, April). Samoan custom and the rights of children. *PIC NZ/Samoan National Women's Synod.* Waitakere, Auckland, New Zealand.

U.S. Census Bureau. (2010). *2010 Census shows more than half of Native Hawaiians and Other Pacific Islanders report multiple races.* Retrieved May 31, 2012 from http://www.census.gov/newsroom/releases/archives/facts_for_features_special_editions/cb12-ff09.htmlup

U.S. Census Bureau (2012a). *The Asian population: 2010.* Washington, DC: U.S. Department of Commerce.

U.S. Census Bureau. (2012b). *Income, poverty, and health insurance coverage in the United States: 2011.* Washington, DC: U.S. Department of Commerce.

U.S. Office of Minority Health. (2011). *Asian American/Pacific Islander profile.* Retrieved from http://minorityhealth.hhs.gov/templates/browse.aspx?lvl=2&lvlid=53

Vakalahi, H. O., Godinet, M. T., & Fong, R. (2006). Pacific Islander Americans. Impact of colonialization and immigration. In R. Fong, R. McRoy, & C. O. Hendricks (Ed.), *Intersecting child welfare, substance abuse, and family violence. Culturally competent approaches* (pp. 319–340). Alexandria, VA: Council on Social Work Education.

Vesneski, W., & Kemp, S. P. (2000). Family group conferencing in Washington State. In G. Burford & J. Hudson (Eds.), *Family group conferences: Perspectives on policy, practice, and research* (pp. 312–323). New York: Aldine de Gruyter.

Walker, L. (2005). A cohort study of Ohana conferencing in child abuse and neglect cases. *Protecting Children, 19*(4), 36–46.

Wesley-Esquimaux, C. C., & Smolewski, M. (2004). *Historic trauma and Aboriginal healing.* Ottawa, Ontario: The Aboriginal Healing Foundation Research Series. Retrieved from http://www.ahf.ca/downloads/historic-trauma.pdf

Yuan, S., Kole, S., & Yuen, S. (2008). *Homeless service utilization report: Hawai'i 2008.* Honolulu, HI: University of Hawaii, Center for the Family.

6

American Indian/ Alaska Native Children and Families

▸ *KATHY DESERLY AND TOM LIDOT*

POPULATION OF ETHNICALLY DIVERSE CLIENTS IN SYSTEM

OVER THE PAST DECADE SIGNIFICANT national attention has been given to the concerns of racial disproportionality and disparities of minority groups throughout various public systems. Although American Indian/ Alaska Native (AI/AN) people represent only a small fraction of the U.S. population, they also represent significant disproportionate and disparate numbers across many systems, including justice, health, education, and child welfare. Considering several centuries of traumatic U.S. historical experiences, intergenerational trauma—also known as "historic trauma"— has emerged as a common intertribal thread, considered by many AI/AN people to be a major factor in the disproportionate representation of Indian people in far too many systems. Consider the data.

Justice

A growing number of studies and reports have made it clear that minority youth in general are more likely than White youth to be arrested, adjudicated, and incarcerated in juvenile justice systems across the United States. Although not as large as those for African Americans, disparities between Native American youth and White youth are alarmingly high and are in need of remediation (Hartney, 2008). In the American justice system, statistics from the National Council on Crime and Delinquency show that Native Americans were arrested at 1.5 times the rate for Whites, with higher disparity for certain violent and public order offenses. Further, Native Americans were admitted to prison at more than four times the rates for Whites, and Native American females were admitted to prison at more than six times the rates for White females (Hartney & Vuong, 2009). Within juvenile justice systems, American Indian youth are grossly overrepresented in state and federal juvenile justice systems and in secure confinement. AI/AN youth are 50% more likely than Whites to receive the most punitive measures. On a given day 1 in 25 American Indians age 18 or older is under the jurisdiction of the criminal justice system—2.4 times the per capita rate of Whites, and nearly a third of all American Indian victims of violence are between ages 18 and 24. This group of American Indians experienced the highest per capita rate of violence of any racial group considered by age, about one violent crime for every four persons of this age. Native American youth represent 1% of the U.S. population, yet they constitute 2–3% of the youth arrested for such offenses as larceny-theft and liquor law violations. In 26 states, Native American youth are disproportionately placed in secure confinement in comparison to their population. For example, in four states (South Dakota, North Dakota, Alaska, and Montana), Native youth account for anywhere from 29–42% of youth in secure confinement. Nationwide, the average rate of new commitments to adult state prison for Native American youth is almost twice (1.84 times) that of White youth. In the states with enough Native Americans to facilitate comparisons, Native American youth were committed to adult prison from 1.3 to 18.1 times the rate of Whites. Of the youth in custody of the Federal Bureau of Prisons, 79% were Native American as of October 2000, an increase of 50% since 1994 (Cross, 2008).

Public Safety/Violence

American Indian and Alaska Native communities have been severely affected by family violence. Especially high and alarming rates of victimization have been found among Native American women on and off reservations. Native American and Alaska Native women are more than 2.5 times as likely to be raped or sexually assaulted than are women in the United States in general. A U.S. Department of Justice study on violence against women concluded that 34.1% of American Indian and Alaska Native women—more than one in three—will be raped during their lifetime; the comparable figure for women in the United States as a whole is less than one in five. Native American women were more likely to be victims of assault and rape/sexual assault committed by a stranger or acquaintance rather than by an intimate partner or family member. In 86% of reported rapes or sexual assaults on Native women, the perpetrators are non-Native. In comparison, only 35% of White rape victims reported that the perpetrator was not White. This disparity is not typical of any other ethnicity because perpetrators are usually found to be the same race as the victim (Judicial Council of California, 2010).

Health

American Indian and Alaska Native people have long experienced lower health status when compared with other Americans. Lower life expectancy and the disproportionate disease burden exist perhaps because of inadequate education, disproportionate poverty, discrimination in the delivery of health services, and because of cultural differences. These are broad quality of life issues rooted in economic adversity and poor social conditions (Grant & Brown, 2003). American Indian/Alaska Native people have higher mortality rates than Whites at each stage of the life span. Some chronic conditions are also particularly high among Native Americans—for example, the highest prevalence of diabetes in the world is found among the Pima Indians of Arizona. American Indian/Alaska Native poorer health indices are related, in part, to their higher poverty rates than Whites. About half (49%) of American Indian/Alaska Native people have job-based or other private coverage, compared to 83% of Whites. Nearly 1 in 5 (17%) of American Indian/Alaska Native people, compared to 5% of Whites, report coverage through Medicaid and other public programs. Medicaid is playing an increasingly larger role in financing AI/AN care and as a revenue source for Indian Health Service (IHS) providers. Almost half (48%) of low-income American Indian/Alaska Natives are uninsured, largely reflecting the low rates of job-based coverage in this income group. Although IHS is a resource for some of the AI/AN population, its reach is limited. Just under half of uninsured American Indian/Alaska Natives identify IHS as a source of coverage of care (Henry J. Kaiser Family Foundation, 2004). Even in health-care funding,

American Indian/Alaska Native people face disparities. A report from the U.S. Commission on Civil Rights compared spending on American Indian health care to other groups for whom the government provides care. In 2003, the government will spend $6,000 for each Medicare recipient, $5,200 for every veteran using the VA, and $3,725 for federal prisoners. For American Indians, the government spent $1,600 per person. IHS spends less on its patients than any other group providing public care—and about 60% less than average per capita health-care costs nationwide (U.S. Commission on Civil Rights, 2003).

Education

In 2003, the Individuals with Disabilities Education Act (IDEA) served 9% of all U.S. children between the ages of 3 and 21 who were enrolled in public elementary and secondary schools. American Indian/Alaska Native and Black children were more likely than other racial/ethnic groups to receive services under the IDEA. About 12% of American Indian/Alaska Native children and 11% of Black children received IDEA services in 2003, compared to 8% of White children, 8% of Hispanic children, and 4% of Asian/Pacific Islander children. In addition, the percentage of American Indian/Alaska Native children served under IDEA increased from 10% in 1998 to 12% in 2003. In 2003, the drop-out rate was 15% for American Indians/Alaska Natives, higher than the 6% for Whites and 4% for Asian/Pacific Islanders. Although the estimate for American Indians/Alaska Natives appears to be higher than the rate for Blacks, the difference is not significant due to the large standard error for American Indians/Alaska Natives. However, American Indian/Alaska Native youth and young adults were less likely to have dropped out than Hispanics (15% vs. 24%). Between 1990 and 2003, the estimates for American Indians/Alaska Natives fluctuated, showing no consistent trend. Teachers in public schools with large American Indian/Alaska Native populations (public schools with 25% or more enrollment of American Indian/Alaska Native students and Bureau of Indian Affairs schools) were more likely to identify serious problems in the school such as students coming to school unprepared, lack of parent involvement, poverty, and student apathy, than were teachers in public schools with less than 25% enrollment of American Indian/Alaska Native students (Freeman and Fox, 2005).

Mental Health

The tragedy of youth suicide in Indian country is so severe that it has prompted North Dakota Senator Bryon L. Dorgan (D-ND) (2010, p.213) to write:

Youth suicides in American Indian and Alaska Native communities have reached epidemic levels over the past 25 years. Federal policymakers and health-care providers urgently need to develop an effective response to repair the broken health-care system that allows this epidemic to persist year after year. The rate of suicide for American Indian and Alaska Natives is far higher than that of any other ethnic group in the United States—70% higher than the rate for the general population of the United States. American Indian and Alaska Native youth are among the hardest hit. They have the highest rate of suicide for males and females, ages 10 to 24, of any racial group. The rate of suicide among Native American youth, ages 15 to 24, is the highest of any racial or age group in the United States. Suicide is the second leading cause of death for Native Americans between the ages of 10 and 34 years. The Native youth have an average suicide rate 2.2 times higher than the national average for their adolescent peers of other races. Native American suicide rates are highest among the 15- to 19-year-old age group. Males account for up to five times more suicides than females in Native American youth. The rate of suicide among American Indian and Alaska Native male youth is two to four times higher than males in other racial groups and up to 11 times higher than females in other racial groups. However, studies have shown female youths may be attempting suicide more often. Regardless, suicide rates for both sexes of Native American youth are higher in comparison to adolescents of any other race in the U.S. In the Great Plains, the area west of the Mississippi River and east of the Rocky Mountains, which includes the states of South Dakota, Wyoming, Montana, Nebraska, Colorado, Kansas, New Mexico, Oklahoma, Texas, and my state of North Dakota, the youth suicide rate has reached epidemic proportions. On certain reservations, the incidence of youth suicide has been documented at 10 times the national average. For example, in North Dakota during 2004, there was an average of six suicide attempts and one completion for every five days. Of these suicides, up to five times more occurred on Indian reservations than on nontribal land. There are several important risk behaviors for suicide, and unfortunately, many of these factors are more prevalent in Indian country.

Child Welfare

Children and families of color, especially African American and American Indian children, experience significantly worse outcomes in the child welfare system than do nonminority children. In fact, the disparities in outcomes are so great that racial/ethnic inequities can best be described as a "chronic crisis." That is, the problem is longstanding, but it is of such urgency that no lasting improvements are possible in child welfare services unless these inequities are reduced and eventually eliminated (Center for Community Partnerships in Child Welfare, 2006).

The most recent statistics on children in foster care indicate that AI/AN children represent 2% of all children in foster care in the United States (U.S. Department of Health and Human Services, 2012). This demonstrates a disproportionate overrepresentation because AI/AN children represent only 1% of the total U.S. child population. At the state level, AI/AN children are represented at a proportion more than five times their number in the general population in certain states, including Iowa, Nebraska, and Washington (Summers, Wood, & Russell, 2012). In Minnesota, the state with the greatest disproportionality, AI/AN children represent only 1.4% of the state's child population, yet they represent 15.2% of children in foster care, a proportion more than 11 times their share of the general population (Summers et al., 2012).

There are many reasons for addressing disproportionality and disparity, and these reasons can be different for tribal and nontribal communities. For nontribal jurisdictions (federal, state, and local), reasons tend to address policy directives and resource limitations. Tribal reasons tend to lean toward community and cultural preservation outcomes. These reasons are a clear extension of the competing value systems that drive programs, systems, and communities. Following is a brief summary of some suggested reasons for comparison.

Nontribal (Federal, State, and Local) Reasons:

1. Shared use of resources (U.S. government and tribal) reduces overall costs for services. Examples include educational tutoring, tribal family services, and tribal health care.
2. Ground level practice changes support current initiatives to enhance culturally appropriate engagement strategies and promote best practices in placement and family reunification (for example, in child welfare cases).

3. Demonstrates local and state efforts to comply with federal and state policy to utilize consultation with tribes and tribal communities.

Tribal (Reservation and Nonreservation) Reasons:

1. Promotes healing and reconciliation of historic traumas by ensuring access to services that utilize culturally centered practice in prevention and intervention efforts.
2. Prevention efforts support cultural preservation and cultural restoration (especially in nonreservation settings) that are critical to tribal identity and survival.
3. Collaboration with local, state, and federal efforts strengthens tribal involvement at the highest level of decision making, ensuring community support and appropriateness.

DEMOGRAPHIC OVERVIEW

The previous section outlines grim statistics related to American Indian/ Alaska Native contacts with public systems, especially when considered in relation to the small population of AI/AN people. The following demographics provide a snapshot of the overall population of AI/ AN people based on the most recent 2010 U.S. Census. As of 2010, the nation's population of American Indians and Alaska Natives, including those of more than one race, was 5.2 million people. They made up 1.7% of the total population. Of this total, 2.9 million were American Indian and Alaska Native only, and 2.3 million were American Indian and Alaska Native in combination with one or more other races. Twenty-two percent of American Indians/Alaska Natives reside on reservation or trust land. There are 566 federally recognized tribes living on 334 federal and state recognized American Indian reservations. As of the 2010 U.S. Census, 15 states have more than 100,000 American Indian and Alaska Native residents: California, Oklahoma, Arizona, Texas, New York, New Mexico, Washington, North Carolina, Florida, Michigan, Alaska, Oregon, Colorado, Minnesota, and Illinois. The proportion of Alaska's population identified as American Indian and Alaska Native was 19.5% as of 2010—the highest rate for this race group of any state. Alaska was followed by Oklahoma (12.9%), New Mexico (10.7%), and South Dakota (10.1%).

Earlier data from the U.S. All Races Index, a standard composite index baseline for comparison with Native Americans was described in "The Context and Meaning of Family Strengthening in Indian America," a 2004 report to the Annie E. Casey Foundation by the Harvard Project on American Indian Economic Development. According to the Harvard Project (2004) report, Native Americans are *twice as likely* to be in poverty as other races. The median household income of Native Americans is 70% that of other races. These economic conditions have a significant impact on children. Native American children are *twice as likely* to be living in poverty. They are almost *twice as likely* to be in a home with neither parent in the labor force. More than 40% of Native American children live in single parent homes (Harvard Project, 2004). These economic conditions impact other areas of child development as well. Native American children are more likely to attempt suicide. The biggest killers for Native Americans are alcoholism, diabetes, and suicide. Native American births are more likely to receive late or no prenatal care and suffer from the consequences of alcohol use during pregnancy. American Indians are more likely than non-Indians to be poor and to have fewer opportunities to increase income and economic assets than non-Indians. For example, American Indians have a birth rate one-sixth greater than that of the population as a whole, and American Indian teens have a birthrate nearly 50% greater than that of their non-Indian peers; a higher share of American Indian births is to a never-married mother (58.4%) than is the case for non-Indians (33.2%). American Indian children are 50% more likely to live in a single parent household. Nearly one in three American Indian children lives in a poor household, almost twice the rate of their non-Indian peers. American Indians are twice as likely as non-Indians to suffer from a serious mental illness. And although less likely than non-Indians to drink alcohol, American Indians who drink are more likely to be heavy drinkers (7% of all American Indians).

Context of Cultural Values and Norms

There is a common misperception that most American Indians live on reservations. Actually, the American Indians living outside the reservations make up the vast majority. The 2010 U.S. Census reports that just 22% of American Indian/Alaska Natives resided on reservations or other trust lands. However, it must be considered that the accuracy of these numbers is only as valid as the number of individuals who respond to the U.S. Census questionnaires. Mistrust of government agencies, including data collectors, continues to profoundly influence the willingness to share personal information. Yet the divide between "on-reservation" and "off-reservation" or "urban" American Indian and Alaska Native people is a key element in the context of American Indian/Alaska Native social issues.

Several generations of Indian families are now part of their cities of residence. Interestingly, often many of these same families continue to point to their tribe and reservation of family origin as the place "they are from." These linkages are obvious in the reservation-bound migration any time jobs become more available. American Indian individuals or urban programs are secondary to tribal political entities in federal policy. Federal assistance programs are slow to seek out the Native urban populations (Indian Country Today, 2005).

Access to resources, such as health services and housing, is challenging for off-reservation AI/AN people. Indian Health Services are generally located on or in closer proximity to reservation communities. Federal funding resources for tribal education, health, social services, and other services are designated for reservation communities, bypassing the critical needs experienced by off-reservation Indian people. To further exacerbate the situation, urban Indian people are often considered an "invisible" minority. Due to lack of adequate research and data, their needs often go unmet in their communities. The 2010 U.S. Census reports statistics for American Indian/Alaska Native people are not defined by the individual's residential location—urban or reservation. However, rates of disproportionality and disparities describe the situation of American Indian/Alaska Native people who are in off-reservation circumstances.

For American Indian/Alaska Native people who reside on reservations, there is rarely a homogenous population of tribal members. In all tribal communities, intermarriage with non-Native people or with people of other tribes occurs. However, for those who live on the reservation, a tribally elected government provides governance for the tribal members, based on tribal law and code. A variety of services, such as law enforcement, housing, social services, and education, are delivered through a network of programs and agencies (with funding provided by federal, state, and other organizations, such as through the Bureau of Indian Affairs) under the oversight of tribal leadership. Tribal laws do not bind tribal members who reside off-reservation in urban areas. Instead, they must follow state, county, and local laws that pertain to all citizens of the community. There are no elected tribal leaders who oversee the population of tribal members living off-reservation. Instead, in some areas where there are large numbers of urban Indian people, such as Los Angeles, Seattle, and Minneapolis, there are "Indian centers" that serve as resource and advocacy centers for Native people. These centers provide support through employment resources, cultural activities, social services, and other resources that provide connections to Indian people who are far from their homelands. Fundamentally, urban Indian organizations are an important support to Native families and individuals seeking to maintain their values and ties with each other and with their cultures. As they became established, urban Indian centers often provided a wide range of culturally sensitive programs to a diverse clientele. These programs became vital to the well-being of Native children and families because they provide safe and welcoming places, meals, counseling services, educational services, and economic development opportunities (National Urban Indian Family Coalition, 2008). The centers serve individuals who come from a multitude of tribes throughout the nation. These centers may also be a point of contact for American Indian/Alaska Native people who need assistance because they have been involved with systems such as law enforcement, health access, education, and child welfare. Sometimes advocates are able to intervene on their behalf.

However, whether on or off the reservation, American Indian /Alaska Native people—from all corners of the "lower 48" as well as throughout the expanse of Alaska—share very little cultural, linguistic, or social characteristics beyond the classification of "Native American." What is shared, however, is a common historical experience of oppression, loss of land base, loss of language, loss of children to government boarding schools, and a centuries-old link to federal treaties, policies, and legislation.

For example, the poor health experience that is common to American Indians and Alaska Natives, although obscuring their diversity, highlights their shared sociocultural experience (Office of Research on Women's Health, 1998). Group memories of widespread loss of children and other historical traumas remain strong in tribal groups and in American Indian communities. The forced removal of Indian children to boarding schools continued well into the 20th century, and the involuntary adoption of Indian children to non-Indian families still was widespread in the late

1970s. Thus, these experiences may remain fresh in the memories of many contemporary American Indian families. Research shows that group experiences of child removals result in many contemporary families being unable to trust and engage with their child welfare workers in ways necessary to successfully reunify with their children. This mistrust and fear is exacerbated by the child welfare system's ignorance of American Indian cultural values and practices, the imposition of dominant culture norms as the standard of child well-being, and by the lack of knowledge of resources (Lucero, 2007). These shared experiences in turn create some common contexts of American Indian/Alaska Native communities—on and off reservations.

EXPLANATION OF WITHIN GROUP ETHNIC DIVERSITY

Today it has become common for many to refer to American Indians/ Alaska Natives as simply "Native Americans" rather than by their own tribal name. But the term "Native American" is where the commonality ends. No single criterion exists for determining who is an American Indian. Each Indian nation sets its own criteria for membership. Most tribal nations require that a person document a certain percentage of American Indian/Alaska Native heritage to be considered a member; this is referred to as blood quantum. Some tribal nations require that ancestry be traced to someone who was on a tribal census in a particular year. Other nations trace descent only through the mother or only through the father. Criteria for citizenship in Indian nations may or may not be directly linked to biological heritage or to cultural identification. Only the nations themselves are capable of setting standards for citizenship, and these standards are subject to change, just like any other policy (Management Sciences for Health, 2005).

Diversity, rather than commonality, in language and culture across tribes is the norm rather than the exception. Differences in language dialects as well as cultural values *within* tribes and tribal bands also exist for most tribes. Within every tribe exists a continuum of cultural practices, from those members who are firmly rooted in their traditional culture beliefs, language, religion, and values to those who are at the far side of this spectrum—practicing few cultural traditions and leaning more heavily toward Christian-based religion and values. American Indians may identify themselves according to their particular nation rather than as members of a broad category such as American Indian. For some people, membership in a band or a clan may be equally or more important than membership in a nation as a primary source of identity. Bands or clans are groups of extended family networks.

The transition of many Native people from reservation to off-reservation life was significantly increased by the federally sponsored Relocation Project. A side effect of the transition to urban areas for many Native people was the loss of connection with extended family, cultural activities, and community. Living in such a foreign community took its toll on many families. Some had run-ins with law enforcement and Child Protective Services (CPS), possibly beginning the first steps toward racial disproportionality and disparities within these systems.

It was after recognizing the loss of so many Native children to state and county child welfare systems during the 1960s and 1970s that tribes rallied for the passage of the Indian Child Welfare Act (ICWA, Public Law 95-608). This law is applicable only to state/county child welfare agencies that have the authority to remove children to foster or adoptive placements. The Indian Child Welfare Act provides tribes with the authorization to intervene in these cases or to transfer their tribal members back to their tribal communities. Today, tribes throughout the country respond to thousands of ICWA notices that arise from all 50 states.

BRIEF HISTORY RELATED TO SOCIAL AND ECONOMIC JUSTICE

This agency forbade the speaking of Indian languages, prohibited the conduct of traditional religious activities, outlawed traditional government, and made Indian people ashamed of who they were. Worst of all, the Bureau of Indian Affairs committed these acts against the children entrusted to its boarding schools, brutalizing them emotionally, psychologically, physically, and spiritually. Even in this era of self-determination, when the Bureau of Indian Affairs is at long last serving as an advocate for Indian people in an atmosphere of mutual respect, the legacy of these misdeeds haunts us. The trauma of shame, fear, and anger has passed from one generation to the next, and manifests itself in the rampant alcoholism, drug abuse, and domestic violence that plague Indian country. Many of our people live lives of unrelenting tragedy as Indian families suffer the ruin of lives by alcoholism, suicides made of shame and despair, and violent death at the hands of one another. So many of the maladies suffered today in Indian country result from the failures of this agency. Poverty, ignorance, and disease have been the product of this agency's work. . . . and so today, I stand before you as the leader of an institution that in the past has committed acts so terrible that they infect, diminish, and destroy the lives of Indian people decades later, generations later. . . . Let us begin by expressing our profound sorrow for what this agency has done in the past. On behalf of the Bureau of Indian Affairs, I extend this formal apology to Indian people for the historical conduct of this agency (Gover, 2000).

The current challenges of racial disproportionality and disparities within American Indian and Alaska Native communities have evolved through a long and painful journey of American history. Although the United States has gradually become a racially and ethnically diverse country, its original inhabitants now represent less than 2% of the total population. There are innumerable history books, documents, and media that describe how throughout U.S. history disease as well as the impact of institutions such as churches, schools, and government agencies have decimated American Indian tribes, communities, and cultures.

By the end of the 18th century, the once abundant population of Native peoples had been reduced to 10% of its original size. Policies of extermination and seizure of lands were common in the history of the United States' interaction with American Indian tribes. Even after being forced onto reservation lands, many Indian families experienced disruption of their cultural traditions. Many American Indian children were deliberately taken from their homes and forced to attend boarding schools where they were not allowed to speak their native language or practice their traditions. The children usually spent a minimum of eight continuous years away from their families and communities. American policies of assimilation have had a pervasive impact on Native peoples and their way of life. The U.S. citizenship of American Indians was not recognized until 1924 when the Citizenship Act was passed. In addition, American Indians' religious freedoms were not recognized until 1978 when the American Indian Religious Freedom Act was passed, guaranteeing Native peoples the constitutional right to exercise their traditional religious practices for the first time in more than a century. These are but a few examples of historical factors that have affected American Indians psychologically, economically, and socially for generations. Although the experiences of many American Indians have changed as circumstances and policies changed, historical factors and the process of acculturation remain as powerful influences on the lives of many Indian people faced with difficult choices about who they are and how they want to live (Garrett, 1996). Today, survival of Native people is remarkable given that entire tribal cultures were destroyed.

PROBLEMS/ISSUES FACING THESE CLIENTS RELATED TO DISPROPORTIONALITY AND DISPARITIES

Using a systems perspective, theories about causation of disproportionality can be classified into three types: parent and family risk factors, community risk factors, and organizational and systemic factors. According to theories about *parent and family risk factors*, children of color are overrepresented in the child welfare system because they have disproportionate needs. They are more likely to have risk factors such as unemployment, teen parenthood, poverty, substance abuse, incarceration, domestic violence, mental illness, and so on, that result in high levels of child maltreatment. Proponents of *community factors* assert that overrepresentation has less to do with race or class and more to do with residing in neighborhoods and communities that have many risk factors, such as high levels of poverty, welfare assistance, unemployment, homelessness, single-parent families, and crime and street violence that make residents more visible to surveillance from public authorities. In contrast, theories about *organizational and systemic factors* contend that racial overrepresentation results from the decision-making processes of CPS agencies, cultural insensitivity and biases of workers, governmental policies, and institutional or structural racism.

Although these factors focus on overrepresentation of minorities in the child welfare system, it is likely that each could also be considered a factor in overrepresentation of any social system. However, not enough research has been conducted that focuses solely on the issues and outcomes of American Indian/Alaska Native disproportionality and disparities across-systems.

Anecdotally, in many jurisdictions, particularly in those jurisdictions where the disproportionality of Native people in public systems is high, there is generally a perception by Native people that they are negatively singled out by authority figures, such as law enforcement, medical professionals, teachers, and social workers. The fact that Native people are overrepresented in jails, prisons, foster care, and so on is a sad fact of life in most tribal communities.

Periodically, non-Native individuals or organizations exert efforts to fight on behalf of the Native overrepresentation, but there often is not always a concerted effort by tribal leaders to "go to battle" on behalf of tribal members residing off-reservation. However, off-reservation Native organizations throughout the country frequently challenge these public systems on behalf of Native people. Sometimes they are joined by on-reservation tribal leaders, or by members of on-reservation tribal programs, to support the efforts to address disproportionality and disparities.

CULTURALLY COMPETENT ASSESSMENTS AND INTERVENTIONS

The ICWA offers the clearest example of a message to federal and state child protection service agencies in addressing the disproportionate foster and adoptive placement of American Indian/Alaska Native children. Active efforts by the state or county child protection agency are required in every ICWA case to *prevent* AI/AN children from ever entering foster care. Active efforts are also important when children are removed from their parents and reunification efforts must be made. The "active efforts" requirement means that a more intense effort should be made than the "reasonable efforts" prescribed by other federal child welfare legislation. For example, active efforts would involve assisting families with services that meet their specific needs, not simply referring them to another community agency. Preventing a foster care placement through family preservation efforts is a critical first step in intervening in the cycle of disproportionality for American Indian/Alaska Native people.

Although the ICWA's active efforts do not apply to other public systems, the importance of connecting Native family with culturally appropriate advocacy or support services may further reduce the number of American Indian/Alaska Natives overrepresented in a multitude of systems. Family preservation and support services are critical for vulnerable Native families.

Interventions

Early identification of American Indian children entering CPS systems is a critical early step in effective family preservation work. However, often families' Indian status is not ascertained until well into the case and after many important opportunities to implement culturally responsive services have passed. Because of this, their Indian status receives no further consideration. In other instances, workers determine children's Indian status solely on physical characteristics and thus do not inquire about Native heritage if children do not "look" Indian.

In Colorado, for example, formalized protocols for identifying Indian children at the departmental level were made mandatory by state statute. Child welfare and court personnel are required to ask at first contact about children's Indian status and to continue to ask until the ICWA status of cases has been ruled upon definitively. Several CPS departments have developed further system-specific protocols that include referral of families with Native heritage to community-based partner agencies that serve American Indian families, commitment to including extended family members in case planning and services, and development of culturally appropriate family service plans. The experience of the Denver Indian Family Resource Center, in partnership with CPS departments in the metro Denver area, shows that early identification has made a huge impact on decreasing the number of Indian children who "fall through the cracks" and thus fail to benefit from the ICWA and culturally appropriate services. The number of family placements and reunifications with parents or caregivers increased greatly once departments began to identify families at a very early stage. In Denver County, for example, out-of-home nonkinship placements of American Indian children decreased by 76.8% in the two-year period FY 2003 to FY 2005. Early identification allowed extended family members to be contacted almost immediately, and parents or caregivers were able to receive referrals (Lucero, 2007).

Cross-Systems Collaborations

Although focused on child protection systems, the following strategies outlined by Lucero (2007) in "Working with Urban American Indian Families with Child Protection and Substance Abuse Challenges," can serve as a guide in cross-systems partnerships.

One of the most important steps that a CPS system and individual workers can take is to encourage collaborative partnerships with community-based agencies serving American Indians, American Indian service providers (such as psychologists and therapists), and tribes. These collaborative partnerships benefit Indian families and children by making available specialized and culturally appropriate programs and services. Providing the services to support change in the lives of American Indian parents and caregivers who have child protection and substance abuse issues requires an intensive level of clinical intervention. Partnerships with community-based agencies can support workers by helping share some of the workload. Collaborative efforts among CPS, community-based agencies serving Indian families, and tribes should begin by focusing on developing protocols for identifying American Indian families upon first contact with the department. Additional benefits to CPS departments can come from collaborative working relationships with community-based agencies. These agencies may be able to act as a bridge between CPS and tribes, provide cultural consultation and culturally appropriate service plans, suggest to workers ways they can engage in "active efforts to preserve Indian families" as required by the ICWA, assist CPS in identifying and supporting kinship placements, work together to ensure that children are safe and that cultural connections are initiated, and maintain community-based agencies serving American Indians. The latter can play a crucial role in supporting the integration of child welfare and substance abuse services precisely because of their work with clients connected to both systems. A natural linkage can be accomplished through the advocacy efforts of community agencies on behalf of parents or caregivers with child protection and substance abuse challenges. Intensive case management provided from the CPS system or through a collaborative arrangement with community-based agencies should be thought of as the underpinning of all cases involving American Indian families with child protection and substance abuse challenges. Because parents or caregivers in this segment of the population may lack family and other support systems, an active support team similar to that used in the wraparound services model can be a critical element for success. Wraparound teams can recreate support systems that are missing or have never been present in the parents' or caregivers' lives. The presence of an American Indian advocate as a member of the wraparound team is essential and indispensable. This individual serves as the cultural resource person for the group, and many times a trust develops between parents or caregivers and the American Indian advocate (Lucero, 2007).

In other systems, efforts are being made to intervene and address the disproportionality of AI/AN people. For example, in 2008, the North Dakota Supreme Court approved $100,000 in funding for a pilot program to address the overrepresentation of Native American youth in the juvenile justice system, and the program received state general fund appropriations beginning July 1, 2011. The program focuses on two counties with large Native American youth populations not living on a reservation. Native American youth represent 6.1% of the at-risk youth population but make up 26.5% of court referrals in the designated counties. The program focuses on several different points along the continuum, including prevention, diversion, and post-adjudication efforts to prevent placement. A crisis management component focuses on adjudication efforts to prevent placement and on preventing Native American youth from entering the system when they cannot be immediately and safely returned to their parents. A case management component focuses on diversion and the enhancement of services in order to prevent formal adjudications resulting in out-of-home or correctional placements. The program is also developing culturally relevant support services that could have a greater impact on delinquency prevention and early intervention than commonly used one-on-one counseling approaches (National Juvenile Justice Network, 2011).

Assessments

In California, a unique approach to assessing and addressing AI/AN disproportionality began in 2008. The Academy for Professional Excellence, San Diego State University School of Social Work was awarded a five-year grant in 2003 from the Administration for Children, Youth, and Families, to improve outcomes for tribal rural foster youth who are transitioning to adulthood. Because of difficulty in attracting knowledgeable applicants for this program, the need to have authentic engagements and relationships with tribal communities became evident. The academy sought advice and guidance from their tribal partners, Indian Health Council, Inc., and Southern Indian Health Council Inc., both within San Diego County. This process resulted in the development of the tribal Successful Transitions for Adult Readiness (STAR) program, which provides training and technical assistance to county social workers for five southern California counties: San Diego, Riverside, San Bernardino, Orange, and Imperial (Academy for Professional Excellence, 2008).

By conducting focus groups in each county and meeting with county social workers and tribal ICWA advocates and social workers, a number of themes began to emerge. Communication was lacking or strained between the counties and tribes or tribal representatives, which was magnified by recent or historic events. County social workers were largely unaware of the resources available to tribal youth in their care and often requested additional training and awareness to assist in future communication and engagement. Tribal children were also not being identified in the system and were often misplaced with no connections to their cultural origins.

In July 2008, a collaboration led by Casey Family Programs coalesced to fund and support the California Disproportionality and Disparities Project, an effort to improve outcomes for American Indian/Alaskan Native and African American children and families in the child welfare system. The project was based on Breakthrough Series Collaborative methodology emphasizing small tests of change to implement rapidly for practice improvement (Miller & Ward, 2003).

Members of the project reached out to the American Indian community to participate as faculty in the 24-month-long effort and recruited the leadership from the tribal STAR. As a result of this Breakthrough Series Collaborative, the California American Indian Enhancement Project (AIE) evolved and developed a tool kit to assist counties in putting their ICWA-related efforts into perspective. Central to the tool kit is a framework called the *Continuum of Readiness* that was developed to assist counties in their collaborative efforts with tribes and urban Indian programs. The framework's approach is to implement a simple assessment that determines the top priorities of interested counties in the following areas:

1. Awareness of culturally relevant resources to support addressing disproportionality (clinics, ICWA services, American Indian and tribal services, tribal TANF [Temporary Assistance for Needy Families], etc.)
2. Awareness of American Indian culture, history, and values that can increase culturally responsive social welfare practice
3. Establish relationships with American Indian agencies, community members, community leaders, and providers that serve youth in the system

4. Support for developing realistic and achievable goals and/or objectives in their county System Improvement Plan, which includes American Indian/tribal stakeholders

5. Improving ICWA compliance

6. Technical assistance and support for future or existing coalitions that are working to address gaps and challenges faced by county child welfare systems and local American Indian ICWA service providers

7. "Other" self-identified efforts that must be clearly related to supporting collaboration with Tribes and American Indian programs

The objective is to support county readiness for addressing disproportionality through collaboration. The ultimate goal of all technical assistance is to establish trust-based relationships among county principals, American Indian communities, and ICWA service agencies. Today the AIE continues as a collaboration with the Administrative Office of the Courts, California Child Welfare Co-Investment Partnership, California Department of Social Services, California Social Work Education Center, Casey Family Programs, Child and Family Policy Institute of California, the National Resource Center for Tribes, Stuart Foundation, and tribal STAR (Lidot, Orrantia, & Choca, 2011).

SPOTLIGHT: PROMISING PRACTICES

Three examples are provided that demonstrate interventions at different levels of their respective systems. They show the impact of community engagement to affect policy and systems change and the ability to affect outcomes within multiple systems (child welfare, education, health, mental health, and justice). Due to the impact of historic traumas on AI/AN communities, this chapter has illuminated the impact on justice, public safety/violence, health, education, mental health, and child welfare. Therefore it makes sense that to effect change in any disparate indicator, the collaborate effort of multiple systems at multiple levels may be required, from entry, service provision, policy, and procedures, to post-intervention services.

Because of a long history of broken treaties, attempted genocide, and federal policies that broke apart Native families, Native communities are hesitant to collaborate with health departments, nontribal social service agencies, and academic institutions (Lidot & Kolb, 2005). In order for nontribal agencies and organizations to work successfully with American Indian/Alaska Native communities, the worker and the agency must establish trust. This requires agencies to make a commitment to culturally competent practices and for workers to learn appropriate engagement skills that focus on trust building. The three promising practice examples—Tribal Court/State Court Forums, Talking Circle, and Lakota Oyate Wakanyeja Owicaki-yapi (LOWO)—have demonstrated commitment to cultural competence and appropriate engagement. Further, the Talking Circle and LOWO models have integrated cultural values into their foundation of operational policies and program design.

Tribal Court / State Court Forums

A state forum is a body of state and tribal court representatives convened by the state chief justice to find mutually acceptable and practical solutions to conflicts between the two court systems. An action agenda covers educational needs, child welfare, ICWA compliance, proposals for legislation and state and tribal court rules, suggestions for intergovernmental agreements, preparation of a tribal court handbook, approaches to improved communication and cooperation, encouragement of cross-visitations and information sharing, and indications of other actions that should reduce conflicts. Various forums have obtained pertinent legislation and court rules, annual law school symposia on Indian law topics, an institutional mechanism to update a tribal court directory, a growing state library of tribal codes and appellate court decisions, chief justice visitations to tribal courts, and invitations of tribal judges to state judicial conferences, among other accomplishments. Further, the informal working relationships that have developed have allowed numerous intercourt problems to be settled by what one forum chair refers to as a simple telephone call (Grandy & Rubin, n.d.).

This cross-system collaboration, initiated at the judicial level, can have a powerful impact on the day-to-day functioning of the child welfare system. A judge who understands and insists on ICWA compliance will shape the behavior of case workers and supervisors who report to the court. Usually, all it takes is one embarrassing interaction at court to ensure that a mistake will not be repeated. Thus improved ICWA compliance, resulting from systems collaboration, has very clear and life-changing implications for AI/AN children, their families, and their tribes.

Talking Circle—Multidisciplinary Culturally Based Substance Abuse Intervention

The Talking Circle prevention intervention (Lowe, Liang, Riggs, Henson, & Elder, 2012) has its origins in the Teen Intervention Project that was built on the standardized student assistance program (SAP) designed to help adolescents address alcohol and substance abuse problems. The SAP is an evidenced-based program endorsed by the Substance Abuse Mental Health Service Administration (SAMHSA) as a model program. The SAP involves a 10-session motivational, skills-building group intervention and utilizes a traditional group setting, approach, and process. The Talking Circle intervention merges the core ideas of the SAP with Native American values. The Talking Circle prevention intervention requires groups of 15–20 participants to meet for ten 50-minute sessions over a 10-week period. The 10-week group sessions, which are conducted in the culturally congruent format of a talking circle, are guided by a manual that can be tailored for a specific tribal group. The Talking Circle intervention uses the "self-reliance" theory as its foundational theoretical underpinning. This is a cultural theory first designed for Cherokee and Keetoowah Cherokee youth that has evolved to a "Native self-reliance" theory that can be used with youth from multiple and diverse tribes. This model utilizes the collaborative support of the educational, mental health, and substance abuse systems.

Lakota Oyate Wakanyeja Owicakiyapi—Tribal and State Child Welfare Collaboration

Lakota Oyate Wakanyeja Owicakiyapi (LOWO) provides services based on the foundation of Lakota cultural practices and on healing through the Oglala Lakota Practice Model, which incorporates the use of traditional ceremonies and healings to promote the health and well-being of children and families (Casey Family Programs, 2012). Families are given the choice of utilizing cultural services, a combination of cultural services and Western clinical services, or solely Western clinical services to promote and improve holistic wellness. Historically, there had never been an agreement to allow the state of South Dakota to do child welfare work on the reservation. One of the most significant accomplishments of LOWO has been the establishment (in 2008) of a formal agreement with the South Dakota CPS for LOWO to provide foster care services for the Pine Ridge Tribe, thus ending more than 40 years of state supervision over Oglala Sioux child welfare cases. Policy development recognizing government-to-government relationships supports multilevel systemic changes within tribal and nontribal federal, state, and local government efforts. The program builds success on frontline interaction and culturally appropriate engagement.

FUTURE DIRECTIONS

In order to address the extraordinary challenges faced by American Indians/Alaska Natives in their overrepresentation in public systems, it is crucial to examine all avenues that may impact the reduction of minority disproportionality and disparities, whether those efforts are specific to American Indian/Alaska Natives or to all minority people. For example, federal efforts are improving to promote general child well-being in child welfare systems as well as improved tribal-state collaboration through the 2008 Fostering Connections to Success and Increasing Adoptions Act (Public Law 110-351). Increasingly, federally recognized American Indian/Alaska Native tribal governments have access to Title IV-B, Part 1 and Part 2, funding that supports the development of tribal family preservation and support projects. Although these funds are limited, they are flexible dollars that can help provide much needed culturally appropriate and tribally driven services to keep Native children out of foster care systems. Tribes also access Indian Child Welfare Act, Title II funding through the Bureau of Indian Affairs to help them address the numerous ICWA notices they receive annually regarding their tribal members. Unfortunately, neither of these funding opportunities is available to off-reservation urban Indian organizations. This lack of funding severely impedes the ability of these organizations to serve or to advocate for AI/AN families who are involved with child welfare or any other public system.

In order to appeal to funders, it is also critical to be able to articulate the dire community needs. However, research and data about the overrepresentation and disparities affecting American Indians/Alaska Native is very limited, which further reduces the exposure that this topic receives at the local, state, and national level. In the 2001 study, "Child Abuse and Neglect among American Indian/Alaska Native Children: An Analysis of Existing Data," the authors described the policy implications of lack of data for American Indians:

> U.S. policy toward Indian nations is broadly affected by available data, which are used to allocate funding, services, and staff to address problems of abuse and/or neglect. Misleading or inaccurate statistics regarding child abuse and neglect may lead to underfunding of programs (Earle & Cross, 2001, p. 60).

The report goes on to further recommend that data from the Bureau of Indian Affairs, Indian Health Service, and Department of Health and Human Services be combined with other data sources to present an accurate picture of child abuse and neglect among American Indian/Alaska Natives.

Collaboration among agencies at all levels is imperative to raise awareness and address the crisis of American Indian/Alaska Native disproportionality and disparities across systems. For example, together, the federal Children's Bureau and the Bureau of Indian Affairs may find common ground in developing strategies to address the disproportionality of AI/AN children in state child welfare systems because these cases form the center of Indian Child Welfare Act case practice.

American Indian/Alaska Native people have survived more than five centuries of outside contact and influence. This contact has forever changed, and in some cases erased, tribal communities, culture, and traditions. The historic collision of cultures has also resulted in the near destruction of Native communities. Yet in spite of the overwhelming disproportionate numbers and disparate treatment of Native people, American Indian/Alaska Natives remain strong, vibrant people—many who continue to speak their language, adhere to customs and traditions, and work hard each day to raise strong and healthy families. The complete story of disproportionality cannot be told without also telling the story of human resilience.

Addressing disproportionality through collaboration between nontribal and tribal systems requires intention and perseverance. Cross-system efforts that support multiple agendas and recognition of competing values ensure tribal community support while addressing local, state, and federal directions. Ultimately, when these efforts are successful, families are preserved and individual, family, and community wellness is achieved, increasing the potential for continued prevention and reduction of disparity and disproportionality. Recommendations for future directions include the following.

STRATEGIES FOR ADDRESSING AND ELIMINATING DISPROPORTIONALITY AND DISPARITIES

1. Increase awareness of disparities as systemic problems that represent some of the most pressing challenges for American Indians/Alaska Natives. Community awareness must begin at many levels—from the tribal leadership level to the tribal (reservation) community level, at the urban Native organizational level, as well as among Native and non-Native agencies at the local, state, and federal levels. Attention must include accurate and current data related to the issue.
2. Engage tribal leaders and off-reservation Native leaders as well as community advocates and community members in a common mission to reduce disproportionality of AI/AN across all systems, with an initial national focus on child welfare systems.
3. Form community partnerships that include Native and non-Native agency leaders who are committed to the long and difficult challenges of systems change. Include mechanisms to gather data and track the effectiveness of the work.
4. Conduct culturally appropriate agency and community assessments followed by community driven and multisystem strategic planning.
5. Conduct research to learn tribal, state, and national efforts to reduce the overrepresentation of AI/AN people, always documenting lessons learned in order to share successful prevention and intervention strategies.
6. Increase funding for off-reservation and on-reservation services that are designed to address community needs and to prevent the flow of American Indian/Alaska Native people into public systems, such as the criminal justice system, child welfare system, and so on.

REFERENCES

Academy for Professional Excellence. (2008). *Tribal STAR, Children's Bureau Discretionary Grants Program, final evaluation report.* San Diego, CA: San Diego State University, School of Social Work.

Casey Family Programs. (2012). *Lakota Oyate Wakanyeja Owicakiyapi (LOWO) Transformation Report.* Retrieved from http://www.casey.org/Resources/Publications/pdf/LOWO-TransformationReport.pdf

Center for Community Partnerships in Child Welfare. (2006). *Places to watch: Promising practices to address racial disproportionality in child welfare services.* Washington, DC: Casey-CSSP Alliance for Racial Equity.

Cross, T. L. (2008). Native Americans and juvenile justice: A hidden tragedy. *Poverty & Race, 17*(6), 19–22.

Dorgan, B. L. (2010). The tragedy of Native American youth suicide. *Psychological Services, 7*(3), 213–218.

Earle, K. A., & Cross, A. (2001). *Child abuse and neglect among American Indian/ Alaska Native children: An analysis of existing data.* Seattle, WA: Casey Family Programs.

Freeman, C., and Fox, M. (2005). *Status and trends in the education of American Indians and Alaska Natives* (NCES 2005-108). U.S. Department of Education, National Center for Education Statistics. Washington, DC: U.S. Government Printing Office.

Garrett, M. T. (1996). "Two people": An American Indian narrative of bicultural identity. *Journal of American Indian Education, 36*(1), 1–21.

Gover, K. (2000). Remarks of Kevin Gover, Assistant Secretary-Indian Affairs: Address to tribal leaders. *Journal of American Indian Education, 39,* 4–6.

Grandy, H. C., & Rubin, T. E. (n.d.). Tribal court—state court forums: A how-to-do-it guide to prevent and resolve jurisdictional disputes and improve cooperation between tribal and state courts. Retrieved from http://www.walkingoncommon ground.org/files/Resources%201%20TribalCourtStateForumHow2Guide.pdf

Grant, J., & Brown, T. (2003). *American Indian and Alaska Native resource manual.* Arlington, VA: National Alliance on Mental Illness.

Hartney, C. (2008). *Native American youth and the juvenile justice system.* Washington, DC: National Council on Crime and Delinquency.

Hartney, C., & Vuong, L. (2009). *Created equal: Racial and ethnic disparities in the U.S. criminal justice system.* Washington, DC: National Council on Crime and Delinquency.

Harvard Project on American Indian Economic Development. (2004). *The context and meaning of family strengthening in Indian America.* Baltimore, MD: Annie E. Casey Foundation.

Henry J. Kaiser Family Foundation. (2004). *American Indians and Alaska Natives: Health coverage and access to care.* Retrieved from: http://kaiserfamilyfoundation. files.wordpress.com/2013/01/american-indians-and-alaska-natives-health-coverage-access-to-care.pdf

Indian Country Today. (2005, Feb. 23). The seamless Indian community: Reservation to city and back again. *Indian Country Today (Lakota Times)*. Retrieved from http://indiancountrytodaymedianetwork.com/ictarchives/2005/02/23/the-seamless-indian-community-reservation-to-city-and-back-again-94545

Judicial Council of California, Administrative Office of the Courts. (2010). *Native American communities justice project—Beginning the dialogue: Domestic violence, sexual assault, stalking & teen-dating violence policy paper*. San Francisco: Author.

Lidot, T. & Kolb, K. (2005). *Tribal STAR tips for following protocol when working with tribal communities*. Retrieved from University of California at Berkeley Web site: http://calswec.berkeley.edu/files/uploads/pdf/CalSWEC/AIE/AIE_CET_Tips_Protocol.pdf

Lidot, T., Orrantia, R.M., & Choca, M. (2011). *Continuum of readiness for collaboration*. ICWA Compliance & Reducing Disproportionality, unpublished.

Lowe, J., Liang, H., Riggs, C., Henson, J., & Elder, T. (2012). Community partnership to affect substance abuse among Native American adolescents. *The American Journal of Drug and Alcohol Abuse, 38*(5): 450–455.

Lucero, N. (2007). *Resource guide: Working with urban American Indian families with child protection and substance abuse challenges*. Denver, CO: Rocky Mountain Quality Improvement Center.

Management Sciences for Health. (2005). *American Indians and Alaska Natives: Health disparities overview*. Retrieved from http://erc.msh.org/provider/informatic/AIAN_Disparities_CAM.pdf

Miller, O. A., & Ward, K. J. (2003). Disparate outcomes in child welfare: The results of a National Breakthrough Series Collaborative. *Child Welfare, 87*, 211–240.

National Juvenile Justice Network. (2011). *Advances in juvenile justice reform—North Dakota 2009*. Retrieved from http://www.njjn.org/our-work/juvenile-justice-reform-advances-north-dakota#ND2009

National Urban Indian Family Coalition. (2008). *Urban Indian America: The status of American Indian & Alaska Native children & families today*. Baltimore, MD: Annie E. Casey Foundation.

Office of Research on Women's Health. (1998). *Management sciences for health, American Indians and Alaska Natives: Health disparities overview*. Bethesda, MD: Author.

Summers, A., Wood, S., & Russell, J. (2012). *Disproportionality rates for children of color in foster care.* Reno, NV: National Council of Juvenile and Family Court Judges.

U.S. Commission on Civil Rights, (2003). *A Quiet Crisis: Federal Funding and Unmet Needs in Indian Country.*

U.S. Department of Health and Human Services, Administration for Children and Families, Administration on Children, Youth and Families, Children's Bureau. (2012). *The AFCARS report: Preliminary FY 2010 estimates as of July 2012.* Retrieved from http://www.acf.hhs.gov/programs/cb/stats_research

PART 3

Cross Systems

7

Disproportionality and Disparities in the Public Child Welfare System

▸ *LAWANNA LANCASTER AND ROWENA FONG*

DESCRIPTION OF THE SYSTEM AND THE ETHNIC MINORITY POPULATIONS IN THE SYSTEM

SINCE AT LEAST THE EARLY 1600s, there has been a debate about what to do with children whose parents are unable to take care of them. During the 1600s and 1700s, few options were available other than almshouses and orphanages. In the mid-1800s, Charles Loring Brace, in an effort to avoid the use of institutional care, developed the idea of "placing out," which was the precursor to the current U.S. foster care system (Myers, 2004). The Child Abuse Prevention and Treatment Act was passed in 1974, which established the National Center on Child Abuse and Neglect. Currently, there are four primary reasons a child might be removed from his or her family of origin and placed in the foster care system: physical abuse, sexual abuse, emotional/psychological abuse, and neglect. Physical abuse encompasses any nonaccidental physical injury inflicted on a child by an adult (Crosson-Tower, 2007; Myers, 2004). Sexual abuse is any sexual activity between a child and an adolescent or adult (Myers, 2004). Emotional or psychological abuse can be more difficult to define than other types of abuse but encompasses a destructive pattern of behavior designed to make a child feel worthless (Crosson-Tower, 2007; Myers, 2004). Neglect is a broad term that represents the inability or unwillingness of parents to provide the basic needs for their child. This includes shelter, food, clothing, medical care, and so on (Crosson-Tower, 2007; Myers, 2004). One of the issues in the foster care system during the late 1970s was the length of time children were being retained in the system.

Since 1980, several child welfare laws have been passed in an effort to reduce the time children spend in the public welfare system and to better plan for permanency for these children (Crosson-Tower, 2007).

In addition to the fight to reduce the length of time children spend in temporary foster care placements, attention has been paid to the rate at which children from various racial/ethnic groups are entering into the public child welfare system. More than 100 years after the concept of placing out, the first legislation was developed specifically related to foster care policies for children of color, the Indian Child Welfare Act (ICWA) of 1979 (Crosson-Tower, 2007; Myers, 2004). This act marked the first step in addressing disparities that were occurring for children of color in the public child welfare system. The purpose of the ICWA was to keep Native children from being placed in White homes and to require that Native tribes be allowed to make placement decisions for their children. The ICWA was the first piece of child welfare legislation directly addressing a specific racial/ethnic group. In 1994, the Multiethnic Placement Act was passed and further amended in 1996 to be the Interethnic Placement Act (Samantrai, 2004). This law bridged the gap between legislation related to permanence for all children in foster care and the specific challenges related to permanence experienced by children of color. Specifically, it prevents placement and adoption decisions from being based on race, color, or national origin except in very rare circumstances (Samantrai, 2004). Yet despite efforts to address permanency and the specific needs of children of color, children from non-White populations continue to be overrepresented in America's public child welfare system.

Generally speaking, the many resources that discuss the issue of disproportionality in child welfare do not explain why disproportionality is a problem that should be reduced or eliminated. That may be because the authors and researchers anticipate that the reason for eliminating disproportionality in child welfare is obvious. Certainly, the Social Work Code of Ethics indicates that social workers should not only avoid practicing discrimination but also "prevent and eliminate domination of, exploitation of, and discrimination against any person, group, or class on the basis of race, ethnicity, national origin . . ." (National Association of Social Workers, 2008, Section 6.04). Based on the reports of many authors that discrimination and bias are contributors to racial disproportionality in child welfare (Barth, 2005; Chibnall et al., 2003; Clegg & Associates, Inc. & Wanda Hackett Enterprises, 2004; Curtis & Denby, 2011; Derezotes & Poetner, 2005; Dettlaff et al., 2011; Dettlaff & Rycraft, 2008; Hill, 2006; Knott & Giwa, 2012; Miller, 2009;

Miller & Gaston, 2003), social workers have a responsibility to understand and address racial disproportionality in any system, including child welfare.

However, not all authors support a focus specifically on the issue of disproportionality in the child welfare system. Elizabeth Bartholet (2009) has stated that an overreliance on the belief that child welfare systems are flawed in removing children of color at a greater rate than White children will cause other areas of disparity to be overlooked. One concern is that by focusing exclusively on disproportionality rates in child welfare, the actual causes of disparate maltreatment rates will be ignored. Bartholet's perspective is that the focus of concern should be on reducing maltreatment in families of color rather than on reducing placement in the child welfare system.

Although Bartholet's perspective has been a point of controversy in the disproportionality discussion, it is an important part of the conversation. Her writings on disproportionality and disparity in child welfare identify the importance of looking beyond the time that children of color spend in the foster care system to their complete interactions with the child welfare system and the issues that put them at risk for those interactions. The recent focus of research on racial disproportionality in child welfare has provided a conduit whereby disparity and disproportionality in other areas are being identified and addressed. Additionally, social workers, agencies, counties, and states are developing strategies to address issues of disparity and disproportionality for families who are at risk of interactions with the child welfare system, particularly families of color. These strategies are not only designed to mitigate disparity during the out-of-home placement experience for children but also to prevent placement for children and to address disparities that occur in American society in general for families of color. Specific strategies are discussed later in this chapter.

Ethnic Minority Populations in the System

According to statistics compiled by the Annie E. Casey Foundation and the U.S. Department of Health and Human Services (Lorthridge, McCrosky, Pecora, Chambers, & Fatemi, 2012),

> Children of color (including those classified as Hispanic of any race and excluding those whose exact racial background was not known) accounted for 44% of the U.S. child population in 2009 and made up 53% of all children in foster care as of July 2010. (p. 281)

A report by Casey Family Programs (2007) identifies African Americans, Native Americans, and Hispanics/Latinos as the three groups who are over-represented in child welfare. However, the bulk of the research that has been conducted and the literature that has been written about disproportionality focuses on African Americans. In part, this is likely due to the fact that the disproportionality rate for African Americans is higher than the rate for the other two groups. Hill (2006) also suggests that this focus may be due, in part, to the fact that most of the research has been national in nature rather than based on individual states or regions. In looking at national numbers, the disproportionality rates are minimal for people of color who are not African American. Lu et al. (2004) went so far as to indicate that African Americans were the only racial group overrepresented in child welfare in some of the early decision-making points. An additional problem identified by Hill (n.d.) is the lack of research related to groups other than African Americans. This has made it difficult for conclusions to be drawn about the significance of disproportionality for other populations of color.

Although most of the literature on disproportionality in child welfare is related to the overrepresentation of African Americans or Blacks in foster care, Latinos, Native Americans, Alaskan Natives, and those identified as Native Hawaiian/Other Pacific Islanders are overrepresented in foster care as well. Although this may not be observed at the national level for some populations, it has been demonstrated at the state or regional level (Hill, 2006; Hines, Lemon, Wyatt, & Merdinger, 2004).

Hill (n.d.) also points out the need for research on the disproportional-ity encountered by Native Americans, in large part because of the dearth of research related to this group of people. The National Incidence Study (NIS) has been a primary source of data for many who completed early research about disproportionality (Barth, 2005; Derezotes & Poetner, 2005; Gryzlak, Wells, & Johnson, 2005; Sedlak & Schultz, 2005a; Sedlak & Schultz, 2005b). However, a significant concern about the most recent NIS, completed in 2010, is the inaccurate portrayal of disproportionality for American Indians and Alaskan Natives (Cross, 2011). As a result of small samples in several racial groups, the NIS-4 focused exclusively on three categories: White non-Hispanic, Black non-Hispanic, and Hispanic (Cross, 2011). Cross (2011) also mentions the exclusion of important rural data embedded within the NIS-4 as it relates to American Indian and Alas-kan Native families.

Recent regional-specific research has begun to shed light on how certain populations other than African Americans experience disproportionality in foster care in areas of the United States where they are a significant portion of the population (Dougherty, 2003; Godinet, Arnsberger, Li, & Kreif, 2010). For example, research completed in Hawaii indicates that individuals identified as Native Hawaiian, along with other Pacific Islander groups, are overrepresented in the Hawaii foster care system (Dougherty, 2003; Hawai'i Department of Human Services; Godinet et al., 2010). This is despite the overwhelming statistics from most disproportionality research that indicate the underrepresentation in the child welfare system of those included in the classification of Asian (Cheung & LaChapelle, 2011).

UNDERSTANDING THE PROBLEMS AND NEEDS OF ETHNIC MINORITY POPULATIONS IN THE SYSTEM

Native Americans and Alaskan Natives

There are many general pieces of information about Native Americans/ American Indians that need to be understood as a foundation for understanding the overrepresentation of this population in foster care. Some researchers indicate that "Child abuse and trauma have been shown to be elevated in some tribal communities" (Libby et al., 2006, p. 628). According to some, this is a recent phenomenon. Cross, Earle, and Simmons wrote an article in 2000 discussing child abuse and neglect in Indian communities. In that article, they indicate that Indian child-rearing practices have historically focused on teaching children self-discipline rather than on parental discipline as is the dominant child-rearing practice in the United States. As a result, historically child abuse and neglect were rare in tribal settings because of the lack of corporal punishment as part of the disciplinary process. Children were taught self-discipline by many members of the child's extended family, which served as a barrier to child abuse or neglect. This system of childrearing created an inherent child protection system within Indian communities.

The trend of removing Indian children from their families and tribes, which occurred during the 1800s, began affecting the natural child protection in Indian communities. Native children were placed with White families and in White boarding homes. The rationale behind the removal of Indian children was that the children would become civilized away from their families and tribes. As Indian tribes were moved onto reservations and the Indian people had their rights taken away by the federal government, some of their natural child protections began to erode. Throughout the first half of the 20th century, "oppression, alcoholism, disease, and poverty were allowed to flourish and child abuse and neglect had fertile ground in which to take root" (Cross et al., 2000, p. 50).

Some of the same problems encountered by today's larger society also impact Indian communities but at higher levels. For example, 45% of Indian mothers have their first child before they are 20 years old compared to 24% of mothers of other races. The poverty rate for Indian children aged 6–11 is 38%, whereas it is 18% in the general population. Finally, 27% of Indian families are headed by a single female compared to 16% of families in the general population (Cross et al., 2000). These community problems may contribute to the incidence of child abuse or neglect in Indian communities. Also, many tribal communities exist in rural areas, which often impedes the ability of the residents to access any public services, particularly those designed to help families stay together.

Not all Indians live on reservations, in part as a result of the relocation programs of the 1800s and 1900s. Living in urban locations, however, has consequences for Indian families, just as living in very rural locations can impact them. Cross et al. (2000) suggest that child abuse and neglect among urban Indian families may be a result of the trauma they encounter by living in urban areas and the lack of family support that exists outside of the reservation. High levels of abuse and neglect among Indian people can also be attributed to the many years Indian children spent in boarding schools where abuse, both sexual and physical, were prevalent. "Personal experiences such as these, coupled with the breakdown of the extended family and spiritual belief systems, the loss of tribal economies, and the introduction of alcohol, served to create an environment where child abuse and neglect could develop and continue to exist in Indian communities" (Cross et al., 2000, p. 53).

Although the ICWA was a positive step toward helping the Indian people to retain the care for Indian children and the right to be part of the decision-making process, Indian tribal communities needed funding to be able to adequately meet the needs of all of their Indian children. Adequate funding, however, was not provided to tribal communities. The legislation and programs designed to provide funding for child welfare, Title IV-E,

Title IV-B parts 1 & 2, and Title XX, include little to no funding specifically designated for the care of Indian children or child welfare among Indian tribal communities. Plantz, Hubbell, Barret, and Dobreec reviewed the status of the ICWA in 1988 and found that the number of Indian children in foster care rose throughout the early 1980s (Mannes, 1993). They indicate that this increase is likely due to the placement decisions made by the tribal systems and not by state systems because state systems had actually decreased the number of Indian children placed. Plantz et al. further mention that tribes seemed to be taking over the decision making for Indian children as the ICWA required, but they continued to do what state systems had been doing—splitting Native families and placing Indian children in foster care. As with Cross et al. (2000), Mannes attributes this, in part at least, to the limited financial resources available for tribal systems. Also, this can be attributed to "insufficient use of placement prevention practices" (Mannes, 1993, p. 145).

In a recent article, Cross (2011) further explains some of the damage done systemically through the early placement of Indian children into White homes. That placement process created a mindset for people in state and federal agencies that Indian children could escape the "poverty and other social ills affecting Indian people" by being placed into White homes (Cross, 2011, p. 114). That mindset continues to drive practice, consciously or subconsciously, in public child welfare agencies today. Understanding some of the history related to Indian child welfare is crucial to understanding the issue of the current overrepresentation of Native Americans in any foster care system.

Blacks/African Americans

It is now widely accepted by researchers in the child welfare field that African Americans are disproportionately represented in the child welfare system. Additionally, disparate outcomes for this population have been found at virtually every step of the child welfare process from referral to case outcomes (Earth, 1997; Goerge & Bilaver, 2005; Gryzlak et al., 2005; Hill, 2005a; Rolock & Testa, 2005; Sedlak & Schultz, 2005b). In most cases, there are connections identified between race and other factors such as substance use and poverty. However, systemic issues likely also play a role in the experiences of African Americans who interact with the child welfare system.

According to Rolock and Testa (2005), African American families were more likely to have an allegation substantiated regardless of the race of the investigator. Results from several studies have indicated that African American children are reunited at a slower rate than White children (Goerge and Bilaver, 2005; Hill, 2005b). For African American children who are not reunited with their families, they are more likely to remain in care than to be adopted, while White children are more likely to be adopted than to remain in care.

Poverty was one factor that has been identified as a potential cause of disproportionality for African American children in foster care (Clegg & Associates, Inc. & Wanda Hackett Enterprises, 2004; Chibnall, et al., 2003; Curtis & Denby, 2011; Derezotes & Poetner, 2005; Hill, 2006; Lemon, D'Andrade, & Austin, 2005; Miller, 2009). In addition to the risk of abuse or neglect, which can be attributed to the mechanics of living in poverty, families in poverty also have a high level of risk for being reported to the child welfare system by other systems because they are being served by those systems and are highly visible to those systems. Although poverty itself can be a contributing factor for disproportionality, Miller and Gaston (2003) identified society's view of people in poverty as lazy, deficient in character, or immoral as the contributing factor to disproportionality rather than poverty itself. This belief reflects the reality that racism and bias are additional contributing factors to disproportionality in child welfare for African Americans.

Several authors have determined that racism, institutional or personal, or racial bias play a part in the level of disproportionality in the child welfare system (Barth, 2005; Chibnall et al., 2003; Curtis & Denby, 2011; Derezotes & Poetner, 2005; Dettlaff et al., 2011; Hill, 2006; Knott & Giwa, 2012; Miller, 2009; Miller & Gaston, 2003). Although some authors do not necessarily label their concerns as institutional racism, they describe processes that could be included in this concept. For example, Morton (1999) expresses concern that biased risk assessment tools are a contributing factor to disproportionality in the child welfare system. Chibnall et al. (2003) mentions the definitions that are used to identify abuse or neglect as a possible contributor to disproportionality. These definitions are based on White middle-class ideals. It is also important to recognize that the racism and bias that exists in child welfare, although sometimes linked with the prevalence of poverty for African Americans, is not always present in conjunction with poverty. The examples from Morton (1999) and Chibnall et al. (2003) reflect this as does the research from Knott and Giwa (2012) and Curtis and Denby (2011). Knott and Giwa (2012) hypothesized that discrimination against African American families impacts the amount of services that are provided for those families and keeps them in the child welfare system longer. Denby and Curtis found "social workers resist targeting family preservation services (services aimed at preventing the disruption of the family due to maltreatment) to African American children and their families" (Curtis & Denby, 2011, p. 119).

In the book *Shattered Bonds*, Dorothy Roberts (2002) confronts the difficult issue of disproportionality and places the blame for it on child welfare policies, both past and current. She uses the stories of several Black women to describe how individual racism and institutional racism have combined to destroy Black families by involving them in the child welfare system. Several times throughout the book, Roberts makes the claim that the system is arranged intentionally to divide Black families and that the division of Black families is seen as a positive, or at least neutral, issue by the broader society. She reviews recent child welfare policy changes, including the Adoption and Safe Families Act (ASFA) and the Multiethnic Placement Act (MEPA), and explains how these policies specifically target Black families in an attempt to destroy them. She also reviews the change from Aid to Families with Dependent Children (AFDC) to Temporary Assistance for Needy Families (TANF) and the Welfare-to-Work program and how that adds to the number of Black children being placed in foster care and to the destruction of Black families. Although Roberts does reference the disparate outcomes that African American children experience in comparison to White children once they enter the foster care system, her focus is on the way they enter the system.

Latinos

Research related to disproportionality in child welfare among Latinos is sparse. Additionally, most of the existing research indicates that Latinos are underrepresented in the child welfare system. This is largely due to the national nature of that research (Hill, 2006). Several researchers, however, have pointed out the importance of studying Latinos in the child welfare system (Dettlaff, 2011; Hill, n.d.; Hines, Lee, Osterling, & Drabble, 2007; Hines, Lemon, et al., 2004).

> Nationally, Latino children constitute the second largest group in the child welfare system and in states with a large Latino representation (e.g., California, Texas and New Mexico) Latino children are the majority, and exhibit placement characteristics that mirror those of African American children. (Hines, Lee, et al., 2007, p. 276)

Although this population has traditionally been underrepresented in the foster care system nationwide, state-by-state comparisons indicate that Latinos are overrepresented in foster care in some states (Dettlaff, 2011).

One concern related to the underrepresentation of Latinos in the child welfare system is whether or not the representation is as it should be. Dettlaff (2011) mentions the possibility that the underrepresentation of Latinos in foster care may be as a result of less maltreatment, but it might also be a result of underreporting. Any research moving forward in the area of disproportionality for Latinos should include considerations about the consequences of under- and overrepresentation.

Asians/Pacific Islanders

If the amount of research encompassing disproportionality and Latinos can be considered sparse, research related to disproportionality and Asian or Pacific Islander populations is virtually nonexistent. Much of the existing disproportionality research indicates that children identified as Asian or Pacific Islander are underrepresented in child welfare (Hill, 2006). As with Latinos, Cheung and LaChapelle (2011) identify a concern that although underrepresentation in child welfare may be due to a lower rate of maltreatment among Asian families, it may instead be related to underreporting. The study by Godinet et al. (2010) mentioned earlier lends credence to this concern. Cheung and LaChapelle indicate that the underreporting of Asian families may be related to biases held by many White Americans that Asians are a "model minority" (2011, p. 132). Further research is needed to fully understand the impact of disproportionality and disparity on Asian and Pacific Islander families in the United States. Even though the experiences for each population group are unique, bias is a factor in how all of them experience the public child welfare system.

SYSTEMS EFFORTS TO ADDRESS DISPROPORTIONALITY AND DISPARITIES: GENERAL BARRIERS AND ETHNIC-SPECIFIC BARRIERS FACED AND CHALLENGES ENCOUNTERED

Many barriers exist for families of color in their interactions with the child welfare system. In part, the barriers could be linked to some of the proposed causes of disproportionality in child welfare. Many of the reasons for disproportionality in foster care are related to barriers experienced by families of color and the ways that the child welfare system is designed to address those barriers. For example, as was mentioned earlier, poverty has been identified as a potential cause of disproportionality and has been described as either an individual/family issue (Chibnall et al., 2003; Derezotes & Poetner, 2005; Hill, 2006), a neighborhood or community issue (Hill, 2006; Lemon et al., 2005), or a broad societal problem (Clegg & Associates, Inc. & Wanda Hackett Enterprises, 2004; Miller, 2009). Families in poverty face a high level of scrutiny because they are receiving services, in many cases TANF, that increase the likelihood that they will be reported for child abuse or neglect. Families of color are more likely to experience poverty than White families (Chibnall et al., 2003; Hill, 2006). "According to the GAO (2007), African Americans are nearly four times more likely than others to live in poverty" (Green, 2011, p. 156). This also means that families of color are more likely to be reported to the child welfare system via other systems as a result of their increased visibility (Chibnall et al., 2003; Hill, 2006). This is not to say that families of color actually have a higher incidence of abuse and neglect than White families. Potentially, it is the perceptions of poverty that lead to increased reports of abuse or neglect among families of color.

Increased visibility by alternate systems is not just an issue related to poverty but also to the justice system. Many families of color live in communities or neighborhoods that have high levels of poverty, homelessness, unemployment, single-parent families, domestic violence, and community violence—all of which increase the visibility of families and communities to police and to the courts. These factors increase the level of visibility of the members of that community or neighborhood, and they put children at an increased level of risk for abuse or neglect (Hill, 2006; Lemon et al., 2005). Chibnall et al. (2003), Dettlaff and Rycraft (2008), Hill (2006), Lemon et al. (2005), and Barth (2005) use the term "disproportionate need" as a way to describe how personal or family issues put families of color at greater risk for being involved with the child welfare system. The term disproportionate need encompasses the idea that families of color are more likely to experience circumstances such as poverty, teen- and single-parenthood, substance abuse, incarceration, and so on, which are all considered risk factors for child abuse or neglect. Consequently, families of color are more likely than White families to experience abuse or neglect (i.e., they have a higher level of need for service). Cross (2011) identifies a caution in accepting the idea of disproportionate need as an explanation for racial disproportionality in foster care. He indicates, "We have to look closer to the complex linkages between poverty, race, and worker perceptions" (Cross, 2011, p. 113). His comment is important in considering barriers encountered by populations of color in relation to the child welfare system.

Barth (2005), Chibnall et al. (2003), Clegg & Associates, Inc., and Wanda Hackett Enterprises (2004), Derezotes and Poetner (2005), Dettlaff et al. (2011), Hill (2006), Miller (2009), and Miller and Gaston (2003) all discuss that racism, institutional or personal, or racial bias play a part in the level of disproportionality in the child welfare system is another significant barrier. At the institutional level, factors such as biased risk assessments or the definitions of abuse or neglect may contribute to disproportionality and may impact certain populations more than others. At the individual level, racial bias would connote a phenomenon whereby, given equivalent levels of risk, children of color are more likely to enter the child welfare system than White children as a result of implicit or explicit biases on the part of caseworkers (Dettlaff & Rycraft, 2008).

Public perception is a significant barrier for families of color and many social service systems. Gilens (2003) and Avery and Peffley (2003) reviewed the effects of media on public perceptions about poverty, race, and welfare reform. Gilens (2003) reviewed media sources from the last 40 years to determine how poverty had been portrayed in the media and whether or not there were differences related to race. He found that when media stories about poverty were sympathetic or when the public was sympathetic to the poor, most of the families portrayed in poverty were White. In fact, prior to the 1960s and the War on Poverty, it was almost as if poor Black families did not exist. In the mid-1960s, the public feeling about poverty changed and so did the media portrayal of families experiencing poverty. Media stories about poverty became unsympathetic, and the public was unsympathetic to poverty. During that time, the media also began to portray Black families as part of the poor population. Gilens (2003) makes the point that it is not necessarily bad that Blacks are portrayed as a significant portion of the poor in America; what is unfortunate is that they are portrayed in such a negative manner.

Avery and Peffley (2003) also discuss the issues of media portrayal of poverty and welfare reform as they relate to race. They conducted a study where they submitted several different scenarios to respondents. In some cases, the welfare recipient was Black and in some the recipient was White. The stories were also separated into those that portrayed welfare reform as a success and those that portrayed welfare reform as problematic; thus, there were four comparison stories. The results of this study support the notion that race does have an impact on how the public views welfare. Using seven-point semantic differential scales, respondents were asked to determine who would be at fault if the woman in the story lost her job (the woman or welfare reform), whether the woman would be likely to look for another job or go back on welfare, whether the five-year time limit on welfare was too long or too short, whether they strongly agreed or strongly disagreed with the statement "'Most people on welfare could get by without it if they really tried,'" and whether they would like to see welfare spending decrease or increase.

In response to who was at fault if the woman in the story lost her job, when welfare reform was portrayed as a success, the respondents placed equal blame on the mother and on welfare regardless of race. When welfare reform was portrayed as having problems, the respondents believed that the mother was to blame if she was Black but that welfare reform was to blame if she was White. When responding to whether the woman was likely to get another job or return to welfare, both Blacks and Whites were considered more likely to go back on welfare if welfare reform was portrayed as problematic. If welfare reform was portrayed as a success, respondents determined that the woman was more likely to find another job. However, Blacks were ranked more likely than Whites to go back on welfare regardless of the tone of the story (Avery & Peffley, 2003).

When asked about time limits on welfare, the results were similar to the results for the first question. There was no difference based on race in how respondents felt about the time limits on welfare when the story was positive. When welfare reform was portrayed as having problems, however, the respondents were more likely to say that the time limit of five years was too long if the welfare mother was Black and too short if the mother was White. In response to whether people could get by without welfare, the respondents were more likely to agree that they could if the mother was Black than if the mother was White. Finally, there was no difference in how respondents felt about the amount of money spent on welfare related to race or to the tone of the story. In all cases, the respondents rated the questions slightly below the midpoint (Avery & Peffley, 2003).

These two studies demonstrate different aspects of how media portrayals of poverty can affect public opinions. The chapter by Avery and Peffley (2003) demonstrates how the negative portrayals described in Gilens' (2003) writing can impact public opinion about race, poverty, and welfare. There has been a great deal of debate in the last 20 years about the effects of the media on a variety of social problems. These two studies combine to demonstrate that the media does effect public opinion and often not in a positive way. If what Gilens (2003) and Avery and Peffley (2003) found is accurate, then the way the media portray Black families and individuals (and potentially all individuals of color, regardless of race) impacts how policy decisions are made and what policies members of the broader society are willing to support. The impact of race on public welfare policy decisions likely extends to child welfare policies. Miller and Gaston (2003), in their article "A Model of Culture-Centered Child Welfare Practice," went so far as to indicate that disproportionality was likely less due to poverty than to society's views of those in poverty. If Black families and individuals are portrayed as being responsible for their own poverty, members of the broader society will be less likely to support policies that provide financial support for them. Additionally, they will likely be less willing to support policies that include a drive to keep children with their parents.

Schram (2003) explains that as a result of the historical treatment of people of color, they tend to have a lower level of access to the resources needed to stay off of welfare; consequently, they are overrepresented in the welfare system. Unfortunately, this means that they are depicted by the media as being deficient or lazy, which makes the public less likely to support welfare reform that actually helps welfare recipients. As a result, the stereotypes and policies that have led to the overrepresentation of people of color in the welfare system are reinforced and continued by the public at large. The researcher's point about this is that, rather than pretending this issue does not exist because it is more comfortable to do so, it needs to be discussed if the makeup of America's welfare population is ever going to change.

Public perceptions about race and welfare have often translated to policy support or decisions. Fording (2003) considered how race was related to state decisions to adopt federal waivers in the AFDC/TANF program. He found that states with a higher percentage of Blacks were more likely to adopt federal waivers, which are used to limit who can receive welfare and for how long. Black political representation, however, seems to mitigate the effects of race on the adoption of federal waivers.

In the same way that families of color are disproportionately impacted by welfare policies because they are overrepresented in the welfare system, families of color are disproportionately affected by child welfare policy. Families of color are disproportionately poor, thus they are disproportionately represented in the welfare system. It is also known that they are disproportionately represented in the child welfare system. Additionally, families in the child welfare system are more likely than not to be poor and to be receiving services from the welfare system. Thus, the same families are impacted by the negative media portrayals of families of color who use either system and by the impact of those portrayals on policy development and enactment. By virtue of their poverty, families of color also tend to have less voice when attempting to advocate for themselves and for their own needs. These factors combine to create a situation where families of color have the least voice, the least resources, and are the least able to garner empathy for their situations. Understanding the connection between what happens in the welfare system and what happens in the child welfare system is crucial to understanding the issue of disproportionality in child welfare.

In 1997, President Clinton signed the Adoption and Safe Families Act into law. This law was designed to push children toward permanency (Pecora, Whittaker, Maluccio, Barth, & Plotnick, 2000); however, Roberts (2002) indicates that when people talk about permanency, they mean permanency through adoption. Her point is that African American children are disproportionately impacted by the focus on permanency because they are less likely to experience reunification than White children. That means they are more likely to be adopted and probably adopted into White homes. Roberts (2002) indicates that the child welfare system and policymakers tout ASFA as being a wonderful piece of legislation, but, in her view, it increased the amount of damage to African American families under the guise of "the best interests of the child."

Two important barriers for families of color can be learned by looking at the interaction of race and the educational system. Mary Lee Brady (1984) and Richard Baker (1997) both discuss the impact of race on the educational system, although in very different circumstances. Brady (1984) emphasizes the challenge of teaching minority children because they have often been taught to mistrust the system, especially if the educator in that system is White. Even very young children enter the school system with questions about those who are different than they are and different than others in their community, which is typical for young children and not necessarily related to race. However, these young children can also be influenced by older siblings and parents who have had negative experiences with the dominant society and with the educational system. Baker (1997) writes of his findings from a qualitative study about discrimination in an educational system in rural Idaho. He found that some of the discrimination against students of color was a systemic issue, but some of it was individual bias on the part of the teachers. Both institutional and individual racism need to be considered to understand the overall impact of racism in the educational system.

There are two ways in which understanding how education is influenced by race can inform an understanding of racial/ethnic disproportionality in child welfare. First, the distrust of the system, which is taught and learned at an early age and sometimes reinforced in educational settings, has a strong possibility of influencing a person's life as they become an adult. If children of color do not trust the system, then when they become adults and need services and support to maintain their children in their homes, they may be unlikely to ask for help. Additionally, the learned mistrust of social systems may impact how they respond to a child protection worker and to a case plan. Because children of color are more likely to be taught to distrust the system, they may be less likely to request abuse prevention services or to use the services provided once a child is removed.

A key barrier for each non-White racial/ethnic group is an expectation by the system of uniformity. Baker (1997) and Brady (1984) both discuss this in their research. The educational system in the United States is designed to teach children to be the same. As a result, adults raised in this educational system will likely look for uniformity among families referred to the child welfare system. This also has implications for how the definitions of child abuse or neglect are developed and enforced. People from diverse cultures are likely to be perceived in particular ways because they do not fit the uniformly accepted idea of good parenting. However, the history and challenges of each racial/ethnic group is not necessarily the same as all other groups. For example, the colonization experience by the American Indian and Alaskan Native populations has not been experienced by other non-White populations in the United States. Brayboy (2005), in a discussion of Tribal Critical Race Theory (TribalCrit), includes statements about the expectation of the assimilation of American Indians, policies of the United States which are rooted in White supremacy, the desire of indigenous people to maintain autonomy, and the idea that understanding indigenous people requires an understanding of their beliefs, customs, traditions, and so on. The educational upbringing of most Americans may cause them to avoid considering the unique circumstances experienced by American Indians when making decisions about child welfare.

Latinos have also had unique experiences as a part of American society. They encounter immigration, migration, and language barriers that are not experienced by other non-White populations. Villalpando (2003) identifies that these experiences are directly related to the oppression experienced by Latinos. Lavergne, Dufour, Trocmé, and Larrivée (2008), in a study of Child Protective Services (CPS) in Canada, emphasize that immigrants face unique issues, not just because of being in a new environment but also because they are subject to the parenting norms of the majority population, which could impact their rate of referral to CPS. Dettlaff (2011) further emphasizes the importance of using culturally competent assessments with Latino families, particularly those who are recent immigrants. He also mentions a crucial point about difference within groups and how those differences need to be appreciated in addition to the differences between groups. He says, "Perhaps most importantly, when conducting assessments of Latino families, caseworkers need to be aware of the vast heterogeneity of the Latino population . . . Latinos are a highly diverse group, representing more than 20 countries of origin . . ." (Dettlaff, 2011, p. 124).

As has been mentioned, the educational expectation of uniformity pre-pares children to become adults who do not see differences or who see dif-ferences as something to be quashed. Not long ago, a common response by individuals discussing diversity was to say that "we are all the same, why do we have to focus on difference?" The attempt to make everyone the same has the potential to be a significant barrier for families of color as they encounter the child welfare system. There are some similarities in the oppression and discrimination experienced by all non-White popula-tions in the United States. However, there are also many differences and those differences need to be taken into account when developing strate-gies for serving individual population groups in child welfare. According to the U.S. Census Bureau (Green, 2011) the percentage of people of color is growing and "by the year 2050 a majority of this nation's population will be people of color" (p. 163). As the population of the United States, and the populations of individual communities, becomes more diverse, the need for specialized child welfare approaches increases.

CHANGING MACROSYSTEMS: CURRENT PRACTICES AND PREVENTIVE SYSTEMS EFFORTS TO ADDRESS DISPROPORTIONALITY AND DISPARITIES

Many ideas for how to address or reduce racial/ethnic disproportional-ity in the child welfare system have been suggested by recent authors and researchers. Overall, these recommendations can be categorized into four areas: training, collaboration, evaluation, and access to services and resources; some solutions fit into more than one area. A few of these solu-tions are discussed in greater detail here. The vignette that follows illus-trates how a Latino family might interact with the child welfare system and how one of the solutions, the Point of Engagement program, as presented in Chapter 3 and later in this chapter, could be used to help a parent retain custody of her children.

Training

One strategy for addressing disproportionality is increased training for child welfare workers, supervisors, and others involved in the child welfare system. There are many things that can be accomplished through training,

CASE EXAMPLE: THE RODRIGUEZ FAMILY

The Rodriguez family was reported to the public child welfare agency when Hector, age six, came to school one Monday reporting that he had not eaten since he left school the previous Friday. When the social worker went to the home to complete the initial investigation, she found a dilapidated trailer with several broken windows and an only partially existing roof. The door was answered by three-year-old Lucia; Mrs. Rodriguez was home but sleeping. She did get up after becoming aware that another adult was in the home. The social worker determined that Mrs. Rodriguez had been sleeping since Hector went to school that morning and that neither he nor Lucia had eaten recently. Mrs. Rodriguez explained that they were very poor. Her husband had recently been arrested and was in the process of being deported due to being an undocumented immigrant. He had been the sole income provider for their family. Mrs. Rodriguez expressed feeling very depressed since his arrest, stating that she and her kids would likely die of starvation in the next couple of weeks. When the social worker expressed her concerns about supervision for Lucia, Mrs. Rodriguez's apparent state of mind, and the condition of the home, Mrs. Rodriguez seemed open to receiving help, stating, "I just don't know where to begin."

The social worker reported to her supervisor, and they called a multidisciplinary team meeting to discuss the Rodriguez family. Using a systems approach, the team identified three primary concerns for the Rodriguez family: Mrs. Rodriguez's probable depression, their extreme poverty, and the recent arrest of Mr. Rodriguez. They also developed a list of possible community resources that might be accessed to address these three concerns. Mrs. Rodriguez was invited to join the team in discussing how to proceed with her case. The local homeless shelter was full, but the Rodriguez family was placed on a waiting list. In the interim, Mrs. Rodriguez was provided with emergency food stamps and a list of soup kitchens within walking distance of her home.

Additionally, she was referred to a faith-based organization in the area that provides home repairs for individuals and families in need. They were able to find someone to fix the broken windows in her trailer and to provide a temporary fix for the roof. Mrs. Rodriguez was also referred to a county clinic for a depression assessment, after which she was able to get free medication and counseling. Finally, one of the team members identified a lawyer in the community who specialized in immigration law and was often willing to take cases pro bono for families just like this one.

The social worker made regular visits to the home over the coming six months and was impressed by the improvement in the Rodriguez family. After receiving medication for her depression, Mrs. Rodriguez was better able to address the physical needs of her children. They were eventually able to get a place in the local homeless shelter and, by the end of the six months, all were doing well. Mr. Rodriguez was being represented by the local attorney, and it seemed likely that he would be able to return home soon. By using a multidisciplinary team, involving Mrs. Rodriguez in her own solutions, and accessing multiple community-based resources (both formal and informal), the child welfare agency was able to help the Rodriguez children remain at home.

including knowledge about the issue of disproportionality (Casey—CSSP Alliance for Racial Equity, 2006; Miller & Ward, 2008, 2011), an understanding of institutional racism (Miller, 2009; Miller & Ward, 2008, 2011), identification of personal biases and the consequences of those biases (Clegg & Associates, Inc. & Wanda Hackett Enterprises, 2004), and an increased knowledge of culturally competent practice, oppression, and specific cultural groups encountered by the workers (Lemon et al., 2005; Richardson, 2008, 2011). Miller and Gaston (2003) stated that "workers must fundamentally reorient themselves toward the cultural worldviews of the communities with whom they work" (p. 247). Training is one way that this goal can be accomplished. In most of these articles, the importance of helping child welfare workers understand their own biases and the need to be more culturally sensitive is either alluded to or mentioned outright. Clark, Buchanan, and Legters (2008, 2011); James, Green, Rodriguez, and Fong (2008, 2011); and Miller and Ward (2008, 2011) specifically identified the use of *Undoing Racism* workshops, put on by the People's Institute for Survival and Beyond, and the *Knowing Who You Are* materials developed by Casey as methods for increasing workers' knowledge about racism and their own biases. Miller and Ward (2008, 2011) also included judges in their list of who needed increased education about disproportionality. The goal of this education was to help judges understand the ramifications of their decisions related to permanency and the impact their decisions have on families.

Collaboration

The need for increased collaboration has also been addressed as a solution to disproportionality. One area in which collaboration needs to increase is between the agencies and the families they are serving. Crampton and Jackson (2007), Dettlaff (2011), Dougherty (2003), and Lemon et al. (2005) all mentioned the use of Family Group Decision Making (FGDM) as a strategy that can mitigate the effects or extent of disproportionality in the child welfare system. In recent research, systems of care and FGDM have both been found to improve disproportionality rates for Latinos specifically (Dettlaff, 2011). Generally, enhanced identification and engagement of family members and collaboration around decision-making was a significant part of many plans to address disproportionality (James et al., 2008; Marts, Lee, McRoy, & McCroskey, 2008, 2011; Miller & Ward, 2008, 2011). An additional area for collaboration is between public and private agencies (Chibnall et al., 2003) and between the child welfare agency and communities, especially communities of color or community-based organizations (Casey—CSSP Alliance for Racial Equity, 2006; Chibnall et al., 2003; Clegg & Associates, Inc. & Wanda Hackett Enterprises, 2004; James et al., 2008; Marts et al., 2008; Miller, 2009; Miller & Ward, 2008; Richardson, 2008). Lemon et al. (2005) recommend collaboration with community-based services as a way of preserving families so that the children never need to enter the child welfare system. Additionally, they suggest locating child welfare workers in these community agencies so that they are working within the communities that are at greatest risk for having children in the child welfare system. Lemon and colleagues also recommend the development of ethnic-specific agencies so that the cultural needs of families of color can be better addressed.

A similar approach to collaboration was identified and studied by Belanger, Copeland, and Cheung (2011). They studied the possible connection between faith and a desire or willingness to adopt among African American families. An increase in the number of African American families willing to adopt has the potential to improve the disproportionality rate for African American children in foster care. Part of what is advocated in this chapter is connecting with faith communities of color to increase the number of adoptive parents of color, thereby providing more homes for children of color out of the foster care system.

Evaluation

Improving evaluation in two areas has also been identified as an important strategy for addressing disproportionality in child welfare. First, two reports from Casey mention the collection and use of data as a way to understand disproportionality and what approaches are being used to address disparate outcomes in child welfare (Casey—CSSP Alliance for Racial Equity, 2006; Miller, 2009). Cross (2011) and Dettlaff (2011) also identify increased data on specific racial/ethnic populations as a crucial element in the fight against racial/ethnic disproportionality in child welfare. Additionally, this research can be used to educate stakeholders, community members, and others who have an interest in the child welfare system. Evaluation as a means of tracking disproportionality rates and the progress that is being made to improve those rates is the second area of evaluation. Evaluation can be used to track referral patterns and service provision by race, to assess the level of cultural competence among the workers and the extent to which child welfare workers acknowledge their biases, and to determine the level of diversity among staff (Casey—CSSP Alliance for Racial Equity, 2006; Clegg & Associates, Inc. & Wanda Hackett Enterprises, 2004; Miller & Gaston, 2003). Another recommendation related to evaluation included the use of the Racial Equity Scorecard to identify disparities in the initial decision points of the child welfare process and to assess progress in addressing such disparities (Derezotes, Richardson, Bear King, Kleinschmit-Rembert, & Pratt, 2008, 2011). The Racial Equity Scorecard can be used to pinpoint where in the decision-making process strategies can be implemented to reduce disparity at given decision points. Miller and Ward (2008, 2011) also recommend the use of evaluation in the hiring process in order to hire people who are aware of disproportionality issues and who understand how to work with diverse populations, along with regular employee evaluation to determine cultural competence. The primary idea behind these evaluation strategies is that increased knowledge about disproportionality and what is being done to address it can help agencies continue to implement effective strategies.

Access to Services and Resources

Service and resource accessibility is another issue that has been identified as a way of reducing disproportionality in the child welfare system.

As was noted previously, Lemon et al., (2005) had some ideas about ways that services to families of color could be increased. Additionally, Casey—CSSP Alliance for Racial Equity (2006), Chibnall et al. (2003), Clegg & Associates, Inc. and Wanda Hackett Enterprises (2004), and Lemon et al. (2005) suggested the expansion of services and an improvement in the accessibility of those services for groups experiencing significant levels of disproportionality. Some specific strategies that were identified were providing a higher level of service for kinship families, having better coordination with TANF, developing a system through which families are assigned an advocate who will help them navigate the system (Clegg & Associates, Inc. & Wanda Hackett Enterprises, 2004), and using a differential response system (Lemon et al., 2005). A differential response system means that child welfare workers would respond differently to the various types of child maltreatment forms rather than having a standard response plan regardless of the type of maltreatment. Differential response provides a way for agencies to meet a family's needs without necessarily pursuing an investigation against that family. It involves providing culturally appropriate services to meet families' needs, in some cases before they are ever reported to the agency for abuse or neglect. Clark et al. (2008, 2011) further address this point by recommending a program called Champions for Permanence. Through this program, "twenty-five Native children were targeted for a higher level of intervention to improve their permanency outcomes . . ." (Clark et al., 2008, p. 328). While the outcomes of this program have not been tested, anecdotal information seems to support the effectiveness of this strategy (Clark et al., 2008, 2011).

Systemic Strategies

Several additional strategies were mentioned, either as a separate plan or as a part of a larger systemic change plan. Some of the additional strategies mentioned were working to make policy and legislative changes that are culturally sensitive (Casey—CSSP Alliance for Racial Equity, 2006; Miller & Gaston, 2003), involving fathers in the lives of the children (Clegg & Associates, Inc. & Wanda Hackett Enterprises, 2004; Lemon et al., 2005), and holding contracted agencies accountable for racially equitable service provision (Miller & Ward, 2008, 2011). Clark et al. (2008, 2011) developed the use of benchmark hearings as a way to improve attention paid to ensuring permanency. Benchmark hearings ensure that all dependency cases receive in-court reviews, thereby ensuring that all children come before a judge and shining the spotlight on the need for permanency for each child.

Value-based leadership development was another strategy identified that has been used to address the issues of disproportionality (James et al., 2008, 2011). Leadership development is considered a crucial part of an organizational shift to family-centered practice. The rationale for enhancing value-based leadership is that focusing on important values can help organizational leaders to support staff "in the cultural change process so that cultural competence, family support, and strengths-based work underlie and define the way work is done throughout the organization" (2008, p. 289). Similarly, Green discusses the use of value-driven decisions. She provides the reader with a variety of case examples where the social work core values could be used to respond to families in contact with the child welfare system. For example, she uses the value of social justice to consider the connection between poverty and the involvement of families of color in the child welfare system. Using the value of social justice, Green (2011) advocates for education, specifically related to mandated reporting laws, for families who are likely to come in contact with social systems that increase their risk for referral to child welfare. As was previously discussed, families involved in the public welfare system and other social systems are at increased risk of referral due to higher exposure to social service personnel. Green's point is that families who are at higher risk for being affected by the child welfare system need to be aware of the interactions among the various social systems of which they are a part.

Point of Engagement

One unique solution to the issue of disproportionality was developed in the Compton office of the Los Angeles County Department of Child and Family Services (Marts et al., 2008). This solution is called point of engagement (POE). The basic idea of POE is that each case is approached from a team perspective utilizing a multidisciplinary approach and the collaboration of community-based resources, both formal and informal. Through the POE model, various procedures were developed to help families who have been referred for child abuse and neglect. These procedures are designed to help families retain custody of their children while keeping the children safe. A variety of mechanisms were put in place to connect the family with informal resources, such as churches or food pantries, and with formal community-based resources. Additionally steps were taken to create opportunities for families to participate in the decision-making process regarding their child/children in order to keep families connected and to reduce possible future occurrences of abuse or neglect. Finally, a series of strategies were developed for families who had children removed to improve their ability to regain custody of their children in a timely manner and to receive the services necessary to facilitate their reunification (Marts et al., 2008).

Enhanced Service Provision

One category of strategies designed to address the issue of disproportionality in child welfare is enhanced service provision. There have been a number of implementation strategies for states looking to improve how services are provided to children and families encountering the public child welfare system. The Denver Indian Family Resource Center (DIFRC) is one such strategy. The DIFRC worked in collaboration with county departments of human services in a program designed specifically for helping American Indian children remain in their families and culture. The purpose of this program was to work with families who were connected to the child welfare system and who also had substance abuse issues. This program had promising outcomes; in some cases, using "intensive case management," it was possible to prevent the removal of a child. In other cases, success was identifying relatives with whom to place a child and providing support for a parent who needed substance abuse treatment (Child Welfare Information Gateway, 2011).

An alternative response approach has been used in Ohio to improve service provision for families in the child welfare system and to address issues of disproportionality. Using this approach, families referred for child abuse or neglect have a choice of participating in a "noninvestigative, family-friendly assessment" (Child Welfare Information Gateway, 2011, p. 11). The purpose of this program is to provide services before children become at risk for placement in the child welfare system. Although the alternative response system can be used for all families, it was implemented in an effort to reduce disproportionality for African American families in the Ohio child welfare system.

A multifaceted approach has been used in a couple of locations as a way to address disproportionality within their child welfare systems. In Texas, various agencies collaborated statewide to address disproportionality across all stages of the child welfare system (Child Welfare Information Gateway, 2011). They had five primary approaches that utilized previously identified suggestions for how to mitigate the effects of disproportionality in child welfare, including training and collaboration. Their first approach was to provide cultural competence training, for frontline workers and for managers. This included utilization of *Undoing Racism*. The second strategy was to work with a program entitled "One Church, One Child" to increase the number of foster and adoptive parents. A "community advisory committee" was developed and specialists in the area of disproportionality were hired at the state and local levels. Finally, an effort was made to increase the diversity of the child welfare staff. These strategies resulted in a decrease of removal rates across the state for African American children (Child Welfare Information Gateway, 2011).

The Pomona office in Los Angeles County, California, implemented a multifaceted, community-based approach using six primary strategies to reduce racial disproportionality in their child welfare system (Lorthridge et al., 2012). The first two strategies were to implement the Casey Family-to-Family practice model and to conduct an examination of child outcome data. Part of the purpose for reviewing this data was to clarify the disparity that was occurring in their child welfare system. Additionally, they were able to demonstrate to community agencies the importance of using a multifaceted approach to system changes. Training and conversation in the area of racial disparity was implemented as well. A Youth Permanency Unit was created to focus on the needs of older youth in foster care, with the intention of improving the outcomes for African American youths. The last two strategies were think tank days—caseworkers, supervisors, and community partners all worked together to brainstorm ideas and to discuss outcomes for children in their care—and peer learning. The purpose of the peer-learning approach was to connect with various community partners, such as judges, probation officers, legislators, and so forth, to have ongoing conversations about disparity, risk factors, and strategies to reduce disparities (Lorthridge et al., 2012).

In both of the systems where a multifaceted approach was implemented, value was placed on building and maintaining connections with community partners. Additionally, effort was made to address risk factors at multiple levels. Overall, the ideas for how disproportionality might be reduced were diverse and have been making some impact on agency functioning. Interestingly, the implementation of these solutions spans the country, coming from Washington, California, Indiana, Iowa, Louisiana, Texas, and other areas. Additionally, some strategies have predominantly been used to address disproportionality for Blacks/African Americans (Belanger et al., 2011; Clark et al., 2008, 2011; James et al., 2008, 2011), and others have focused on Native American children (Clark et al., 2008; 2011; Derezotes et al., 2008, 2011). As more potential solutions to the problem of disproportionality are developed, hopefully their effectiveness can be thoroughly assessed and determinations can be made about which strategies are most effective for which populations. Hill (2008) reports that there are many articles explaining promising practices but very few that assess the effect of those practices, particularly through the use of comparison groups or quasi-experimental methods. There are still many gaps in the research, and enhanced research on these practices will improve our ability to draw conclusions about how best to address issues of disproportionality for all populations.

SPOTLIGHT: PROMISING PRACTICES TO ADDRESS DISPROPORTIONALITY IN CHILD WELFARE

- Increased collaboration at all levels: between the child welfare agency and the families they serve; between private and public agencies serving families at risk for involvement in the child welfare system; between the child welfare agency and the community, especially communities of color; between the child welfare agency and community or neighborhood-based services; and between the child welfare agency and faith communities, particularly those specifically connected with specific ethnic populations
- Training to help workers understand their own biases, the role of racism in the issue of disproportionality, and the populations of color with which they are likely to work; specific use of the *Undoing Racism* workshop and the *Knowing Who You Are* course
- Enhanced service provision through intensive case management and working with children and families before the children are at risk for placement in the child welfare system

- Evaluation of outcomes for children; assessment of data to determine the successfulness of programs designed to reduce disparate outcomes; increased data about specific ethnic populations to better understand the experiences of members of those populations; and use of evaluation strategies to increase knowledge about disproportionality for specific populations
- Differential responses to cases, which includes varied responses to each type of child maltreatment, providing prevention services with families so that children do not enter the child welfare system, providing culturally appropriate services for families of various ethnic or cultural populations, using a multidisciplinary approach to meet the needs of families, and involving families in the decisions about the solutions to their cases
- Using a multifaceted approach to address each level of risk and need for families who are at risk for having a child placed in the public child welfare system; developing system approaches that include collaboration with community partners, training for child welfare workers, and education for community members to enhance understanding about disproportionality and disparate outcomes for children of color

CROSS SYSTEMS EFFORTS AND CULTURALLY COMPETENT SERVICES OFFERED

Greater collaboration has been identified as an important strategy for addressing disproportionality in child welfare; few articles, however, have discussed collaboration between the child welfare system and other large systems in which populations of color also experience disproportionality. Hill (n.d.) and McRoy (2008, 2011) both connect child welfare to the educational, welfare, and criminal justice systems. Both the welfare and criminal justice systems contribute to some people being involved in the child welfare system, and they are both a possible result of someone being involved in the child welfare system.

As was previously discussed, Black families are disproportionately poor and are disproportionately portrayed in negative media portrayals of poverty. Currently, they are overrepresented in those portrayals; although prior to the 1960s, portrayal of the poor included virtually no Black families (Gilens, 2003). There are also a few connections between disparate treatment and outcomes for people of color in the criminal justice system and racial/ethnic disproportionality in child welfare. One connection is the likelihood that parents who are incarcerated will have their children placed in foster care. People of color are disproportionately represented in the criminal justice system, which could be contributing to the disproportionality of those same minority groups in child welfare (Hines, Lemon, et al., 2004). Another connection has to do with the judicial system. Levine (2000) conducted a study of juries and found that White and non-White jurors enter the jury box with different backgrounds and look at cases through different lenses, although most people are reticent to acknowledge how those lenses create bias. Levine's conclusion is that there will continue to be verdicts influenced by race as long as it is not acknowledged that they currently are influenced by race. Those same biases translate to other social arenas, including child welfare. Much of the research on the child welfare system identifies decision making and assessment as key contributors to disproportionality in child welfare. However, Levine's (2000) study of juries demonstrates that people often do not realize that their behavior and decisions are being influenced by what they have learned or been taught about race/ethnicity. This means that a key factor in understanding decision making in child welfare is the people involved in the decision-making process.

In many states, the legal system plays a significant role in the investigation and removal phases of the child welfare process in addition to its role in the ongoing determination of outcomes for children. Two recent publications address the connection between the justice or legal system and the child welfare system. Busch, Wall, Koch, and Anderson (2008, 2011) explain the Indiana Disproportionality Committee (IDC) as a strategy to address disproportionality in the state of Indiana. They explain that shortly after its inception, the IDC began partnering with the Indiana Criminal Justice Institute. In fact, the IDC includes members from a variety of systems, including the Indiana Department of Education and the Indiana Minority Health Coalition. They are working to address disparity within multiple systems in Indiana.

Gatowski and Dobbin (2011) also discuss the connections between the legal system and the child welfare system. The National Court Appointed Special Advocate Association is working to increase knowledge about disproportionality and disparity in child welfare through training and collaboration with Casey Family Programs to enhance the use of Casey's training *Knowing Who You Are*. The American Bar Association advocates for and supports policy changes designed to decrease the levels of disproportionality in the child welfare system. They also advocate for practice changes "such as encouraging state and local governments to aggressively search for maternal and paternal kin and consider kinship placements as early as possible after a child becomes known to the child welfare agency and/or court" (Gatowski & Dobbin, 2011, p. 320). One limitation identified by Gatowski and Dobbin (2011) is that although there are many changes that have occurred in the judicial system, there has not been an assessment of the impact of those changes on disproportionality and disparity for people of color (2011). Additionally, there appears to be a commitment on the part of the legal system to address the issue of racial disparity in the justice and child welfare systems. Specific practices, however, have not been identified to confront and change those disparities (Gatowski & Dobbin, 2011). This is a significant need for future work in the collaboration between the child welfare system and the legal system.

FUTURE DIRECTIONS

It has been nearly 35 years since the first legislation was passed related to a specific non-White population, with the Indian Child Welfare Act of 1979 (Crosson-Tower, 2007; Myers, 2004). However, most of the literature related to disproportionality in child welfare has been published since 2001 (Wells, 2011). There continue to be many questions about why disproportionality exists for given populations, the prevalence of over- or underrepresentation for particular racial/ethnic groups in regions of the United States, and which solutions are proving to be the most effective in reducing the disparities experienced by children of color in the public child welfare system. There are a number of efforts that can be taken to address and ultimately eliminate disproportionality. The following recommendations summarize the efforts that have been suggested by child welfare scholars in addressing this topic.

- Gather additional data related to American Indian and Alaskan Native populations (Cross, 2011).
- Conduct research that explores the connections between multiple systems and social problems, including poverty, substance abuse, and criminal justice (Cross, 2011).
- Conduct additional research on the contributors to disproportionality among Latinos and the development of strategies for that population with specific consideration of barriers, such as language, encountered by Latinos (Dettlaff, 2011; Lancaster, 2011).
- Develop practices that are evidence-based and designed to address the unique needs of specific cultural groups (Green, 2011).
- Conduct research on disproportionality at state, regional, and county levels to ensure accurate depictions of disparity for all racial and ethnic populations (Hines, Lemon, et al., 2004; Lancaster, 2011).
- Conduct research so that significant samples of multiple populations of color can be assessed (Bullard, 2011). This can be accomplished in part through research being conducted where significant pockets of particular racial/ethnic groups are present (Derezotes & Hill, 2004; Hill, n.d.).
- Continue to assess strategies that have been developed to address issues of racial disproportionality in the child welfare system.
- Include the characteristics of child welfare workers, such as race/ethnicity, level of experience, and cultural sensitivity, in future studies of disproportionality in child welfare (Cross, 2011; Lancaster, 2011).
- Develop cross-systems connections with areas such as juvenile justice, welfare, or education, to improve issues of disparity across all social systems.
- Conduct studies that include the impact of systemic factors such as poverty and rurality on the issue of disproportionality within the child welfare system (Lancaster, 2011).

REFERENCES

Avery, J. M., & Peffley, M. (2003). Race matters: The impact of news coverage of welfare reform on public opinion. In S. F. Schram, J. Soss, & R. C. Fording (Eds.), *Race and the politics of welfare reform* (pp. 131–150). Ann Arbor: University of Michigan Press.

Baker, R. (1997). *Mexican American students: A study of educationally discounted youth.* Dubuque, IA: Kendall/Hunt.

Barth, R. P. (2005). Child welfare and race: Models of disproportionality. In M. F. Testa, J. Poetner, & D. M. Derezotes (Eds.), *Race matters in child welfare: The overrepresentation of African American children in the system* (pp. 25–46). Washington, DC: Child Welfare League of America (CWLA) Press.

Bartholet, E. (2009). The racial disproportionality movement in child welfare: False facts and dangerous directions. *Arizona Law Review, 51,* 871–932.

Belanger, K., Copeland, S., & Cheung, M. (2011). Addressing disproportionality through communities of faith. In D. K. Green, K. Belanger, R. G. McRoy, & L. Bullard (Eds.), *Challenging racial disproportionality in child welfare: Research, policy, and practice.* (pp. 249–259). Washington, DC: CWLA Press.

Brady, M. L. (1984). Understanding the minority child in the American educational system. *Education, 105,* 21–33.

Brayboy, B. M. J. (2005). Toward a tribal critical race theory in education. *The Urban Review, 37,* 425–446.

Bullard, L. (2011). Mitigating racial disproportionality in residential care. In D. K. Green, K. Belanger, R. G. McRoy, & L. Bullard (Eds.), *Challenging racial disproportionality in child welfare: Research, policy, and practice* (pp. 211–218). Washington, DC: CWLA Press.

Busch, M., Wall, J. R., Koch, S. M., & Anderson, C. (2008). Addressing disproportionate representation: A collaborative community approach. *Child Welfare, 87*(2), 255–278.

Busch, M., Wall, J. R., Koch, S. M., & Anderson, C. H. (2011). Addressing disproportionate representation: A collaborative community approach. In D. K. Green, K. Belanger, R. G. McRoy, & L. Bullard (Eds.), *Challenging racial disproportionality in child welfare: Research, policy, and practice* (pp. 233–247). Washington, DC: CWLA Press.

Casey–CSSP Alliance for Racial Equity (2006). *Places to watch: Promising practices to address racial disproportionality in child welfare services.* Retrieved from www.casey.org/Resources/Publications/pdf/PlacesToWatch.pdf

Casey Family Programs. (2007, March 14). Disproportionality: The disproportionate representation of children of color in foster care. Retrieved from http://www.ncjfcj.org/sites/default/files/CASEY_disproportionality_fact_sheet_31407.pdf

Cheung, M., & LaChapelle, A. (2011). Disproportionality from the other side: The underrepresentation of Asian American children. In D. K. Green, K. Belanger, R. G. McRoy, & L. Bullard (Eds.), *Challenging racial disproportionality in child welfare: Research, policy, and practice* (pp. 131–139). Washington, DC: CWLA Press.

Chibnall, S., Dutch, N. M., Jones-Harden, B., Brown, A., Gourdine, R., Smith, J., et al. (2003, December). Children of color in the child welfare system: Perspectives from the child welfare community. Retrieved from http://www.child welfare.gov/pubs/otherpubs/children/children.pdf

Child Welfare Information Gateway. (2011, January). Addressing racial disproportionality in child welfare. Retrieved from www.childwelfare.gov/pubs/issue_briefs/racial_disproportionality

Clark, P., Buchanan, J., & Legters, L. (2008). Taking action on racial disproportionality in the child welfare system. *Child Welfare, 87*(2), 319–334.

Clark, P., Buchanan, J., & Legters, L. (2011). Taking action on racial disproportionality in King County. In D. K. Green, K. Belanger, R. G. McRoy, & L. Bullard (Eds.), *Challenging racial disproportionality in child welfare: Research, policy, and practice* (pp. 309–318). Washington, DC: CWLA Press.

Clegg & Associates, Inc., & Wanda Hackett Enterprises. (2004, November). Racial disproportionality in the child welfare system in King County, Washington. Retrieved from catalystforkids.org/KingCountyReportonRacial Disproportionality.pdf

Crampton, D., & Jackson, W. L. (2007). Family group decision making and disproportionality in foster care: A case study. *Child Welfare, 86*(3), 51–69.

Cross, T. (2011). Disproportionality in child welfare: An American Indian perspective. In D. K. Green, K. Belanger, R. G. McRoy, & L. Bullard (Eds.), *Challenging racial disproportionality in child welfare: Research, policy, and practice* (pp. 111–118). Washington, DC: CWLA Press.

Cross, T. A., Earle, K. A., & Simmons, D. (2000). Child abuse and neglect in Indian country: Policy issues. *Families in Society: The Journal of Contemporary Human Services, 81*(1), 49–58.

Crosson-Tower, C. (2007). *Exploring child welfare: A practice perspective* (4th Ed.). Boston: Pearson.

Curtis, C. M., & Denby, R. W. (2011). African American children in the child welfare system: Requiem or reform. *Journal of Public Child Welfare, 5*, 111–137. doi:
10.1080/15548732.2011.542731

Derezotes, D. M., & Hill, R. B. (2004). Examining the disproportionate representation of children of color in the child welfare system. *Race Matters
Consortium*.

Derezotes, D. M., & Poetner, J. (2005). Factors contributing to the overrepresentation of African American children in the child welfare system. In M. F. Testa,
J. Poertner, & D. M. Derezotes (Eds.), *Race matters in child welfare: The overrepresentation of African American children in the system* (pp. 1–24). Washington, DC: CWLA Press.

Derezotes, D., Richardson, B., Bear King, C., Kleinschmit-Rembert, J., & Pratt, B.
(2008). Evaluating multisystemic efforts to impact disproportionality through
key decision points. *Child Welfare, 87*(2), 241–255.

Derezotes, D. M., Richardson, B., Bear King, C., Kleinschmit, J., & Pratt, B.
(2011). Evaluating multisystemic efforts to impact disproportionality through
key decision points. In D. K. Green, K. Belanger, R. G. McRoy, & L. Bullard
(Eds.), *Challenging racial disproportionality in child welfare: Research, policy,
and practice* (pp. 179–186). Washington, DC: CWLA Press.

Dettlaff, A. J. (2011). Disproportionality of Latino children in child welfare. In
D. K. Green, K. Belanger, R. G. McRoy, & L. Bullard (Eds.), *Challenging racial
disproportionality in child welfare: Research, policy, and practice* (pp. 119–129).
Washington, DC: CWLA Press.

Dettlaff, A. J., Rivaux, S. R., Baumann, D. J., Fluke, J. D., Rycraft, J. R., & James,
J. (2011). Disentangling substantiation: The influence of race, income, and risk
on the substantiation decision in child welfare. *Children and Youth Services
Review, 33*, 1630–1637.

Dettlaff, A. J., & Rycraft, J. R. (2008). Deconstructing disproportionality: Views
from multiple community stakeholders. *Child Welfare, 87*(2), 37–58.

Dougherty, S. (2003). Practices that mitigate the effects of racial/ethnic disproportionality in the child welfare system. Seattle, WA: Casey Family Programs.

Earth, R. P. (1997). Effects of age and race on the odds of adoption versus remaining in long-term out-of-home care. *Child Welfare, 76*, 285–308.

Fording, R. C. (2003). "Laboratories of democracy" or symbolic politics? The
racial origins of welfare reform. In S. F. Schram, J. Soss, & R. C. Fording (Eds.),
Race and the politics of welfare reform (pp. 72–97). Ann Arbor: University of
Michigan Press.

Gatowski, S. I., & Dobbin, S. A. (2011). National judicial initiatives to reduce racial disproportionality and disparities in the dependency court system. In D. K. Green, K. Belanger, R. G. McRoy, & L. Bullard (Eds.), *Challenging racial disproportionality in child welfare: Research, policy, and practice* (pp. 319–326). Washington, DC: CWLA Press.

Gilens, M. (2003). How the poor became black: The racialization of American poverty in the mass media. In S. F. Schram, J. Soss, & R. C. Fording (Eds.), *Race and the politics of welfare reform* (pp. 101–130). Ann Arbor: University of Michigan Press.

Godinet, M. T., Arnsberger, P., Li, F., & Kreif, T. (2010). Disproportionality, Ohana conferencing, and the Hawai'i child welfare system. *Journal of Public Child Welfare, 4*, 387–405.

Goerge, R. M., & Bilaver, L. M. (2005). The effect of race on reunification from substitute care in Illinois. In M. F. Testa, J. Poertner, & D. Derezotes (Eds.), *Race matters in child welfare: The overrepresentation of African American children in the system* (pp. 201–214). Washington, D C: Child Welfare League of America.

Green, D. K. (2011). Value-driven decisions: Reducing disproportionality through practice. In D. K. Green, K. Belanger, R. G. McRoy, & L. Bullard (Eds.), *Challenging racial disproportionality in child welfare: Research, policy, and practice* (pp. 155–165). Washington, DC: CWLA Press.

Gryzlak, B. M., Wells, S. J., & Johnson, M. A. (2005). The role of race in child protective services screening decisions. In M. F. Testa, J. Poertner, & D. Derezotes (Eds.), *Race matters in child welfare: The overrepresentation of African American children in the system* (pp. 63–96). Washington, DC: CWLA Press.

Hill, R. B. (2005a). The role of race in foster care placements. In M. F. Testa, J. Poertner, & D. Derezotes (Eds.), *Race matters in child welfare: The overrepresentation of African American children in the system* (pp. 187–200). Washington, DC: CWLA Press.

Hill, R. B. (2005b). The role of race in parental reunification. In M. F. Testa, J. Poertner, & D. Derezotes (Eds.), *Race matters in child welfare: The overrepresentation of African American children in the system* (pp. 215–230). Washington, DC: CWLA Press.

Hill, R. B. (2006, October). Synthesis of research on disproportionality in child welfare: An update. *Race Matters Consortium.*

Hill, R. B. (2008). Gaps in research and public policies. *Child Welfare, 87*(2), 359–367.

Hill, R. B. Race Matters Consortium Working Papers. (n.d.). Disproportionality of minorities in child welfare: Synthesis of research findings. *Race Matters
Consortium*.

Hines, A. M., Lee, P. A., Osterling, K. L., & Drabble, L. (2007). Factors predicting family reunification for African American, Latino, Asian, and White
families in the child welfare system. *Journal of Child and Family Studies, 16*,
275–289.

Hines, A. M., Lemon, K., Wyatt, P., & Merdinger, J. (2004). Factors related to
the disproportionate involvement of children of color in the child welfare system: A review and emerging themes. *Children and Youth Services Review, 26*,
507–527.

James, J., Green, D., Rodriguez, C., & Fong, R. (2008). Addressing disproportionality through undoing racism, leadership development, and community
engagement. *Child Welfare, 87*(2), 279–296.

James, J., Green, D. K., Rodriguez, C., & Fong, R. (2011). Innovations in Texas:
Undoing racism, developing leaders, and engaging communities. In D. K.
Green, K. Belanger, R. G. McRoy, & L. Bullard (Eds.), *Challenging racial dis-
proportionality in child welfare: Research, policy, and practice* (pp. 285–295).
Washington, DC: CWLA Press.

Knott, T., & Giwa, S. (2012). African American disproportionality within CPS
and disparate access to support services: Review and critical analysis of the
literature. *Residential Treatment for Children & Youth, 29*(3), 219–230. doi:
10.1080/0886571X.2012.697434

Lancaster, L. (2011). *Racial disproportionality in the Idaho foster care system: A focus
on Latinos and Native Americans.* Unpublished doctoral dissertation. The University of Texas at Austin, Austin, TX.

Lavergne, C., Dufour, S., Trocmé, N., & Larrivée, M. C. (2008). Visible minority,
aboriginal, and Caucasian children investigated by Canadian protective services. *Child Welfare, 87*(2), 59–76.

Lemon, K., D'Andrade, A., & Austin, M. J. (2005, July). Understanding and
addressing disproportionality in the front end of the child welfare system.
Retrieved from http://cssr.berkeley.edu/bassc/public/EvidenceForPractice3_
Disproportionality_FullReport.pdf

Levine, J. P. (2000). The impact of racial demography on jury verdicts in routine
adjudication. In M. W. Markowitz, & D. D. Jones-Brown (Eds.), *The system
in black and white: Exploring the connections between race, crime, and justice*
(pp. 153–169). Westport, CT: Praeger.

Libby, A. M., Orton, H. D., Barth, R. P., Webb, M. B., Burns, B. J., Wood, P., et al. (2006). Alcohol, drug, and mental health specialty treatment services and race/ ethnicity: A national study of children and families involved with child welfare. *American Journal of Public Health, 96*, 628–631.

Lorthridge, J., McCroskey, J., Pecora, P. J., Chambers, R., & Fatemi, M. (2012). Strategies for improving child welfare services for families of color: First findings of a community-based initiative in Los Angeles. *Children and Youth Services, 34*, 281–288. doi: 10.1016/j.childyouth.2011.10.025

Lu, Y., Landsverk, J., Ellis-MacLeod, E., Newton, R., Ganger, W., & Johnson, I. (2004). Race, ethnicity, and case outcomes in child protective services. *Children and Youth Services Review, 26*, 447–461.

Mannes, M. (1993). Seeking the balance between child protection and family preservation in Indian child welfare. *Child Welfare, 72*, 141–152.

Marts, E. J., Lee, E. O., McRoy, R., & McCrosky, J. (2008). Point of engagement: Reducing disproportionality and improving child and family outcomes. *Child Welfare, 87*(2), 335–358.

Marts, E. J., Lee, E. O., McRoy, R. G., & McCroskey, J. (2011). Poing of engagement: Reducing disproportionality and improving outcomes. In D. K. Green, K. Belanger, R. G. McRoy, & L. Bullard (Eds.), *Challenging racial disproportionality in child welfare: Research, policy, and practice* (pp. 167–178). Washington, DC: CWLA Press.

McRoy, R. G. (2008). Acknowledging disproportionate outcomes and changing service delivery. *Child Welfare, 87*(2), 205–210.

McRoy, R. G. (2011). Contextualizing disproportionality. In D. K. Green, K. Belanger, R. G. McRoy, & L. Bullard (Eds.), *Challenging racial disproportionality in child welfare: Research, policy, and practice* (pp. 67–71). Washington, DC: CWLA Press.

Miller, O. A. (2009). *Reducing disproportionality and disparate outcomes for children and families of color in the child welfare system* (Appendix A: A Disproportionality Breakthrough Series Collaborative Framework for Change). Retrieved from Casey Family Programs website: http://www.casey.org/resources/publications/BreakthroughSeries_ReducingDisproportionality_process.htm

Miller, O. A., & Gaston, R. J. (2003). A model of culture-centered child welfare practice. *Child Welfare, 82*, 235–250.

Miller, O. A., & Ward, K. J. (2008). Emerging strategies for reducing racial disproportionality and disparate outcomes in child welfare: The results of a national breakthrough series collaborative. *Child Welfare, 87*(2), 211–240.

Miller, O. A., & Ward, K. J. (2011). Emerging strategies for reducing disproportionality: The results of a breakthrough series collaborative. In D. K. Green, K. Belanger, R. G. McRoy, & L. Bullard (Eds.), *Challenging racial disproportionality in child welfare: Research, policy, and practice* (pp. 271–283). Washington, DC: CWLA Press.

Morton, T. D. (1999). The increasing colorization of America's child welfare system: The overrepresentation of African-American children. *Policy & Practice of Public Human Services, 57*(4), 23–30.

Myers, J. E. B. (2004). *A history of child protection in America.* Bloomington, IN: Xlibris.

National Association of Social Workers. (2008). Code of Ethics of the National Association of Social Workers. Retrieved from http://www.naswdc.org/pubs/code/code.asp

Pecora, P. J., Whittaker, J. K., Maluccio, A. N., Barth, R. P., & Plotnick, R. D. (2000). Understanding the policy context for child welfare. In *The child welfare challenge: Policy, practice, and research* (pp. 21–63). New York: Aldine De Gruyter.

Richardson, B. (2008). Comparative analysis of two community-based efforts designed to impact disproportionality. *Child Welfare, 87*(2), 297–318.

Richardson, B. (2011). Working with youth and families to impact disproportionality. In D. K. Green, K. Belanger, R. G. McRoy, & L. Bullard (Eds.), *Challenging racial disproportionality in child welfare: Research, policy, and practice* (pp. 187–197). Washington, DC: CWLA Press.

Roberts, D. (2002). *Shattered bonds: The color of child welfare.* New York: Civitas.

Rolock, N., & Testa, M. F. (2005). Indicated child abuse and neglect reports: Is the investigation process racially biased? In M. F. Testa, J. Poertner, & D. Derezotes (Eds.), *Race matters in child welfare: The overrepresentation of African American children in the system* (pp. 119–130). Washington, DC: CWLA Press.

Samantrai, K. (2004). *Culturally competent public child welfare practice.* Pacific Grove, CA: Brooks/Cole.

Schram, S. F. (2003). Putting a black face on welfare: The good and the bad. In S. F. Schram, J. Soss, & R. C. Fording (Eds.), *Race and the politics of welfare reform* (pp. 196–221). Ann Arbor: University of Michigan Press.

Sedlak, A. J., & Schultz, D. (2005a). Race differences in risk of maltreatment in the general child population. In M. F. Testa, J. Poertner, & D. Derezotes (Eds.), *Race matters in child welfare: The overrepresentation of African American children in the system* (pp. 47–62). Washington, DC: CWLA Press.

Sedlak, A. J., & Schultz, D. (2005b). Racial differences in child protective services investigation of abused and neglected children. In M. F. Testa, J. Poertner, & D. Derezotes (Eds.), *Race matters in child welfare: The overrepresentation of African American children in the system* (pp. 97–118). Washington, DC: CWLA Press.

Villalpando, O. (2003). Self-segregation or self-preservation? A critical race theory and Latina/o critical theory analysis of a study of Chicana/o college students. *Qualitative Studies in Education, 16*, 619–646.

Wells, S. J. (2011). Disproportionality and disparity in child welfare: An overview of definitions and methods of measurement. In D. K. Green, K. Belanger, R. G. McRoy, & L. Bullard (Eds.), *Challenging racial disproportionality in child welfare: Research, policy, and practice* (pp. 3–12). Washington, DC: CWLA Press.

8

Disproportionality and Disparities in the Juvenile Justice System and the Courts

▸ *HENRIKA MCCOY AND ELIZABETH BOWEN*

DESCRIPTION OF THE SYSTEM AND THE ETHNIC MINORITY POPULATIONS IN THE SYSTEM

Creation of the Court

THE FIRST JUVENILE COURT WAS established in 1899 in Cook County, Illinois (Snyder & Sickmund, 2006), with the philosophy of *parens patriae*, "the state must care for those who cannot take care of themselves" (Campbell, 1991, p. 769). That philosophy enabled the state to take on a parental role for children who had not reached the age of full legal capacity (Snyder & Sickmund, 2006). Prior to that, juveniles who committed crimes were handled in the criminal (adult) justice system where they were allowed to plead "infancy" as their defense (Gardner, 1997). By 1945, juvenile courts had been established in every federal and state jurisdiction, as well as most European nations (Gardner, 1997). Those courts had a goal of rehabilitation, and juveniles were considered malleable children who were neither fully responsible for their actions nor fit to be punished (Gardner, 1997).

However, in 1967, with the Supreme Court case, *In re Gault*, there was a clear movement away from *parens patriae* (Feld, 1993). In 1968, the Juvenile Delinquency Prevention Control Act of 1968 was created, which recommended that status offenses be handled outside of the juvenile court (Snyder & Sickmund, 2006). It was followed by the Juvenile Justice and Delinquency Prevention Act of 1974 (JJDPA), which required the deinstitutionalization of all status offenders and the discharge of all juveniles detained in jails and adult lockdown facilities (Snyder & Sickmund, 2006).

During the 1980s, there was a change and juveniles were increasingly being seen in criminal (adult) court; the juvenile court was gradually transforming into a mirror of the criminal court, and the discretion of juvenile court judges was reduced. Finally, by 1997, most states had made changes in sentencing authority, transfer provisions, victim's rights, correctional programming, and in confidentiality provisions (Snyder & Sickmund, 2006). Currently, all states have upper age limits for juvenile court jurisdiction (e.g., 15, 16, or 17 depending on the state), although there are instances where juveniles who are younger than the upper age limit can be transferred to criminal court (Adams & Addie, 2011). Ultimately, current sentencing practices are based on a juvenile's prior criminal record and their current offense versus the original approach of prioritizing what is in the juvenile's best interest (Feld, 1993).

Progression through the Court

The organization of the juvenile court and how a juvenile progresses through the court varies by state (Sacks & Reader, 1992); however, there are generally three phases: intake, adjudication, and disposition (Ratner, 1992). During intake, the police investigate and decide whether a juvenile should be released to their parents, referred to community services, or detained and referred to court (Siegel & Senna, 1991) for processing (informal or formal) or if the case should be dismissed (Puzzanchera, Adams, & Sickmund, 2010). Cases handled informally can lead to a juvenile being referred to social services, required to pay restitution, or being given informal probation (Puzzanchera et al., 2010). Cases handled formally are petitioned and scheduled for a fact-finding hearing—adjudication—where it is determined whether the juvenile committed the alleged act. During the hearing, the case can be dismissed, the juvenile adjudicated to be a delinquent or status offender, or the case continued while the judge determines whether to dismiss the case (Puzzanchera et al., 2010). Post-adjudication, or once a juvenile admits guilt, the case moves forward and a disposition (sentence) is made that can include a youth being: (1) given probation (intensive or regular); (2) sent to a nonsecure facility such as a foster home, group home, or a training school program; (3) sent to a secure facility such as juvenile detention or a boot camp; (4) fined or required to provide restitution, assigned community service, given supervision, or sent to a diversion program; (5) transferred to the adult criminal justice system (Siegel & Senna, 1991); or (6) referred to mental health services or day treatment (Puzzanchera et al., 2010).

Each state also has instances where a juvenile can be transferred to criminal court: *judicial waiver, prosecutorial discretion* or *concurrent jurisdiction*, and *statutory exclusion (automatic transfer)* laws (Adams & Addie, 2011). The most common, *judicial waivers,* are managed on a case-by-case basis and authorize or require judges to transfer certain youth to criminal court; these waivers can be *discretionary, presumptive,* or *mandatory* (Adams & Addie, 2011). Cases that are transferred under *prosecutorial discretion* or *concurrent jurisdiction* laws are under complete authority of the prosecutor (Adams & Addie, 2011). *Statutory exclusion* laws allow criminal courts to have exclusive jurisdiction over cases involving juveniles that meet certain criteria (Adams & Addie, 2011).

Juveniles can also be impacted by *once adult/always adult, reverse waiver,* and *blended sentencing* laws (Adams & Addie, 2011). *Once adult/always adult* laws prevent juveniles who have been prosecuted in criminal court and who then commit new crimes from having any new cases heard in juvenile court, regardless of the type or level of seriousness of the crime committed (Adams & Addie, 2011). *Reverse waiver* laws allow juveniles the opportunity to petition to have their cases transferred back to juvenile court (Adams & Addie, 2011). Finally, *blended sentencing* laws allow juvenile courts to include criminal court sentencing options (*juvenile court blended sentencing*) and allow criminal courts to include juvenile court sentencing (*criminal court blended sentencing*) into dispositions (Adams & Addie, 2011).

Ethnic Minority Populations

In nearly every state, youth of color are significantly more likely than White youth to be arrested, detained, prosecuted, incarcerated, given probation, or transferred to adult court (Models for Change, 2011a). Youth of color are also likely to be involved in the child welfare system (Models for Change, 2011b), have unmet mental health needs (Teplin, 2000), and to experience difficulties in school (National Council of La Raza [NCLR], 2011)—all of which can lead to involvement in the juvenile justice system. In 2009, there were approximately 1.5 million delinquency cases nationwide with a racial breakdown of 64% White, 34% Black, 1% Native American, and 1% Asian/Native Hawaiian/Pacific Islander (Puzzanchera & Kang, 2011). Those statistics are in stark contrast to the 2009 racial breakdown for juveniles in the greater population, which was 77% White, 16% Black, 1% Native American, and 5% Asian/ Native Hawaiian/Pacific Islander (Puzzanchera & Adams, 2011). The numbers of Latino youth in the juvenile justice system are not discernible in federal reports because the Office of Juvenile Justice and Delinquency Prevention (OJJDP) typically includes Latinos in the racial category of White (Puzzanchera et al., 2010). However, researchers from nongovernmental organizations have noted that when Latino youth are compared to White youth they are more likely to be arrested, prosecuted as adults, imprisoned, admitted to state facilities when charged with the same offense, and receive longer sentences; they also had higher rates for drug, violent, property, and public order offenses (Villarruel & Walker, 2001).

OJJDP reports do include Native American youth, although a large number are actually seen in federal court. For this reason, federal courts are disproportionately comprised of Native American youth (Motivans & Snyder, 2011). In 2008, of the 152 juveniles seen in federal court, 70 (46%) were Native American (Motivans & Snyder, 2011). Any crime committed on tribal lands is a federal offense and even those that would typically be subject to local and state laws when not committed on tribal lands (Short & Sharp, 2005) are investigated by the Federal Bureau of Investigation and the Bureau of Indian Affairs (Motivans & Snyder, 2011). Juveniles with these cases can be given the same sanctions as those seen in the juvenile justice system (Motivans & Snyder, 2011).

UNDERSTANDING THE PROBLEMS AND NEEDS OF ETHNIC MINORITY POPULATIONS IN THE SYSTEM

The needs of ethnic minorities in the juvenile justice system must be understood in light of two types of disparities. The first is the overrepresentation of youth of color, particularly African Americans and Latinos, at all stages of the juvenile justice system. The second is disparities in other systems, such as child welfare, that may increase the likelihood of involvement in criminal activity and the justice system. Given that juvenile justice system involvement has been associated with several negative future outcomes for youth, including increased likelihood of arrest and conviction for criminal activity as an adult (Petitclerc, Gatti, Vitaro, & Tremblay, 2013), the prevention and elimination of racial disparities is vital to improving outcomes and to ensuring justice for vulnerable youth. Applying a systems perspective is useful to understanding how deficiencies in other systems contribute to disparities in juvenile justice and to designing cross-systems interventions to reduce disparities and to ultimately improve outcomes for youth and families (Northey, Primer, & Christensen, 1997).

Two case vignettes help to illustrate the cross-systems interconnections between juvenile justice and other systems that impact youth and families. These vignettes are used throughout this chapter to convey how racial disparities in the juvenile justice system develop and to describe potential solutions to eliminating disparities and their root causes. The first case study, "Ana" is fictional, while the second, "Stephen," is adapted from a real case reported by the Advancement Project/Civil Rights Project (2000), with some added content for illustrative purposes.

CASE EXAMPLE: ANA

"Ana" is a 14-year-old Mexican American young woman who entered the child welfare system one year ago following her mother's incarceration. After moving in with a foster family, Ana showed signs of depression, including low energy, frequent crying, and spending hours alone in her room. She began skipping class to drink and smoke marijuana and cigarettes with a few classmates in a parking lot behind her school. Her caseworker recommended family therapy to address Ana's depression and to help her adjust to living with her new foster family, but the family was put on a wait list to start therapy with a Spanish-speaking therapist (Spanish is the first language of Ana's foster parents and Ana is bilingual). One afternoon, Ana and a classmate were arrested for marijuana possession, underage drinking, and truancy by police patrolling the area near the school. Later, when Ana and her classmate were sentenced, the court recommended probation for Ana's classmate but ordered Ana's placement to be switched to a group home that would provide more supervision, citing concerns about her needs and the level of supervision that her foster parents would be able to provide.

CASE EXAMPLE: STEPHEN

In Mississippi, "Stephen," an African American male student, accidentally hit his Caucasian female school bus driver with a peanut that he was aiming at a friend. The driver immediately pulled the bus over and called the police. Ultimately, Stephen and four friends, all African American males between the ages of 17 and 18 (juniors and seniors), were arrested for felony assault, for which the maximum penalty is five years in prison. After community pressure and the involvement of an attorney, the charges were dropped but the young men lost their bus privileges. They all ultimately dropped out of school because they were unable to locate affordable transportation (each was a low-income student), which was needed to travel the 30 miles to school. Stephen had been an "A" student in math and had wanted to go to college, but he was reduced to just hanging out—putting him at great risk for getting into trouble.

As these vignettes convey, three of the most important systems relevant to disparities in juvenile justice are child welfare, mental health, and education. Next, we describe in detail how each contributes to disproportionality and disparities in the juvenile justice system.

The Child Welfare System

Research indicates that the overrepresentation of youth of color in the child welfare system, particularly African Americans, is related to disparities in juvenile justice. A large number of youth in the juvenile justice system are simultaneously involved in the child welfare system; they are called crossover or dually involved youth (Herz et al., 2012). This phenomenon likely occurs because youth involved in the child welfare system have often experienced neglect and physical abuse, both of which increase the possibility of a youth becoming involved in the juvenile justice system (Models for Change, 2011b). In addition, crossover youth who are moved deeper into the juvenile justice system are not likely to have their complex needs stemming from their delinquent behavior and history of maltreatment resolved or attended to (Ryan, Herz, Hernandez, & Marshall, 2007).

For example, a recent study in Illinois found that children involved in the child welfare system were more than twice as likely as other juveniles to receive a formal delinquency petition, even when controlling for age, race, gender, and offense type (Models for Change, 2011b). Such outcomes potentially occur because (1) court systems might be less likely to release juvenile offenders who are living in foster homes, (2) in some cases a youth's foster family does not want to become involved in the justice system, or (3) in others the court erroneously assumes the foster family does not want to remain involved (Ryan et al., 2007). As a result, these youth are more likely to enter residential or group settings where they can be exposed to negative peer influences (Ryan et al., 2007). In sum, as Ana's case study illustrates, the trauma of family separation, as well as biases within the justice system, contribute to disparities for child welfare-involved youth, such as increased likelihood of out-of-home placement. These outcomes may in turn increase the potential of such youth to become involved in the juvenile justice system and ultimately to recidivate.

The Mental Health System

Youth of color are underserved by mainstream mental health care systems, and researchers have suggested that such unmet needs can lead to involvement in the juvenile justice system (Teplin, 2000). For example, despite similar levels of need, African American and Latino youth involved in the child welfare system access specialty mental health services at lower rates than White youth (Martinez, Gudiño, & Lau, 2013). In Ana's case, this was due to a lack of linguistically and culturally competent mental health service providers. One can speculate that effective mental health treatment to address Ana's depression and trauma would have greatly reduced her likelihood of engaging in delinquent behaviors (skipping school, substance use) and prevented her entry into the justice system.

Researchers have begun to closely examine the relationship between unmet mental health needs and disparities in the juvenile justice system (Cauffman & Grisso, 2005). In fact, some have suggested that juveniles with mental health disorders are remanded to detention facilities for reasons other than their criminal behavior, such as the failure of the mental health system to meet their needs (Teplin, 2000). When state budgets for public mental health care services are cut, many families turn to the juvenile justice system as an entry point for obtaining mental health services (Chapman,

Desai, & Falzer, 2006). Because of those service cuts, many youth are left without an appropriate setting to meet their needs and therefore either fall through the cracks or are eventually placed in the juvenile justice system (Teplin, 2000). This is not uncommon, and some local law enforcement agencies indicate that their juvenile justice systems serve as a primary referral source for youth with psychiatric disorders (Grisso, 2004). Additionally, some research suggests that courts are more likely to refer White youth who have committed an offense to psychiatric facilities, although African American youth are more likely to be deemed "disorderly" and referred to correctional facilities (Cauffman & Grisso, 2005).

The School-to-Prison Pipeline

The creation and utilization of zero tolerance laws has led to tremendous racial and ethnic disparities and marginalization of youth of color in the nation's school system via high rates of school suspensions, expulsions, and eventual school-based arrests (NCLR, 2011), which can lead to them permanently dropping out of school (Goodman, 2005) and being referred to the juvenile justice system (Nicholson-Crotty, Birchmeier, & Valentine, 2009). The school's decision to involve these students with the criminal justice system (Anderson, 2004) creates a clear pathway for their involvement in the *school-to-prison pipeline* (Christle, Jolivette, & Nelson, 2005). This is dramatically illustrated by Stephen's case study, in which the school's disciplinary response to a minor behavioral infraction—tossing a peanut at a classmate—had devastating and potentially lifelong consequences for Stephen and his peers. Youth with these experiences demonstrate an increased likelihood of becoming incarcerated (Martin, 2001). Unfortunately, some schools are no longer viewed as places designed to support, develop, and nurture a youth's development, and instead youth are treated as adversaries who must be removed in order to maintain a good school environment (Advancement Project, 2010).

SYSTEMS EFFORTS TO ADDRESS DISPROPORTIONALITY AND DISPARITIES: GENERAL BARRIERS AND ETHNIC-SPECIFIC BARRIERS FACED AND CHALLENGES ENCOUNTERED

Multiple challenges exist that lead to the disproportionate representation of youth of color in the juvenile justice system. Those barriers are systematic and contextual and can eventually lead to diminished long-term opportunities. Applying a systems theory approach, we can identify barriers at multiple levels of the environment, including: (1) barriers related to the formal juvenile justice system; (2) barriers related to accessing culturally competent and responsive services; (3) barriers related to stereotypes; and (4) barriers related to socioeconomic status.

System Barriers Related to the Formal Juvenile Justice System

In 1988, Congress made a series of amendments to the JJDPA including the requirement that any state participating in the Formula Grants Program determine the extent of *disproportionate minority confinement* (DMC) in their system and subsequently create and implement reduction strategies (Devine, Coolbaugh, & Jenkins, 1998). DMC was defined as occurring when the proportion of confined or detained minorities in secure detention facilities exceeded the proportion of minorities in the general population (Children's Defense Fund, 2000). That amendment was followed by the creation of the DMC Initiative, a pilot project started by OJJDP in 1991 to help states become compliant; through a competitive process, Arizona, Florida, Iowa, North Carolina, and Oregon were chosen as the first states to participate. During the first 18 months, those states assessed the extent of DMC; during the second 18 months, they created and implemented a corrective plan (Devine et al., 1998). Each state was required to collect the appropriate data and analyze their system's decision-making process (Roscoe & Morton, 1994).

In 1992, another amendment was made to JJDPA that required states to address DMC in order to be eligible for additional funding (Hsia & Hamparian, 1998). By 1994, as a requirement of the JJDPA Formula Grants Program, all states were required to determine if DMC was a problem in their state (Roscoe & Morton, 1994); if they identified a problem, they needed to identify the cause, create and implement a corrective action plan (Leiber, 2002), and include ongoing monitoring of the intervention (Crane & Ellis, 2004). As a result, between 1997 and 2002, the government provided almost 80 technical assistance grants to states in order to address DMC (Hsia, Bridges, & McHale, 2004). The amendment's requirements were initially focused on the racial disparities related to the confinement of juveniles in secure detention facilities and, in 2002, JJDPA reauthorized the use of the Formula Grants Program to support state and local delinquency prevention and intervention efforts and juvenile justice system improvements including DMC (Hsia, 2004). Also in 2002, DMC was changed from its original idea of *disproportionate minority confinement* to (OJJDP, 2009) *disproportionate minority contact* in recognition that race directly and indirectly impacts the outcome of numerous juvenile court decisions throughout the process (Roscoe & Morton, 1994).

States and localities have differed in their priorities and in the particular interventions they implemented to address DMC. For example, as of 2008, 25 states were funding programs that would provide alternatives to detention as a way of reducing DMC at the confinement stage, while 15 states were conducting cultural competency trainings or assessments within their juvenile justice systems (OJJDP, 2009). Yet other states created early intervention programs designed to prevent crime and delinquency; specialized courts, as well as sentencing guidelines; recommended sanctions; and rehabilitative interventions for youth who committed particular offenses (Mears, 2002).

OJJDP has provided grants to create evaluation partnerships at the state and local level (Hsia et al., 2004), provided in-service training and technical assistance to states, developed a research agenda, created a pool of DMC researcher consultants for state and local use, awarded funding for the development of accurate data collection methods, launched a Web-based data entry system for the repository of state and local data, and has continued to publish reports about the status of DMC in various locales (Coleman, n.d.). But, in spite of these efforts, DMC remains a significant problem; therefore, empirical studies and reports evaluating the progress of the attempts to reduce DMC continue to be generated.

Barriers Related to Accessing Culturally Competent and Responsive Services

One of the barriers that youth of color experience is the lack of culturally competent or responsive practice being utilized in the juvenile justice system. Culturally competent and responsive service provision should be considered at two levels and should take into account: (1) how services can be delivered in a culturally competent and responsive manner to youth and families who are already involved in the juvenile justice system and

(2) how culture can be used as the foundation for prevention strategies to avert youth from entering the system.

For the juvenile justice system to provide culturally competent and responsive services, at minimum it must ensure that youth and families of all racial, ethnic, linguistic, cultural, and economic backgrounds receive equitable treatment and have equitable access to resources and support at all decision points throughout the system. Juvenile justice systems also need to consider the numerous ways in which culture can affect how youth participate (or do not participate) in available services. A culturally competent and responsive approach to juvenile justice should also consider how culture and community resources can enhance protective factors and reduce risk factors for young people's involvement in criminal and delinquent behaviors. Researchers and advocates such as Williams (2010) have suggested that culturally rooted programming may be what is missing (but needed) from most youth interventions.

Regarding the provision of culturally competent and responsive mental health services in the juvenile justice system, it has been suggested that some African American men and boys adopt a *cool pose*, a coping mechanism that involves minimizing their problems or emotions (Majors & Billson, 1992), or they believe that having a mental health disorder is unacceptable and that they need to maintain their tough persona (Shelton, 2004). Having those beliefs or adopting that cool pose could be related to the tendency of African American males in the juvenile justice system to minimize symptoms on mental health screenings and to give socially desirable responses (McCoy, 2011). The design of culturally competent and responsive mental health services in the juvenile justice system should consider ways of addressing these barriers to ensure that youth who need services are identified through culturally sensitive screenings and that they be given the opportunity to access treatment that is culturally responsive.

As we acknowledge the increasing importance of culturally competent and responsive services, one key area is the intersection between immigration and the juvenile justice system. In an analysis of juvenile court decisions for youth in the Phoenix, Arizona, area, Rodriguez (2007) writes that immigration and border security is such a salient issue in the region that courts can be influenced to perceive Latino youth as threatening, regardless of their economic background or the neighborhood where they reside. The belief exists that immigrants are responsible for committing larger numbers of crimes (Arya, Villarruel, Vilanueva, & Augarten, 2009). Although entrenched socioeconomic issues such as the concentration of poverty or public concerns about immigration are not easily changed, service providers cannot afford to lose sight of how these issues directly or indirectly contribute to DMC. It is important to recognize and value cultural differences. This is highlighted by the need to ensure that a youth's linguistic and cultural needs are met (Arya et al., 2009).

Barriers Related to Stereotypes

There is the existing perception that youth who have committed crimes are released back into the community without having engaged in appropriate services and have not been rehabilitated (Soler & Garry, 2009). Youth of color are heavily influenced by stereotypes that associate youth of color, in particular African American and Latino males, with criminal behavior. These stereotypes are often reinforced by the way that crime is covered in the media. This often occurs because crime coverage on television and in print media generally focuses on violent crime, leading people to believe that violent crime occurs much more frequently than it actually does (Soler & Garry, 2009). The media disproportionately represents people of color as the perpetrators of crime while underrepresenting them as victims, and it disproportionately associates youth, especially young people of color, with violent acts (Soler & Garry, 2009). As a result, the public often holds negative and fearful attitudes about youth of color and crime. For example, in a report of results from a national poll, approximately one-third of respondents reported believing that African American youth were more likely to engage in criminal activities than White youth (Soler & Garry, 2009). It is important to understand how such a belief system can serve as one pathway to creating or supporting the disproportionate representation of youth of color in the juvenile justice system.

Barriers Related to Socioeconomic Status

Not to be ignored is the impact of socioeconomic status (SES) on many youth of color, particularly because they are disproportionately represented in lower socioeconomic levels. Jargowsky, Desmond, and Crutchfield (2005) argue that the concentration of poverty in urban neighborhoods that are primarily African American or Latino has contributed to higher crime rates in these areas and can result in disparities if youth from these neighborhoods are treated differently in the justice system because they are profiled as residents of "bad" neighborhoods. The negative impact of socioeconomic status can be reflected in a judge's unwillingness to release a youth to a single parent home in an impoverished neighborhood because they believe the youth will have inadequate parental supervision and guidance (Kakar, 2006). In addition, parents who earn low wages may also find it difficult to attend court hearings; this failure can erroneously appear to be a lack of parental support and can be considered negatively in sentencing decisions (Kakar, 2006). Situations like these can lead to the perception that the state must take responsibility for the youth and therefore assign him or her to an out-of-home placement (Kakar, 2006). Finally, low SES can lead to increased vulnerability because low-income communities are often policed at higher rates. This policing strategy increases the likelihood of a youth having contact with the juvenile justice system (Primm, Osher, & Gomez, 2005).

CHANGING MACROSYSTEMS: CURRENT PRACTICES AND PREVENTIVE SYSTEM EFFORTS TO ADDRESS DISPROPORTIONALITY AND DISPARITIES

Many current major initiatives to address DMC are the result of funding by foundations and are the work of community organizations. Some of the most influential include the MacArthur Foundation's Models for Change Initiative, the Annie E. Casey Foundation's Juvenile Detention Alternatives Initiative, and the W. Haywood Burns Institute's programming. With a focus on community engagement, transparency, and demonstrating outcomes, these initiatives are beginning to build an evidence base of best practices for reducing DMC.

The MacArthur Foundation's Models for Change Initiative

The John D. and Catherine T. MacArthur Foundation's Models for Change Initiative supports system-wide reform in juvenile justice. One aspect of the initiative is to work toward the fair treatment of juveniles at all stages of the system, particularly the elimination of biases related to factors such as

The DMC Action Network

The DMC Action Network was started in 2007 through funding from the John D. and Catherine T. MacArthur Foundation and is managed by the Center for Children's Law and Policy (2010). It brings together state and local leaders to share information in an attempt to accelerate the reduction of DMC in the juvenile justice system. The network seeks to work collaboratively and to identify the most sustainable and effective tools and ideas for reducing DMC. In order to accomplish that goal, each site implements four "strategic innovations." These are specifically designed to result in measurable outcomes through collaboration to address and resolve the barriers and challenges encountered during implementation and in the development of practical lessons that can inform the knowledge base at the national level about effective DMC reduction strategies at the state and local levels: (1) to collect and analyze data about DMC that can lead to reform, (2) to strengthen the knowledge base about culture and the community, (3) to address arrest and pre-adjudication through diversion and risk screening, and (4) to examine post-disposition decisions.

- Data collection and analysis: The network uses a data-driven model to reduce the disproportionate overrepresentation of youth of color, particularly by focusing on reducing the entrance of youth of color into the system who have been charged with technical violations or low-level offenses. Each network site collects and reports data about DMC and identifies areas for reform. Data about arrests, secure detention, and detention alternatives are regularly collected for analysis and strategic use and then disaggregated by race, ethnicity, gender, location, offense, and probation violations that lead to detention. Because there are no widely used or accepted performance measures, the network quantifies results from sites that have implemented reform—in practice, program, or policy.
- Culture and community: The network focuses on ensuring that system processes and community programs are culturally competent and responsive to youth of color and their families. Sites focus on capacity-building so parents and caregivers can become fully involved in the judicial process. They identify the best practices for improving linguistic services for youth and families who have limited English proficiency (LEP), and they focus on the best practices

for counting the underidentified Hispanic population in the juvenile justice system. The network also works to engage nontraditional partners (e.g., youth, advocates, grassroots organizations) when addressing DMC and uses services and interventions that can support parents when they access and navigate the juvenile justice system.

- Arrest and pre-adjudication: Network sites focus on implementing new or expanding existing school-based diversion programs in an effort to decrease the number of youth arrested for school discipline issues. In addition, efforts focus on improving perceptions and relationships between youth and law enforcement, designing and implementing objective screening tools to measure risk of reoffending or the potential to not appear in court, and developing or expanding community supervision programs, such as evening report centers, for pre-adjudicated youth.
- Post-disposition: A primary focus is the development of graduated responses that consider risk to public safety and seriousness of a probation violation. In addition, issues that impact reentry, such as system policies and post-dispositional placement, are explored.

race and gender (Griffin, Torbet, Thomas, Snyder, & Halemba, 2004). As of 2011, 16 states were engaging in system reforms through this initiative, including four "core" states of Illinois, Louisiana, Pennsylvania, and Washington (Griffin, 2011).

Models for Change emphasizes local, community-led, and collaborative responses that effectively consider and address the context of disparities. An example of one community-based project supported through the initiative is a partnership between the National Council of La Raza's (NCLR) Philadelphia Latino Juvenile Justice Network and one of its member organizations, *Men in Motion in the Community*. Through the partnership, *Men in Motion in the Community* has created mentoring programs to promote constructive youth development and prevent delinquency and has hosted training that brings Latino youth together with local law enforcement to build more positive relationships (NCLR, 2011). One indicator of the program's impact is that 30 of 32 youth participating in the first year of the mentoring program graduated from eighth grade although they had been previously classified by school administrators as among the most likely to drop out (NCLR, 2011).

Models for Change maintains an extensive database and has generated multiple research reports to document the impact of the programming it supports. One of their unique programs is in Jefferson Parish, Louisiana, where public school staff were trained in alternative discipline practices. Jefferson City schools constitute the primary referral sources for youth arrests, with more than 80% involving youth of color, but the result was a 16% reduction in school-referred arrests (Griffin, 2010). Programs like this one can have a great impact on reducing DMC.

The Annie E. Casey Foundation's Juvenile Detention Alternatives Initiative

Launched in 1992 by the Annie E. Casey Foundation, the Juvenile Detention Alternatives Initiative (JDAI) aims to promote fairness, to foster opportunities for healthy development, and to reduce unnecessary detentions for youth in the juvenile justice system. Programs have focused on reducing DMC primarily at the level of confinement. Core change strategies include using data to accurately identify disparities in the justice system, establishing clear criteria for making decisions about detention in order to reduce biases that contribute to DMC, and creating opportunities for collaboration among multiple systems and stakeholders such as families and community-based organizations (Annie E. Casey Foundation, 2009).

Like Models for Change, JDAI has prioritized the evaluation and documentation of outcomes in order to establish evidence of programs and policies that reduce DMC. Justice systems that have adopted the initiative's strategies have achieved several target outcomes, including reducing the overall number of youth of color held in detention, reducing the proportion of detained youth who are minorities, and leveling the odds so that youth of color who are arrested for delinquency are no more likely to be detained than their White counterparts (Annie E. Casey Foundation, 2009). For example, one site in Multnomah County, Oregon, reduced the average total number of youth detained per day from 96 to 33 and the proportion of detained youth of color from 73% to 50%. Furthermore, although 42% of youth of color were detained following arrest for delinquency, compared with 32% of White youth, systems-level interventions through JDAI lowered the likelihood of detention to 22% for both groups (Annie E. Casey Foundation, 2009).

The W. Haywood Burns Institute for Juvenile Justice Fairness & Equity

The W. Haywood Burns Institute is a San Francisco-based nonprofit organization that works to reduce disparities in the juvenile justice system related to race and ethnicity, gender, and socioeconomic status. One of its key programs, the Community Justice Network for Youth, supports community organizations in their efforts to reform the juvenile justice system and reduce DMC and its causes in 21 states (Barrows, Garza, Gomez, Williams, & Rahimi, 2010). Much of the Burns Institute's work connects disparities in the juvenile justice system with inequalities in other systems, such as education and employment, with an emphasis on grassroots community leadership to lead cross-systems reform.

Among the Burns Institute's strategies is advocating for restorative justice, an approach that emphasizes dialogue among multiple stakeholders to address the harms created by violent or criminal behavior as an alternative to punishing and stigmatizing offenders. Restorative justice approaches have demonstrated effectiveness in outcomes related to DMC, such as reducing recidivism for youth of diverse backgrounds (Schwalbe, Gearing, MacKenzie, Brewer, & Ibrahim, 2012). The Burns Institute reports that a school-based restorative justice pilot program in Peoria County, Illinois, resulted in a 43% reduction in detentions of African American youth for fighting in school (W. Haywood Burns Institute, n.d.).

CROSS SYSTEMS EFFORTS AND CULTURALLY COMPETENT SERVICES OFFERED

Clinicians and policymakers alike have long recognized that disparities in the juvenile justice system do not develop in a vacuum. It is clear that because youth in the juvenile justice system are frequently involved in the child welfare system, have high rates of mental health problems including substance use, and face challenges in their educational environments, each of these systems must collaborate with each other (Herz et al., 2012). As a result, efforts to reduce DMC have increasingly focused on collaborating with other service systems including the child welfare, mental health, and educational systems in order to help prevent and reduce disparities before, during, and after youth and families come in contact with the justice system.

Collaboration with the Child Welfare System

Disproportionality in the juvenile justice and child welfare systems has long been recognized, but only recently have leaders from both systems begun to address how the disparities are interrelated. Several states are now working to improve system collaboration and reduce disparities. For example, Texas and Michigan have passed laws mandating reports about disproportionality in systems that serve children and families, specifically child welfare and juvenile justice (Bilchik, 2009). Improved reporting and data collection are viewed as important for understanding and calling attention to disparities across systems and as a first step for designing effective cross-systems interventions. Some jurisdictions such as King County, Washington, have prioritized multisystem case coordination by creating procedures for coordinating assessment and case management among youth involved in both systems in addition to collecting and sharing data (Griffin, 2010).

Another key target for intervention is changing each system's organizational culture. In many states, the child welfare and juvenile justice systems are unaccustomed to working with one another and may not always recognize how collaborating to reduce racial and ethnic disparities fits with their respective missions. But in Iowa, leaders of both systems are working to change this through a *de-categorization initiative* (Bilchik, 2009). Representatives of the child welfare and juvenile justice systems meet regularly to build relationships and to design policies and programs to prevent youth from entering either system when possible (Bilchik, 2009). Such collaboration has the potential to produce better outcomes for young people like Ana, whose complex family circumstances may otherwise contribute to disparities.

Collaboration with the Mental Health System

Because of the large number of youth with mental health disorders in the juvenile justice system, collaborative efforts between the juvenile justice and mental health systems are critical. Numerous strategies have been recommended at national and local levels. For example, at the federal level, the Technical Assistance Partnership for Child and Family Mental Health, a program of the U.S. Department of Health and Human Services, has published a brief on strategies and benefits of collaborations between mental health and juvenile justice systems. One recommendation is to co-locate staff, for example by having a trained clinician serve as a liaison to the mental health system for juvenile courts or probation departments (Shufelt, Cocozza, & Skowyra, 2010). Another strategy is to use a *braided funding* approaching in budgeting, which allow systems that would normally be siloed (such as child mental health care and juvenile justice) to combine their funding streams, creating a pool of resources that can be used for a variety of services to help families or youth (Shufelt et al., 2010). As Ana's story suggests, service access is key because quality and culturally competent mental health care has the potential to prevent behavioral problems that can lead to young people's initial contact with the justice system.

At a more local level, juvenile justice systems are considering how to best provide effective treatment and care for the youth in their care who are experiencing mental health problems. A key priority is to develop sensitive screening procedures for mental disorders, taking into account that race and culture can influence how people exhibit symptoms of depression, anxiety, and other disorders (Hicks, 2004). For example, African American boys in the juvenile justice system often show a stronger tendency than White males to give socially desirable responses on mental health screenings, which may reduce the likelihood that they will be identified and ultimately receive appropriate treatment (McCoy, 2011). Once mental health disorders are diagnosed, it is important for the juvenile justice and mental health systems to work together to ensure that all youth are able to access effective, evidence-based treatments, whether in the community or within detention facilities. Research suggests that access to specialized outpatient treatment for youth with mental health needs who have been involved in either the juvenile justice or child welfare systems can lead to improved outcomes, including reduced odds of future out-of-home placements (Glisson & Green, 2006).

Collaboration with the Education System

There are several cross-systems national collaborations under way to address the connection between educational policies and racial disparities in the juvenile justice system. One notable example is the Advancement Project (2010), which has conducted research documenting how zero tolerance policies are often implemented in ways that disproportionately target youth of color, as exemplified in Stephen's case study. The Advancement Project advocates for the formation of community-based working groups including parents, students, and teachers to create disciplinary alternatives, therefore reducing expulsions and referrals to law enforcement and helping to prevent and de-escalate potentially problematic behaviors. Such measures could have led to drastically different outcomes for students like Stephen and his peers, who faced a serious legal challenge and ultimately dropped out of school as a result of disciplinary actions. This strategy has been used in areas such as the Los Angeles Unified School District, where Community Asset Development Redefining Education, a community-based advocacy group, has worked with the school district to create an evidence-based disciplinary policy that emphasizes support and early intervention in addressing misbehaviors (Advancement Project, 2010).

Culturally Competent and Responsive Service Provision

Providing services that acknowledge culture are important because youth of color are likely to have additional unique needs that have the potential for being misunderstood and misinterpreted (Pattison, 1998). Toward meeting the goal of culturally competent and responsive services, some juvenile justice departments have prioritized hiring diverse staff to reflect the diversity of their communities and training staff to reduce potential biases that can contribute to disparities. For example, the juvenile justice system of Santa Cruz, California, committed to a staffing plan in which the proportion of staff who are Latino and/or Spanish-speaking matches or exceeds the proportion of youth in the system who are Latino (Cox & Bell, 2001). Some programs focus on primary prevention, aiming to keep children from entering the juvenile justice system, while others seek to reduce recidivism among youth who have already been involved in the system. Three programs that exemplify the use of culture as a core prevention tool are the Connections Program in Chicago, the Omaha Nation Community Response Team in rural Nebraska, and Programa Shortstop in Orange County, California. These programs are not only community-based but are largely community-led, and at the core of each initiative is engagement with young people, families, and local institutions.

The Connections Program is one of a few community-based prevention programs nationwide that draws on aspects of African and African American culture in order to reduce crime and delinquency and encourage positive development for youth. The Connections Program is located in West Englewood, a predominately African American and low-income community with a high crime rate. The program aims to prevent violence and delinquency by introducing youth to an "Afro cultural tool kit" that emphasizes traditional Afrocentric values and principles that can help young people respond successfully and prosocially to institutional racism and other types of oppression, and to become community leaders (Williams, 2010). For example, the program requires all participants to complete 75 hours of community service annually and develops community service projects in Chicago and Africa. Locally, community service projects can increase bonds among neighbors and can help to reduce crime by promoting a sense of collective efficacy among neighbors, while youth also gain pride and a deep sense of community on a global scale from their service work in Africa. Further research and evaluation is needed, but the Connections Program is a promising example of a culturally and community-based program's potential to reduce DMC and empower youth from oppressed groups on individual and community levels.

This approach is also found in the work of the Omaha Nation Community Response Team, a small nonprofit organization based on the Omaha Reservation in rural Nebraska. The organization has embraced a *culture as prevention* approach to reducing substance abuse and other delinquent behaviors among youth in the Omaha Tribe (Penn, Doll, & Grandgenett, 2008). The model emphasizes family resilience, spiritual beliefs, and connection to traditional Omaha culture as protective factors for young people. Importantly, the organization made a deliberate choice to view youth substance abuse and violence as community problems with community-level solutions. Workshops were organized with local leaders to define target problems, their causes, and potential solutions. Subsequently, activities such as after-school programming and summer leadership camps were developed to support youth, encourage their connection with Omaha culture, and to build community capacity. The response team also collaborated with the tribal justice system to provide appropriate, culturally meaningful responses to youth who were found engaging in delinquent behaviors such as fighting at school (Penn et al., 2008). This model demonstrates many key elements of culturally competent prevention, including focusing on strengths and assets, actively involving multiple community stakeholders, and developing activities that strengthen young people's connections to their cultures, histories, and traditions.

Programa Shortstop was created as a family-based, Spanish language, culturally sensitive program to address the needs of first-time offender Latino youth in Orange County, California (Cervantes, Ruan, & Dueñas, 2004). Youth were referred from their local police department and court systems. The program grounded their approach in using a culturally focused intervention and sought to decrease delinquency, increase prosocial behaviors, decrease substance use, improve academic performance, and improve self-identity and personal decision making. Of the 321 youth who participated, 89% failed to have a subsequent referral to probation and 79% were not re-arrested within one year of program completion. In addition, 95% of the participants' parents felt that their children's high-risk behaviors had decreased. This program highlights the value and potential of emphasizing and including culturally sensitive and community-based strategies for Latino youth.

FUTURE DIRECTIONS

It has been more than 20 years since the issue of DMC rose to national prominence and states were required to address the disproportionate confinement of minority youth (Leiber & Rodriguez, 2011). The efforts that we have described in this chapter have made strides in documenting how DMC occurs, who it affects, and in identifying strategies for addressing DMC and its underlying causes. However, the challenge of ending DMC is far from over. It is important to understand and address the policies and practices that work to maintain DMC (Bilchik, 2008).

Despite the best efforts of countless stakeholders, one of the reasons why ending DMC remains a challenge is that the juvenile justice system has always been tasked with simultaneously satisfying multiple goals. The system's goals include maintaining public safety, punishing criminals, rehabilitating and supporting those who have committed crimes to make more positive choices, and maintaining a sense of fairness and equality while simultaneously acknowledging the individual factors that make each case unique (Mears, 2002). Are some of these goals inherently in conflict with each other? Can the same system punish and rehabilitate and do so in a way that is fair and equitable? What would a system that is truly fair to youth from all races, ethnicities, and socioeconomic backgrounds look like? These are some of the questions that must continue to be debated, reflected upon, and ultimately answered if we are to move toward the development of a juvenile justice system that does not include DMC. We propose the following recommendations to guide further action, advocacy, and research.

STRATEGIES FOR ADDRESSING AND ELIMINATING DISPROPORTIONALITY AND DISPARITIES

Social workers must work within and across systems to foster collaboration. Many systems, including juvenile justice, child welfare, and education, are often perceived as "broken" and as having many internal problems, such as large caseloads, chronic funding shortages, and inflexible bureaucratic cultures that would presumably impede collaboration. While addressing these internal issues, stakeholders ranging from on-the-ground caseworkers to top-level administrators should commit to maintaining a collaborative mindset, so that working across systems to better serve youth and families becomes the rule rather than the exception.

Collaboration can and should occur not only across systems but also among concerned youth and their families, community groups, and funders. Social workers and other practitioners should advocate to ensure that disenfranchised individuals and communities, such as the young people of color who have been most directly affected by DMC, have a strong voice in all efforts to reform the juvenile justice system.

Research, policy, and services addressing DMC need to reflect an understanding of the multidimensionality of culture and oppression. Programs serving youth, whether within or outside of the justice system, need to consider how different aspects of young people's identities—including race, ethnicity, gender, sexual orientation, socioeconomic background, religion, neighborhood, country of origin, and immigration status—can intersect and may influence outcomes and experiences related to juvenile justice. Justice systems should collect and analyze data on less commonly documented facets of identity, for example ethnic identity (e.g., "Mexican American"), in addition to acknowledging Hispanic/Latino youth separately from those youth classified as White.

Stereotypes that convey strong associations between youth of color (particularly African American males) and crime foster an environment in which DMC is able to thrive (Soler & Garry, 2009). Although it can be difficult to challenge widely held stereotypes and public attitudes, striving to change perceptions should be an important part of the DMC elimination agenda. This task might begin by having conversations in the classroom or workplace to address perceptions and stereotypes; critically considering the ways in which media portrayals and public attitudes may differ from reality when it comes to youth, race, and crime; and thinking about how this can translate into disparities for youth in the juvenile justice system.

Culturally rooted programming shows great promise for preventing DMC and empowering vulnerable individuals and communities and is also consistent with the social work profession's focus on strengths-based practice. Further research and evaluation are needed to identify the key components of culturally specific programs and to examine how they can be replicated and adapted for different locales to improve outcomes for young people of color and their families.

Efforts should be made to continue to evaluate and disseminate innovations for reducing DMC at all systems levels. Building an evidence base of best practices for reducing DMC is challenging because the context and factors contributing to DMC vary considerably among jurisdictions and systems. However, tools such as the OJJDP's Model Programs Guide (http://www.ojjdp.gov/mpg) are useful for practitioners who wish to examine what programs and policies have been successful in reducing DMC in other areas and to evaluate how they could be adapted in their own settings.

REFERENCES

Adams, B. & Addie, S. (2011). *Delinquency cases waived to criminal court, 2008.* (Report No. NCJ 236481). Retrieved from http://www.ojjdp.gov/pubs/236479.pdf

Advancement Project. (2010, March). *Test, punish, and push out: How "zero tolerance" and high-stakes testing funnel youth into the school-to-prison pipeline.* Retrieved from http://www.advancementproject.org/resources/entry/test-punish-and-push-out-how-zero-tolerance-and-high-stakes-testing-funnel

Advancement Project and The Civil Rights Project (2000). *Opportunities suspended: The devastating consequences of zero tolerance and school discipline.* Boston, MA: Harvard University.

Anderson, C. L. (2004). Double jeopardy: The modern dilemma for juvenile justice. *University of Pennsylvania Law Review, 152,* 1181–1219.

Annie E. Casey Foundation. (2009). *Detention reform: An effective approach to reduce racial and ethnic disparities in juvenile justice.* Retrieved from http://www.aecf.org/~/media/Pubs/Initiatives/Juvenile%20Detention%20Alternatives%20Initiative/DetentionReformAnEffectiveApproachtoReduce Rac/JDAI_factsheet_3.pdf

Arya, N., Villarruel, F., Vilanueva, C., & Augarten, I. (2009). *America's invisible children: Latino youth and the failure of justice.* Washington, DC: National Council of La Raza.

Barrows, T., Garza, M., Gomez, C., Williams, O., & Rahimi, S. (2010). *Stopping the rail to jail: The foundations of a movement known as the Community Justice Network for Youth.* Retrieved from the W. Haywood Burns Institute for Juvenile Justice Fairness & Equity Web site: http://www.burnsinstitute.org/publications/cjny-publication-stopping-the-rail-to-jail/

Bilchik, S. (2008). Is racial and ethnic equity possible in juvenile justice? *Reclaiming Youth, 17*(2), 19–23.

Bilchik, S. (2009). Policy reforms to address racial and ethnic disparity and disproportionality in the child welfare and juvenile justice systems: Federal, state, and local action. In *Racial and ethnic disparity and disproportionality in the child welfare and juvenile justice systems: A compendium* (pp. 55–77). Retrieved from Center for Juvenile Justice Reform Web site: http://cjjr.georgetown.edu/pdfs/cjjr_ch_final.pdf

Campbell, H. (1991). *Black's law dictionary* (6th ed.). St. Paul, MN: West.

Cauffman, E., & Grisso, T. (2005). Mental health issues among minority offenders in the juvenile justice system. In D. F. Hawkins & K. Kempf-Leonard (Eds.), *Our children, their children* (pp. 390–412). Chicago, IL: University of Chicago Press.

Center for Children's Law and Policy (2010). *DMC Action Network.* Retrieved from http://www.cclp.org/DMC_Action_Network.php

Cervantes, R.C., Ruan, K., & Dueñas, N. (2004). Programa Shortstop: A culturally focused juvenile intervention for Hispanic youth. *Journal of Drug Education, 34*(4), 385–405.

Chapman, J. F., Desai, R. A., & Falzer, P. R. (2006). Mental health service provision in juvenile justice facilities: Pre- and postrelease psychiatric care. *Child and Adolescent Psychiatric Clinics of North America, 15*, 445–458.

Children's Defense Fund (2000). Disproportionate minority confinement (DMC). Retrieved April 21, 2000, from http://www.childrensdefense.org/juvenilejusitice/confinement.html

Christle, C. A., Jolivette, K., & Nelson, C. M. (2005). Breaking the school to prison pipeline: Identifying school risk and protective factors for youth delinquency. *Exceptionality: The Official Journal of the Division for Research of the Council for Exceptional Children, 13*(2), 69–88.

Coleman, A.R. (n.d.). *A disproportionate minority contact (DMC) chronology: 1988 to date.* Retrieved from http://ojjdp.ncjrs.org/dmc/about/chronology.html http://www.ojjdp.gov/dmc/chronology.html

Cox, J. A., & Bell, J. (2001). Addressing disproportionate representation of youth of color in the juvenile justice system. *Journal of the Center for Families, Children & the Courts, 3*, 31-43.

Crane, K. D., & Ellis, R. A. (2004). Benevolent intervention or oppression perpetuated: Minority overrepresentation in children's services. *Journal of Human Behavior in the Social Environment, 9*(1/2), 19–38.

Devine, P., Coolbaugh, K., & Jenkins, S. (1998). Disproportionate minority confinement: Lessons learned from five states. *Juvenile Justice Bulletin.* Washington, DC: U. S. Department of Justice, Office of Justice Programs, Office of Juvenile Justice and Delinquency Prevention.

Feld, B. (1993). Criminalizing the American juvenile court. *Crime and Justice, 17*, 197–280.

Gardner, M. R. (1997). The juvenile court movement. In *Understanding juvenile law* (pp. 179–198). New York: Matthew Bender.

Glisson, C., & Green, P. (2006). The role of specialty mental health care in predicting child welfare and juvenile justice out-of-home placements. *Research on Social Work Practice, 16*(5), 480–490.

Goodman, J. W. (2005). *Leandro v. State* and the constitutional limitation on school suspensions and expulsions in North Carolina. *North Carolina Law Review, 83*, 1507–1525.

Griffin, P. (2010, November). *Models for Change: Innovations in practice.* Retrieved from Models for Change Web site: http://www.modelsforchange.net/publications/287

Griffin, P. (2011). *Adding up Models for Change: Initial findings from the Models for Change database.* Retrieved from Models for Change Web site: http://www.modelsforchange.net/publications/325

Griffin, P., Torbet, P., Thomas, D., Snyder, H., & Halemba, G. (2004, April 12). *Models for Change framework.* Retrieved from Models for Change Web site: http://www.modelsforchange.net/about/Background-and-principles.html

Grisso, T. (2004). Reasons for concern about mental disorders of adolescent offenders. In *Double Jeopardy* (pp. 3–26). Chicago: The University of Chicago Press.

Herz, D., Lee, P., Lutz, L., Stewart, M., Tuell, J., & Wiig, J. (2012). *Addressing the needs of multi-system youth: Strengthening the connection between child welfare and juvenile justice.* Washington, DC: Center for Juvenile Justice Reform.

Hicks, J. W. (2004). Ethnicity, race, and forensic psychiatry: Are we color blind? *Journal of the American Academy of Psychiatry and Law, 32*(1), 21–33.

Hsia, H., Bridges, G. S., & McHale, R. (2004). *Disproportionate minority confinement 2002 update.* Washington, DC: U. S. Department of Justice, Office of Justice Programs, Office of Juvenile Justice and Delinquency Prevention.

Hsia, H. M. (2004). *OJJDP Formula Grants Program overview.* (Report No. FS-200402). Retrieved from https://www.ncjrs.gov/pdffiles1/ojjdp/fs200402.pdf

Hsia, M., & Hamparian, D. (1998). *Disproportionate minority confinement: 1997 update.* Washington, DC: U.S. Department of Justice, Office of Juvenile Justice and Delinquency Prevention.

Jargowsky, P. A., Desmond, S. A., & Crutchfield, R. D. (2005). Suburban sprawl, race, and juvenile justice. In D. F. Hawkins & K. Kempf-Leonard (Eds.), *Our children, their children* (pp. 167–201). Chicago, IL: University of Chicago Press.

Kakar, S. (2006). Understanding the causes of disproportionate minority contact: Results of focus group discussions. *Journal of Criminal Justice, 34,* 369–381.

Leiber, M. J. (2002). Disproportionate minority confinement (DMC) of youth: An analysis of state and federal efforts to address the issue. *Crime & Delinquency, 48*(1), 3–45.

Leiber, M., & Rodriguez, N. (2011). The implementation of the disproportionate minority confinement/contact (DMC) mandate: A failure or success? *Race and Justice, 1*(1), 103–124.

Majors, R., & Billson, J. M. (1992). *Cool pose: The dilemmas of black manhood in America*. New York: Touchstone.

Martin, R. C. (2001). *Zero tolerance policy*. Chicago: American Bar Association.

Martinez, J. I., Gudiño, O. G., & Lau, A. S. (2013). Problem-specific racial/ethnic disparities in pathways from maltreatment exposure to specialty mental health service use for youth in child welfare. *Child Maltreatment, 18*(2), 98–107.

McCoy, H. (2011). A path analysis of factors influencing racial differences on the MAYSI-2. *Journal of Offender Rehabilitation, 50*(3), 119–141.

Mears, D. P. (2002). Sentencing guidelines and the transformation of juvenile justice in the 21st century. *Journal of Contemporary Criminal Justice, 18*(1), 6–19.

Models for Change. (2011a). *Knowledge brief: Are minority youths treated differently in juvenile probation?* Retrieved May 30, 2012, from http://www.modelsforchange.net/publications/314

Models for Change. (2011b). *Knowledge brief: Is there a link between child welfare and disproportionate contact in juvenile justice?* Retrieved May 30, 2012, from http://www.modelsforchange.net/publications/317

Motivans, M., & Snyder, H. (2011). *Summary: Tribal youth in the federal justice system.* (Report No. NCJ 234218). Washington, DC: U.S. Department of Justice, Office of Justice Programs, Bureau of Justice Statistics.

National Council of La Raza. (2011). *Men in Motion in the Community and the Philadelphia Latino Juvenile Justice Network: Reducing disproportionate minority contact, strengthening reentry, and building community.* Retrieved from Models for Change Web site: http://www.modelsforchange.net/publications/327

Nicholson-Crotty, S., Birchmeier, Z., & Valentine, D. (2009). Exploring the impact of school discipline on racial disproportion in the juvenile justice system. *Social Science Quarterly, 90*(4), 1003–1018.

Northey, W. F., Primer, V., & Christensen, L. (1997). Promoting justice in the delivery of services to juvenile delinquents: The ecosystemic natural wraparound model. *Child & Adolescent Social Work Journal, 14*(1), 5–22.

Office of Juvenile Justice and Delinquency Prevention. (2009, October). *OJJDP in focus: Disproportionate minority contact.* Retrieved from https://www.ncjrs.gov/pdffiles1/ojjdp/228306.pdf

Pattison, B. (1998). Minority youth in juvenile correctional facilities: Cultural differences and the right to treatment. *Law and Inequality, 16*, 573–599.

Penn, J., Doll, J., & Grandgenett, N. (2008). Culture as prevention: Assisting high-risk youth in the Omaha Nation. *Wicazo Sa Review, 23*(2), 43–61.

Petitclerc, A., Gatti, U., Vitaro, F., & Tremblay, R. E. (2013). Effects of juvenile court exposure on crime in young adulthood. *Journal of Child Psychology and Psychiatry, 54*(3), 291–297.

Primm, A. B., Osher, F. C., & Gomez, M. B. (2005). Race and ethnicity, mental health services and cultural competence in the criminal justice system: Are we ready to change? *Community Health Journal, 41*(5), 557–569.

Puzzanchera, C., & Adams, B. (2011). *Juvenile arrests 2009.* (Report No, NCJ 236477). Washington, DC: U.S. Department of Justice, Office of Justice Programs, Office of Juvenile Justice and Delinquency Prevention.

Puzzanchera, C., Adams, B., & Sickmund, M. (2010). *Juvenile Court statistics 2006–2007.* Pittsburgh, PA: National Center for Juvenile Justice.

Puzzanchera, C., & Kang, W. (2011). *Easy access to Juvenile Court statistics: 1985–2009.* Retrieved from http://www.ojjdp.gov/ojstatbb/ezajcs/

Ratner, R. A. (1992). Role of the psychiatrist. In M. G. Kalogerakis (Ed.) *Handbook of psychiatric practice in the juvenile court* (pp. 25–36). Washington, DC: American Psychiatric Association.

Rodriguez, N. (2007). Juvenile court context and detention decisions: Reconsidering the role of race, ethnicity, and community characteristics in juvenile court processes. *Justice Quarterly, 24*(4), 629–656.

Roscoe, M., & Morton, R. (1994). *Disproportionate minority confinement.* Washington, DC: U.S. Department of Justice, Office of Justice Programs, Office of Juvenile Justice and Delinquency Prevention.

Ryan, J. P., Herz, D., Hernandez, P. M., & Marshall, J. M. (2007). Maltreatment and delinquency: Investigating child welfare bias in juvenile justice processing. *Children and Youth Services Review, 29*, 1035–1050.

Sacks, H., & Reader, W. D. (1992). Procedures in the juvenile court. In M. G. Kalogerakis (Ed.), *Handbook of psychiatric practice in the juvenile court* (pp. 13–19). Washington, DC: American Psychiatric Association.

Schwalbe, C. S., Gearing, R. E., MacKenzie, M. J., Brewer, K. B., & Ibrahim, R. (2012). A meta-analysis of experimental studies of diversion programs for juvenile offenders. *Clinical Psychology Review, 32*(1), 26–33.

Shelton, D. (2004). Experiences of detained young offenders in need of mental health care. *Journal of Nursing Scholarship, 36*(2), 129–133.

Short, J., & Sharp, C. (2005). *Disproportionate minority contact in the juvenile justice system.* Washington, DC: Child Welfare League of America.

Shufelt, J. L., Cocozza, J. J., & Skowyra, K. R. (2010, September). *Successfully collaborating with the juvenile justice system: Benefits, challenges, and key strategies.*

Retrieved from the Technical Assistance Partnership for Child and Family Mental Health Web site: http://www.tapartnership.org/docs/jjResource_collaboration.pdf

Siegel, L. J., & Senna, J. J. (1991). An overview of the juvenile justice system and its goals. In *Juvenile delinquency: Theory, practice & law*, 4th ed. (pp. 397–426). St. Paul, MN: West.

Snyder, H. N., & Sickmund, M. (2006). *Juvenile offenders and victims: 2006 national report*. Washington, DC: U. S. Department of Justice, Office of Justice Programs, Office of Juvenile Justice and Delinquency Prevention.

Soler, M., & Garry, L. (2009, September). *Reducing disproportionate minority contact: Preparation at the local level*. Retrieved from Office of Juvenile Justice and Delinquency Prevention Web site: https://www.ncjrs.gov/pdffiles1/ojjdp/218861.pdf

Teplin, L. A. (2000). Juvenile justice and identification of mental health needs. In *U. S. Public Health Service, report of the Surgeon General's conference on children's mental health: A national action agenda*. Washington, DC: Department of Health and Human Services.

Villarruel, F. A., & Walker, N. E. (2001). *¿Dónde está la justicia? A call to action on behalf of Latino and Latina Youth in the U.S. justice system*. Retrieved from http://www.cclp.org/documents/BBY/Donde.pdf

W. Haywood Burns Institute. (n.d.). *Fact sheet: Disproportionate minority confinement/contact (DMC)*. Retrieved from http://www.burnsinstitute.org/services/success/

Williams, L. (2010). Cultural interventions for reducing violence among young, African American males. In W. E. Johnson, Jr. (Ed.), *Social work with African American males: Health, mental health, and social policy* (pp. 265–291). New York: Oxford University Press.

9

Disproportionality and Disparities in the Educational System and Schools

▸ DEENA HAYES AND ANGELA M. WARD

DESCRIPTION OF THE SYSTEM AND THE ETHNIC MINORITY POPULATIONS IN THE SYSTEM

THE AMERICAN EDUCATION SYSTEM IS based on the factory model of the industrial age. Students are expected to fit a mold. Typically, the mold is not one that considers race, ethnicity, gender, sexual orientation, religion, level of ability, or the overall background a child brings to the classroom. Yet schools function in a manner that requires a child and the family of that child to conform to the Americanized way of socializing, learning, and coping with daily life. Students of color, particularly Black and Latino, face educational disparities the second they enter educational environments. Gilliam's (2005) national study on preschool expulsions found that suspension and expulsion rates were highest for African American children and were higher in preschool programs than in K–12. In any discussion on disproportionality with regard to the schooling of children, it is difficult to exclude race because where African American children are enrolled in schools across our country, disproportionality exists in their access to a high-quality education. In this Americanized education system, "Black males are more likely than any other group to be suspended and expelled from schools . . . more likely to be classified as mentally retarded or suffering from a learning or emotional disability and placed in special education . . . [and] are least likely to be enrolled in advanced placement and honors courses. . . ." (Delpit, 2012, p. 15). Primarily, this reality breaches the access to a quality education that should be guaranteed to every student. Second, it deprives the nation of the gifts, talents, and competencies of Black males and overburdens multiple systems as a result. As they matriculate through the Americanized education system, students of color are historically less likely to receive a high-quality instructor who uses culturally responsive pedagogy for instructional delivery and are less likely to have an instructor who understands the complex history of race in America and the role it plays in the everyday existence of students of color. Socioeconomic status is often mentioned as a larger issue than race, yet when race is layered over socioeconomic status, African American students still rank well below other students of color and White students of the same socioeconomic class.

Racial disproportionality and disparities need to be addressed in the education system because we are losing an entire generation of Black and Latino boys to the disconnected, unstructured White industrial educational system. The impact of disparities is discussed throughout this chapter. The overall impact is that the disparities give the "appearance" that there are students at the "top." Public school systems along with the juvenile justice and child welfare systems are designed to keep White children on the top. The top is relative to the disparities, meaning that when the "top" is pulled out as its own group and compared to other "tops" (especially globally), they become the bottom.

The Federal government provides Title I and Title II for student achievement and professional learning at schools with a large demographic of students with lower socioeconomic status. Those funds, instead of enhancing and innovating, are going toward the maintenance of disparities instead of eliminating them. The system is not functioning optimally. The system in its current state perpetuates a culture that disenfranchises students of color. Those disenfranchised children drop out at an early age, and some turn to a life that is very unproductive for American society. If disparities persist in the education system, children of color will not grow into productive adults of color. The impact on African American and Latino boys is the increased likelihood of involvement in the criminal justice system, the child welfare system, the social services system, the healthcare system, the public housing/homeless system, and so on. There is a social and economic cost to ignoring disproportionality and disparity.

Students of color have suffered negative stigmas as related to their interest in and commitment to education. The results are lowered expectations and patronizing instructional efforts. Latino families who make a living as migrant workers are stigmatized as not valuing education because many members of the family have to work to make ends meet. Conversations with teachers in our factory model of schooling reveal that they find it difficult to empathize with a parent who needs their teenage child to work. These same teachers do not feel it is their role to help the child and parent find a solution that increases the child's ability to learn as well as a solution that helps the family. Urban schools are filled with programs that allow students to learn a trade or go to school part time to earn a diploma and work part time to assist the family, but the system often fails to make these programs available to those who need them. Addressing racial disproportionality and disparities will assist in achieving educational equity for students of color, undoubtedly increasing the educational outcomes for all students. As Gloria Ladson-Billings once shared,

> Before I stepped into my first classroom as a teacher, I thought teaching was mainly instruction, partly performing, certainly being in the front and at the center of classroom life. Later, with much chaos and some pain, I learned that this is the least of it—teaching includes a more splendorous range of actions. Teaching is instructing, advising, counseling, organizing, assessing, guiding, goading, showing, managing, modeling, coaching, disciplining, prodding, preaching, persuading, proselytizing, listening, interacting, nursing, and inspiring (Sennett, 2004, p. 42).

In order for students of color to receive an adequate education, teachers and school administrators must adopt the belief that their role has changed. Teachers have to do more with less, and it is true that not everyone can teach. Teaching is an art, a passion, and a calling. Education is a process of acquiring information through learning and sharing and is experienced in multiple ways.

1. Formally through institutions (structural systems) and schools—public and private/curriculum/design/methods
   a) Standard (mainstream)
   b) Alternative (nontraditional)
   c) Special education (special learning needs)
2. Independent (experiential/self-directed)
   a) Homeschooling
   b) Social Education—informal groups, associations

Ethnic Minority Populations in the System

The Census Bureau released its new statistics on the nation's children and school enrollment and it showed something momentous. For the first time since this annual data series has been released, fewer than half of all the children (49.9%) in the youngest age group shown, three-year-olds, were White.

Whites still comprised a small majority of four-year-olds and increasing shares of older ages. Of those three-year-olds who did attend school—preK and kindergarten—Whites were still in the majority. (Whites still comprise 58.8% of students of all ages.)

Yet these statistics finally confirm the beginning of an oft-predicted trend— a truly multiethnic school age population that will continue to pour into our grade schools, high schools, and beyond in the coming decade. The trend is most pronounced in eight states and the District of Columbia, where the preK and kindergarten populations are already majority students of color. In an additional nine states, Latinos, Blacks, Asians, and other races—comprise over four in ten students (Frey, 2011).

This tipping point came in the midst of the state by state release of 2010 census race-ethnic redistricting data that reinforced the picture of an increasingly multiethnic American youth. In just the first four states released in this process—New Jersey, Louisiana, Mississippi, and Virginia— declines were found in the population of White youth (under age 18) since 2000. This may not come as much of a surprise in the two Gulf Coast states, which were ravaged by Hurricane Katrina—but it also applies to the other two more "suburban" states. According to the 2010 census, more than three-in-ten young people in New Jersey were either Latino or Asian, as is the case for more than one-in-six in Virginia.

According to the *Enrollment in the Texas Public School System Report* from 2000–01 through 2010–11, between 1998 and 2008, the percentages of [Latino] students increased in the four most populous states in the country, as well as the United States as a whole, and in each case, the percentage-point increase was the largest for any racial/ethnic group. The proportion of enrollment accounted for by Latinos rose from 38.6% to 47.9%

(9.3 percentage points) in Texas, and from 14.9% to 21.5% (6.6 percentage points) nationwide. During the same period, the proportion of enrollment accounted for by White students decreased from 44.1% to 34.0% in Texas and from 63.0% to 54.9% nationwide. This downward trend also held true in California, Florida, and New York. Throughout the period, Texas and California had much higher percentages of [Latino] students and lower percentages of White students than the nation as a whole (Texas Education Agency, 2011, p. 43).

With these data trends, our public schools are becoming less diverse as White families choose suburban public schools and private schools. Texas had six school districts make the list of graduation rates for the 24 largest central city districts, 2002–2003.

Of those districts in Dallas, El Paso, and Santa Ana, 100% of Latino students attend schools that are predominantly [students of color], and in 15 [of the largest central city districts], more than 90% of Latino students attend schools where more than half of their peers are [students of color]. These districts . . . for the most part, are high poverty. . . . Among these large districts, all of those with the lowest high school completion rates are central city systems with very high levels of segregation (Orfield & Lee, 2005, p. 37).

According to the National Center for Education Statistics, revenues for public elementary and secondary schools amount to $525 billion for the school year 2011–2012. Current expenditure per pupil is projected at around $10,591. In September 1993, Texas instituted the Robin Hood Law, which required property rich urban school districts such as Austin, Houston, and Dallas to send a large portion of their yearly revenue to property poor school districts. The Robin Hood plan is the result of *Edgewood v. Kirby*.

A suit filed against education commissioner William Kirby in 1984, by the Mexican American Legal Defense and Educational Fund (MALDEF) on behalf of the Edgewood Independent School District in San Antonio, alleging discrimination against students in poor school districts. The plaintiffs in the Edgewood case contested the state's reliance on local property taxes to finance its system of public education, contending that this method was intrinsically unequal because property values varied greatly from district to district, thus creating an imbalance in funds available to educate students on an equal basis throughout the state. These differences produced disparities in the districts' abilities to hire good teachers, build appropriate facilities, offer a sound curriculum, and purchase such important equipment as computers. In its original 1984 brief, MALDEF had declared that such gaps amounted to the denial of equal opportunity in an "increasingly complex and technological society," and asserted that this was contrary to the intent of the constitution's Texas Education Clause (Acosta, 2012).

Laws such as this one add to the disproportion by limiting the funding available to districts such as those urban school districts in Texas. Sending more than $100 million dollars annually back to the state on top of billions of dollars in cuts to the state education fund severely cripples the urban school district's ability to provide an equitable educational opportunity to all students.

With the issue of funding in mind, it is incumbent upon our nation's largest school districts to set a new standard for recruiting and retaining high-quality teachers. The majority of the teachers are young, White, and middle class, yet often they are not adequately prepared to teach our most needy populations found largely in urban schools, which can create a strain on the professional development budget of a large urban district. According to Tatum,

> . . . the number of young people of color entering the teaching profession is still too small to meet the demand . . . [and] many White teachers will still be needed to replace retiring teachers in the coming years. Schools concerned about meeting the needs of an increasingly diverse student population should be looking specifically for teachers of all backgrounds with demonstrated experience in working with multiracial populations, with courses on their transcripts like Psychology of Racism; Race, Class, Culture, and Gender in the Classroom; and Foundations of Multicultural Education, to name a few (Tatum, 1999, p. 125).

Tatum recognizes that the problem of disproportionality and disparities begins in the classroom, particularly when unchecked bias drives instruction, interaction, and classroom management. For example, this bias is exemplified in the following case example common in Americanized schools.

CASE EXAMPLE: BILLY

A preK White girl says to a little boy, "I don't want to play with you because you are Black." The teacher scolds the girl for not being nice to "our" friends. Billy, a Black boy in the same class, calls a White boy fat and Billy receives lunch and recess time out with a note home to his parents. Instances like this persist in his school and Billy, now in third grade, is labeled a bad kid and feels targeted by the adults in the school. He can do nothing right and gives up on being a good boy because the teachers don't like him.

Children like Billy have a threshold set between preK and second grade. The ability to plug in and attach to this educational experience has been negative causing them to unplug. Little boys of all races enter kindergarten and early childhood with the idea of wanting to be a superhero or fireman. Disproportionate discipline experiences distance students from the innocence and optimism with which they enter school. Trying to determine where they fit in, some little boys of color turn to strumming beats and writing lyrics. Others may choose one of three paths (1) they float through school or just get by; (2) they display underachievement in school and life; or (3) as unsupervised teenagers, they are disenfranchised from the education system and become a menace. In the education system, we see high dropout rates in the eighth and ninth grades as a result of the path chosen.

Guilford County, North Carolina, schools have found a solution that is working for their children and families. Dr. Terry Grier, former Guilford County school superintendent, became the superintendent of the Houston Independent School District in Texas. Realizing that many of our teachers, administrators, and staff enter the education system ill-equipped to meet the sociocultural needs of students, he enacted a professional learning program to address disparities. During his tenure in the Greensboro, North Carolina, school district, he initiated cross-systems cultural competency training, *Undoing Racism*, conducted by the New Orleans, Louisiana–based People's Institute for Survival and Beyond. He scheduled training that involved school social workers, district senior cabinet staff, and school resource officers (SRO). The second year, he implemented antiracism training for all Title I Schools that were part of a district initiative to increase student achievement. The current superintendent of Guilford County schools has continued to support racial equity/antiracism training and additionally has launched an effort to address African American male student achievement based on the antiracism analysis of examining structural barriers for students of color while addressing individual student's needs.

Hiring staff who are mentally prepared to service the educational needs of students of color and providing professional learning opportunities that require critical self-reflection on bias and prejudice increases the district's chances of maintaining a high standard of education in every classroom and of eliminating disproportionality and disparities for students of color.

UNDERSTANDING THE PROBLEMS AND NEEDS OF ETHNIC MINORITY POPULATIONS IN THE SYSTEM

To fully understand the issues facing people of color in the Americanized system of education, one must focus on the buzz words often used to legitimize the disproportion that exists. The "achievement gap" refers to racial and ethnic educational disproportionality and disparities among and between White and African American and White and Latino students. The Association for Supervision and Curriculum Development (ASCD) coined the phrase "the learning gap" to capture the low existence of teachers who have demonstrated experience instructing multiracial populations (Hayward, 2010). Also, to bring light to the fact that undergraduate work often inadequately prepares teachers to teach in an urban system, ASCD along with other professional learning organizations such as Learning Forward (formerly the National Staff Development Council) provide school systems with cutting-edge resources to enhance the teaching and learning of their staff. Learning Forward provides national standards for professional development, and innovation configurations help educators understand and visualize the practical application of the standards.

In virtually every indicator of academic and educational success, Black, Latino, and Native American students lag behind their White counterparts. Yet the conversation often overlooked in our data analysis is the White versus Asian achievement gap. Some may say Asian students do not lag behind, but if you do not look at the data in that way, how do you know if disparity exists? Educational success can be measured by overall achievement, advanced placements/honors, graduation, SAT/ACT outcomes, and admission to college, while educational failures are indicated by rates of dropouts, suspensions and discipline, and overrepresentation and overidentification in special education. Students of color do not have the lowest educational capacity and ability and are no more likely to act up, but they are more likely to be suspended and are more likely to receive a low-level education. Failure for these students happens mainly as a result of the school system and not as a result of what happens at home with their families.

> Most Texans who are black, under 21, and being incarcerated, are entering prison with the lowest educational levels in the criminal justice system . . . [the] average level for these inmates, entering the Texas prison system between 2007–2011, was just above a sixth-grade level. White inmates averaged an eighth-grade level . . . inmates with a ninth-grade education had an 18% lower recidivism rate than inmates with a fourth-grade education (Pressley & Skelton, 2013, p. 2).

The Council of State Governments and the Public Policy Research Institute conducted a statewide study in the state of Texas. They wanted to know if school discipline relates to a student's success or failure and to their introduction to the juvenile justice system. The study followed all Texas students in seventh grade for six years beginning during the 2000, 2001, and 2002 school years. Key findings in the report are as follows.

1) The majority of students in the public school system (59.6%) experienced some form of suspension or expulsion in middle or high school.
2) African American students were more likely than students of other races to be disciplined during their seventh- to twelfth-grade school years.
3) Nearly three out of four students who qualified for special education services during the study period were suspended or expelled at least once between their seventh- and twelfth-grade school years. The level of disciplinary involvement by these students, however, varied significantly according to the specific type of educational disability they had.
4) Students who experienced suspension or expulsion, especially those who did so repeatedly, were more likely to be held back a grade or [to] drop out of school than students who were not involved in the disciplinary system.
5) More than one in seven students were in contact with the juvenile justice system between seventh and twelfth grade. Students who were suspended or expelled had a greater likelihood of contact with the juvenile justice

system in their middle or high school years, particularly when they were disciplined multiple times.

6) Schools that had similar student populations and were alike in other important regards varied significantly in how often they suspended or expelled pupils (Council of State Governments Justice Center, 2011).

These findings allude to another "factor contributing to the lowered achievement of students of color . . . institutionalized racism, which we recognize as the unexamined and unchallenged system of racial biases and residual White advantage that persist in our institutions of learning" (Singleton & Linton, 2006, p. 33). Often in urban school settings, because the majority of the educators are White and middle class, students of color are blamed for what amounts to their inability to cope and adapt to the Americanized system. Educators must establish processes and priorities that require a focus on issues of race plaguing students of color in the Americanized system of education.

Root causes of the achievement gap are complex and multifaceted and rarely explored in depth because this requires educators to go beyond social class and to have serious conversations about the intersectionality of identities that include but are not limited to race, ethnicity, gender, and sexual orientation. Access to learning and full educational opportunities was closed to non-Whites for the majority of the history of our nation. Because the school age population is increasingly of color, it is important to expand our view of the historical context of the experience of people of color in the American educational system. We must expand our view in order to provide effective instruction and to interrupt the implicit bias of institutional racism that shapes and informs the delivery of educational goods.

Socioeconomic conditions are frequently cited as compounding the educational barriers that students of color face. Enid Lee shares,

> I have found in my work . . . I often gain a greater understanding of the situations before me when I insert the race lens over the lens of . . . class. For instance, when I am trying to understand why negativity is being expressed against working class parents and their assumed lack of interest in their children's education, I discover that those parents are African American, African Canadian, Native American, Native Canadian, or Latino. I can raise the delicate question of race and help the discussion move forward to a more positive place (Lee, Menkart, & Okazawa-Rey, 2008, p. 405).

The socioeconomic disadvantages experienced by students of color are relevant to the social, political, and economic history of the United States. Eugene Robinson, in his book *Disintegration*, references the 2008 census.

> In 1940, only 15.7% of African American households nationwide were headed by women who were either single, widowed, or abandoned by their spouses. In 1960, just 22% of Black children were growing up in one-parent households. Today, an astounding 54% of all African American children are being raised in single-parent households (Robinson, 2010, p. 130).

In his book, Robinson describes four "Black America's"—one being the Abandoned, a large minority with less hope of escaping poverty and dysfunction than at any time since Reconstruction's end, that makes up one-quarter of the Black population. Robinson goes on to share that "as a result . . . , children of Abandoned families are at a significant disadvantage, compared to their more affluent peers, when they enter school" (Robinson, 2010, p. 131). In the Abandoned families, we find high instances of dysfunction, despair, and little hope. The Moynihan Report of 1965 found the conditions of the disordered single mother and the unemployed absentee father were the manifestations of systemically disparate decisions and not often the cause (Office of Policy Planning and Research, 1965).

> In 1940, Edward Wight Bakke described the effects of unemployment on family structure in terms of six stages of adjustment. Although the families studied were White, the pattern would clearly seem to be a general one, and apply to Negro families as well. The first two stages end with the exhaustion of credit and the entry of the wife into the labor force. The father is no longer the provider and the elder children become resentful. The third stage is the critical one of commencing a new day-to-day existence. At this point two women are in charge. Consider the fact that relief investigators or case workers are normally women and deal with the housewife. Already suffering a loss in prestige and authority in the family because of his failure to be the chief bread winner, the male head of the family feels deeply this obvious transfer of planning for the family's well-being to two women, one of them an outsider. His role is reduced to that of errand boy to and from the relief office (Moynihan, 1970, p. 379).

If the family makes it through this stage, Bakke finds that it is likely to survive, and the rest of the process is one of adjustment. The critical element of adjustment was not welfare payments but work.

> Having observed our families under conditions of unemployment with no public help, or with that help coming from direct [sic] and from work relief, we are convinced that after the exhaustion of self-produced resources, work relief is the only type of assistance which can restore the strained bonds of family relationship in a way which promises the continued functioning of that family in meeting the responsibilities imposed upon it by our culture. Work is precisely the one thing the Negro family head in such circumstances has not received over the past generation. The fundamental, overwhelming fact is that Negro unemployment, with the exception of a few years during World War II and the Korean War, has continued at disaster levels for 35 years (Moynihan, 1970, p. 379).

Through President Roosevelt's New Deal government program and other race-based access and resources, White people were given concrete, tangible, material opportunities, while people of color got and still get programs that can help or hurt. Traditional programs and services are shaped by the needs of constituents often void of racial and historical context. Programs serve to interrupt the cultural buffer that kept marginalized communities together and do more to manage poverty's distress patterns.

People, families, children, and parents are vulnerable for a variety of reasons—economically poor, disabled, uneducated, and unskilled. However, they become at risk when they enter an at-risk system. An at-risk system is a system that chronically produces patterned disparities for groups that share a common condition, as mentioned earlier. When people enter our systems, they become at risk of being underidentified, overidentified, overmedicated, overprosecuted, or underserved. They become at risk of receiving disproportionate services and decision making along patterned lines, most notably racial lines.

The glaring focus of the social and economic realities of students functions as a deterrent to considering the disproportionate social and economic opportunities for White students and their families. The flip side to disproportion has a positive effect on the lives of White children. The African American Policy Forum produced a short animated film titled

The Unequal Race (African American Policy Forum, 2012) that depicts the institutionalized power that historically dominates families of color and that favors White families. Due to inherent (legal) intergenerational and multigenerational inequitable access to structural resources and opportunities, White students are disproportionately (more often) located in families characterized by two-parent or socioeconomically stable households, middle–high income jobs, and longer-term employment with benefits, any of which causes White students not to be at high risk for family uncertainty and collective racial deficiencies. Therefore, White students are less likely to fall victim to inadequate nutrition, vulnerable child-care situations, neglect, poor health, criminal sanctions, and material deprivations. They are less likely to live in substandard crowded quarters, characterized by negative stigmas and low expectations of group values and potential. In *Why Segregation Matters*, Orfield and Lee (2005) purport, "students attending low poverty schools in the South are predominantly White (69%). Because of high White isolation, the average White student attends a school that is 80% White (p. 25)." Additionally, of the 24 largest central cities in America:

> ... the cities with the lowest completion rates are among the country's largest: New York City, Los Angeles, and Chicago. More than three-quarters of the students in these schools are of color. Sadly included in this group is the first city that experienced full urban desegregation outside the South, Denver, which is also the city in which the right of Latino students to desegregated education was established in a decision on the city schools by the U.S. Supreme Court (Orfield & Lee, 2005, p. 37).

As shown in the animated film referred to above, White families' consistent and legal access to educational opportunities positively impacts White students' trajectory from the cradle to college or a career pathway. Knowledge of the historical and current context of the experience of people of color provides the tools for educators to interrupt the implicit bias of institutional racism. Teachers aware of the impact of racial identities and the political, social, and economic meaning of these identities may be able to see their students of color as not being personally responsible for the condition of the family.

SYSTEMS EFFORTS TO ADDRESS DISPROPORTIONALITY AND DISPARITIES: GENERAL BARRIERS AND ETHNIC-SPECIFIC BARRIERS FACED AND CHALLENGES ENCOUNTERED

In our Americanized public educational system, White students collectively are prepositioned to produce better outcomes than marginalized populations. Black and Latino students historically and presently are faring the worst. The disparities in educational experiences and outcomes are a complicated dynamic and are often approached from a very superficial understanding of where the problem originated. As one colleague framed the problem, when one fish in the lake is belly up and is floating dead on the top of the lake, it makes sense to look at the fish to find out its cause of death. When half of the fish in the lake are floating belly up dead at the top, it is time to look at the lake. Unfortunately, public service institutions, training, and practices stress the individual fish approach and not the systemic analysis. Based on the American value of individuality and the focus on meritocracy, we are not encouraged or taught that we must and should examine our institutions so that we can understand how structural/social designs are implicated in these inequities. "One reason for the lack of [Black] academic success in schools is that many poor [Black] students are simply not being taught" (Delpit, 2012, p. 8).

Race versus Racism as a Barrier

If race is indicated in outcomes, as the statistics dictate, then an analysis/examination of race must also be part of the intervention in order for it to adequately address the problem and the population. In order to begin accessing the impact of race, we must have/share a common understanding of race. Often when we are talking about race and racism we are not talking about the same thing. Peggy McIntosh invites people to consider a different definition and understanding of racism. She says, "I was taught to recognize racism only in individual acts of meanness by members of my group, never in individual systems conferring unsought racial dominance on my group from birth" (McIntosh, 1988, p. 17–18). Our education, formal and informal, and training of race and racism has been limited to seeing race in terms of individual behavior and attitudes—such as using the "N" word or laughing at racist jokes. Race is a complicated and loaded issue. Race is a powerful variable of outcomes in institutional experiences as is evident in health and human services, education, the judicial/criminal justice system, and in housing. Yet it is the topic that we are least comfortable discussing. Explanations and definitions of race and racism are often left to our opinion. With such broad differences in exactly what race and racism are, confusion and conflict is usually the result. Families, friends, and systems are careful to avoid the slippery slope of racial differences and the meaning we make of race and racism. Hence we "shush" children when they raise questions about race. Bronson and Merryman (2009) write that people believe that children only see race when it is pointed out to them. They are learning that it is not nice to talk about race. As a matter of fact, historically, we have been taught it can be downright rude to point it out and to notice it. Children naturally categorize things. I remember watching the vignettes on *Sesame Street*, where they present pictures of patterns and themes with one thing out of sequence. The question is, "which one of these things doesn't belong?" When adults fail to facilitate age-appropriate conversations about race with young children, they are left ill-equipped to understand how race has shaped lives and to explain how people have become "differently situated." The issue of race is often left up to children to figure out on their own without the historical context necessary to minimize implicit bias. In the years where children have the greatest capacity to learn the basics of race, they are handicapped and the foundation is set for their inability to understand what is most visible to them.

It is often said that racism is taught at home. Often left out of early childhood experiences is the impact the media has on the creation of racist ideals and values by perpetuating stereotypes. The movie *Crash* brings many of those stereotypes into view and shows the impact they have when microaggressions boil out of control. New York City's Stop and Frisk Law represents real events that create state-sanctioned microaggressions. Understanding race as a social construct that comes with social and institutional power that is historically accessible to the members of the dominant group is a real departure from the interpersonal dynamics and perpetuates barriers that create systemic inequities.

Unexamined History as a Barrier

Tatum (1999) relates this story of her son, Jonathan, who was in day care where he was

> . . . one of few children of color, and the only Black child in his class. Jonathan said, "Eddie says my skin is brown because I drink too much chocolate milk. Is that true?" Eddie was a White three-year-old in Jonathan's class who . . . had observed a physical difference and was now searching for an explanation. "No," I replied, "your skin is brown because you have something in your skin called melanin. Melanin is very important because it helps protect your skin from the sun. Eddie has melanin in his skin, too. Remember when Eddie went to Florida on vacation and came back showing everybody his tan? It was melanin in his skin that made it get darker. Everybody has melanin, you know. But some people have more than others. At your school, you are a kid with the most!" (Tatum, 1999, p. 33–34).

Tatum takes a healthy matter-of-fact approach to talking about race with her child. Another example could be a Black child asking why White people bruise and Black people do not. A parent may explain to the child that Black people do bruise, but because of the melanin in Black skin, bruises do not show up as well on those with darker complexions. Yet not all parents have the forethought or skill set to hold a conversation like this with their children because as Americans we have been conditioned that talk about race is taboo.

Early childhood researchers have been gauging the racial attitudes of children for almost a century, beginning with Mary Goodman in the 1930s (Goodman, 1952). Dr. Kenneth Clark used the Black Doll/White Doll test in the *Brown v. Topeka Board of Education* case to demonstrate that African American children had internalized negative feelings about their racial identity and the relationship of that identity to systems and institutions. Kiri Davis, a young African American film major in New York, readministered the doll test in 2007 to see if children's racial attitudes have been influenced by the progressive advancement and positive images made by African Americans, which also addresses the prevailing social belief in a postracial America. CNN personality Anderson Cooper did a version of the doll test with pictures on a laminated sheet. He included White, Black, and biracial children. Unfortunately, in all of the experiments, the results were similar. Black and White children assigned negative characteristics to the Black doll/picture and positive attributes to the White doll (Davis, 2007).

Without any interruption or correction, these early preferences get reinforced and hardwired in the way that we have come to see and understand race. Tatum's graduate student

> . . . asked . . . three- and four-year-olds to draw a picture of a Native American [and they had difficulty]. . . . When she rephrased the question and asked them to draw a picture of an Indian . . . Almost every picture included one central feature: feathers. . . . Many also included a weapon—a knife or tomahawk—and depicted the person in violent or aggressive terms (Tatum, 1999, p. 4).

Some of these children with biases eventually become teachers, social workers, doctors, nurses, police officers, judges, reporters, and other deliverers of services and information. The question becomes, what happens when the image and appearance of that doll or a Native American is now a client, a student, a patient, a suspect? How do we act on our preferences? How does that early internalized preference or implicit bias impact the decisions that we are going to make? How do we acknowledge and make the teacher aware of their own racial identity and the race of the people they are serving? When we suppress or deny that implicit bias is there, we fail to act in a culturally responsive manner and we increase that bias. For decades, the colorblind campaign told us it was not okay to notice color and race. To effectively and morally serve our children, we must recognize our deepseated internal bias and work to build an awareness of that bias so we and others can interrupt it for the success of children.

In North Carolina, the model court bench card helps judges acknowledge implicit bias and makes race visible in the courtroom. An excerpt from this bench card is shown here.

In the following case example, Judge Trosch, a district court judge in Charlotte, North Carolina, explains how implicit bias can result in disparities, justifying the need for a tool to address the impact of this bias.

PRELIMINARY PROTECTIVE HEARING BENCH CARD

Reflections on the Decision-Making Process that Protect Against Institutional Bias

Ask yourself, as a judge:

What assumptions have I made about the cultural identity, genders, and background of this family?

What is my understanding of this family's unique culture and circumstances?

How is my decision specific to this child and this family?

How has the court's past contact and involvement with this family influenced (or how might it influence) my decision-making process and findings?

What evidence has supported every conclusion I have drawn, and how have I challenged unsupported assumptions?

Am I convinced that reasonable efforts (or active efforts in Indian Child Welfare Act [ICWA] cases) have been made in an individualized way to match the needs of the family?

Am I considering relatives as preferred placement options as long as they can protect the child and support the permanency plan? (Excerpt from National Council of Juvenile and Family Court Judges, 2013).

CASE EXAMPLE: JOHN AND SAM

I was presiding in Juvenile Delinquency Court conducting Detention and First Appearance Hearings. In North Carolina, all juveniles charged with felony offenses must come to court immediately after being charged to be apprised of their charges and legal rights, to inform their parents of expectations for guardians in juvenile court, and to determine whether they should be detained or released to their parents. Depending on the severity of the offense and the juvenile's past delinquency history, they may or may not already be detained. That determination is made based on recommendations from arresting officers and juvenile court counselors (JCC) at the time the juvenile is charged. If the JCC believes the juvenile meets the criteria for detention and is a danger to the community, they seek a secured custody order from a judge, which then allows the juvenile to be arrested and detained pending his/her first appearance. On this particular day, there were a number of juveniles on the first appearance docket with a wide variety of charges. Some were already in detention while others remained home with their families. I began plowing through my cases.

About midway through my afternoon hearings, I called the first of two co-defendants charged with armed robbery. The juvenile came in what I sometimes call door number 2, meaning the bailiffs brought him into the court room from a holding cell. The juvenile was in shackles and had been in custody since he was charged a day earlier. Frankly, I expected him to be in detention, since armed robberies are among the most serious offenses we see in juvenile court. Almost all juveniles charged with this offense are detained at their first appearance. Many remain in detention until their cases are adjudicated and disposed. Others are released at some point prior to adjudication, with very restrictive conditions of release. For example, they might be placed on house arrest with an electronic monitor or released on a very strict supervision plan called the ATD or Alternative to Detention Program. As expected, the young man came into court with the deputies, while his family filed into the courtroom from the lobby. He had a huge number of family and friends supporting him, many more than I usually see. His parents were present, along with aunts, uncles, and grandparents. In addition, his youth pastor was there to speak on the juvenile's behalf. It turns out that the juvenile and his co-defendant "planned," and I use that term loosely, the crime after watching *Oceans 11* or some other heist movie. At any rate, they decided they would conduct their own heist at a local fast food restaurant. They entered with matching Scream Masks on their faces, each of them carrying handguns. Well they turned out to be pellet guns, but they looked like real weapons. It turns out that they were horrible criminals. Both were caught almost immediately and charged. Co-defendant 1, I will call him John, had no delinquent record, was an average student at school, had never been suspended from or expelled from school, had a tremendous family support system, and was extremely active in positive activities in his church. In balancing safety to the community with the strengths of the juvenile and the many positive supports in his life, I recommended an assessment to determine if ATD or other conditions would be appropriate and scheduled a detention hearing four days later. I fully anticipated that the juvenile would be deemed appropriate for our ATD program and released at his next hearing.

Following "John's" hearing I called in his co-defendant, who I will refer to as Sam. When I called in the case, again a huge contingent of family and supporters came into Court on behalf of Sam. Rather than a pastor, a coach from the juvenile's school appeared to attest to his good character. Meanwhile, my bailiff stood in the courtroom next to the holding cell door. After a few moments, I reminded him that we needed the juvenile to be brought into the court room from the holding cell. He said, "Judge we don't have any more juveniles in the back. I think that's the young man you want right there." At that he pointed to a young man in the courtroom, who had come in with the rest of the family. His lawyer agreed that this was "Sam" and ushered him to the defendant's table. The remainder of the hearing was much the same. I found out that Sam had no delinquent record, was an average student at school, had never been suspended from or expelled from school, had a tremendous family support system, and was extremely active in positive activities with his sports team. I also found out that Sam and John had been best friends since first grade, that they lived one street over from one another, and that their families were also friendly with one another. Oddly, no one in my court room (defense attorneys, DAs, JCCs, or anyone else) raised the elephant in the room, namely that John was in detention and Sam was home with his family. So I asked what led to this difference and couldn't find any factor, save one. Besides their very similar backgrounds, both had weapons during the robbery, both participated actively during the crime, and both planned their heist together. The fact that the reader, along with everyone in every audience to whom I've relayed this story, knows that the difference involves race and that John is African American and Sam is White pretty much sums up how implicit bias continues to play a role in our justice system. From my knowledge of those involved, I do not believe that in this case there was any intention to treat these two young men differently, but implicit bias is insidious and leads to many disparities. (Judge Louis A. Trosch, personal communication, July 9, 2013)

Institutions as Barriers

People of color, particularly African Americans, are more likely to experience disparate outcomes at most every point of contact. The child welfare system bears similar racial disparities as does the banking and finance system. There are decades of studies and research that confirm judicial and criminal justice systems are overwhelmed by the disproportionate correlation that people of color have compared to their White counterparts in concurring conditions.

> The desperate conditions created by urban poverty have ensured a constant flow of disordered or self-destructive Black patients to emergency rooms staffed by White and foreign born physicians who draw their own conclusions about racial character. . . . Constant exposure to the self-destructive behaviors indulged in by what appear to be disproportionate numbers of an ethnic group can have a devastating effect on how doctors feel about such people: The patients were there either because they abused drugs, or had an illness like diabetes that they wouldn't take care of, or were alcoholic, or had gotten beaten on the head while they were robbing a store. Almost all of them had self-inflicted illness. It's very hard to get real sympathetic with people who make themselves sick (Hoberman, 2012, pp. 21–22).

This scenario is mimicked in education when we place new, inexperienced teachers in highly impacted schools of color, where they, too, are experiencing a constant flow of chronically disorganized or self-destructive parents, students, and community members that shape their racial imagination. This racial imagination spills over and impacts instructional and educational decisions and expectations. Teachers of color are not immune from this racial imagination. They interpret the world from many of the same perspectives as White teachers. Their racial imagination has been shaped from a similar assessment of the world around them

Law enforcement officers have a comparable experience. Zero tolerance philosophy armed many of our schools with school resource officers that, like Dr. Hoberman's description, are often placed in high poverty, low performing schools and communities where they experience the constant flow. Ron Chisom, founder of the People's Institute for Survival and Beyond, is the community architect of a nationally known training workshop, called *Undoing Racism*. Chisom says when we are employing people who are or who are going to be working with people/communities of color and we provide training and skills, but those skills do not include an understanding of race, history, and culture, then those employees are simply becoming more skillful racists—not in the malicious conscious sense. But they are becoming more skillful at establishing, maintaining, and sustaining the racial inequities of their system.

What is missing from the medical residents, well-meaning teachers, and colorblind school resource officers is an examination of the root causes of the broken infrastructure, the impact that decades of divestment and disempowerment have had in creating the dysfunction that they are witnessing. The concept of race and its political and historical sensitivities make talking about the achievement gap rare and problematic. Historically, in our Americanized system of education, local education agencies have experienced a similar crisis—failure to achieve positive consistent educational results for Black students, primarily, as well as for other students of color. These school systems have recycled a plethora of programs from literacy to behavior modification with inconsistent results and unreliable evaluations. Some districts have had extensive financial resources, materials, supplies, and technology and others have not, yet the racial inequities persist.

Educational successes and failures are measured through examining overall achievement, advance placement/gifted/honors, SAT/ACT, special education/exceptional children, and suspensions/discipline. White is on top in regards to educational outcomes, and Black is at the polar extreme. Other peoples of color may shift in some order throughout the years depending on what political or social shifts we may be experiencing. For example, Mexicans and Asians were considered White until the Supreme Court decided White was whatever the common White man said it was. In *U.S. v. Bhagat Singh Thind*, the Supreme Court (261 U.S. 204, 1923) stated,

> The words of the statute are to be interpreted in accordance with the understanding of the common man from whose vocabulary they were taken. . . . What we now hold is that the words "free White persons" are words of common speech, to be interpreted in accordance with the understanding of the common man, synonymous with the word "Caucasian" only as that word is popularly understood. As so understood and used, whatever may be the speculations of the ethnologist, it does not include the body of people to whom the appellee belongs (261 U.S. 204, 215).

Other races of people are able to shift; however, the arrangement of Black and White stays constant: Slavery, *Dred Scott v. Sanford* (1857)— Blacks are property and are not U.S. citizens and could not be considered free to become citizens; *Brown vs. Topeka Board of Education* (1954)—separate schools are not equal and are detrimental to the well-being of Black children. *Fisher v. University of Texas at Austin* (2012) was a case where the plaintiff challenged any consideration of race in the admissions process. The case operated under the assumption that the system fairly and equitably incorporates a consideration of race in admissions decisions that excludes Whites. White and Black represent the bookends/anchors of the race arrangement in our society; their positions are fixed and seemingly unchangeable under the current racial arrangement.

CHANGING MACROSYSTEMS: CURRENTLY USING PRACTICES AND PREVENTIVE SYSTEMS EFFORTS TO ADDRESS DISPROPORTIONALITY AND DISPARITIES

Educators operate in the macrosystem of Americanized schooling. The national debate around public education is an all too familiar one around the failure of schools to prepare students for the jobs of tomorrow. Currently, our schools do not prepare a majority of students to think creatively, to reason, nor to work productively in a group. The No Child Left Behind Act's focus on achievement has come at the cost of teacher flexibility in the learning environment. School administrators conduct walk-throughs with teams of staff members who leave teachers with notes on how they should improve or berate them for not sticking to the district-adopted scope and sequence. State boards of education are run by White male or upper- to middle-class politicians with no knowledge of or passion for developing an equitable system.

> In 1989, Terry Cross, Executive Director of the National Indian Child Welfare Association, in Portland, Oregon, published a monograph. . . . *Toward a Culturally Competent System of Care* provides several tools for addressing the responses to diversity . . . that many of us encounter in the public school system. Mr. Cross's work focused on mental healthcare; however, his framework . . . has been the basis of a major shift in responding to difference in preK–12 schools, universities, social services. Cultural Proficiency is an approach for responding to the environment shaped by its diversity and provides four tools for a person to develop their own Cultural Proficiency:

- *The Guiding Principles*: Underlying core values of the approach
- *The Continuum*: Language for describing individual values and behaviors and organizational policies and practices
- *The Barriers*: Caveats that assist in responding effectively to forces that undermine Cultural Proficiency
- *The Essential Elements*: Behavioral standards for measuring and planning for growth toward Cultural Proficiency (Nuri-Robins, Lindsey, Lindsey, & Terrell, 2012, p. 3–4)

Although Cross's work has been adapted to educational language, cultural proficiency as a concept has yet to be embraced by the Americanized system of education. Even as the data stares them in the face, educators rationalize that the children lack this, the parents do not support that, and the blame cycle continues. What is working? What programs are making a difference in the community to reduce disproportionality and disparities in the education system? If *working* is the operative term, we would say no programs or policies are working because the data still reflects overwhelming disproportionality for Black and brown children in discipline, special education, and a lack of enrollment in advanced academics.

What we do in the Americanized educational system really impacts the community's ability to participate in the school system as a partner. Education is a system that chronically produces patterned disparities for vulnerable (economically, disabled, etc.) populations. We find in our work with schools and the community that we as adults need to be willing to practice. When we truly make an effort to engage students in learning, what happens at school changes what happens at home. When children, their parents, and their grandparents have a negative educational experience, barriers to collaboration abound. In communities served by public schools across America, there is a deep-seated, historical tension and distrust of the schools by the communities they serve. That distrust and skepticism leaves the field wide open for programs where the district partners with the community to address disproportionality and disparities.

We do believe that every person who makes the commitment to work in the education system has good intentions and has the best interest of children at heart. We also have to be willing to look at ourselves as "at risk" for unconsciously making racially based decisions. The at-risk teacher, counselor, or school resource officer (SRO) who goes through their daily work without ever considering the fact that their entire background and existence is with the White race is at risk of stereotyping and pigeonholing children of color into a box they are conditioned to see. Because the adults are at risk in the education system, programs are not the answer. Ongoing opportunities for professional learning for educators that include community members with focus on personal perspectives and perspectives of others meet the need no program can address. Programs perpetuate the cycle that allows institutional racism to exist unchecked. Programs set the stage for microaggressions to infiltrate the daily life of students at school and school-sponsored events. Community members see through the programs as tools to perpetuate the cycle of disparity that is disenfranchising them.

Eliminating disproportionality and disparities goes well beyond test preparation, tutoring, and mentoring children. Educators must make a long-time commitment to invest in their personal professional learning. Professional learning necessary for the elimination of disproportionality and disparities requires an examination of personal bias, values, and beliefs by each person in the system.

SPOTLIGHT: PROMISING PRACTICES TO ADDRESS DISPROPORTIONALITY
IN THE EDUCATION SYSTEM

Examining the discipline data and revising policies to eliminate the school-to-prison pipeline

Providing antiracist professional learning opportunities for all preservice and current educators

Focusing on early childhood education to give each child a good start

Partnering with child welfare, juvenile justice, police, and other institutions with a vested interest in positive student outcomes

Adopting a focus on culturally responsive teaching and leading

Partnering with and promoting Communities in Schools programs

Adopting a focus on social emotional learning

Partnering with the Anti-Defamation League for the No Place for Hate® Campaign

Preparing healthy food and teaching children how to make healthy choices outside of school

Efforts are being made in the Austin Independent School District to study its history and change the way school business is done for the success of the students and families. In 2010, former Superintendent Meria Carstarphen called for an internal council to devise a plan to reduce disproportionality in Special Education and discipline referrals. She also charged her staff to develop and offer antiracist professional learning opportunities and participated in those activities (M. Carstarphen, personal communication, November 28, 2012).

The Cultural Proficiency and Inclusiveness focus aims to assist staff understanding of ". . . how to interact with students and their families in a manner that considers the diverse needs of all" (Ward, 2012). The district has begun to formulate discussion protocols and professional learning opportunities in collaboration with local universities, and community and state level partners using the Cultural Proficiency Framework as a guide (see Figure 9.1). Campus staff engage in a detailed analysis of academic, discipline, and special education data that reveals biased and racialized data created each year. Staff then develop strategies to eliminate the disproportion they notice in their campus data. The Austin Independent School District (Texas) is focusing on the fact that it takes each adult in the system to first recognize who they are, that is, through what lens they view the world and their place in the world. Before schools in our Americanized system can make meaningful, lasting change, they first must begin the personal journey that a focus on cultural proficiency evokes.

The National Leading with Diversity Culture Standards ask educators to develop cultural awareness:

1) The teacher develops awareness of his or her own cultural identity, values, attitudes, and biases.
2) The teacher is knowledgeable about the culture of the school and seeks ways to accommodate it to students' needs (Trumbull & Pacheco, 2012).

Through an intense focus on self, small groups of educators can begin to make changes in their workspace beyond what any program can teach or mandate. That change ripples to other workspaces within an organization to effect the change needed to reduce disproportionality and disparities in schools.

The Tools of Cultural Proficiency

The Essential Elements—*Standards for Planning and Evaluating*

- **Assess Culture:** Identify the cultural groups present in the system
- **Value Diversity:** Develop an appreciation for the differences among and between groups
- **Manage the Dynamics of Difference:** Learn to respond appropriately and effectively to the issues that arise in a diverse environment
- **Adapt to Diversity:** Change and adopt new policies and practices that support diversity and inclusion
- **Institutionalize Cultural Knowledge:** Drive the changes into the systems of the organization

Cultural Proficiency Continuum

Change Mandated for Tolerance			Change Chosen for Transformation		
Destruction	Incapacity	Blindness	Precompetence	Competence	Proficiency
Eliminate differences: The elimination of other people's cultures	Demean differences: Belief in the superiority of one's culture and behavior that disempowers another's culture	Dismiss differences: Acting as if the cultural differences you see do not matter or not recognizing that there are differences among and between culture	Respond inadequately to the dynamics of difference: Awareness of the limitations of one's skills or an organization's practices when interacting with other cultural groups	Engage with differences using the essential elements as standards: Using the five essential elements of cultural proficiency as the standard for individual behavior and organizational practices	Esteem and learn from differences as a lifelong practice: Knowing how to learn about and from individual and organizational culture; interacting effectively in a variety of cultural environments. Advocating for others.

Reactive Behaviors, Shaped by the **Barriers**

- Unawareness of the need to adapt
- Resistance to change
- Systems of oppression and privilege
- Sense of entitlement

Proactive Behaviors, Shaped by the **Principles**

- Culture is a predominant force
- People are served in varying degrees by the dominant culture
- There is diversity within and between cultures
- Every group has unique culturally-defined needs
- People have personal identities and group identities
- Marginalized populations have to be at least bicultural
- Families, as defined by culture, are the primary systems of support
- The diverse thought patterns of cultural groups influence how problems are defined and solved
- The absence of cultural competence anywhere is a threat to competent services everywhere

CROSS-SYSTEMS EFFORTS AND CULTURALLY COMPETENT SERVICES OFFERED

People of color represent a considerable segment of the U.S. population, enhancing our society with many unique assets, cultural mores, and important experiences. As a segment of the general population, these groups are growing rapidly; current projections show that by 2025, people of color will account for more than 40% of all Americans.

Unfortunately, the educational system has not kept pace with the diverse needs of all racial and ethnic groups, often underserving or inappropriately serving them. Specifically, the system has failed to incorporate mutual respect or understanding of the histories, experiences, and value systems of culturally diverse groups. Overidentification and disparate decision making have led to disproportionate and harmful consequences, including inaptly placing students of color in the juvenile justice systems' trajectory as evidenced in the Breaking Schools' Rules Report. "Nearly 20% of Whites have used cocaine, compared with 10% of Blacks and Latinos. . . . Higher percentages of Whites have also tried hallucinogens, marijuana, pain relievers like OxyContin, and stimulants like methamphetamine. . . . Crack is more popular among Blacks than Whites, but not by much. . . . Still, Blacks are arrested for drug possession more than three times as often as Whites."

These inequitable patterns and processes produce a steady tributary of students of color to our juvenile and adult criminal justice system. "Almost 60 years after *Brown v. Board of Education* ended legal segregation and sought to provide equal educational opportunities to all races, school discipline may be contributing to a school-to-prison pipeline" (Pressley & Skelton, 2013, p. 1). The school-to-prison pipeline begins in deep social and economic inequalities and has taken root in the historic shortcomings of the American education system. This pipeline is ". . . best avoided in the classroom. . . . A teacher's decision to refer students for punishment can mean they are pushed out of the classroom—and much more likely to be introduced into the criminal justice system" (Elias, 2013, p. 39).

The "zero tolerance" policies that today are the most extreme form of mandatory consequences for certain violations were originally written for the war on drugs in the early 1980s and later applied to schools. "These

SPOTLIGHT: EFFORTS IN THE EDUCATION SYSTEM TO ADDRESS THE
SCHOOL-TO-PRISON PIPELINE IN GUILFORD COUNTY, NORTH CAROLINA

Having conversations about race with the community and cross systems

Disaggregating data by race, gender, and offense and looking at patterns and
trajectories.

Implementing an initiative entitled "Achieving Educational Excellence for African
American Males" that focuses on creating systems change through professional
learning in the areas of implicit bias and antiracism

Focusing on literacy and the reduction of suspensions in antiracist school-based
training and professional learning

policies called for mandatory punishment—regardless of accidental mistakes or individual circumstances—for drug use or possession, or weapons
on campus. . . . Over the years, zero tolerance has expanded to include lesser
offenses, such as shoving, disruption of classes, or using profanity" (Pressley & Skelton, 2013, p. 2). As Annette Fuentes (2013), author of *Lockdown
High: When the Schoolhouse Becomes a Jailhouse*, explains, the resulting
extraordinary rates of suspension and expulsion are linked nationally to
increasing police presence, checkpoints, and surveillance inside schools.

As police have set up shop in schools across the country, the definition
of what constitutes a crime as opposed to a teachable moment has changed
in extraordinary ways. In one middle school, a teacher routinely allowed
her students to take single pieces of candy from a big container she kept
on her desk. One day, several girls grabbed handfuls. The teacher promptly
sent them to the police officer assigned to the school. What formerly would
have been an opportunity to have a conversation about a minor transgres-
sion instead became a law enforcement issue.

Children are being branded as criminals at ever-younger ages. *Zero
Tolerance in Philadelphia*, a recent report by Youth United for Change
and the Advancement Project (2011), offers an example:

Robert was an 11-year-old in 5th grade who, in his rush to get to school
on time, put on a dirty pair of pants from the laundry basket. He did not

notice that his Boy Scout pocketknife was in one of the pockets until he got to school. He also did not notice that it fell out when he was running in gym class. When the teacher found it and asked whom it belonged to, Robert volunteered that it was his, only to find himself in police custody minutes later. He was arrested, suspended, and transferred to a disciplinary school (p. 8).

Harsher and racially unequal judicial decisions follow youth into their adult life. One might conclude that the teacher did not have a relationship with Robert due to the consequence that was chosen. Zero Tolerance for a knife must include a thorough review of a preponderance of the evidence. Culturally competent practice requires the juvenile courts to ask about the child's history and to determine if they were ever given a chance to explain or at least given the benefit of the doubt and provided a less harsh consequence by the school. A culturally competent response to eliminate the school-to-prison pipeline requires educators to consistently engage in courageous conversation that checks implicit bias and holds them accountable for their decisions. Educators engage in these conversations with adults from multiple systems, parents, and families of students—for without hearing those perspectives, educators maintain the status quo.

> Even as we recognize that individuals make choices that influence the character of their lives, we must also recognize that the range of choices available is profoundly constrained and shaped by external forces. For this reason, efforts to counter behaviors that are viewed as injurious— whether it be dropping out of school, selling drugs, or engaging in violent behavior—must include efforts to comprehend the logic and motivations behind the behavior. Given the importance of agency and choice, the only way to change behavioral outcomes is to understand the cognitive processes that influence how individuals adapt, cope, and respond (Noguera, 2008, p. 26).

Whites do not experience institutional barriers similar to the obstacles experienced by Blacks. In fact, even Whites with criminal records received more favorable treatment (17%) than Blacks without criminal records (14%) when it comes to employment (Pager, 2003). Students with convictions face barriers to higher education opportunities to employment possibilities, and to securing housing.

In *The New Jim Crow*, Michelle Alexander reports that the United States has the highest rate of incarceration in the world. She goes on to say, in Germany, 93 people are in prison for every 100,000 adults and children compared to 750 for every 100,000 in the U.S. The United States imprisons a larger percentage of its Black population than South Africa did at the height of apartheid. In Washington, D.C., it is estimated that three out of four young Black men (and nearly all those in the poorest neighborhoods) can be expected to serve time in prison (Alexander, 2012, p. 6–7).

Multiple initiatives and programs aimed at improving the services, experiences, and outcomes for students of color have been implemented

CASE EXAMPLE: CROSS-SYSTEMS COLLABORATION

After years of antiracism training, Guilford County Department of Social Services, in collaboration with Dr. Grier's work in the education system, prioritized disproportionality. Posters, conversations, videos, and trainings focused on making key staff and stakeholders aware of the overrepresentation of children and families of color in the child welfare system. They began the disproportionality task by examining portals of entry and contact points by race. At the time, nearly 850 children were in Department of Social Service (DSS) custody. Their first step was to chart their data by race and referral system. The results showed that the school system was the largest mandatory reporter for Black children being referred for neglect or abuse calls. White children were being referred by human service personnel or anonymous, and law enforcement appeared on the chart in the Latino entries. After several presentations, conversations, and racial equity training, school system personnel shared their hesitation in calling Black families when they had concerns about neglect or abuse, and as a result they more often would refer the concern to DSS. This cross-systems analysis and conversation has been a part of several initiatives aimed at reducing disproportionality, which has resulted in the number of children in care dropping below 300.

and resourced yet the results are staggeringly lamentable and significant barriers still remain in access, quality, and outcomes of health care for minorities. As a result, American Indians, Alaska Natives, African Americans, and Latino Americans bear a disproportionate burden. This higher number does not arise from a greater prevalence or severity of illnesses in these populations. Rather it stems from receiving less care and poorer quality of care.

FUTURE DIRECTIONS

If we are to talk about race in education and cross systems, we must address the popular sociopolitical belief that we are now in a post-racial America. When the Supreme Court of the United States (SCOTUS) struck down section 3 of the 1996 Defense of Marriage Act (DOMA) extending federal benefits to same sex couples, in the same week the court invalidated the section 5 preclearance requirement of the Voting Rights Act in *Shelby County Alabama, 2012 v. Eric Holder*. The Shelby County case set in motion the ability for many southern states to enact voter identification laws that suppress the vote for all people of color, women, and young people. With the decision, states do not have to prove that changes to their voting rights laws are nondiscriminatory; they are given carte blanche to enact them at will. With regard to DOMA, if race is not part of the advocacy intervention or initiative, then what is the outcome and what happens to people of color within the gay, lesbian, bisexual, and transgender (GLBT) community? If the issue of marriage equality is about the oppression of people, then the GLBT community would also speak to what is happening with the Voting Rights Act and not separate the two issues. The SCOTUS decision took three steps back on voting equality and one step forward for marriage equality. It seems contradictory for the SCOTUS to allow more rights but to suppress voting rights that allowed new marriage rights to even be considered. SCOTUS has bought in to the post-racial America that does not require checks and balances to make sure that states that historically suppressed the Black vote do not continue to do so.

If we recognize that the SCOTUS rulings mentioned here have a different impact on people based on their race, we have to consider that we do not live in a post-racial America; therefore, we must focus on race in our schools. Educational outcomes are not based on sexual orientation but on race. A post-racial America will see institutions and multimillion dollar corporations led by people of color. The Obama Administration stimulus of $800 billion has built more White wealth because, when the last stimulus occurred, the New Deal was already in place. The civil rights movement did nothing to address the existing wealth disparity so each stimulus continues to build financially sound White families. We have not come very far at all with regard to concrete tangible assets that have an effect on the quality of life for people. An example of this is the American Recovery Reinvestment Act—American Recovery Capital (ARC). The Obama Administration does not report the racial breakdown of who is benefiting from these loans, but data obtained by New America Media (NAM) from the Small Business Administration (SBA) found that of the 4,497 ARC loans where the race of the borrower was reported, 4,104 (more than 91%) went to White-owned firms, 140 (3%) went to [Latino]-owned businesses, and 151 (3%) went to Asian- or Pacific Islander-owned businesses. Only 65 (1.5%) went to Black-owned firms (Glantz, 2009).

True indicators of progress toward a post-racial America will see churches with mixed audiences and a stark reduction in the disproportionate rate of underachievement in schools and in the incarceration of Black males. Because American society holds to the belief that we live in a post-racial America, we are worse off outcome wise. Young people have no language for racial disparities; they are ill-equipped to see how racial disparity plays out, and how the disparities are truly evident in our systems. They are not coming together across racial lines as done in the past. Instead they hang out in common venues, listen to rap music together, shop together, and enjoy each other's company—but only superficially. They do not understand how the SCOTUS rulings affect their rights as people—as young Americans—and they do not know that they should be concerned based on their race.

According to the Center for Public Education (2012), the face of our nation is changing, and nowhere is the change more evident than in Americanized classrooms. Just consider this—compared with the last century, we are increasingly aging and White on the one hand and young and multihued on the other. These changing demographics create a number of challenges for public schools, most markedly:

- The need for educators who understand the historical foundations of race in the United States
- The expertise in early childhood pedagogy and in maintaining the gains made in early childhood programs
- The practice of disaggregating data by race and gender regarding dropout rates, test scores, advanced/honors placement, suspensions/discipline, graduation rates, and college entrance rates and comparing that data to the race and gender of the teaching staff at each campus
- The need for organizing with families and communities of color (collective capacity building)
- The need to be equipped with culturally relevant curricular material and resources (to also understand how to utilize the resources in the context of student self-efficacy and recognizing personal bias and cultural clashes adult to student)
- The need for effective bilingual educators who understand that all students are learning academic English

To this list we would also add:

- The need for culturally responsive adults who recognize their personal bias and values and who also understand that their beliefs can hinder the progress of children of color

Although our schools reflect changing racial and ethnic demographics, our practices, procedures, protocols, and structures have remained the same. School culture is framed and shaped by European culture and orientations. The systems and institutions of today grew from a time of Whites-only citizenship and access. School culture is Americanized White culture, and schools have a fundamental arrangement that was derived from the cultural experience of European Americans. The rules, the perspectives, the practices, and the values are rooted in that reality. School personnel historically and currently are White and female, so female European culture frames and shapes other aspects of school culture, namely behavior in regards to compliance, efficiency, and organization. White females are able to access both the European culture and the female culture for their educational experience. The design is germane, the curriculum is affirming and relevant, the rules are familiar; White females are having the best outcomes in our Americanized educational institutions as a collective. White males are able to access the European culture for their Americanized educational experience, and their behavior does not match the negative consequences of males of color. They are having the second best outcomes, collectively, in our educational institutions. Females of color are more apt to yield to the demands of European culture to fit in, and if they can comply with the rules, are collectively in third place in regards to educational outcomes. Males of color, unable to see their culture reflected academically or behaviorally, struggle to dodge the opposing environment. Often we ask students of color to conform, to assimilate, to abandon their culture to succeed in the Americanized school culture. "The key to making good decisions [for the children in our public school system] is to develop an awareness of the important values of school and home cultures so as to avoid putting students in the position of choosing one system over the other" (Rothstein-Fisch & Trumbull, 2008, p. xix).

Why should we change the system to eliminate disproportionality? We liken the answer to the river story (Rocky Mountain Conference of the United Methodist Church, 2013).

THE RIVER STORY

Once upon a time, there was a small village on the edge of a river. The people there were good and life in the village was good. One day a villager noticed a baby floating down the river. The villager quickly swam out to save the baby from drowning. The next day this same villager noticed two babies in the river. He called for help, and both babies were rescued from the swift waters. And the following day four babies were seen caught in the turbulent current. And then eight, then more, and still more!

The villagers organized themselves quickly, setting up watchtowers and training teams of swimmers who could resist the swift waters and rescue babies. Rescue squads were soon working 24 hours a day. And each day the number of helpless babies floating down the river increased. The villagers organized themselves efficiently. The rescue squads were now snatching many children each day. While not all the babies, now very numerous, could be saved, the villagers felt they were doing well to save as many as they could each day. Indeed, the village priest blessed them in their good work. And life in the village continued on that basis.

One day, however, someone raised the question, "But where are all these babies coming from? Let's organize a team to head upstream to find out who's throwing all of these babies into the river in the first place!"

The seeming logic of the community elders countered: "And if we go upstream who will operate the rescue operations? We need every concerned person here!" "But don't you see," cried the one lone voice, "if we find out who is throwing them in, we can stop the problem and no babies will drown! By going upstream we can eliminate the cause of the problem!" "It is too risky," said the village elders. And so the numbers of babies found floating in the river increase daily. Those saved, but those who drown increase even more.

Clearly, we need to do our part in rescuing those babies found floating down the river. But we also need to take the risk of raising our voices and asking why they're being thrown into the river and what we can do about it!

The education system and the juvenile justice system continue to throw the babies in the water and social services pulls them out. Why should the people who seem to be on the receiving end of these inequitable systems want it to change? In the community, White women and children are not doing well at all; their children are not faring well globally. Education is way below par for White children on a global scale. If we make the disproportion clear across racial lines, then everyone will find a vested interest in focusing on the elimination of disproportionality and disparities. Cross-systems work requires that we focus on advocacy, not just for individual clients but for many clients. Each system must simultaneously translate cases with many common denominators into the larger public conversation. The river story calls for us to look for the root cause of circumstances mobilizing within the institution. Educators must find those common denominators in our respective systems to bring community organizing into the larger system by engaging the adults in deeper analysis. Collective change has to occur.

To eliminate disproportionality and disparitites in the education system we must begin with the adults. Schools no longer focus on professional learning because they are so overwhelmed with tests and accountability measures. Based on what we know about why our education system was formed, we have to refocus the adults on the whole child. Doing so means we have to create the opportunity for educators to critically self-reflect on the images they have in their heads. Educators (i.e., teachers, teachers aides, athletic and academic coaches, tutors, cafeteria staff, custodians, bus drivers, counselors, vice principals, principals, superintendents, etc.) must examine their background, bias, and beliefs. They must examine how their personal preferences impact decisions, interactions, and thoughts about the children and families they serve. We propose an educator's "bench" card, building from the work done by the juvenile justice system, to facilitate this process.

Finally, concluding recommendations for addressing disproportionality and disparities in the education system are provided in the following section.

EDUCATOR'S BENCH CARD

Based on how I identify personally (race, culture, gender, socioeconomic class . . .):

What assumptions have I made about this student's racial, cultural, gender, socio-economic class, identities, and background?

What evidence has supported every conclusion I have drawn?

How have I challenged my unsupported assumptions?

What is my understanding of this student's unique culture and circumstances?

What decisions do I make on a daily basis about this student that might be limiting and/or discouraging this student's participation in the classroom?

Are there persons on this staff with whom I feel comfortable to help me increase my efficacy with this student?

How related is the material I am using in my classroom to this student's culture, experiences, interests?

What strategies/changes might I employ to improve my ability to ensure success for this student? (Adapted from the Educator's Equity Lens Checklist, developed by Monica Walker [2012], Guilford County Schools, Diversity Office.)

- *Start with the leaders of educational systems.* Systemic change in a system as complex as the educational system must begin with the Superintendent, cabinet, and principals. Without buy-in, vision, and focus from this group of key and influential decision makers, the district will not make change.
- *Insist on critical self-reflection about institutional racism.* As stated in the Leading with Diversity Culture Standards, critical self-reflection requires adults to develop a personal awareness of cultural identity, values, attitudes, and biases—also, to become knowledgeable about the culture of the school and to seek ways to accommodate it to the students' needs (Trumbull & Pacheco, 2012). As adults become self-aware, they are able to check their bias in relation to work with students and their families. Checking personal bias is a key step in critical self-reflection about institutional racism. Explore White as a racial identity and how it shows up in the classroom. Acknowledge that a colorblind educator creates disproportionate outcomes for children of color in their care. Acknowledge all the identities each of us hold—for example, race, ethnicity, gender, sexual orientation, and national origin, to name a few. In acknowledging these identities and critically self-reflecting on them, the White educator begins to explore White as a racial identity.
- *Include families and the community in the exploration.* To eliminate the educator's tendency to maintain the status quo, we must invite parents and members of the community into our conversations regarding the elimination of disproportionality and disparities.
- *Conduct equity audits of academic, discipline, and special education data.* Become critical lovers of your school system. Review the data with a focus toward creating an equitable system for children in your care. Require educators to point out and problem-solve ways to eliminate glaring disparities in academics, discipline, and special education.
- *Control data for race, gender, and socioeconomic status.* Race is a factor in the elimination of disproportionality and disparities. No Child Left Behind holds educators accountable by race; therefore, we must review the data first by race, then add other key identities to the review. Only by exploring data through the intersection of identities will we begin to make true change and address disproportion and disparities.

- *Understand the current and historical impact of race on education.* Stay current on and gain a personal and collective understanding of issues of race in American society. National, state, and local issues of race drive the changes in the educational system. Incorporate into professional learning sessions historical and current events relevant to the critical self-reflection of educators.
- *Invest in early childhood.* Hold your school boards and state governments accountable for the funding of early childhood education. Every child, no matter their socioeconomic status or race, deserves a strong start to their education. Also honor the home language and encourage English as a second language rather than the only language.
- *Invest in the professional growth of school staff.* Budget funds and set aside days in the yearly school calendar for all staff to engage in antiracist professional learning. Support the professional growth to build the capacity of central administration staff to conduct antiracist professional learning.

REFERENCES

Acosta, T. P. (2012, October 27). *Texas State Historical Association. Edgewood ISD V. Kirby.* Retrieved from Handbook of Texas Online: http://www.tshaonline. org/handbook/online/articles/jreo2

African American Policy Forum. (2012, October 21). *The unequal race.* Retrieved from You Tube: http://www.youtube.com/watch?v=SFG_VviFnCo

Alexander, M. (2012). *The new Jim Crow: Mass incarceration in the age of colorblindness.* New York: New Press.

Bronson, P., & Merryman, A. (2009). *Nurtureshock: New thinking about children.* New York: Twelve.

Center for Public Education. (2012). *The United States of education: The changing demographics of the United States and their schools.* Alexandria, VA: Author.

Council of State Governments Justice Center in Partnership with the Public Policy Research Institute at Texas A&M University. (2011). *Breaking schools' rules: A statewide study of how school discipline relates to students' success and juvenile justice involvement.* New York: Council of State Governments Justice Center.

Davis, Kiri. (2007). *A girl like me.* Retrieved from http://www.understandingrace. org/lived/video/

Delpit, L. (2012). *Multiplication is for white people: Raising expectations for other people's children.* New York: New Press.

Elias, M. (2013). The school-to-prison pipeline. *Teaching Tolerance, 43,* 39–40.

Frey, W. H. (2011, Feb. 7). A demographic tipping point among America's three-year-olds. *State of Metropolitan America* [Web editorial], The Brookings Institution. Retrieved from http://www.brookings.edu/research/opinions/ 2011/02/07-population-frey

Fuentes, A. (2013). *Lockdown high: When the schoolhouse becomes a jailhouse.* Brooklyn, NY: Verso.

Gilliam, W. S. (2005). *Prekindergarteners left behind: Expulsion rates in state pre-kindergarten programs* (Foundation for Child Development Policy Brief Series No. 3). Retrieved from: http://www.fcd-us.org/usr_doc/ExpulsionComplete Report.pdf.

Glantz, A. (2009, December 17). *Minority businesses shut out of stimulus loans.* Retrieved from http://news.newamericamedia.org/news/view_article.html?article_ id=d40e83db3ee2eb66d27effb8a50ac34f

Goodman, M. (1952). *Race awareness in young children.* Addison-Wesley.

Hayward, C. C. (2010, October 29). Closing the learning gap once and for all. *Education Update, 52.* (ASCD, Ed.) Alexandria, Virginia, United States. Retrieved from http://www.ascd.org/publications/newsletters/education-update/oct10/ vol52/num10/Closing-the-Learning-Gap-Once-and-For-All.aspx

Hoberman, J. (2012). *Black and blue: The origins and consequences of medical racism.* Berkeley: University of California Press.

Lee, E., Menkart, D., & Okazawa-Rey, M. (Eds.). (2008). *Beyond heroes and holidays: A practical guide to K–12 anti-racist, multicultural education and staff development.* Washington, DC: Teaching For Change.

McIntosh, P. (1988). *White privilege and male privilege: A personal account of coming to see correspondences through work in women's studies.* Wellesley, MA: Wellesley College.

Moynihan, D. P. (1970). The Negro family. In P. I. Rose (Ed.), *Slavery and its aftermath* (pp. 357–416). Atherton Press.

National Council of Juvenile and Family Court Judges. (2013, November 17). Retrieved from: http://www.ncjfcj.org/resource-library/publications/right-start-courts-catalyzing-change-preliminary-protective-hearing-o

Noguera, P. (2008). *The trouble with black boys: And other reflections on race, equity, and the future of public education.* San Francisco: Jossey-Bass.

Nuri-Robins, K. J., Lindsey, D. B., Lindsey, R. B., & Terrell, R. D. (2012). *Culturally proficient instruction: A guide for people who teach.* Thousand Oaks, CA: Corwin.

Office of Policy Planning and Research, United States Department of Labor. (1965). *The Negro family: The case for national action.* Washington, DC: U.S. Government Printing Office.

Orfield, G., & Lee, C. (2005). *Why segregation matters: Poverty and educational inequality.* Cambridge, MA: The Civil Rights Project Harvard University.

Pager, D. (2003). The mark of a criminal record. *American Journal of Sociology, 108,* 937–975.

Pressley, S., & Skelton, R. (2013, May 06). *"Tough on crime" is now tough on education.* Retrieved from Dallasnews.com, Education: http://www.dallasnews.com/news/education/headlines/20130503-tough-on-crime-is-now-tough-on-education.ece

Robinson, E. (2010). *Disintegration: The splintering of black America.* New York: Doubleday.

Rocky Mountain Conference of the United Methodist Church. (2013, July 7). Retrieved from Church and Society: http://www.rmcumc.org/new/mission-and-ministry/advocacy/48-church-and-society.html

Rothstein-Fisch, C., & Trumbull, E. (2008). *Managing diverse classrooms.* Alexandria, VA: Association for Supervision and Curriculum Development.

Sennett, F. (2004). *400 quotable quotes from the world's leading educators.* Thousand Oaks, CA: Corwin.

Singleton, G. E., & Linton, C. (2006). *Courageous conversations about race.* Thousand Oaks, CA: Corwin.

Tatum, B. D. (1999). *Why are all the black kids sitting together in the cafeteria?* New York: Basic.

Texas Education Agency, Division of Research and Analysis. (2011). *Enrollment in Texas public schools.* Austin: Texas Education Agency.

Trumbull, E., & Pacheco, M. (2012, October 20). *Leading with diversity cultural competencies.* Retrieved from Education Alliance at Brown University: http://www.brown.edu/academics/education-alliance/publications/leading-diversity-cultural-competencies-teacher-preparation-and-professional-development

United States vs. Bhagat Singh Thind, 202. (Supreme Court, February 19, 1923).

Ward, A. (2012, October 27). *Understanding cultural proficiency and inclusiveness.* Retrieved from Austin Independent School District: http://www.austinisd. org/cpi/understanding

Walker, Monica. (2012). Educator's Equity Lens Checklist, Guilford County Schools, Diversity Office, Greensboro, NC.

Youth United for Change and the Advancement Project. (2011). *Zero tolerance in Philadelphia.* Philadelphia: Author.

10

Disproportionality and Disparities in the Mental Health System

▸ *DANIEL C. ROSEN, ORA NAKASH,*
AND MARGARITA ALEGRÍA

DESCRIPTION OF THE SYSTEM AND THE ETHNIC MINORITY POPULATIONS IN THE SYSTEM

MENTAL HEALTH IS RECOGNIZED AS a central determinant of individual well-being, family relationships, and active engagement within society. The consequences of untreated illness are potentially devastating. Successful treatment is predicated upon the existence of a functional delivery system and the capacity to provide these services in a culturally informed context consistent with professional guidelines (American Psychological Association, 2003) and multicultural counseling competencies (Arredondo et al., 1996).

Mental illness impacts all communities across age, race, and ethnicity. Recent epidemiological studies have found that approximately 27% of adults in the United States experience at least one mood disorder, anxiety disorder, impulse control disorder, or substance use disorder each year, and that more than 11% of adults experience serious psychological distress resulting in significant functional impairment (Substance Abuse and Mental Health Services Administration [SAMHSA], 2010).

To address these and other concerns, the mental health service system in the United States relies on four primary groups of providers (U.S. Department of Health and Human Services [USDHHS], 1999): (1) the specialty mental health sector, such as psychologists, social workers, and psychiatrists with specific training related to the assessment and treatment of mental health conditions; (2) the primary care sector, such as family practice physicians, internists, and naturopaths who care for patients' mental health concerns in the context of a broader medical practice; (3) the human service sector, which encompasses professionals who work within social service organizations, the criminal justice system, school-based settings, and religious institutions; and (4) the voluntary support network, largely organized and operated by volunteers who provide self-help groups (e.g., Alcoholics Anonymous) and peer counseling.

Of those adults treated for a mental health problem in 2005, approximately 28% were treated within the specialty mental health sector (including 16% by nonpsychiatrist mental health professionals and 12% by psychiatrists), 23% within the primary care sector, and 8% within the human service sector (SAMHSA, 2008). There is a growing trend for adults and children to receive care for mental health conditions delivered by nonspecialty service providers (e.g., primary care physicians, emergency rooms) (SAMHSA, 2010).

Different levels and types of care are provided within each of these sectors. The setting in which an individual receives care depends on many factors, including his or her severity of symptoms, impairment of functioning, and access to services. Whereas outpatient care at a mental health clinic may be appropriate for someone with a mild mental health condition, those individuals who are actively suicidal or psychotic often require hospitalization within a psychiatric inpatient unit. Individuals are least likely to be treated within residential or inpatient facilities, which serve approximately 7% of those adults who seek mental health services (SAMHSA, 2010).

Another primary distinction within the mental health delivery system is between the public and private sectors. Those government services that are funded by federal and state resources are regarded as "public" and are delivered by organizations such as county hospitals and state mental hospitals. The public sector often serves those who do not have the resources to afford their own care and provides "safety net" resources for those with severe mental health conditions. The term "private sector" refers to services funded through private resources and delivered through private organizations. Cumulatively, spending for the treatment of mental health within the United States is projected to reach $203 billion by 2014, amounting to 6% of all health-care spending (SAMHSA, 2010).

Like all individuals in the United States, ethnic minority groups suffer from mental health conditions that require treatment and seek care across public and private sectors from all provider groups identified. In the general population, less than half of individuals in need of treatment actually receive it (SAMHSA, 2010), and for ethnic minorities the numbers are even more alarming. African Americans, Asian Americans, and Latinos in need of services are all significantly less likely to utilize mental health services in general, and specialty mental health services in particular, compared to Whites. Further, members of ethnic minority groups often delay entry into treatment longer and thus present with more severe conditions (USDHHS, 2001). As a result, racial/ethnic disparities in mental health care have not only surpassed disparities in many areas of health care (Agency for Healthcare Research and Quality [AHRQ], 2008) but have been enduring over time (Blanco et al., 2007).

For the purposes of this chapter, we use the Institute of Medicine (IOM, 2002) disparities definition originally developed for health service disparities. The IOM model posits that racial/ethnic disparities are unfair even if they arise through racial/ethnic differences in socioeconomic status, insurance, or other mechanisms outside of need and preferences. The IOM disparity definition explicitly distinguishes between a difference and a disparity in use of mental health services among ethnic/racial minority populations by stating that a difference is the simple, unadjusted difference in means or rates of use between two racial/ethnic groups such as non-Latino White and Latino counterparts. This difference does not take into account potential differences in need (e.g., diagnoses, chronic conditions, or level of impairment). Differences between racial/ethnic groups in service utilization might be explained by several sets of factors related to need for services (e.g., differences in parental recognition of child's need or divergent pathways into care between groups). However, only the remainder of the identified difference after adjusting for need is defined as the disparity. The distinctive feature of the IOM definition of disparities is that it includes all racial/ethnic differences in service use that are not attributable to need or preferences, including the differences that are attributable to other sociodemographic factors, family factors, or contextual factors (e.g., where a person resides).

UNDERSTANDING THE PROBLEMS AND NEEDS OF ETHNIC MINORITY POPULATIONS IN THE SYSTEM

Disparities in the mental health system experienced by ethnic minority populations have been well documented and include inequities in access to services, quality of services, and outcomes that result from services (USD-HHS, 2001). The needs of ethnic minority populations within the mental health system mirror each of these disparities. As the serious consequences of unmet needs in ethnic/racial minority populations have been identified (e.g., augmented rates of suicidality, incarceration, lost productivity, and premature death), racial and ethnic disparities and disproportionalities in access to quality behavioral health care have received increasing attention. Although the effort to identify and assess disparities continues, there is lack of recognition that behavioral health equity is an issue of social justice and social welfare. Health equity refers to differences in population health that are linked to systematic—and thus avoidable—unequal economic and social conditions, which are inherently unjust and unfair (Centers for Disease Control [CDC], 2007; Whitehead, 1992). Evidence suggests that disparities are mostly compounded by the limited access that minorities have to the behavioral health system, the suitability of the treatments and providers that are available in these systems, and the structure of care provided to individuals from diverse communities of color. Additionally, more data is demonstrating that these disparities are also intensified by interactions with the health-care system.

The Socio-Cultural Framework for Health Service Disparities (SCF-HSD) (Alegría, Canino, & Pescosolido, 2009; Alegría, Pescosolido, Williams, & Canino, 2011) model offers a contextual and integrated conceptualization of mental health that identifies the root causes of such health disparities from the microlevel of the individual to the macrolevel inequities that exist within the larger society. It elucidates the underlying processes, structures, and mechanisms that give rise to existing mental health disparities by explaining how such problems accumulate over the course of an individual's illness and emerge in relation to the external environment.

The disadvantages experienced by ethnic minority groups arise from a dynamic relationship between an individual's community system and the health-care system at three levels: (1) the societal level, which includes

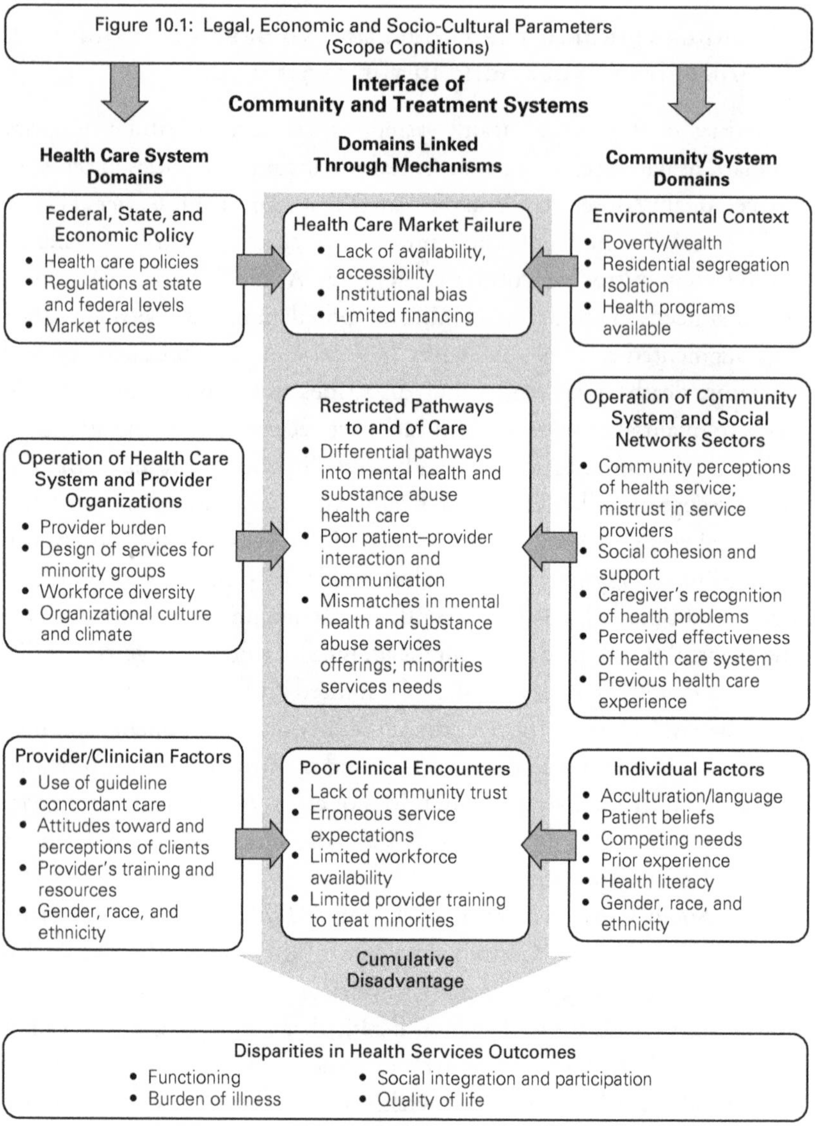

Figure 10.1: Legal, Economic and Socio-Cultural Parameters (Scope Conditions)

Interface of Community and Treatment Systems

Health Care System Domains

Domains Linked Through Mechanisms

Community System Domains

Federal, State, and Economic Policy
- Health care policies
- Regulations at state and federal levels
- Market forces

Health Care Market Failure
- Lack of availability, accessibility
- Institutional bias
- Limited financing

Environmental Context
- Poverty/wealth
- Residential segregation
- Isolation
- Health programs available

Operation of Health Care System and Provider Organizations
- Provider burden
- Design of services for minority groups
- Workforce diversity
- Organizational culture and climate

Restricted Pathways to and of Care
- Differential pathways into mental health and substance abuse health care
- Poor patient–provider interaction and communication
- Mismatches in mental health and substance abuse services offerings; minorities services needs

Operation of Community System and Social Networks Sectors
- Community perceptions of health service; mistrust in service providers
- Social cohesion and support
- Caregiver's recognition of health problems
- Perceived effectiveness of health care system
- Previous health care experience

Provider/Clinician Factors
- Use of guideline concordant care
- Attitudes toward and perceptions of clients
- Provider's training and resources
- Gender, race, and ethnicity

Poor Clinical Encounters
- Lack of community trust
- Erroneous service expectations
- Limited workforce availability
- Limited provider training to treat minorities

Individual Factors
- Acculturation/language
- Patient beliefs
- Competing needs
- Prior experience
- Health literacy
- Gender, race, and ethnicity

Cumulative Disadvantage

Disparities in Health Services Outcomes
- Functioning
- Burden of illness
- Social integration and participation
- Quality of life

government policies and the broader environmental context; (2) the organizational level, which includes the operation of the mental health system and its organizations, as well as community systems and social networks; and (3) the individual level, which includes patient and provider factors. As illustrated in Figure 10.1, each of these levels corresponds to the cumulative disparities that racial and ethnic minorities experience within the mental health system: a failure of the health-care market (at the systemic level), restricted pathways to adequate care (at the organizational level), and poor clinical encounters (at the individual level). Ultimately, disparities related to service access, quality, and outcome result from this dynamic process.

The problems and needs of ethnic minority communities at the societal level include deficiencies within the health-care market, institutional bias, and limited financing (Alegría et al., 2011). A key consideration for access to services in the U.S. health-care system is whether one holds insurance, and ethnic minority populations are more likely to be uninsured or underinsured compared to the majority population due to socioeconomic factors (DeNavas-Walt, Proctor, & Smith, 2012). An inadequate supply of providers in ethnic minority communities also has the potential to restrict access and quality of care (Alegría et al., 2011). Communities with high proportions of African American and Latino residents have been found to be four times as likely as non-Latino Whites to have a shortage of providers, regardless of community income (Putsch & Pololi, 2004). The end result may be insufficient competition that thwarts the power of governments to reform the health-care system.

Experiences of poverty and racism also impact mental health disparities at a systemic level. A clear link has been found between poverty and mental illness, with those in the lowest socioeconomic status nearly three times more likely to have a mental health disorder than those at the opposite end of the spectrum (USDHHS, 2001). The impact of discrimination and racism on the mental health of ethnic minority populations is significant, from both its modern-day manifestations and the historical injustices that preceded them. The impact of these injustices is often intergenerational because atrocities such as slavery, the destruction of American Indian culture, and the *Shoah* (Holocaust) have each inflicted lasting wounds. The impact of racism within the United States has been identified as an ongoing problem for the mental health of affected communities (Carter, 2007). Sue and colleagues (2007) have demonstrated that the daily indignities experienced by people of color, even if unintentional, may have detrimental consequences to one's psychological functioning and well-being.

Social conditions within ethnic minority communities also present significant challenges to accessing quality mental health services at the systemic level. Geographical segregation, often the result of public housing policy that places vulnerable ethnic minority populations in isolation (Alegría, Pérez, & Williams, 2003), can restrict employment opportunities (and thus insurance) and access to mental health services (Alegría et al., 2011). Other problems regarding accessing adequate pathways to care have been documented across multiple systems, including a lower likelihood of receiving services and being referred to services, and a higher likelihood of involuntary psychiatric hospitalization (Alegría et al., 2011).

The problems and needs of ethnic minority communities at the organizational level exist in the areas of provider burden, diversity of the workforce, service design, and the organizational climate of mental health-care organizations (Alegría et al., 2011). Problems in the mental health service delivery system occur at this level for ethnic minority populations when a mismatch is present between services offered and the community's specific needs. In mental health organizations, this mismatch grows when providers and staff are not given the time and resources to meet the needs of their patients, do not represent the racial and ethnic diversity reflected in their communities, and are not equipped to address the specific needs of the populations with whom they work. Clinic policies and procedures regarding the ongoing training of clinicians and staff in culturally relevant issues, the treatments an agency offers, and the availability of clinical resources (e.g., consent forms, patient handouts, psychological testing materials) shape the experience of treatment and its success and may or may not be available in a client's preferred language (Nakash, Rosen, & Alegría, 2009).

Within each community, the level of trust placed within providers and organizations is central to whether its members choose to engage and collaborate with organizations and service providers. Further, the level of social cohesion and support available within the community and the perceived effectiveness of the mental health-care system are each important organizational level factors to consider.

At the individual level, factors relevant to existing health disparities include a client's level of acculturation, language skills, prior experience with the mental health system, and health literacy. The quality of provider–client interactions is significantly diminished when providers fail to adhere to the evidence-based standards of care or otherwise engage in the stereotyping and exclusion of ethnic minority individuals from needed treatments, further compounding mistrust within the community (Alegría et al., 2011). Available treatment recommendations at times fail to consider how mental health conditions uniquely manifest within different communities, and providers may fail to understand the individual's perspective on what gave rise to a particular mental health condition, what treatment options will be most effective, and how to deliver effective care. Further, standards for the culturally competent practice of mental health (Arredondo et al., 1996) require that providers seek to understand each client's behavior within the appropriate cultural context and to develop an awareness of his or her own cultural values and biases related to decision making, problem solving, information processing, communication style, and conflict resolution. Guidelines also recommend that providers acknowledge the limitations of their cultural competence and seek consultation or make necessary referrals when appropriate. If such recommendations are not adhered to, the perpetuation of the mental health disparities is the likely result.

SYSTEMS EFFORTS TO ADDRESS DISPROPORTIONALITY AND DISPARITIES: GENERAL BARRIERS AND ETHNIC-SPECIFIC BARRIERS FACED AND CHALLENGES ENCOUNTERED

The disproportionately higher burden of unmet mental health needs within racial and ethnic minorities includes multiple barriers. Challenges exist that limit access to effective care across the systemic, organization, and individual levels of the system.

Barriers Related to the Health-Care System

State and federal regulations aimed toward cost control may have a disproportionate effect on minorities' access to care because they tend to be overrepresented among the poor. For example, restrictions on Medicaid eligibility criteria, which traditionally gave states flexibility to set their own poverty line, has disproportionately affected minorities and limited their access to care (e.g., Latinos have the lowest rate of health insurance coverage) (Vega & Lopez, 2001). When states limit Medicaid payments or require higher eligibility thresholds, individuals who depend on public insurance are curtailed from service providers who would accept low payments or who might offer them as part of the safety net.

Importantly, reimbursement by the state or the federal government is pertinent in shaping provider burden and service design, which have a direct impact on accessibility and availability of services. For example, health-care policies designed to improve cultural adequacy, such as the culturally and linguistically appropriate services that encourage providers to have trained interpreters when servicing non-English speakers and to provide linguistically and culturally adapted critical health information, have been met with resistance due to, among other factors, their high costs. Lack of compliance with these guidelines results in less diverse workforces and service delivery that is not adapted to the needs of cultural minorities. The scarcity of bicultural and bilingual mental health professionals forms a significant barrier to seeking help. Language difficulties can be particularly challenging for recent immigrants from Spanish-speaking and Asian countries, who may be less likely to enter and stay in treatment due to problems with communication (Leong & Kalibatseva, 2011).

The organizational cultural climate (including attitudes, beliefs, and behaviors) toward minority populations and institutional racism may serve as an additional barrier to care. Minority clients might be viewed as less "appealing" to the mental health providers if they are perceived to have a disproportionately greater risk of requiring more intensive treatment (Johnson, Roter, Powe, & Cooper, 2004). Such attitudes could have an effect on the desirability of treating ethnic and racial minority clients that may translate into negative attitudes, or what has been labeled institutional racism (Alegría et al., 2009).

Although the implementation of evidence-based practice has improved treatment for disadvantaged groups, studies have shown that providers frequently do not adhere to these standards of care when treating minorities (Alegría et al., 2009). Minorities are rarely referred for evidence-based treatments for mental illnesses such as depression, when compared with non-Latino Whites, even when they meet clinical appropriateness criteria and when age, gender, and insurance status are controlled (Alegría & Woo, 2009). Moreover, although a recent meta-analysis provided support for the effectiveness of culturally adapted interventions, especially when they targeted a specific group and were conducted in the clients' native language

(Griner & Smith, 2006), such practices are rarely adopted in the field and result in reduced competence in addressing the needs of minority populations. Similarly, although cultural competence training has received support in addressing some of the barriers to effective communication with minority populations, therapists typically have limited training in cross-cultural assessment, resulting in inadequate definition of the problem and treatment goals.

The Institute of Medicine's (2002) analysis further highlighted the role of provider uncertainty, stereotyping, and biases as potential barriers to competent care for ethnic minorities. Miscommunication or misunderstanding between the client and provider resulting from cultural or language differences may contribute to uncertainty and may result in misdiagnosis and premature termination. Providers may unintentionally or intentionally dismiss minority client's concerns or may not communicate about pivotal health information. This limited inquiry may lead to missed identification of mental health disorders and to lack of referral to specialty services. For example, Alegría et al. (2008b) found that during the intake interview providers consistently gathered scarce diagnostic information about the client's symptom presentation and that discussion of mental health symptoms varied as a result of the client's ethnicity and race. Differential discussion of symptom areas resulted in differential diagnosis and increased likelihood of diagnostic bias. Even with similar information collected, such as history of abuse, clinicians sometimes weighed the information differently to assign a diagnosis depending on the race/ethnicity of the client. In the absence of cultural and contextual information that supplants stereotypes, there is an increased probability of misdiagnoses. For example, Afro-Caribbean clients are three to twelve times more likely to be diagnosed with schizophrenia than their White counterparts, even with similar symptom presentation. As a result, these clients show low service utilization, low retention in care, and disproportionate negative consequences in seeking treatment (Sharpley, Hutchinson, Murray, & McKenzie, 2001).

In a study examining the links between race and ethnicity and outpatient mental health-care use, Elwy, Ranganathan, and Eisen (2008) found that although Black and Latino patients reported worse psychiatric and substance use symptoms, there were no significant racial or ethnic disparities in diagnosis or number of treatment visits, after demographic and diagnosis variables had been controlled for. A similar study by Harman, Edlund, and

Fortney (2004) found that Latinos and African Americans with depression were significantly less likely to fill antidepressant prescriptions than White patients. However, the same study found that those Latinos and African Americans who did fill their antidepressant prescriptions at least once showed no difference in continued use. The authors of both studies speculate that disparities in mental health care and substance use treatment may be due to differences in treatment-seeking behaviors. Indeed, patient–provider language differences have been shown to be among the largest barriers to receiving adequate care. Aratani and Cooper (2012) found that in a study of continuation of children's mental health service use, non-English speakers were 55% less likely than English speakers to continue using community mental health services.

Stereotyping of ethnic and racial minority clients by health-care professionals has also been identified as a potential barrier to delivery of adequate care. Various studies have demonstrated that providers may hold preconceptions about clients based on their group membership, resulting in provider stereotypes. For example, psychiatrists characterized African American clients who were indistinguishable from White clients in sociodemographics and clinical data (except for race) as less articulate, less competent, less introspective, less self-critical, less sophisticated about mental health, and less psychologically minded, and, consequently, less able to benefit from psychotherapy (Burgess, van Ryn, Dovidio, & Saha, 2007; Dovidio, Gaertner, Kawakami, & Hodson, 2002; Dovidio et al., 2008). Cabassa, Zayas, and Hansen (2006) noted that Latinos were more likely to experience delays in receiving care and were less satisfied with the care they did receive. They hypothesize that this difference could have been the result of providers' different approaches to treating minority patients, poor patient–provider communication, and language and cultural differences. Finally, provider biases have also been found to negatively influence clinical decision making. Both over- and underdiagnosis could result from these negative biases (Kirmayer, Groleau, Guzder, Blake, & Jarvis, 2003; Nakash et al., 2009), leading to inappropriate referrals.

Unconscious bias on the part of providers has also been implicated in inadequate treatment recommendations for minority clients. For example, Green et al. (2007) documented that although clinicians expressed no explicit preference for White versus Black clients, their implicit preference for White clients and implicit stereotype of Black clients as less cooperative directly impacted the likelihood of treating the White client and not treating the Black client. Bias may also disrupt the formation of the therapeutic alliance, which is fundamental for successful engagement in treatment (Burgess et al., 2007; Nakash, Saguy, & Levav, 2012). When significant bias is present in treatment, the result may be alienation and lack of trust compounded by cultural misunderstanding.

Barriers Related to the Community System

The larger geographical area in which ethnic minorities live creates a social context that, in itself, may impact access to care. Geographical segregation continues, perhaps even at greater levels than would be expected for minority populations (Alegría et al., 2009). Location of mental health clinics may serve as a significant barrier to accessing care. Many Native Americans, for example, live in rural or isolated areas that do not offer specialty services. The costly and often inconvenient transportation can be a deterrent to seeking treatment.

General education and health literacy play a key role in increasing the knowledge and accessibility of mental health services and in reducing stigmas associated with it. Low literacy skills create barriers to a successful navigation and functioning within the U.S. health-care system. For example, as many as 50% of Latinos lack English skills and 62% lack the necessary literacy skills to successfully navigate the health-care environment (Alegría et al., 2009). Health literacy may indirectly create barriers to health-care use by inhibiting access to care due to a client's inability to register for health insurance; difficulty in interpreting coverage benefits and rules; avoidance or delays in accessing mental health services due to the inability to adequately fill out forms in physician offices; or difficulty following directions to service facilities.

Cultural beliefs and perceptions of what constitutes mental illness and appropriate treatment, as well as the role of extended family members and involvement of community and religious figures in care, may constitute additional barriers to services, particularly if they are discrepant from Western conceptions and values (Alegría et al., 2009). In some Asian cultures, for example, the body and mind are perceived as an undivided unit. However, the dominant Western conceptualization of mental health is based on Cartesian dualism, which views the mind and the body as separate entities.

This difference in the conceptualization of mental illness may explain why some Asian Americans tend to experience psychological distress in somatic terms and seek help only from medical doctors for their psychological problems. Similarly, among Asian, Hispanic, and African Americans, it is often believed that a mental illness can be treated or overcome through willpower and heroic stoicism rather than by seeking professional help (Alegría et al., 2008a).

Cultural values further shape our emotional expressions and communication styles, which are particularly relevant to psychotherapy. For racial and ethnic groups that are oriented more toward collectivistic values, such as Hispanics and Asians, the process of psychotherapy may seem foreign because it traditionally focuses on an individual's internal thoughts and feelings and requires open verbal communication about intimate issues with a person who is not a family member or part of a trusted in-group. The disclosure of personal problems or family dysfunctions to strangers (such as psychotherapists) is highly discouraged in collectivistic cultures (Leong & Lau, 2001).

The willingness to report problems may also be influenced by perceptions of stigma and shame. Among ethnic and racial minorities, in comparison to the majority group, mental illness may be even more stigmatized. For example, the concern for "loss of face" among Asian Americans is key in maintaining group cohesion and requires the social image that is projected by a person to be in accordance with socially approved attributes and functions (Zane & Yeh, 2002).

In addition, multicultural clients' expectations of being stereotyped may lead to distrust in mental health services (Burgess, Fu, & Van Ryn, 2004). For example, African Americans and Latinos have increased odds of feeling unfairly judged or treated by their provider versus their White counterparts (Johnson et al., 2004). Themes of distrust and healthy cultural paranoia have been acknowledged as being culturally relevant in the clinical encounter and crucial for clinicians to appreciate when working with, for example, Black clients (Whaley, 2004).

The health and community systems' factors detailed here do not operate in isolation and are often interrelated. For example, immigrants who live in an ethnic enclave where the primary spoken language is not English may delay accessing care as a result of difficulty communicating their distress but also for fear of being stereotyped by the providers and shamed by their community. Attention should be paid to all factors (from policy to individual-level factors) across the two systems in order to adequately increase accessibility and availability of services.

CHANGING MACROSYSTEMS: CURRENT PRACTICES AND PREVENTIVE SYSTEM EFFORTS TO ADDRESS DISPROPORTIONALITY AND DISPARITIES

As a result of the identified disparities within the mental health system, investigators, health-care providers, and institutions have begun to develop and implement large-scale strategies and more problem-specific interventions to begin addressing these disparities and disproportionalities. Although there is no one-size-fits-all solution that can be applied at the level of the whole health-care system (Alegría, Atkins, Farmer, Slaton, & Stelk, 2010), system-wide policies are crucial to the effort to eliminate disparities.

Our "Sociocultural Framework for Health Service Disparities" identifies multiple points of interaction between the two major systems—community and treatment—and thus multiple opportunities for intervention. This cross-systems dialogue was emphasized in the original *Quality Chasm* report of the Institute of Medicine (2006) that recommended building effective coordination of care across patients, services, and settings, but the evidence about how to accomplish this remains mostly lacking. Therefore, there is a great need to create relational and resource bridges between community and treatment systems to better understand what the community needs, how to intervene to provide it, and how to successfully achieve health equity.

Legislative Interventions

Given the large number of factors that can potentially cause disparities in care, many different solutions will be required to address the overall problem. At the macrosystem level, there are several areas included under the Affordable Care Act (ACA; Public Law 111–148 and Public Law 111–152) legislation of 2010 that are expected to impact the access and financing of mental health and that could potentially reduce disparities. First, the Patient Protection and Affordable Care Act provides access to insurance coverage for people with preexisting behavioral health conditions through the Pre-Existing Condition Insurance Plan (PCIP). It also allows for people ineligible for Medicaid and with incomes up to 400% of the federal poverty level (FPL) to obtain premium subsidies through tax credits through state health insurance exchanges. Medicaid will likely be amplified to cover an estimated 16–24 million individuals not previously covered with incomes at or below 133% of the FPL (Ku, 2010). These expansions are expected to disproportionally benefit access to behavioral health care for ethnic and racial minority groups.

The Mental Health Parity and Addiction Equity Act (2008) requires "parity," or equivalence, in annual and lifetime dollar limits on mental health benefits with medical benefits. It could also improve access to care for people with behavioral health conditions and be used as leverage for reducing disparities in access and quality for ethnic/racial minorities who have a greater burden of higher copayments, deductibles, and limits on the number of visits for behavioral health services when accessed as compared to general medical needs. This is increasingly important because mental health expenditures by all types of behavioral health payer sources increased from 1986 to 2005 but declined or remained flat as a share of all health expenditures (SAMHSA, 2012).

Incentive Systems

Payment bonuses/incentives for insurers have been considered as a way to reduce disparities (Chien, Chin, Davis, & Casalino, 2007; Millett, Netuveli, Saxena, & Majeed, 2009) in both access and quality; but at the present time, there is limited data on which to judge such interventions in behavioral health care. However, in other areas, such as coronary artery bypass or diabetes, the results are not promising, leading the authors to conclude that the incentive system could potentially widen disparities. Given the negative findings of increasing disparities, Chien and colleagues (2007) suggested several ways of using performance incentive programs to reduce disparities, such as emphasizing clinical measures that target conditions that are more prevalent in minority populations, instituting national disparities guidelines or "scorecards," and rewarding improvement in care instead of comparing hospitals and providers using absolute disparities measures that do not take into account different resource levels and diverse patient populations. Millett and colleagues (2009), on the other hand, emphasized that health-care planners should design incentive systems with an understanding of how they might impact already existing disparities or even create disparities where they had not existed before.

Blustein, Weissman, Ryan, Doran, and Hasnain-Wynia (2011) also examined the development and effectiveness of Medicaid pay-for-performance measures targeting racial and ethnic disparities in a study in Massachusetts. Problems with Medicaid's program to eliminate disparities arose for multiple reasons. The use of only five fairly specific clinical measures meant that sample sizes were low and required the Medicaid office to alter its methods for determining performance after data had been collected. Furthermore, the requirement of documentation for structural improvements was complex, and many hospitals' documentation was deemed inadequate in the first year of implementation. Hospital administrators interviewed by the authors also commented that the Medicaid office seemed to be playing a regulatory role instead of working with hospitals to improve care. Finally, they suggested that many hospitals in Massachusetts do not serve large minority populations; therefore, it would make more sense to see whether there are large quality gaps between hospitals that serve large minority populations and those that do not.

Quality Improvements

Two reviews of interventions designed to reduce disparities in behavioral health care show that integration of evidence-based interventions are effective in improving access and quality of care for minority patients (Schraufnagel, Wagner, Miranda, & Roy-Byrne, 2006) and that multicomponent interventions (addressing disparities at the system, provider, and patient levels simultaneously) are most effective (Van Voorhees, Walters, Prochaska, & Quinn, 2007). Quality improvements have also been shown to eradicate disparities in the quality of care. Wells and colleagues (2004) intervened by providing a quality improvement (QI) program for patients with depression that included cultural sensitivity training for providers and additional support for patients such as telephone-based medication adherence. In a 57-month follow-up, the percentage of minority patients still showing symptoms of depression was almost identical to the percentage for non-Latino White patients, suggesting that QI would be an effective way to reduce disparities in quality of care.

In contrast with other researchers' advocating for quality improvements based on integrating evidenced-based treatments, Kirmayer (2012) argued that although evidence-based practice and the use of cultural competence training have positive effects on reducing disparities, they are based on particular claims that originate from within a specific mainstream culture. He emphasized that it is important to keep in mind that the purpose of using the combination of evidence-based practice and cultural competence training is to improve care for minorities but that the use of such methods creates the potential risk of dominating other cultures or invalidating their systems of knowledge and belief. He concluded by recommending that providers should keep in mind the fact that patients may have different ideas of mental health problems and potential solutions that, although not necessarily useful in a medical sense, must be respected in order to ensure quality treatment.

Community-Based Programs

Engaging communities to increase their involvement in decision making and promotion of culturally adapted services and pathways into care is essential to improve health equity for ethnic minority populations. Such involvement can include actions needed (within mental health services and outside of them) to give all communities genuine opportunities to influence mental health policy and provision and to promote mental health and recovery. Engaging communities is essential to identify unmet needs and different models of service provision that may be applicable to the problem and to uncover any nonstatutory sector expertise that may be better placed to offer support (McKenzie, 2008).

The building of knowledge and links in the community is a way of developing capacity through education and creating networks of people interested in reducing the burden of mental health challenges. Successful interventions in this regard have increased awareness of availability of mental health care to reduce stigma at the community level and increased the likelihood that minorities will recognize the need for and initiate use of mental health services (Elwy et al., 2008). When necessary, a public awareness campaign requires a properly targeted message. Community organizations can help reduce stigma against mental health services by promoting education about mental health disorders as well as addressing the negative connotations of some terminology—for example, the word "mental"—and by promoting culturally sensitive support groups.

Efforts to reduce inequity need to be supported by work across disciplines, directorates, and services so they are better placed to influence statutory services. Some investigators suggest that providing more mental health services in primary care settings and launching public health campaigns targeting specific ethnic and racial groups will increase visibility for mental health among minority groups (Cabassa et al., 2006) and could be a cost-effective mechanism to eradicate behavioral health disparities. Of particular importance is the role of primary care physicians (PCPs) in light of research showing that ethnic minorities are more likely to present their mental health concerns to their PCP and are less likely to have been treated for their psychological problems (Bach, Pham, Schrag, Tate, & Hargraves, 2004; Borowsky et al., 2000). Many PCPs who are not trained in assessing mental health issues fail to recognize psychiatric symptoms, particularly among ethnic minorities (Borowsky et al., 2000). Initial support has been documented for the effectiveness of providing integrative care in which mental health services are located within the primary care clinic (compared with the regular referral model) to reduce inequities particularly to minority groups (Ayalon, Areán, Linkins, Lynch, & Estes, 2007). Integrative care can also more effectively address comorbid disproportionate health conditions that are more prevalent among certain minority groups. For example, African Americans are disproportionately represented among type 2 diabetes patients that have poor glycemic control (Harris, Eastman, Cowie, Flegal, & Eberhardt, 1999). Using a model of integrative care for diabetes and depression within primary care clinics was more effective in reducing symptoms of depression as well as glycemic control among members of this ethnic group (Bogner & de Vries, 2010).

Overall, this review emphasizes the limited progress in disparities interventions achieved over the last decade.

CROSS-SYSTEMS EFFORTS AND CULTURALLY COMPETENT SERVICES OFFERED

Consistent with the systemic and integrative lens taken to understand mental health disparities, efforts that address the needs of ethnic minorities across various community systems are essential to ensuring optimal care.

Multiple scholars from within the field of mental health have called upon practitioners to adopt a social justice perspective for their work (Aldarando, 2007; Toporek, Gerstein, Fouad, Roysircar, & Israel, 2006), with some arguing that professionals must engage in systemic efforts to promote patient wellness (Prilleltensky, Dokecki, Frieden, & Ota Wang, 2007). Advocacy competencies focused on promoting client empowerment across systems have been adopted by the American Counseling Association (2003). Consistently, psychologists and other mental health professionals engage in work across numerous systems to reduce disparities, including public policy, within traditionally closed health-care settings (e.g., cardiology), and the child welfare system (Harris & Hackett, 2008). The following case illustrates an example of one such effort.

Disproportionate Minority Contact in the Juvenile Justice System: The Case of Drug Offenders

The link between substance use and mental health disorders is well documented in community (Swendsen et al., 2010) and clinical samples (Robinson, Sareen, Cox, & Bolton, 2009) and provides a case example of a cross-systems effort by mental health professionals. Studies have found a high risk for drug use in subjects with mental illness and a high frequency of psychopathology triggered by drug use. The National Survey on Drug Use and Health (NSDUH) estimates that 2.7 million adults in the United States over the age of 18 have experienced a co-occurring major depressive episode and alcohol use disorder during the previous year (Office of Applied Studies, 2007a). A similar picture arises among young adults. Among youths aged 12 to 17 who were at risk for illicit drug initiation, those who experienced a past year major depressive episode were more than twice as likely to have initiated use of an illicit drug as those who had not experienced a depressive episode in the past year (16.1 vs. 6.9%; Office of Applied Studies, 2007b).

Despite the high prevalence of these co-occurring disorders, nearly half of all individuals with co-occurring depressive and alcohol abuse disorders fail to receive treatment for either disorder (Office of Applied Studies, 2007a). This is in part due to long-standing separations in treatment systems for substance use and mood disorders (Kilbourne, Greenwald, Bauer, Charns, & Yano, 2012; Darghouth, Nakash, Miller, & Alegría, 2012), which disproportionately affect minority youth. This is particularly important in light of recent data showing that young people of different ethnicities report engaging in illicit drug use and report selling drugs at similar rates, yet young people of color comprise nearly two-thirds of the youth detained for drug offenses (Annie E. Casey Foundation, 2009). Beyond the legal, ethical, and social implications related to this disproportionate representation, the mental health consequences are severe because detention significantly limits the likelihood of minority youth receiving appropriate mental health care for either the depressive or drug abuse problems.

This complex case vignette illustrates the importance of a cross-systems effort to help Carlos. Efforts need to be simultaneously directed to the individual/family system addressing financial and relational stressors the

CASE EXAMPLE: CARLOS

Carlos is a 16-year-old Mexican American teenager who was referred to the mental health clinic at a local hospital by the court after being arrested for suspected involvement in gang activity and drug possession. Carlos immigrated to the United States with his family (parents and two younger sisters) when he was seven years old. Since then, his parents separated (although they still live in close proximity to each other), and Carlos spends most days of the week with his mother. The family life he had known back in Mexico (e.g., having family meals every night) had changed dramatically since they moved to the United States, partly due to the fact the both parents worked two jobs to maintain the family and left the home early in the morning, returning late at night. As the oldest son, Carlos felt a duty to care for his family and was torn between the need to find a job and help his family financially and continuing his studies. Carlos also frequently functioned as the "foreign ambassador" of the family, helping his parents negotiate their needs with officials because they both did not speak English well. Carlos lives in a low socioeconomic neighborhood that had a relative high crime rate and some gang activity. Carlos was a victim of violence twice, being robbed while walking back home from school. In order to protect himself, he started carrying a knife. In addition, he began dealing drugs—partly due to social pressures—and associating with the dominant gang members in the community.

family is facing as well as targeting agents within the school setting to help improve school performance and reduce work-school conflict in addition to targeting the legal and local community systems to examine the continuum of detention alternatives. For example, evening reporting centers operated by a neighborhood nonprofit community-based organization can be an effective intervention to reduce the risk of youth reoffending.

Cross-Systems Intervention: Cook County, Illinois

Increases in the severity and enforcement of drug laws over the last two decades led to explosive growth of the criminal justice system with disproportionate overrepresentation of minority youth, particularly African Americans, among drug offenders (Short & Sharp, 2005; Whitney, 2005). In 2002, federal legislation that broadened the scope of the examination of minority youth in the justice system to include all decision-making stages encouraged states to develop comprehensive plans that address disparity across the stages of decision making and the continuum of services. Critical components of these efforts include organizational responsibility, data collection and analysis, prioritization and consensus building that are based in the community, intensive training, and increased access to counsels and evaluation (Short & Sharp, 2005). An example of a successful model to reduce disproportionality among drug offenders was developed and implemented in Cook County, Illinois (Hoyt, Schiraldi, Smith, & Ziedenberg, 2003; Short & Sharp, 2005; Whitney, 2005).

In sum, the county formed community coalitions that contributed to the diversification of services available to detained youth. Cook County reduced disproportionate minority contact throughout the system. It also achieved the goals of reduction of the average daily detention population and improved outcomes for detained youth through this comprehensive approach to reform.

FUTURE DIRECTIONS

Ethnic and racial service disparities in behavioral health care continue to surpass disparities in many other areas of health care (AHRQ, 2008). Over a decade ago, the President's Commission on Mental Health (2003) called for launching federal policies to reduce behavioral health service disparities.

SPOTLIGHT: PROMISING PRACTICE TO ADDRESS DISPROPORTIONALITY IN THE MENTAL HEALTH SYSTEM CROSS-SYSTEMS INTERVENTION

The cross-systems initiative in Cook County began with the establishment of a "Disproportionate Representation Committee." The committee included diverse members and stakeholders including a presiding judge, representatives of court services and probation, the public defender, juvenile detention staff, police, state's attorneys, community-based service providers, and leaders of advocacy groups. Such a community-inclusive steering composition is advantageous to the development and expansion of community-based services and programs such as detention alternatives and supports for youth and families within the least restrictive settings. The committee aimed to reduce the overall number of youth detained and focused on helping individuals who were detained to reduce adversity and improve outcomes. First, the county developed a successful train-the-trainer model, which focused on racial stereotypes and biases that affected decision making. The training also focused on increasing cultural competence and communication and provided participants with the opportunity to learn from one another. The training facilitated the development of a more positive work culture.

In addition, a new risk assessment tool was developed to help improve the cultural adaptability of the decisions to detain a youth. The new tool was designed to heighten awareness of the context of the lives of minority youth and the comprehensive risk factors that underlie delinquent behavior. Moreover, the county significantly expanded the social support system provided for offenders during the court process. As part of this support system, paralegals interviewed detained youth prior to hearings, verified community ties, contacted families to stress the importance of their presence and involvement at hearings, and provided information about procedural and behavioral expectations during the hearing. In addition, paralegals helped bridge the gap and develop connections and direct communication among families, the community, and the court.

The most prominent detention reform strategy was the development of a continuum of detention alternatives. Community-based organizations run by members of ethnic and racial groups in the community increased their activities and improved their cultural competence. Nonprofit community-based organizations in neighborhoods with high rates of minority youth detainees developed and operated evening reporting centers to reduce the risk of youth reoffending. These centers provided potent, individualized supervision during the peak hours of criminal and delinquent activity while the youth's delinquency proceedings were pending. They also ensured that youth appeared in court while remaining in school and living at home.

But as Stone (2006) suggests, it has not been until recently that service disparities have been reframed as a moral issue that requires state governments to accelerate interventions to reduce these disparities (Alegría, 2009; Kilbourne, Switzer, Hyman, Crowley-Matoka, & Fine, 2006). Given that predictors of disparities have been identified at multiple levels, it is surprising that the progress has been limited in behavioral health care (see Blanco et al., 2007; Cook, McGuire, & Miranda, 2007), especially with a greater awareness of negative impacts and better tracking by the federal government (AHRQ, 2008). Thus, we propose the following future directions to address the existing barriers and remedy limited progress:

STRATEGIES FOR ADDRESSING AND ELIMINATING DISPROPORTIONALITY AND DISPARITIES

- Promote national attention to support recognition that behavioral health equity is an issue of social justice and social welfare that has negative repercussions for all.
- Redesign public and employer-based payment rules to offer alternative payment methods that allow for greater coverage of QI in behavioral health services for ethnic and racial minorities, especially services outside of the clinic walls (e.g., telepsychiatry, employer-based behavioral health services, in-home counseling, and school services) proven to be effective treatments for behavioral health problems.
- Revise Medicaid and other state payment policies so they do not dramatically limit the types of personnel that can be reimbursed in community health centers (where ethnic/racial minorities overwhelmingly receive their care) and the types of effective behavioral health services that can be covered.
- Build a diverse workforce of ethnic/racial minority professionals and para-professionals that is continuously trained and retrained in evidence-based behavioral health treatments and supervised to provide quality care—one that is committed to at least five years of service to poor, people of color, and/or Medicaid patients.
- Require insurers to offer psychosocial education and health literacy training for improving ethnic/racial minority patients' empowerment and self-management of their conditions, as well as increasing their knowledge base so that they can

register for public insurance programs, navigate the health-care system (and acquire skills to solve bureaucratic barriers to health care), and self-monitor to prevent relapse.

- Guarantee sufficient resources for social and economic assistance programs (e.g., supported employment, earned income tax credit, after-school preventive programs) that can buffer the social conditions of ethnic/racial minorities.

- Ensure adequate and continued funding for community health clinics through federal stimulus funds devoted to community health centers so that they can continue augmenting access to behavioral health services for racial and ethnic minorities (McCarthy et al., 2007).

- Incentivize organizations that intervene with bias at several levels (e.g., practitioner, practice network or program, and community) with QI programs and subsequently evaluate the program's contribution to particular forms of bias in behavioral health care.

- Tackle the lack of institutional cultural competence, addressing discrimination and stereotyping in behavioral health care, increasing access to minority providers, and improving ways for evaluating the mechanisms of disparities in their own institutions.

- Target political actors with authority and power to make health policy changes directed at behavioral health disparities so they continuously advocate the moral case of behavioral health inequities (Stone, 2006).

- Align treatment options with the needs of families of color, ensuring that their voices are valued in the process of decision making. Community liaisons or community partner research can serve as translators of how best to evaluate "evidence" of evidence-based interventions in the community system and to identify the steps necessary to implement these treatments by community and behavioral health providers.

- Evaluate the number of providers at the state and county level accepting new Medicaid patients on an annual basis to ensure a sufficient distribution of providers capable of serving behavioral health patients. Only one-third of primary care physicians (PCPs) report being able to successfully obtain outpatient behavioral health services for their primary care patients (Cunningham, 2009).

REFERENCES

Agency for Healthcare Research and Quality. (2008). *National healthcare dispari-ties report, 2008*. Rockville, MD: Agency for Healthcare Research and Quality.

Aldarondo, E. (Ed.) (2007). *Advancing social justice through clinical practice*. Mah-wah, NJ: Lawrence Erlbaum.

Alegría, M. (2009). *AcademyHealth 25th Annual Research Meeting chair address: From a science of recommendation to a science of implementation. Health Services Research, 44*(1): 5.

Alegría, M., Atkins, M., Farmer, E., Slaton, E., & Stelk, W. (2010). One size does not fit all: Taking diversity, culture and context seriously. *Administration and Policy in Mental Health and Mental Health Services Research, 37*(1–2), 48–60. PMCID: PMC2874609

Alegría, M., Canino, G. P., & Pescosolido, B. (2009). A socio-cultural frame-work for mental health and substance abuse service disparities. In B. J. Sadock, V. A. Sadock, & P. Ruiz (Eds.), *Comprehensive textbook of psychiatry* (pp. 4370–4379). Baltimore: Wolters Kluwer Health, Lippincott Williams & Wilkins.

Alegría, M., Canino, G., Shrout, P. E., Woo, M., Duan, N., Vila, D., et al. (2008a). Prevalence of mental illness in immigrant and non-immigrant U.S. Latino groups. *American Journal of Psychiatry, 165*(3), 359–369.

Alegría, M., Nakash, O., Lapatin, S., Oddo, V., Gao, S., Lin, J., et al. (2008b). How missing information in diagnosis can lead to disparities in the clini-cal encounter. *Journal of Public Health Management and Practice, 14*, Suppl: S26–35.

Alegría, M., Pérez, D., & Williams, S. (2003). The role of public policies in reduc-ing disparities in mental health status for people of color. *Health Affairs, 22*(3), 51–64.

Alegría, M., Pescosolido, B., Williams, S., & Canino, G. (2011). Culture, race/ethnicity and disparities: Fleshing out the socio-cultural framework for health services disparities. In B. Pescosolido, J. Marin, J. McLeod, & A. Rogers (Eds.), *Handbook of the sociology of health, illness, and healing: A blueprint for the 21st century* (pp. 363–382). New York: Springer.

Alegría, M., & Woo, M. (2009). Conceptual issues in Latino mental health. In J. Grau, M. Azmitia, N. Cabrera, G. Carlo, J. Chain, & F. A. Villarruel (Eds.), *Handbook of Latino psychology: Community and developmental perspectives*. Thousand Oaks, CA: Sage.

American Counseling Association (2003). *Advocacy competencies.* Alexandria, VA: Author. Retrieved June 1, 2012, from http://www.counseling.org/docs/competencies/advocacy_competencies.pdf?sfvrsn=3

American Psychological Association. (2003). Guidelines on multicultural education, training, research, practice, and organizational change for psychologists. *American Psychologist, 58*, 377–402.

Annie E. Casey Foundation. (2009). Detention reform: An effective approach to reduce racial and ethnic disparities in juvenile justice. Baltimore, MD: Annie E. Casey Foundation.

Aratani, Y., & Cooper, J. (2012). Racial and ethnic disparities in the continuation of community-based children's mental health services. *Journal of Behavioral Health Services & Research, 39*(2), 116–29.

Arredondo, P., Toporek, R., Brown, S. P., Jones, L., Locke, D. C., Sanchez, J., et al. (1996). Operationalization of the multicultural counseling competencies. *Journal of Multicultural Counseling and Development, 24*, 42–78.

Ayalon, L., Areán, P. A., Linkins, K., Lynch, M., & Estes, C. L. (2007). Integration of mental health services into primary care overcomes ethnic disparities in access to mental health services between black and white elderly. *American Journal of Geriatric Psych, 15*(10), 906–912.

Bach, P. B., Pham, H. H., Schrag, D., Tate, R. C., & Hargraves, J. L. (2004). Primary care physicians who treat blacks and whites. *New England Journal of Medicine, 351*(6), 575–584.

Blanco, C., S. Patel, L. Liu, H. Jiang, R. Lewis-Fernandez, A. Schmidt, et al. (2007). National trends in ethnic disparities in mental health care. *Medical Care* 45(11): 1012–1019.

Blustein, J., Weissman, J. S., Ryan, A. M., Doran, T., & Hasnain-Wynia, R. (2011). Analysis raises questions on whether pay-for-performance in Medicaid can efficiently reduce racial and ethnic disparities. *Health Affairs, 30*(6), 1165–1175.

Bogner, H. R., & de Vries, H. F. (2010). Integrating type 2 diabetes mellitus and depression treatment among African Americans a randomized controlled pilot trial. *The Diabetes Educator, 36*(2), 284–292.

Borowsky, S. J., Rubenstein, L. V., Meredith, L. S., Camp, P., Jackson-Triche, M., & Wells, K. B. (2000). Who is at risk of nondetection of mental health problems in primary care? *Journal of General Internal Medicine, 15*(6), 381–388.

Burgess, D., van Ryn, M., Dovidio, J., & Saha, S. (2007). Reducing racial bias among health care providers: Lessons from social-cognitive psychology. *Journal of General Internal Medicine, 22*(6), 882–887.

Burgess, D. J., Fu, S. S., & Van Ryn, M. (2004). Why do providers contribute to disparities and what can be done about it? *Journal of General Internal Medicine, 19*(11), 1154–1159.

Cabassa, L., Zayas, L., & Hansen, M. (2006). Latino adults' access to mental health care: A review of epidemiological studies. *Administration and Policy in Mental Health, 33*(3), 316–330.

Carter, R. T. (2007). Racism and psychological and emotional injury: Recognizing and assessing race-based traumatic stress. *The Counseling Psychologist, 35,* 13–105.

Centers for Disease Control. (2007). Unnatural causes: Is inequality making us sick? Retrieved from http://www.cdc.gov/pcd/issues/2007/oct/07_0144.htm

Chien, A. T., Chin, M. H., Davis, A. M., and Casalino, L. P. (2007). Pay for performance, public reporting, and racial disparities in health care: How are programs being designed? *Medical Care Research and Review, 64*(5 suppl): 283S–304S.

Cook, B., T. McGuire, and J. Miranda. (2007). Measuring trends in mental health care disparities, 2000–2004. *Psychiatric Services, 58*(12): 1533–1539.

Cunningham, P. J. (2009). Beyond parity: Primary care physicians' perspectives on access to mental health care. *Health Affairs, 28*(3), 490–501.

Darghouth, S., Nakash, O., Miller, A., & Alegría, M. (2012). Assessment of co-occurring depression and substance use in an ethnically diverse patient sample during behavioral health intake interviews. *Drug and Alcohol Dependence.*

DeNavas-Walt, C., Proctor, B. D., & Smith, J. C. (2012). *U.S. Census Bureau, current population reports, P60-243, income, poverty, and health insurance coverage in the United States: 2011.* Washington, DC: U.S. Government Printing Office.

Dovidio, J. F., Gaertner, S. L., Kawakami, K., & Hodson, G. (2002). Why can't we just get along? Interpersonal biases and interracial distrust. *Cultural Diversity and Ethnic Minority Psychology, 8,* 88–102.

Dovidio, J. F., Penner, L. A., Albrecht, T. L., Norton, W. E., Gaertner, S. L., & Shelton, J. N. (2008). Disparities and distrust: The implications of psychological processes for understanding racial disparities in health and health care. *Social Science and Medicine, 67*(3), 478–486.

Elwy, A., Ranganathan, G., & Eisen, S. (2008). Race-ethnicity and diagnosis as predictors of outpatient service use among treatment initiators. *Psychiatric Services, 59*(11), 1285–1291.

Green, A. R., Carney, D. R., Pallin, D. J., Ngo, L. H., Raymond, K. L., Iezzoni, L. I., et al. (2007). Implicit bias among physicians and its prediction of thrombolysis decisions for black and white patients. *Journal of General Internal Medicine, 22*(9), 1231–1238.

Griner, D., & Smith, T. B. (2006). Culturally adapted mental health intervention: A meta-analytic review. *Psychotherapy: Theory, research, practice, training, 43*(4), 531.

Harman, J., Edlund, M., & Fortney, J. (2004). Disparities in the adequacy of depression treatment in the United States. *Psychiatric Services, 55*(12), 1379–1385.

Harris, M. I., Eastman, R. C., Cowie, C. C., Flegal, K. M., & Eberhardt, M. S. (1999). Racial and ethnic differences in glycemic control of adults with type 2 diabetes. *Diabetes Care, 22*(3), 403–408.

Harris, M. S., & Hackett, W. (2008). Decision points in child welfare: An action research model to address disproportionality. *Children and Youth Services Review, 30*, 199–215.

Hoyt, E. H., Schiraldi, V., Smith, B. V., & Ziedenberg, J. (2003). Pathways to juvenile detention reform: Reducing racial disparities in juvenile detention. Baltimore, MD: The Annie E. Casey Foundation.

Institute of Medicine. (2002). *Unequal treatment: What health care system administrators need to know about racial and ethnic disparities in healthcare.* Retrieved June 28, 2011, from http://www.iom.edu/~/media/Files/Report%20Files/2003/Unequal-Treatment-Confronting-Racial-and-Ethnic-Disparities-in-Health-Care/DisparitiesAdmin8pg.pdf

Institute of Medicine. (2006). *Improving the quality of health care for mental and substance-use conditions: Quality chasm series.* Washington, DC: Institute of Medicine.

Johnson, R. L., Roter, D., Powe, N. R., & Cooper, L. A. (2004). Patient race/ethnicity and quality of patient-physician communication during medical visits. *American Journal of Public Health, 94*(12), 2084–2090.

Kilbourne, A., Greenwald, D., Bauer, M., Charns, M., & Yano, E. (2012). Mental health provider perspectives regarding integrated medical care for patients with serious mental illness. *Adm. Policy Ment. Health, 39*, 448–457.

Kilbourne, A. M., Switzer, G., Hyman, K., Crowley-Matoka, M., and Fine, M. J. (2006). Advancing health disparities research within the health care system: A conceptual framework. *American Journal of Public Health 96*(12): 2113.

Kirmayer, L. J. (2012). Rethinking cultural competence. *Transcultural Psychiatry*, *49*(2), 149–164.

Kirmayer, L. J., Groleau, D., Guzder, J., Blake, C., & Jarvis, E. (2003). Cultural consultation: A model of mental health service for multicultural societies. *The Canadian Journal of Psychiatry/La Revue canadienne de psychiatrie, 48*(3), 145–153.

Ku, L. (2010). Ready, set, plan, implement: Executing the expansion of Medicaid. *Health Affairs, 29*(6), 1173–1177.

Leong, F. T. L., & Kalibatseva, Z. (2011). *Cross-cultural barriers to mental health services in the United States*. Retrieved April 23, 2014, from http://www.ncbi. nlm.nih.gov/pmc/articles/PMC3574791/

Leong, F. T. L., & Lau, A. S. L. (2001). Barriers to providing effective mental health services to Asian Americans. *Mental Health Services Research, 3*(4), 201–214.

McCarthy, J., Blow, F., Valenstein, M., Fischer, E., Owen, R., Barry, K., et al. (2007). Veterans Affairs health system and mental health treatment retention among patients with serious mental illness: Evaluating accessibility and availability barriers. *Health Services Research, 42*(3), 1042–1060.

McKenzie, K. (2008). Improving mental healthcare for ethnic minorities. *Advances in Psychiatric Treatment, 14*(4), 285–291.

Millett, C., Netuveli, G., Saxena, S., & Majeed, A. (2009). Impact of pay for performance on ethnic disparities in intermediate outcomes for diabetes: A longitudinal study. *Diabetes Care. 32*(3): 404–409.

Nakash, O., Rosen, D., & Alegría, M. (2009). The culturally sensitive evaluation. In P. Ruiz & A. Primm (Eds.), *Disparities in psychiatric care: Clinical and cross-cultural perspectives*. Baltimore, MD: Wolters Kluwer Health, Lippincott Williams & Wilkins.

Nakash, O., Saguy, T., & Levav, I. (2012). The effect of social identities of service-users and clinicians on mental health disparities: A review of theory and facts. *Israel Journal of Psychiatry, 49*, 202–210.

Office of Applied Studies, Substance Abuse and Mental Health Services Administration. (2007a). *National Survey on Drug Use and Health (NSDUH)'s report: Co-occurring major depressive episode (MDE) and alcohol use disorder among adults*. Rockville, MD: Substance and Mental Health Services Administration.

Office of Applied Studies, Substance Abuse and Mental Health Services Administration. (2007b). *National Survey on Drug Use and Health (NSDUH)'s report: Depression and the initiation of alcohol and other drug use among youths aged 12 to 17*. Rockville, MD: Substance and Mental Health Services Administration.

Paul Wellstone and Pete Domenici Mental Health Parity and Addiction Equity Act of 2008. (2008). Retrieved from the Centers for Medicare & Medicaid Services Web site: https://www.cms.gov/HealthInsReformforConsume/Downloads/MHPAEA.pdf

President's Commission on Mental Health. (2003). *Final report for the President's New Freedom Commission on Mental Health*. Retrieved from http://govinfo.library.unt.edu/mentalhealthcommission/reports/FinalReport/toc.html

Prilleltensky, I., Dokecki, P., Frieden, F., & Ota Wang, V. (2007). Counseling for wellness and justice: Foundations, practice, and ethical dilemmas. In E. Aldarondo (Ed.), *Social justice and mental health practices* (pp. 19–42). Mahwah, NJ: Lawrence Erlbaum.

Putsch, R. W., & Pololi, L. (2004). Distributive justice in American healthcare: Institutions, power, and the equitable care of patients. *The American Journal of Managed Care, 10*, 45–53.

Robinson, J., Sareen, J., Cox, B., & Bolton, J. (2009). Self-medication of anxiety disorders with alcohol and drugs: Results from a nationally representative sample. *Journal of Anxiety Disorders, 23*(1), 38–45.

Schraufnagel, T. J., Wagner, A. W., Miranda, J., & Roy-Byrne, P. P. (2006). Treating minority patients with depression and anxiety: What does the evidence tell us? *General Hospital Psychiatry, 28*(1), 27–36.

Sharpley, M. S., Hutchinson, G., Murray, R. M., & McKenzie, K. (2001). Understanding the excess of psychosis among the African–Caribbean population in England: Review of current hypotheses. *The British Journal of Psychiatry, 178*(40), s60–s68.

Short, J., & Sharp, C. (2005). *Disproportionate minority contact in the juvenile justice system*. The Child Welfare League of America. Retrieved April 4, 2012 from http://www.cwla.org/programs/juvenilejustice/disproportionate.pdf

Stone, D. (2006). Reframing the racial disparities issue for state governments. *Journal of Health Politics, Policy and Law, 31*(1), 127–152.

Substance Abuse and Mental Health Services Administration. (2008). *Results from the 2007 National Survey on Drug Use and Health: National findings*. (NSDUH Series H-34, DHHS Publication No. SMA 08-4343). Rockville, MD: Substance Abuse and Mental Health Services Administration, Office of Applied Studies.

Substance Abuse and Mental Health Services Administration. (2010). *Mental health, United States, 2008*. HHS Publication No. (SMA) 10-4590, Rockville,

MD: Center for Mental Health Service, Substance and Mental Health Services Administration.

Substance Abuse and Mental Health Services Administration. (2012). *Mental health, United States, 2010*. HHS Publication No. (SMA) 12-4681. Rockville, MD: Substance Abuse and Mental Health Services Administration.

Sue, D. W., Capodilupo, C. M., Torino, G. C., Bucceri, J. M., Holder, A. M. B., Nadal, K., et al. (2007). Racial microaggressions in every day life: Implications for clinical practice. *American Psychologist, 62*, 271–286.

Swendsen, J., Conway, K., Degenhardt, L., Glantz, M., Jin, R., Merikangas, K., et al. (2010). Mental disorders as risk factors for substance use, abuse, and dependence: Results from the 10-year follow-up of the National Comorbidity Survey. *Addiction, 105*(6), 1117–1128.

Toporek, R. L., Gerstein, L. H., Fouad, N. A., Roysircar, G. S., & Israel, T. (2006). *Handbook for social justice in counseling psychology: Leadership, vision, & action.* Thousand Oaks, CA: Sage.

U.S. Department of Health and Human Services. (1999). *Mental health: A report of the Surgeon General.* Rockville, MD: U.S. Department of Health and Human Services, Substance Abuse and Mental Health Services Administration, Center for Mental Health Services, National Institutes of Health, National Institute of Mental Health.

U.S. Department of Health and Human Services. (2001). *Mental health: Culture, race, and ethnicity—A supplement to mental health: A report of the Surgeon General.* Rockville, MD: U.S. Department of Health and Human Services, Public Health Service, Office of the Surgeon General.

Van Voorhees, B. W., Walters, A. E., Prochaska, M., & Quinn, M. T. (2007). Reducing health disparities in depressive disorders outcomes between non-Hispanic whites and ethnic minorities: A call for pragmatic strategies over the life course. *Medical Care Research and Review, 64*, 157S–194S.

Vega, W. A., & Lopez, S. R. (2001). Priority issues in Latino mental health services research. *Mental Health Services Research, 3*(4), 189–200.

Wells, K. B., Sherbourne, C., Schoenbaum, M., Ettner, S., Duan, N., Miranda, J., et al. (2004). Five-year impact of quality improvement for depression. *Archives of General Psychiatry, 61*, 378–386.

Whaley, A. L. (2004). Paranoia in African-American men receiving inpatient psychiatric treatment. *Journal of the American Academy of Psychiatry and the Law Online, 32*(3), 282–290.

Whitehead, M. (1992). The concepts and principles of equity and health. *International Journal of Health Services, 22*(3), 429–445.

Whitney, T. (2005). *Disproportionate sentencing of minority drug offenders in Illinois: Report on changes in drug laws 1985–2002.* Retrieved from http://www.icjia.state.il.us/public/pdf/ResearchReports/Disproportionate%20Sentencing%20Report.pdf

Zane, N., & Yeh, M. (2002). The use of culturally-based variables in assessment: Studies on loss of face. In K. S. Kurasaki, S. Okazaki, and S. Sue (Eds.), *Asian American mental health: Assessment theories and methods. International and cultural psychology series* (pp. 123-138). New York: Kluwer Academic/Plenum Publishers.

11

Disproportionality and Disparities in the Health-Care System

▸ *SUSAN J. WELLS, SARAH GIRLING, AND ANDREW VERGARA*

DESCRIPTION OF THE SYSTEM AND THE ETHNIC MINORITY POPULATIONS AFFECTED BY THE SYSTEM

THE HEALTH SYSTEM IN ANY society is a product of economic, social, cultural, and political forces that combine to create the family and community context in which people grow and develop and the network of health services that influence individual health and mental health status for a lifetime. For example, early childhood education programs for children in low income neighborhoods can have a significant impact on later health outcomes. A Cochrane systematic review of research on the effectiveness of early childhood day care for pre-school children targeting diverse populations or low socioeconomic status (SES) neighborhoods found diminished likelihood of later teenage pregnancy, decreased criminal behavior, and greater likelihood of higher SES (Zoritch, Roberts, & Oakley, 2000) decreasing the likelihood of health problems associated with these behaviors and conditions. Health is therefore influenced not only by health services. Factors including family, social network, neighborhood, and larger community, in combination with health promotion efforts and health service delivery systems, support to a greater or lesser extent community residents' health and well-being.

One of the most significant characteristics of the U.S. health service delivery system is its lack of any overarching organization. Shi and Singh (2008) outline the following health services and describe mechanisms of service delivery. Health services include: preventive care, primary care, specialized care, chronic care, long-term care, subacute care, acute care, rehabilitative care, and hospice care. These services are delivered by a diverse array of private enterprises, agencies, and organizations, including, for example, doctors' offices, community clinics, walk-in clinics, hospitals, outpatient surgical centers, rehabilitation centers, and long-term care facilities. Additionally, health services may be delivered at home by trained medical personnel. These services are comprised of an often accidental combination of public and private payment and service delivery systems. Local and regional health systems may be more or less organized in any one of a number of models. Four examples of highly organized systems are offered by Shih et al. (2008): (1) integrated delivery system or large multispecialty practice, with a health plan and one type of a health maintenance organization (HMO), for example Kaiser Permanente; (2) integrated delivery system or large multispecialty group practice, without a health plan, such as the Mayo Clinic; (3) private network of independent providers, such as an independent practice association; and (4) government-facilitated network of independent providers, such as Community Care of North Carolina.

Health services in the United States have generally been funded by a combination of private insurers through places of employment and government programs for selected populations such as the very poor, severely disabled, veterans, and persons over 65 years old. The largest funding sources for medical care are Medicaid, Medicare, and insurance paid by employers and employees. Medicaid services vary by state, depending on the degree to which the state supplements federal funding. The federal funding guidelines are complex but generally are intended to provide for families with extraordinarily limited incomes, children whose family income is under 133% of the U. S. federal poverty level—$23,050 for a family of four in the continental United States in 2012 (United States Department of Health and Human Services [USDHHS], 2012a), and others with proof of citizenship or immigration documentation who have very low incomes and who meet other eligibility criteria such as a specified level of disability (Klees, Wolfe, & Curtis, 2011). Medicare benefits are also complex but are generally thought of as funding medical care for those aged 65 and over. Depending on the type of coverage, services may include hospital care, home health care, physician's fees, outpatient care, and pharmaceuticals for U. S. citizens and selected legal aliens. Other publicly funded health services include specialized populations such as the Children's Health Insurance Program (CHIP), Department of Defense, and Veteran's Affairs. (See Klees et al. for an excellent overview of the very complex world of federal government funding under Titles XVIII and XIX of the Social Security Act.)

Spiraling health-care costs and concurrent lack of health care coverage for large portions of the population are noted by many as the most challenging problems in the U.S. health-care system (Hellander, Himmelstein, & Woolhandler, 2013). In 2010, an estimated $2.6 trillion was spent on health care in the United States (Centers for Medicare and Medicaid Services, 2011), an average of more than $8,000 per person (The World Bank, 2012). Almost 33% of health care costs were paid by private insurers, 20% by Medicare, more than 15% by Medicaid, and almost 4% was from publicly funded programs such as CHIP, Department of Defense, and Veteran's Affairs. Approximately 12% of health-care costs in 2010 came from out-of-pocket costs to the consumer and almost 11% was from other blended public and private payers such as workman's compensation (Kaiser Family Foundation, 2012).

Despite the amount spent and the apparent abundance of programs, reports for 2012 (Cohen & Martinez, 2012) showed that 59.7 million, almost 20% of the population, had been uninsured for at least part of the year prior and 34.6 million, or 11% of the population, had been uninsured for more than a year. About 15% of the population had no usual place to go for health care. By race and ethnicity, 24% of Hispanic people of any race, 17% of non-Hispanic Black persons, and 12% of non-Hispanic White persons had no usual place to go for health care. At the same time, 6% of the population failed to obtain needed medical care over the preceding year due to cost. This was true for 6% of the White population and almost 8% of the non-Hispanic Black and Hispanic populations.

The requirement for legal immigration status means that the many persons who do not have such status do not have any health insurance coverage. Additionally, many "working poor" are not able to afford insurance. For people who are not eligible for federally funded programs and who have no or few financial resources, health care is often provided at emergency rooms in hospitals that do not turn away those without insurance.

The complexity of health disproportionality and disparities in the United States is immediately apparent in a quick review of selected statistics reported in Robert Wood Johnson Foundation's (RWJF, 2012) *Disparities Fast Facts*.

- Infant Mortality Rates

  Large disparities in infant mortality rates persist. From 2000–2007, infants born to Black women were 1.5 to 3 times more likely to die than those born to women of other races and ethnicities.

  Source: Centers for Disease Control and Prevention

- Chronic Illness Disparities

  Elevated rates of chronic illness due to health disparities will cost the U.S. health care system an estimated $337 billion from 2009–2018. About $220 billion of that cost will be incurred by Medicare.

  Source: The Urban Institute

- Black Population has Higher Death Rate

  In 2009, the age-adjusted death rate for the non-Hispanic Black population was 26.6% higher than that of the non-Hispanic White population.

  Source: Centers for Disease Control and Prevention

- Minorities Experience Higher Rates of Illness and Death

  At no time in U.S. history has the health status of minority populations equaled or even approximated that of Whites. With few exceptions, all racial and ethnic minorities experience higher rates of illness and death than non-minorities.

  Source: Institute of Medicine

- Disparities among Minorities in Health and Health Care

  Racial and ethnic minorities suffer from worse health and receive lower-quality care than Whites—regardless of where they live, their income, or their health insurance coverage.

  Source: Institute of Medicine

- Worse Cardiovascular Care

  African Americans are less likely to receive recommended cardiovascular medications like beta blockers, blood clot drugs, or aspirin.

  Source: Institute of Medicine

- Appropriate Procedures and Therapies

  African Americans with coronary artery disease or heart attacks are significantly less likely than Whites to receive appropriate procedures or therapies.

  Source: Institute of Medicine

- Hispanics Less Likely to Get Major Procedures

  Hispanics are less likely than non-Hispanics to receive major procedures in 38 of 63 different disease categories.

  Source: Institute of Medicine

- Inequities in Therapeutic Care
  African Americans are significantly less likely than Whites to receive major therapeutic procedures in almost half of 77 disease categories.
  Source: Institute of Medicine
- Disparities in Cardiac Care
  Minorities are less likely to be given appropriate cardiac medications or undergo bypass surgery.
  Source: Institute of Medicine
- Unequal Quality of Care
  Even when access to care is equal, racial and ethnic minorities tend to receive a lower quality of health care than Whites.
  Source: Institute of Medicine
- Diabetes Causes More Deaths for Hispanics
  Hispanics are almost twice as likely as non-Hispanic Whites to die from diabetes.
  Source: Institute of Medicine
- Disproportionate Deaths among American Indians
  American Indians disproportionately die from diabetes, liver disease and cirrhosis, and unintentional injuries.
  Source: Institute of Medicine
- More Deaths from Disease
  African Americans die more frequently from heart disease, cancer, diseased blood vessels in the brain, and HIV/AIDS than any other U.S. racial or ethnic group.
  Source: Institute of Medicine
- Communities of Color are More Likely to be Uninsured
  People from communities of color are more likely to be uninsured. In 2009, 32.4% of Hispanics, 21% of African Americans, and 17.2% of Asians were uninsured compared with 12% of non-Hispanic Whites.
  Source: U.S. Census Bureau
- The Impact of Health Care Expenses
  High health care expenses impact poor people at a rate of five times that of high-income earners.
  Source: Agency for Healthcare Research and Quality

From: Robert Wood Johnson's *Disparities Fast Facts*, 2012. *Robert Wood Johnson Foundation.*
Used with permission from the Robert Wood Johnson Foundation.

This rather lengthy list reflects only a portion of the disparities experienced by different racial and ethnic groups in the United States.

To provide an idea of how the health status and well-being of various populations experience disparities, it is instructive to look at the Kaiser Family Foundation's (KFF) study of men's health-care disparities (James, Salganicoff, Ranji, Goodwin, & Duckett, 2012). In this study, minority men were self-identified as Black, Hispanic, Asian and Native Hawaiian or other Pacific Islander (NHPI), and American Indian/Alaska Native. There is also a KFF study specific to women, published in 2009, but for the purposes of illustrating some of the social, economic, and health system influences on minority populations, the men's study contains some of the most recent data analyses currently available on this topic. Data were largely collected from Behavioral Risk Factor Surveillance System (BRFSS) and the Current Population Survey (CPS) for men ages 18–64 in the years 2006–2008. There were several additional sources of information such as the *National Survey on Drug Use and Health*. New AIDS cases rates for 2004 were generated with data from the Centers for Disease Control and Prevention (CDC). The U.S. Census and other government reporting systems such as the American Community Survey, CDC health surveillance systems, and Bureau of Justice Statistics were also used. "The disparities rates were calculated by weighted average of the ratio of the mean prevalence for each racial and ethnic group divided by the mean prevalence for non-Hispanic White men in that state. Weights for averaging were based on the proportion of the state's minority population" (James et al., 2012, pp. 65–66). Selected items such as median household income and wage gap were reversed to maintain consistency with the higher number being the least favorable; for example, higher rates of disease prevalence for minority men indicated a disparity that was captured by a score in which one equaled no disparity in rates of disease and scores higher than one indicated a disparity.

Indicators of health disparities were divided into three dimensions: health status; access to, and utilization of, health care; and social determinants of poorer health. Ten indicators of health status were selected for their association with "health problems, premature death, and disability" (James et al., 2012, p. 4). They included, for example, self-reported poor or fair health status, unhealthy days, limited activity days, serious psychological distress, smoking, binge drinking, and health problems such as diabetes and cardiovascular disease. Health-care access and utilization included health insurance, a primary physician or health-care provider, regular checkups, dental checkups, colorectal cancer screening (ages 50–64), and not visiting the doctor due to cost. The social determinants of health included poverty, median household income, no high school diploma, unemployment, wage gap, and incarceration rate per 100,000 men.

Overall, men of color fared considerably worse than their White counterparts. Often, in states that did not have disparities or where the disparity favored men of color, both Whites and men of color were doing very poorly. For those with higher disparities, self-reported fair or poor health status was double for all minority men (17%) than for non-Hispanic White men (8.5%). Almost 16% of non-Hispanic White men lacked health insurance coverage, while the rates for Black, American Indian and Alaska Native, and Hispanic men were 28.8%, 38.5%, and 46%, respectively. Likewise, 8.7% of non-Hispanic White men were lacking a high school diploma. The percentages of men lacking high school diplomas were 16.2%, 21.9%, and 38.6% for Black men, American Indian men and Hispanic men, respectively. Of 50 states and the District of Columbia (DC), 16 states and DC had overall disparities of 2:1 or greater, with the disparities for unfavorable health status, care, and social determinants of ill health at almost 6:1. That is, minority men were almost six times more likely to suffer ill health, to be at greater risk for ill health, and to lack access to sufficient medical care. Notably, "in every state and among every social determinant indicator, men of color fared worse than White men" (James et al., p. 5), unlike in the health status and access dimensions, where a small number of indicators were found to be slightly higher in White men. "The highest disparity scores were found for no high school diploma (disparity score 2.96), incarceration (disparity score 2.76), and poverty (2.09) where minority men had rates that were twice as high as or greater than that of White men. The smallest disparities were found for wage gap (disparity score 1.46) and unemployment (disparity score 1.55)" where rates for minority men were one- and-one-half times that of White men (James et al., p. 5).

Each racial and ethnic group faced distinct health, health-care, and socioeconomic challenges. Although it is not desirable to group many different peoples into single groups, for example, Hawaiians and Pacific Islanders with Asian Americans (see for example, Srinivasan & Guillermo, 2000), and all Hispanics, regardless of country of origin (Jerant, Arellanes, & Franks, 2008), the small numbers of the former and the absence of sufficient detail in some studies often do not support separate analyses. One should be cautioned, then, against assuming that these numbers represent the various subgroups within the larger group sample.

- The significant health and socioeconomic struggles that many American Indian and Alaska Native men faced was striking. Native American men had higher rates of health and access challenges than men in other racial and ethnic groups on all the health indicators with the exception of self-reported health status and new AIDS cases. This pattern was generally evident throughout the country. The high rates of smoking and obesity among Native American men were also notable given the widespread impact of these indicators. They also had the highest poverty rate and the second poorest educational attainment, unemployment rate, and incarceration rate among men.
- For Hispanic men, access and utilization were consistent problems. More than 40% of Latino men lacked insurance, a personal doctor/health care provider, delayed or went without care because of cost, or did not have timely colon cancer screening. Latino men also had the lowest median household income, the largest wage gap, and the lowest educational status.
- Black men experienced consistently higher rates of problems associated with social determinants of health than Whites. Black men also experienced unemployment and incarceration rates that far exceeded any other racial or ethnic group. They also had high rates of poverty and low median household income compared to other groups. The most striking health disparity was the extremely high rate of new AIDS cases among Black men.
- Asian American, Native Hawaiian, and Pacific Islander men had the lowest rate of health problems and the fewest barriers to access of all subgroups of men, even White men. While their access measures were often comparable to those of White men, their experiences often varied considerably by state. This group also fared comparably or better than White men on most of the social determinants (James et al., 2012, p. 3 [This information was reprinted with permission from the Henry J. Kaiser Family Foundation.[1]]).

---

1   The Kaiser Family Foundation, a leader in health policy analysis, health journalism and communication, is dedicated to filling the need for trusted, independent information on the major health issues facing our nation and its people. The Foundation is a non-profit private operating foundation, based in Menlo Park, California.

UNDERSTANDING THE PROBLEMS AND NEEDS OF ETHNIC
MINORITY POPULATIONS IN THE SYSTEM

It is apparent that disproportionality and disparity in health status and heath care permeate society. From societal factors such as the effects of poverty and the experience of discrimination on health status (Pratto et al., 2000; Wilkinson & Pickett, 2009; Williams & Eberhardt, 2008), to inequities in health-care delivery, people who live in poverty and those who represent visible minorities or ethnic groups suffer disproportionate rates of disease and ill health leading to disproportionate rates of chronic disease, disability, and early death. Poverty and rural residence are notably associated with some risks, but ethnicity and race alone, or in combination with other risk factors, often add significantly to the risk burden. Health status is threatened by lack of resources (for example, safe housing and adequate nutritional food), lack of education, historic trauma, stresses associated with living in poverty, stresses associated with prejudice and discrimination, inequitable availability of health supports, inequitable health care, and many other societal threats to well-being (Adler & Newman, 2002; Gans et al., 2009; Krieger & Higgins, 2002; Machenbach et al., 2008; Macinko & Starfield, 2002; National Prevention Council, 2011; Starfield, 2007).

Teasing apart the effects of poverty and race/ethnicity, Nazroo (2003) and Ram (2005), among others, independently and through different approaches, support the impact of race on health inequities when controlling for income. Historically, Blacks, American Indians/Aboriginal peoples, and immigrants have very different histories and current conditions, but they are more likely than White citizens of Canada and the United States to suffer myriad inequities in the social determinants of ill health, with American Indians/Aboriginal peoples often faring worst of all (Ng, Wilkins, Gendron, & Berthelot, 2005; Smiley, 2009). Braveman (2007) suggests it is not just an issue of race or one's ethnic identity but an issue of power and exclusion. Accepting that as true (Galabuzi, 2005, 2009), racism and the "racializing" of ethnic and cultural groups (Cobas, Duany, & Feagin, 2009; Razack, 2008) is one of the major sources of reinforcing existing power structures and perpetrating exclusion (Nelson, 2009; see also, examples such as Centre for Equality Rights in Accommodation, 2009). For example, when a person or group is assigned a subordinate rank within a society, poor health is likely to result when harassment and a lack of social support are also present (Green & Darity, 2010).

Those with power within a social structure are more likely to control and access resources and to maintain the structure in a way that perpetuates the system and preserves bias in favor of their own views and preferences. It follows that, given the history of race in the United States, initial access to the health system is restricted for racial and ethnic minorities through limited coverage or resources and through other pervasive barriers such as inadequate transportation options to allow them to access clinics or other services (Institute of Medicine [IOM], 2011). Even when health services are accessed, they are tailored toward the prevailing ideas of health and may not take into account cultural needs and practices of minorities, such as through a perceived lack of respect for traditional Aboriginal approaches to healing (see Health Council of Canada [HCC], 2012, for examples).

It is apparent that people experience health care at many levels. The most familiar experience is one of discrimination by an individual—for example, direct or indirect racial discrimination by frontline health services staff. The larger picture is one of systemic or institutional discrimination, and one expression of this is what Gee, Ro, Shariff-Marco, and Chae (2009) call the "discrimination iceberg" (see also Gee & Ro, 2009). Discrimination exists at various levels, with the tip of the iceberg being overt racial or ethnic bias but with less overt discrimination being the most prevalent.

More overt or direct discrimination within the health-care setting would include negative social stereotypes, which are recognized to influence the behaviors of health professionals and providers in their interactions with clients, whether consciously or unconsciously (Anderson et al., 2003). An example of this would be the withholding of pain killers for a client in pain due to a mistaken assumption that ethnic minorities are likely to become addicted if provided with certain pain medications (see HCC, 2012, and Anderson et al., 2003, for this and other examples).

Structural discrimination and institutional racism within health services, such as restricted access to the system as previously highlighted, would be classified by Gee et al. (2009) as part of the iceberg lurking below the water line, and until this less obvious discrimination is dealt with, there will be no major change in health disparities. In a racialized society, race, ethnicity, and culture together constitute a powerful pathway to increased likelihood of experiencing social determinants of health inequities and the resulting imbalance in health status (Access Alliance Multicultural Community Health Centre, 2005). A further related consideration in designing health-care systems is that of the expectation of bad treatment as an understandable response to previous bad experiences. Given all of the barriers identified, it is the responsibility of the health-care practitioner and the system at large to ensure that the client does not feel alienated or judged but safe and understood within the health-care setting (HCC, 2012).

CASE EXAMPLE: THE DEATH OF ANNA BROWN

The cost of hospital care and societal attitudes about people who are poor and Black can easily interact to result in dire consequences for those unlucky enough to need medical care.

Anna Brown, a 29-year-old Black woman, died in jail after making three attempts to seek health care at two different hospitals in the days preceding her death. In her third, and last, attempt to seek care, she told hospital personnel at an emergency room that her legs hurt so badly she couldn't walk. After examination including an ultrasound of her legs, doctors discharged Ms. Brown but she returned eight hours later and was again discharged. However Ms. Brown refused to leave the hospital until she received adequate medical attention.

Eventually, police were called to the scene, and the doctor assured them Ms. Brown was sufficiently healthy to leave the hospital and be taken to jail. Despite Ms. Brown telling police she was unable to stand due to the pain in her legs, she was arrested for trespassing and taken from the emergency room to a jail cell. Ms. Brown was taken by law enforcement officers into the police station, carried by her arms and legs into a cell and left there on the floor. Less than an hour later, Ms. Brown died where she had been left.

The autopsy revealed blood clots had started in her legs, likely causing the pain she had been seeking assistance for, before travelling to her lungs and causing her death. Despite both the hospital and police suspecting that Ms. Brown was using drugs, there were no intoxicating or illegal substances in her system. (Summarized from Byers 2012.)

It appears that Ms. Brown had wider social and medical issues such as homelessness and possible—but undiagnosed—mental health issues that could have affected professionals' perceptions of her and their beliefs that she might be on drugs or seeking drugs. Whatever the assumptions were, these beliefs appeared to halt any search for medical explanations for her pain and may have led them to think the pain was not real. Giving Ms. Brown the benefit of the doubt and believing her accounts of pain might have led staff to keep her under observation in the hospital for at least 24 hours, in case she did continue to deteriorate, rather than concluding that she was not in genuine need of assistance and therefore needed to leave.

It is possible that the treatment of a White woman in the same circumstances as Ms. Brown would have been the same. However, when the larger picture is considered, it becomes clear that ethnic minorities are disproportionately at risk of situations similar to those leading to the death of Ms. Brown in the circumstances described here.

There are also reports of far more directly expressed discrimination, such as the 2012 report by the Health Council of Canada detailing the story of an Aboriginal man who entered an emergency department after being assaulted. When a physician attended and asked the nurse why the patient—whom the nurse had not allowed to lie on the bed—was in a chair, the nurse stated that he was dirty, and that, in any case, when he left the hospital, he would only return to the street to engage in the same risky behaviors that had caused him to come into the emergency department on this occasion. In fact, the man had been assaulted on his way home from work. It appears unlikely that the nurse would have made such an assumption for every person who entered the emergency room after being assaulted.

These cases capture some of the complexities of racial and ethnic disparities in health and health services. Racial and ethnic minorities are significantly more likely to be unemployed or to receive lower wages than their White counterparts and therefore more likely to struggle financially and be at greater risk of homelessness. In addition, statistics also detailed previously show that minorities are significantly more likely to suffer ill health, to be at greater risk for ill health, and to lack access to sufficient medical care than White persons. Racial bias by health service professionals, whether conscious or unconscious, is a relevant factor. A 2007 study found unconscious or implicit bias among physicians in favor of White men over

Black men in terms of treatment offered for chest pain based on a picture of the patient's face and a description of presentation at a hospital with sharp chest pain; the higher the level of bias, the higher the likelihood of treating White patients and not treating Black patients. Implicit stereotypes of Black Americans as less cooperative with medical procedures and overall were also identified (Green et al., 2007).

SYSTEMS EFFORTS TO ADDRESS DISPROPORTIONALITY AND DISPARITIES: GENERAL BARRIERS AND ETHNIC-SPECIFIC BARRIERS FACED AND CHALLENGES ENCOUNTERED

Systems efforts need to deal with institutional and direct service issues in order to address health and health service disparities. The creation of the Office of Minority Health (OMH) in 1986 was one of the early federal efforts to address health disparities. The OMH was established in response to the 1985 *Secretary's Task Force Report on Black and Minority Health* (USDHHS, 1985). The office of the assistant secretary for health supports the mission of the secretary of the USDHHS, along with the offices of the surgeon general, adolescent health, women's health, and others. The mission of OMH is to improve the health of racial and ethnic minorities through promoting policies and activities to collect relevant data, increase awareness, promote networks and collaboration, foster research and demonstration projects, and to serve as a general catalyst for change by partnering with public and private organizations in the health sector and across departments. For well over 25 years, various agencies, departments, and offices in the federal government have each, within their own mission, identified and reported on the nature, extent, and consequences of health disparities (IOM, 2012). A few of the seminal moments among these developments follow.

In 2000, the National Center for Minority Health and Health Disparities (NCMHD) was created in the National Institutes of Health with a focus on research and training, and the Agency of Healthcare Research and Quality (AHRQ) was authorized to monitor and report on progress in the reduction of health disparities (IOM, 2012). Since that time, AHRQ's biennial publication of a *National Healthcare Disparities Report* has continued to document the degree to which racial and ethnic minorities suffer inequalities in health and health care from birth to death. In

2003, with *Unequal Treatment; Confronting Racial and Ethnic Dispari-ties in Health Care*, the Institute of Medicine (IOM, 2003) assembled and published data documenting the extent of disparities in access to and qual-ity of health care for racial and ethnic minorities. This publication inten-sified the effort to identify the nature of and reason for the problem and to develop methods to ensure equitable health care and health status to all. The IOM (2012) cites Howard Koh, Assistant Secretary for Health, USDHHS, detailing a number of federal initiatives to address and amelio-rate health disparities. In one example, the 2008 Medicare Improvements for Patients and Providers Act (MIPPA) required USDHHS to enhance its capabilities for documenting racial and ethnic health disparities. Many efforts during this time were focused on better understanding the extent, nature, and causes of the problem.

At the same time the government was increasingly recognizing and addressing disparities and inequalities, a number of private foundations and health organizations were also active in supporting research to inform policy and practice. The Robert Wood Johnson Foundation, Kaiser Family Foundation, and W. K. Kellogg Foundation represent just three of these.

Yet with all this activity, in a 2010 review of progress to date, IOM Roundtable (IOM, 2012) participants cited minimal gains since the year 2000 and identified the numerous barriers to achieving equality for all. Some of the gains noted included increasing knowledge about health inequality and its causes, more public awareness of these inequalities and their consequences, and increasing efforts to involve communities at all lev-els of government in planning solutions.

The barriers to successfully alleviating health disparities and inequalities recognized at the IOM Roundtable (IOM, 2012) include the current state of the economy, ongoing socioeconomic disadvantage, racism, local and regional environmental factors including continued housing segregation, the need to raise public awareness, and the absence of a unified approach to "health in all policies" crossing institutional barriers.

With respect to attempting to change the service delivery model, uni-versal or nearly universal systems efforts to improve health status and health care range from federal legislation such as the Affordable Care Act (ACA, 2010), which expands government funding to provide more health-care coverage to more people, to efforts among employers to foster wellness at work. Universal efforts to reach all people in a system may not address all aspects of disparities such as racial bias, but they will be inclusive of many more minority persons than has been true to date.

However, the national dialogue about the Affordable Care Act (ACA, 2010) revealed additional political and economic barriers to more holistic approaches to supporting good health for everyone. Some of the difficulties encountered in attempting to expand coverage include the reticence of Americans to support universal, government-funded benefits for people in poverty and specifically for those who are different from themselves. The news media is replete with concerns over the extent of the ACA. For example, Campbell (2012) writes that the health care reform "was limited by the terms of the debate, particularly the enduring belief that markets are always more efficient than government. . . ." To date, the ACA has withstood attempts at repeal and a challenge in the Supreme Court (Campbell, 2012). Yet there are continuing concerns regarding the future extent of employer health coverage under the ACA and the degree to which some recalcitrant states will refuse to expand Medicaid coverage in accordance with the Supreme Court decision allowing such a refusal.

In addition to the political sensibilities of Americans with respect to individual responsibility, concerns among the states regarding unfunded federal mandates, and the vested interests of many in the health industry, there are structural barriers to racial and ethnic equality. Jones (2006) traces the history of health disparities of indigenous peoples in the New World, suggesting that reasons given for such disparities were more often products of the culture and time in which they were offered than helpful insights regarding the actual forces at play. In a more pragmatic look at how current systems perpetuate inequality, Trahant (2009) identifies the funding for the Indian Health Service as one source of injustice. Alaska Natives or American Indians who live on reservations and those who are recognized members of a tribe or group under federal supervision are served by the Indian Health Service of the federal government. The Indian Health Service provides health services to about two million Alaska Natives and American Indians, 600,000 of whom are served through 33 urban clinics (USDHHS, 2012b). Yet these services are woefully underfunded. In fact, Indians suffer some of the worst health and health risks in spite of this "universal" coverage. Trahant (2009) describes the paradox of the Indian Health Service, noting that they are given a fraction of the per capita resources available to the larger population, yet they have accomplished amazing things with these limited resources. By focusing on infrastructure, they were able to reach the entire population and reduce illness. For example, in one initiative, by ensuring running water and appropriate sewage systems, it radically reduced the rate of gastrointestinal disease among American Indians and Alaska Natives. In spite of notable successes, the level of funding keeps equitable health-care coverage out of reach.

The experience of Hispanic peoples may depend largely on their country of origin (including the United States), immigration status, where they live (for example, the degree of inhospitable laws and policies in a state or community), how long their families have resided in the United States, their degree of acculturation, and family income (see for example, Acevedo-Garcia, Bates, Osypuk, & McArdle, 2010; Jerant et al., 2008; Lebrun, 2012). For those who are primarily Spanish speaking and for others who speak English as a second language, systemic barriers may involve the availability of linguistically appropriate services as much as larger systems issues that are at issue for many visible minorities.

Using the equal protection clause of the Fourteenth Amendment to the U.S. Constitution, in 1996, Menefee posited that systemic barriers to equitable health care for Black people are woven into the fabric of medical education, the development of medical centers, and into health-care financing in the United States. He proposed using the Fourteenth Amendment to examine the system in its entirety, rather than focusing only on its unfortunate outcomes. Other ongoing systemic challenges such as disproportionate arrest rates of Black men and lack of investment in neighborhood-building have required that systemic efforts not only attend to the provision of health services but that they also address the socioeconomic well-being of the people to be served to stem the tide of poor health for these populations.

The aim of culturally competent health care is to ensure that any care given is appropriate to each client whatever their race or ethnic background and to reduce mistakes or misunderstandings caused by poor understanding due to cultural differences or lack of knowledge regarding relevant cultural aspects of client care (Anderson et al., 2003). An important aspect of policy development is addressing the direct service experience for

individuals, for example, through action to reduce the incidence of negative stereotyping by medical professionals (such as the previous example
relating to pain medications being withheld for ethnic minorities). Cultural competence applies not only to direct contact by health professionals
with individuals but also to the health system overall. Although approaches
such as attending to offering frontline services in a culturally competent
and linguistically appropriate way will have less broad ranging impact than
wider systemic changes, they can also be more immediately addressed than
those systemic barriers ingrained in our society that may require many years
to overcome. Addressing systemic and institutional discrimination longer term will require a holistic, collaborative approach to health involving
not only health-care services but wider community organizations such as
housing and education as some of the numerous factors influencing health.
Attempts to change service delivery models and the potential expansion of
government funding to extend health-care coverage to the entire population are examples of potential systematic efforts to address current racial
and ethnic disparities.

CHANGING MACROSYSTEMS: CURRENT PRACTICES AND PREVENTIVE SYSTEM EFFORTS TO ADDRESS DISPROPORTIONALITY AND DISPARITIES

In 2010, NCMHD became a full-fledged institute in the National Institutes of Health (NIH, 2013) and is now the National Institute on Minority Health and Health Disparities (see NIMHD, n.d.). NIMHD's mission
is to support research on better understanding of disparities and inequalities and to identify effective mechanisms for addressing them. A number of federal, state, and local agencies, organizations, and offices track
health disparities. At the federal level, this charge is addressed jointly by
OMH, CDC, and AHRQ, among others. The CDC now complements
the AHRQ biennial report with the *CDC Health Disparities & Inequalities Report* (CDC, 2011), which analyzes health disparities by sex, race
and ethnicity, income, education, disability status, and other social characteristics. Other current federal efforts include focusing more attention
on electronic data collection, supporting community initiatives through
a variety of mechanisms (IOM, 2012), and the development of a National

Partnership for Action to End Health Disparities, which has supported the development of a recent *Action Plan to Reduce Racial and Ethnic Health Disparities* that, based on the information gleaned over the years, focuses specifically on developing action plans and on assigning areas of responsibility for implementation.

Most notably, current systemic efforts to address barriers to health care and to improve health status are being implemented through the ACA (2010). One of the principal goals of the ACA legislation is to aid those without health insurance and to expand Medicaid to cover more low-income children and families. The ACA specifically provides consumer protections to ensure ongoing coverage in the face of chronic health problems, preexisting conditions, prohibition of lifetime dollar limits on coverage, and other limitations imposed by the insurance industry. In 2011, people with Medicare received selected preventive services and discounts on brand-name drugs. In 2011 and 2012, emphasis had also been placed on improving quality and lowering costs, for example, undertaking federal initiatives to improve health-care quality and efficiency. In 2013, among other measures, the law provided for the expansion of Medicaid funding to preventive care and increased reimbursement rates for physicians who provide Medicaid services. In 2014, along with continued emphasis on improving quality and lowering costs, Americans who earn less than 133% of the poverty level are eligible for Medicaid. (See also, HealthCare.gov, 2012, for more information.) By targeting people who have systematically fallen through the "safety net," it is hoped this law will lift health-care access and health status of all people in need. It is not the single payer approach that many would like to see, but it will begin to cover many people who have always been without.

To address prevention, the U. S. Office of the Surgeon General hosted a National Prevention Council (2011) that released a report detailing a National Prevention Strategy to achieve better health and wellness. This report identifies critical issues and provides a blueprint for a coordinated effort between the government and community partners including policymakers, service purchasers, employers, funders, researchers, providers, and health educators. In one example, speaking to the community context of health care, the report addresses enforcement of environmental standards and regulations; promoting safe, affordable, and accessible housing;

strengthening state, tribal, local, and territorial public health departments; and also addresses enhancing cross-sector collaboration, among other recommendations. These recommendations are based on current research findings; along with recommendations, health indicators for the recommendations are identified. As part of this strategy, the council recommended the following strategies to eliminate health disparities in the United States:

- *Ensure a strategic focus on communities at greatest risk*, including identifying levels of risk and enlisting the participation of community leaders as well as engagement with the local culture and people.
- *Reduce disparities in access to quality health care* by broadening the scope of preventative care, increasing access, improving health information, and providing outreach and support services; tailoring of services to the needs of specific peoples is also recommended.
- *Increase the capacity of the prevention workforce to identify and address disparities* by ensuring this workforce is "culturally competent" and diverse, reflecting the richness of varied community characteristics.
- *Support research to identify effective strategies to eliminate health disparities* because research on effective ways to address the needs of diverse peoples is often lacking.
- *Standardize and collect data to better identify and address disparities*— improving the standardization of data collected will improve the ability of the government and its partners to better identify and target efforts to address disparities.

Many recommended actions in the report are intended to reduce disparities. Among these, the federal government commits to supporting cross-sector activities to enhance access to high quality education, jobs, economic opportunities, and healthy living; identifying and mapping high-need areas and aligning existing resources to meet those needs; and to developing and evaluating community-based interventions to reduce health disparities. Selected examples of actions partners can take include maximizing use of health data collection and analysis, providing for workplace prevention activities, and hiring more health-care staff from underrepresented racial and ethnic minorities. These efforts do not encompass a revisualizing of medical education and facility development, but they do offer a practical place to begin.

CROSS-SYSTEMS EFFORTS AND CULTURALLY COMPETENT SERVICES OFFERED

The need to address racial and ethnic disparities and disproportionality in health and health services is widely recognized and, in light of the scale of the problem as detailed earlier, is clearly an issue that negatively impacts a large percentage of the population. The World Health Organization (2013) references in its constitution the highest attainable standard of health as a fundamental right of every human being. Successfully tackling health disparities would benefit not only those individuals currently experiencing such health or health service issues but also the wider community—for example, by reducing the overall cost of health care for all and increasing productivity of individuals (IOM, 2011), as well as reducing the costs of those medical errors or unnecessary treatments caused by lack of culturally competent treatment and services previously highlighted. In 2009, Waidmann estimated the financial cost of preventable disease among minorities over the subsequent ten years to be approximately $337 billion.

Nationally and locally some cross-systems efforts to provide culturally competent services have been made at the direct services level and at broader systemic and institutional levels. Federal efforts in cross-systems coordination are embodied in the USDHHS Health Disparities Council, created by the ACA (2010). The council will coordinate activities across federal agencies and departments and will aid in developing a coordinated effort to support activities to reduce health disparities. The IOM (2011) refers to the National Center for Healthy Housing (NCHH) in Columbia, Maryland, a nonprofit organization aiming to combat housing inadequacies and to provide healthy, safe, and environmentally sound homes to families regardless of income (NCHH, 2008). The NCHH has worked with the public health, housing, and environmental sectors to tackle problematic policies and practices and to conduct research into aspects of housing and health. Its various aims include increasing the evidence base for new policies and standards.

At the state and local levels, numerous initiatives are also underway. One example of a community-based effort is the combined Phillips-Powderhorn Experience and the Allina Backyard Project in Minneapolis, Minnesota (IOM, 2011). In a 2009 meeting, the mayor of Minneapolis described coordinated efforts to engage in community building with the neighborhoods that suffered from the greatest unemployment, poorest housing, and greatest health disparities. The city, with its partners, focused on housing, access to healthy food, access to health care, job training, and job placement. They also worked with juvenile justice to launch a public health approach to youth violence, engaging the community in planning a comprehensive approach. Additionally, they have implemented Safe Routes to School, a federal program to ensure safe passage of students on their way to and from their schools. Allina, the health-care organization based in the neighborhood, has also funded a number of health-related initiatives that will specifically target neighborhood residents.

The Food Trust is another nonprofit organization referred to by the IOM (2011). Based in Philadelphia, they collaborated with the Greater Philadelphia Urban Affairs Coalition, recognizing the need for broad policy changes and investment in providers of healthy foods to underserved communities (The Food Trust, 2012). The Food Trust has worked with residents and the wider community, including schools, grocers, farmers, and policymakers locally and nationally, achieving improved community access to, and affordability of, healthy foods. The involvement of a research and evaluation team has also assisted in creating models for replication, and the project has since been replicated in other communities.

Another notable program is the African American Health Disparity Project (AAHDP) in San Francisco, California, that aims to improve the health status of African Americans and to eliminate any institutional racism within the local health-care system (AAHDP, n.d.a), referencing collaboration with the African American community and those organizations and individuals who are currently advancing health (AAHDP, n.d.a). The Hospital Council of Northern and Central California and every hospital in San Francisco formed the AAHDP (AAHDP, n.d.b), which supports various public health services and other agencies or community groups, including theater groups, the YMCA, and housing projects (AAHDP, n.d.c). Hospitals involved in the project have reported findings such as the need for health-care providers to commit to tackling health and health service disparities long-term, pointing to the long-term buildup of distrust by African American clients of prominently Caucasian-driven health provision overall and the commonly recognized importance of "buy in" by staff when implementing changes (AAHDP, n.d.a).

In 2007, Minyard and colleagues reported lessons learned from Local Access Initiatives across the United States aimed at responding to disparities in health-care access and assisting uninsured and medically indigent people to health-care services and health insurance. A number of policy implications were identified including the possibility that some proposed policy changes to narrow eligibility to coverage programs would increase the need for community initiatives, and that without increased resources the current reliance of community initiatives on volunteerism could be stretched.

Communities from California, New Jersey, Massachusetts, Florida, and other locations also have reported on local initiatives to address disparities. Their systems recommendations include, for example, enhancing leadership and strategy development, promoting information availability, establishing sustainable funding mechanisms to support community health and preventions, collaborating across disciplines for holistic results, expanding community mapping of health indicators, and providing technical assistance and tools to support community-level efforts (IOM, 2011).

Efforts to identify effective culturally competent and linguistically appropriate services were recently undertaken by Wells and Dettlaff (Wells, Vergara, Dettlaff, Janke, & Doyle-Waters, 2011) in a systematic review of research in health and mental health services. The team initially sought to identify all manner of micro to macro adaptations of health and mental health services but found that the most rigorous research yielding evidence about effectiveness was largely found at the micro level (Healey et al., 2012). Although all manner of service adaptations exist, those that were most rigorously tested focused largely on interactions between the health provider or educator and the service recipient. These were often prevention activities to encourage healthy habits or to deter substance use or abuse.

Adaptations of service delivery included in the studies were: (1) consultation with the community or target group, (2) translation of intervention materials, (3) adaptations to the physical location of the service or intervention, (4) the provision of supplementary services, (5) matching service providers and service recipients in language, race, culture, or gender, (6) changes to the way in which service providers interacted with service recipients, and (7) adaptations to the content of the intervention to include culturally or racially specific information.

The outcomes researched in the most rigorous studies included: (1) provider awareness, knowledge, and attitudes; (2) service uptake: completion/participation in the intervention; (3) service recipient awareness, knowledge, and attitudes; (4) health behavior; and (5) indicators of health status. There was not one clear finding about what works in these situations, but the evidence suggests that further understanding and development of targeted interventions that take into account acculturation, identity, and other characteristics may be the most promising in direct interactions or in health promotion.

SPOTLIGHT: PROMISING PRACTICES TO ADDRESS DISPARITIES IN THE HEALTH-CARE SYSTEM

- The combined efforts of the Phillips-Powderhorn Experience and the Allina Backyard Project in Minneapolis, Minnesota, coordinating to engage in community building with the neighborhoods that suffered from the greatest unemployment, poorest housing, and greatest health disparities
- The Food Trust, in collaboration with the Greater Philadelphia Urban Affairs Coalition, working with residents and the wider community, including schools, grocers, farmers, and policymakers both locally and nationally
- The National Center for Healthy Housing (NCHH) in Columbia, Maryland, working with the public health, housing, and environmental sectors to tackle problematic policies and practices
- The African American Health Disparity Project in San Francisco, California, referencing collaboration with the African American community and those organizations and individuals who are currently advancing health. The Hospital Council of Northern and Central California and every hospital in San Francisco formed the AAHDP, which supports various public health services and other agencies or community groups, including theater groups, the YMCA, and housing projects.

FUTURE DIRECTIONS

Systems efforts to address disproportionality and disparities are entwined with efforts to improve health and heath care of the entire population. Because disparities are closely tied to the factors that affect health care for all, such as limited income and lack of health-care benefits at work, addressing the financial and structural barriers to health care for the population at large will also reach many who suffer disproportionately due to being disproportionately represented among the poor and the near poor, and among those with insufficient health benefits. Possible indicators to watch for results of the efforts made include:

1) The proportion of racial and ethnic minority adults in fair or poor health
2) The proportion of individuals who are unable to obtain or who delay obtaining needed health care, prescription, or dental care due to inability to pay
3) The proportion of racial and ethnic minority people who report their health-care provider always listens carefully

The plan that is unfolding is largely reflected in the *HHS Action Plan*:

- Improve the social and economic well-being of the poor—and of racial and ethnic minorities in particular (for example, through housing, education, employment)
- Ensure implementation of efforts to improve public awareness of disparities, to improve health literacy, and to engage racial and ethnic minorities in preventive health behaviors
- Improve access and engagement in health services
- Improve direct interaction with racial and ethnic minorities through increased cultural competency and linguistic appropriateness
- Use increased knowledge available through health monitoring and research to support effective policy changes such as payment reform, regulatory changes, health information technology, and other such initiatives (Shih et al., 2008; for full plan see USDHHS, 2011)

With respect to collaboration, the developments and activities reported suggest that each level of government will need to develop integrative communication among existing departments, with the community, and with partners in the private sector. The federal government's council suggests this is happening at the federal level. The states vary considerably, but vehicles for communication among states (such as the state legislatures) support the idea that developments in individual states can be effectively shared among states and built upon for more effective results. Examples from local communities such as Minneapolis also suggest that the local coordination will need to be specifically tailored to each community and its needs but that it should include principal actors such as health providers, community members, juvenile justice, housing, education, and others. In this analysis, Menefee's (1996) thoughts about going to the very structure of the entire system—including, for example, education of professionals—will be the most effective way to ensure enduring change both at a structural and a direct service level.

The IOM (2011) suggests a number of things that need to be achieved and maintained in order for equitable health to be achieved, including strengthening communities and health system infrastructure, improving access to culturally competent health care and preventative services for those in underserved communities, and supporting local community efforts. The importance of knowledge translation should also not be underestimated. As the body of knowledge in the area of health and health service disproportionality and disparities strengthens, effective translation and dissemination of recommendations and evidence-based practices within a systems theory framework will be key to the successful reduction in, and eventual elimination of, such disparities (See Benjamin, 2010, and Canadian Institutes of Health Research, 2013). Ruffin (2010) highlights that knowledge translation to various communities requires an understanding of each community's unique cultures and attitudes; this bolsters the importance of community engagement and also culturally competent practice, not only in health-care systems but within any efforts to inform and assist communities. Going beyond the aims of the HHS action plan, Anderson et al. (2003) go further in describing factors that contribute to a culturally competent health-care setting (for example, a culturally diverse staff reflective of the client community) and offer details of how services may become culturally and linguistically appropriate (for example, providing instructional literature consistent with a client's cultural norms). Another more specific way of ensuring that the wishes and needs of people of different cultural and socioeconomic backgrounds are better understood in the health-care setting could be, for example, to have patient advocates on staff who would be available and take time that perhaps medical staff may not have to understand the person's point of view and to address any communication issues between them and the medical staff. In sum, we propose the following future directions:

STRATEGIES FOR ADDRESSING AND ELIMINATING DISPROPORTIONALITY AND DISPARITIES

- Engage in a holistic approach, including collaboration with organizations and systems outside of the immediate health providers.
- Educate professionals.
- Develop and implement strategies for effective knowledge translation.
- Invest in community initiatives, particularly those involving cross-systems collaboration.
- Increase the understanding and implementation of various other factors contributing to culturally competent services and practices.
- Engage in collaborative, cross-systems efforts to strengthen communities.

REFERENCES

Access Alliance Multicultural Community Health Centre. (2005). *Racialised groups and health status: A literature review exploring poverty, housing, race-based discrimination and access to health care as determinants of health for racialised groups.* Toronto, Canada: Author.

Acevedo-Garcia, D., Bates, L. M., Osypuk, T. L., & McArdle, N. (2010). The effect of immigrant generation and duration on self-rated health among US adults 2003–2007. *Social Science & Medicine, 71*(6), 1161–1172. DOI: 10.1016/j.socscimed.2010.05.034

Adler, N. E., & Newman, K. (2002). Socioeconomic disparities in health: Pathways and policies. *Health Affairs, 21*(2), 60–76.

African American Health Disparity Project San Francisco. (n.d.a) *Four year project report.* Retrieved from http://www.healthmattersinsf.org/javascript/htmleditor/uploads/AAHD_Four_Year_Report.pdf

African American Health Disparity Project San Francisco. (n.d.b) *Project description.* Retrieved from http://www.hospitalcouncil.net/sites/main/files/file-attachments/description_page.pdf

African American Health Disparity Project San Francisco. (n.d.c) *AAHDP sponsored projects at a glance for 2010.* Retrieved from http://www.healthmattersinsf.org/javascript/htmleditor/uploads/AAHDP_Sponsored_Projects_At_A_Glance_082910__2_.pdf

Anderson, L. M., Scrimshaw, S. G., Fullulove, M. T., Fielding, J. E., Normand, J., and the Task Force on Community Prevention Services. (2003). Culturally competent healthcare systems, a systematic review. *American Journal of Preventative Medicine, 24*(3S), 68–79.

Benjamin, R. (2010). Reflections on addressing health disparities and the national agenda. *American Journal of Public Health, 100*(S1), S7. DOI:10.2105/AJPH.2010.195503

Braveman, P. (2007). We also need bold experiments: A response to Starfield's "Commentary: Pathways of influence on equity in health." *Social Science & Medicine, 64,* 1363–1366. DOI:10.1016/j.socscimed.2006.11.028

Byers, C. (2012, March 25). Woman unhappy with care at St. Mary's hospital is arrested for trespassing, dies in jail. *St Louis Post-Dispatch.* Retrieved from http://www.stltoday.com/news/local/crime-and-courts/woman-unhappy-with-care-at-st-mary-s-hospital-is/article_ed640f3d-64a0-516c-88ff-fb770b5e9677.html

Campbell, A. L. (2012, August 13). The future of U.S. health care. *Boston Review.* Retrieved from http://www.bostonreview.net/us/future-us-health-care-andrea-louise-campbell

Canadian Institutes of Health Research (CIHR). (2013). *More about knowledge translation at CIHR.* Retrieved from http://www.cihr-irsc.gc.ca/e/39033.html

Centers for Disease Control and Prevention (CDC). (2011). *CDC health disparities & inequalities report (CHDIR).* Atlanta, GA: Author. Retrieved from http://www.cdc.gov/minorityhealth/CHDIReport.html

Centers for Medicare & Medicaid Services (CMS) Office of the Actuary, National Health Statistics Group. (2011, July 28). *National Health Expenditure Projections 2010–2020.* Baltimore, MD: Author. Retrieved from http://www.cms.gov/Research-Statistics-Data-and-Systems/Statistics-Trends-and-Reports/NationalHealthExpendData/downloads/proj2010.pdf

Centre for Equality Rights in Accommodation. (2009). *"Sorry, it's rented." Measuring discrimination in Toronto's rental housing market.* Toronto: Centre for Equality Rights in Accommodation. Retrieved from http://www.equalityrights.org/cera/docs/CERAFinalReport.pdf

Cobas, J. A., Duany, J., & Feagin, J. R. (2009). *How the United States racializes Latinos: White hegemony and its consequences.* Boulder, CO: Paradigm.

Cohen R. A., & Martinez M. E. (2012, September). *Health insurance coverage: Early release of estimates from the National Health Interview Survey, January–March 2012.* National Center for Health Statistics. Retrieved from: http://www.cdc.gov/nchs/nhis/releases.htm

The Food Trust. (2012). *Making Healthy Food Available to All.* Retrieved from http://thefoodtrust.org/

Galabuzi, G. E. (2005). *Canada's economic apartheid: The social exclusion of racialized groups in the new century.* Toronto, Canada: Canadian Scholars' Press.

Galabuzi, G. E. (2009). Social Exclusion. In Raphael, D. (Ed.), *Social determinants of health: Canadian perspectives* (2nd Ed.) (pp. 252–268). Toronto, Canada: Canadian Scholars' Press.

Gans, K. M., Risica, P. M., Strolla, L. O., Fournier, L., Kirtania, U., Upegui, D., et al. (2009). Effectiveness of different methods for delivering tailored nutrition education to low income, ethnically diverse adults. *International Journal of Behavioral Nutrition and Physical Activity, 6(24).* DOI: 10.1186/1479-5868-6-24

Gee, G. C. & Ro, A. (2009). Racism and discrimination. In Trinh-Shevrin, C. Islam, N.S. Rey, M.J. (Eds.), *Asian American Communities and Health: Context, Research, Policy and Action.* San Francisco, CA: Jossey Bass.

Gee, G. C., Ro, A., Shariff-Marco, S., & Chae, D. (2009). Racial Discrimination and Health Among Asian Americans: Evidence, Assessment, and Directions for Future Research. *Epidemiologic Reviews, 31,* 130-11. DOI:10.1093/epirev/mxp009

Green, A. R., Carney, D. R., Pallin, D. J., Ngo, L. H., Raymond, K. L., Iezzoni, L. I., et al. (2007). Implicit Bias among Physicians and its Prediction of Thrombolysis Decisions for Black and White Patients. *Journal of General Internal Medicine, 22(9).* 1231–1238. DOI:10.1007/s11606-007-0258.5

Green, T. L. & Darity, W. A., Jr. (2010). Under the Skin: Using Theories From Biology and the Social Sciences to Explore the Mechanisms Behind the Black-White Health Gap. *The American Journal of Public Health, 100 (S1).* S36–S40.

Healey, P., Dettlaff, A. J. Jantz, I., Vergara, A., Janke, R., Jantz, I. Caplan, D. . . . Wells, S. J. (2012). *Effectiveness of Adaptations to Enhance Cultural Competence, Appropriateness, and Safety of Health and Mental Health Services.* Kelowna, BC: Centre for the Study of Services to Children and Families, University of British Columbia.

HealthCare.gov. (2012, October). *Key features of the Affordable Care Act, by year.* Washington, DC: U.S. Department of Health and Human Services. Retrieved from http://www.healthcare.gov/law/features/index.html

Health Council of Canada. (2012). *Empathy, dignity and respect. Creating cultural safety for Aboriginal people in urban health care.* Retrieved from http://www.healthcouncilcanada.ca/rpt_det.php?id=437

Hellander, I., Himmelstein, D., & Woolhandler, S. (2013). Health crisis by the numbers: Data update from the physicians for a national health program's newsletter editors. In C. Estes & E. Williams (Eds.), *Health Policy: Crisis and Reform* (6th Ed.). Sudbury, MA: Jones & Bartlett Publishers.

Institute of Medicine (IOM). (2003). *Unequal treatment: Confronting racial and ethnic disparities in healthcare.* Washington, DC: The National Academies Press.

Institute of Medicine (IOM). (2011). *State and local policy initiatives to reduce health disparities.* Washington, DC: The National Academies Press. Retrieved from http://www.nap.edu/catalog.php?record_id=13103

Institute of Medicine (IOM). (2012). *How far have we come in reducing health disparities? Progress since 2000 Workshop summary.* Washington, DC: National Academies Press.

James, C., Salganicoff, A., Ranji, U., Goodwin, A., and Duckett, P. (2012, September). *Putting men's health care disparities on the map: Examining racial and ethnic disparities at the state level.* Menlo Park, CA: Kaiser Family Foundation. Retrieved from http://www.kff.org/minorityhealth/8344.cfm

Jerant, A., Arellanes, R., & Franks, P. (2008). Health status among US Hispanics: Ethnic variation, nativity, and language moderation. *Medical Care, 46*(7), 709–717. DOI: 10.1097/MLR.0b013e3181789431

Jones, D. S. (2006). The persistence of American Indian health disparities. *American Journal of Public Health, 96*(12), 2122–2134. DOI: 10.2105/AJPH.2004.054262

Kaiser Family Foundation. (2012, May). *Health care costs: A primer; key information on health care costs and their impact.* Menlo Park, CA. Figure 9: Percent Distribution of National Health Expenditures, by Source of Funds, 1960–2010, p. 18. source: Kaiser Family Foundation calculations using NHE data from Centers for Medicare and Medicaid Services, Office of the Actuary, National Health Statistics Group, at http://www.cms.hhs.gov/NationalHealthExpend Data/ (see Historical; National Health Expenditures by type of service and source of funds, CY 1960–2010; file nhe2010.zip).

Klees, B. S., Wolfe, C. J., & Curtis, C. A. (2011, November 1). *Brief summaries of Medicare & Medicaid Title XVIII and Title XIX of The Social Security Act as of November 1, 2011*. Washington, DC: Office of the Actuary Centers for Medicare & Medicaid Services Department of Health and Human Services. Retrieved from http://www.cms.gov/Research-Statistics-Data-and-Systems/Statistics-Trends-and-Reports/MedicareProgramRatesStats/Downloads/MedicareMedicaidSummaries2011.pdf

Krieger, J. & Higgins, D.L. (2002). Housing and Health: Time Again for Public Health Action. *American Journal of Public Health, 92(5)*, 758–768.

Lebrun, L. A. (2012). Effects of length of stay and language proficiency on health care experiences among immigrants in Canada and the United States. *Social Science & Medicine, 74(7)*, 1062–1072. DOI: 10.1016/j.socscimed.2011.11.031

Machenbach, J. P., Stirbu, I., Roskam, A-J. R., Schaap, M. M., Menvielle, G., Lelnsalu, M., et al. (2008). Socioeconomic Inequalities in Health in 22 European Countries. *The New England Journal of Medicine, 358*, 2468-2481. DOI:10.1056/NEJMsa0707519

Macinko, J. A., & Starfield, B. (2002). Annotated bibliography on equity in health, 1980–2001. *International Journal for Equity in Health, 1*, 1–20. DOI:10.1186/1475-9276-1-1

Menefee, L. T. (1996). Are Black Americans entitled to equal health care? A new research paradigm. *Ethnicity & Disease, 6(1–2)*, 56–68.

Minyard, K., Chollet, D., Felland, L., Lonergan, L., Parker, C., Anderson-Smith, T., et al. (2007). *Lessons from Local Access Initiatives: Contributions and Challenges*. New York: The Commonwealth Fund.

National Center for Healthy Housing (NCHH). (2008). *Who We Are*. Retrieved from http://www.nchh.org/who-we-are.aspx

National Institute on Minority Health and Health Disparities (NIMHD). (n.d.). *About NIMHD*. Retrieved from http://www.nimhd.nih.gov/default.html

National Institutes of Health (NIH). (2013). *The NIH Almanac. National Institute on Minority Health and Health Disparities*. Retrieved from http://www.nih.gov/about/almanac/organization/NIMHD.htm

National Prevention Council. (2011). *National prevention strategy*. Washington, DC: Author. Retrieved from http://www.healthcare.gov/prevention/nphpphc/strategy/report.pdf

Nazroo, J. Y. (2003). Public health matters: The structuring of ethnic inequalities in health: Economic position, racial discrimination, and racism. *American*

Journal of Public Health, 93, 277–284. Retrieved from http://www.ncbi.nlm.
nih.gov/pmc/articles/PMC1447729/

Nelson, T. (2009). *Handbook of prejudice, stereotyping and discrimination.* New
York, NY: Psychology Press, Taylor & Francis Group.

Ng, E., Wilkins, R., Gendron, F., & Berthelot, J. M. (2005). *Healthy today, healthy
tomorrow? Findings from the national population health survey.* Ottawa, Canada:
Statistics Canada.

Pratto, F., Liu, J. H., Levin, S., Sidanius, J., Shih, M., Bachrach, H., et al.
(2000). Social dominance orientation and the legitimization of inequality across cultures. *Journal of Cross-Cultural Psychology, 31*, 369–409. DOI:
10.1177/0022022100031003005

Ram, R. (2005). Income inequality, poverty, and population health: Evidence
from recent data for the United States. *Social Science & Medicine, 61*,
2568–2576.

Razack, S. H. (2008). *Casting out: The eviction of Muslims from western law &
politics.* Toronto, Canada: University of Toronto Press.

Robert Wood Johnson Foundation. (2012). Health Policy Disparities Fast
Facts. Web page. Princeton, NJ: Author. Retrieved from http://www.rwjf.
org/en/topics/rwjf-topic-areas/health-policy/disparities/DisparitiesFast
Facts.html

Ruffin, J. (2010). The Science of Eliminating Health Disparities: Embracing a New
Paradigm. *American Journal of Public Health, 100(S1).* S8–S9.

Shi, L. & Singh, D. A. (2008). *Delivering health care in America.* Boston: Jones and
Bartlett Publishers.

Shih, A., Davis, K., Schoenbaum, S. C., Gauthier, A., Nuzum, R., & McCarthy,
D. (2008). *Organizing the U.S. health care delivery system for high performance.*
New York: The Commonwealth Fund.

Smiley, J. (2009). The health of Aboriginal people. In D. Raphael (Ed.), *Social
determinants of health: Canadian perspectives (2nd Ed.)* (pp. 280–301). Toronto,
Canada: Canadian Scholars' Press.

Srinivasan, S. & Guillermo, T. (2000). Toward improved health: Disaggregating
Asian American and Native Hawaiian/Pacific Islander data. *American Journal
of Public Health, 90(11),* 1731–1734. DOI: 10.2105/AJPH.90.11.1731

Starfield, B. (2007). Pathways of influence on equity in health. *Social Science &
Medicine, 64,* 1355-1362. Baltimore: John Hopkins School of Hygiene and
Public Health.

Trahant, M. (2009, September 16). The Indian Health Service Paradox. *Kaiser Health News.* http://www.kaiserhealthnews.org/Columns/2009/September/091709Trahant.aspx

United States Department of Health and Human Services (USDHHS). (1985). *Report of the Secretary's Task Force Report on Black and Minority Health.* Washington, DC: U.S. Government Printing Office. Retrieved from http://health-equity.pitt.edu/3005/

United States Department of Health and Human Services (USDHHS). (2010). *Affordable Care Act of 2010* (P.L. 111–148, P.L. 111–152) (ACA). Retrieved from http://www.healthcare.gov/law/full/index.html

United States Department of Health and Human Services (USDHHS). (2011, April) *HHS action plan to reduce racial and ethnic disparities: A nation free of disparities in health and health care.* Washington, DC: U.S. Department of Health and Human Services.

United States Department of Health and Human Services (USDHHS). (2012a). The poverty guidelines updated periodically in the *Federal Register* by the U.S. Department of Health and Human Services under the authority of 42 U.S.C. 9902(2). Retrieved from http://aspe.hhs.gov/poverty/12poverty.shtml

United States Department of Health and Human Services (USDHHS). (2012b). American Indian/Alaska Native profile. In Data/Statistics on The Office of Minority Health website. Retrieved from http://minorityhealth.hhs.gov/templates/browse.aspx?lvl=2&lvlID=52

Waidmann, T. (2009). Estimating the Cost of Racial and Ethnic Health Disparities. *The Urban Institute.* Retrieved from http://www.urban.org/uploadedpdf/411962_health_disparities.pdf

Wells, S.J., Vergara, A.T., Dettlaff, A., Janke, R., & Doyle-Waters, M. (2011). *Interventions to enhance cultural competence of service systems and reduce health inequities: a multidisciplinary perspective; protocol for a systematic review.* Kelowna, BC: Centre for the Study of Services to Children and Families, University of British Columbia.

Wilkinson, R. G., & Pickett, K. E. (2009). Income inequality and social dysfunction. *Annual Review of Sociology, 35,* 493–511. DOI:10.1146/annurev-soc-070308-115926

Williams, M. J., & Eberhardt, J. L. (2008). Biological conceptions of race and the motivation to cross racial boundaries. *Journal of Personality and Social Psychology, 94,* 1033–1047. DOI:10.1037/0022-3514.94.6.1033

The World Bank. (2012). Health expenditure per capita (current US$). Washington, DC: Author. Retrieved from http://data.worldbank.org/indicator/ SH.XPD.PCAP

World Health Organization. (2013). *Health and Human Rights*. Retrieved from http://www.who.int/hhr/en/

Zoritch, B., Roberts, I., & Oakley, A. (2000 [3]). Day care for pre-school children. Cochrane Database Syst Rev. CD000564.

Conclusion

12

A Case Study:
The Texas Story

▸ ALAN DETTLAFF, ROWENA FONG, JOYCE JAMES,
AND CAROLYNE RODRIGUEZ

DISPROPORTIONALITY IN CHILD WELFARE AND other social service systems has been recognized as a nationwide problem for decades. In 1985, a report from the U.S. Department of Health and Human Services revealed a disparity in health status for minority populations compared to the White population (Heckler, 1985). Subsequently, national data has continued to elaborate on the presence of these disparities within and across health and social service systems. As additional data became available, Texas was identified as one of 46 states in which African American children appeared disproportionately in the foster care system (Texas Health and Human Services Commission [THHSC], 2006a). Texas state officials responded by establishing the Office of Minority Health in 1993, and the Office for the Elimination of Health Disparities a decade later, in 2003. The purpose of these new offices was to address health disparities and the unmet needs of the populations identified as marginalized (THHSC, 2006a).

In 2005, the 79th Texas Legislature passed Senate Bill 6, requiring comprehensive reform of the state's Child Protective Services (CPS) system. A significant component of this reform required the state to address the issue of racial disproportionality within this system. Specifically, the state was mandated to "analyze data regarding child removals and other enforcement actions taken by the department during fiscal years 2004 and 2005" and to "determine whether enforcement actions were disproportionately initiated against any racial or ethnic group, in any area of the state, taking into account other relevant factors," (Texas Health and Human Services

Commission [THHSC], 2006a, p. 3). If this examination revealed that disproportionality was present within the child welfare system, the department was required to develop and implement a remediation plan to address this issue and to prevent racial or ethnic disparities from affecting further enforcement actions.

The resulting analyses found that African American children were over-represented in the CPS system, and that the level of disproportionality increased at each stage of the service delivery system. In 2004, African American children represented 12% of the child population in Texas but comprised 19% of children reported for alleged maltreatment, 21% of children investigated, 26% of children removed from their homes, and 29% of children in foster care. African American children were removed from their homes at a rate more than double that of White and Latino children, who were both underrepresented at each stage of the system. Further analyses found that even when controlling for other factors including family income, age of the child, type of maltreatment, and source of report, African American children spent significantly more time in foster care, were less likely to be reunified with their families, and waited longer for adoption than White or Latino children (THHSC, 2006a).

Following these analyses, which confirmed the existence of racial disproportionality, plans were developed to address disproportionality throughout the state. These plans involved sweeping system changes as well as significant cultural shifts within the agency concerning agency practices and service delivery. In doing so, Texas became one of the leading states to address the problem of racial disproportionality in its child welfare system and a national exemplar for systems change. This chapter will provide a historical overview of the Texas child welfare system's efforts to address racial disproportionality, the resulting impact of those efforts, and how this work led to the state's current efforts to address racial disproportionality and disparities across service systems.

EARLY EFFORTS TO ADDRESS DISPROPORTIONALITY

Efforts to address disproportionality in Texas began as early as 1996, nearly a decade before the legislative mandate passed in 2005. At that time, CPS staff in the East Texas region of Beaumont, headed by Program Administrator Joyce James, recognized that more than half of all children entering foster care were African American, and African American children remained in foster care longer than their White counterparts (Belanger, 2002). To understand more about why this was occurring, the administration partnered with researchers from Stephen F. Austin University to examine the factors contributing to the high number of African American children entering the system in that region. This research found that African American children within this region were reported to CPS at a rate more than double that of White children, with this imbalance increasing at each subsequent stage of service delivery (Belanger, 2002). The study identified high rates of poverty and a lack of supportive services in many of the communities within the region as significant contributors to the observed disproportionality (Belanger, 2002). This research, the first of its kind in Texas, raised awareness of the overrepresentation of African American children in this system and developed into a commitment among the administration and staff in this region of the state to continue to explore and address this disproportional representation.

By 2002, James had become the regional director, and the administration partnered with Lamar University to conduct additional research to identify a specific community to begin the agency's efforts to address disproportionality, resulting in the identification of Port Arthur, a small community in Jefferson County. Recognizing the need for the involvement of community stakeholders in these efforts, Regional Director James held the first community forum to raise awareness and educate the community about the issue of disproportionality. Participants included parents, youth, and representatives from education, health, juvenile justice, law enforcement, housing, court appointed special advocates, city and county government, court personnel, and other community systems. During the forum, representatives from CPS shared their data on the overrepresentation of African American children and discussed potential solutions with community members (Casey Family Programs, 2010). This forum and subsequent community discussions led to the establishment of Project HOPE (Helping Our People Excel) in Port Arthur, an asset-based, one-stop service center designed to strengthen the community and provide needed resources. This model of engaging the community in strategies to address the shared concern of racial disproportionality became a model for later efforts to address disproportionality throughout the state (Casey Family Programs, 2010).

During the same time that Project HOPE was launching in the Beaumont region, the state agency that oversees the CPS system—the Texas Department of Family and Protective Services (TDFPS)—participated in the federally mandated Child and Family Services Review. This is a periodic review of state child welfare systems conducted by the federal government to assess the systems' progress in meeting federal child welfare requirements as they concern outcomes for children and families. The result of this review identified the need for improvements in the state's kinship care programs, including training and supportive services for kinship caregivers (Casey Family Programs, 2007).

Following this review, Texas entered into collaboration with Casey Family Programs (dubbed the Texas State Strategy) to address these issues as well as other system improvements. A leadership team was formed, which brought together leaders from both agencies to design and implement a statewide systems-change strategy to improve outcomes for children in the foster care system. In April 2004, Joyce James became the assistant commissioner of the Texas CPS system, bringing her knowledge and understanding of disproportionality at the regional level and a desire to examine this issue statewide. The Texas State Strategy was the perfect vehicle through which to approach the expansion James had in mind when accepting the state-level position, and Casey Family Programs' systems improvement team in Texas, under the leadership of Carolyne Rodriguez, was eager to engage in the discussion.

In May 2004, members of the leadership team met to examine the current data and to discuss the steps necessary to address disproportionality at the state level. Important priorities were identified in this meeting that shaped the state's approach to addressing disproportionality, including (1) the need to educate CPS administration, staff, and the public about disproportionality; (2) the need to develop and modify policy and practices to bring more awareness to disproportionality; and (3) the need to include consumers' voices in the planning and implementation process (TDFPS, 2004). At the same time, the success of Project HOPE in Port Arthur led Joyce James and other CPS and community stakeholders to develop plans to expand this work and to draft recommendations for system reform that addressed disproportionality. These recommendations were ultimately included in Senate Bill 6, the statewide CPS system reform bill (Casey Family Programs, 2007).

Beginning with the formation of the leadership team, change efforts were directed from the highest levels of the agency's administration. Leaders indicated that, in order to effectively address disproportionality, the internal culture of the agency needed to change. Thus, their role was to clarify expectations for administrators and staff at the regional and county levels and to reinforce the agency's commitment to addressing the issue of disproportionality. Building from the previously identified needs to inform system improvement efforts, the following frameworks were used by state administrators to guide the work throughout the state: (1) training based on antiracist principles, (2) values-based leadership development, (3) community engagement, (4) the use of data-driven strategies, and (5) the promotion of legislative mandates.

STRATEGIES FOR CHANGE—THE TEXAS STATE STRATEGY

Training Based on Antiracist Principles

At an early point in these efforts, the leadership team recognized that in order to address disproportionality, the issues of race and institutional racism would need to be discussed and addressed openly. Building from this, CPS entered into collaboration with the People's Institute for Survival and Beyond (PISAB) and adopted their approach to addressing racism to inform their work. PISAB was founded in 1980 and is an international collective of community organizers and educators dedicated to social change (PISAB, 2006). The philosophy of the People's Institute states that racism is "the single most critical barrier to building effective coalitions for social change," and that racism "can be undone only if people understand what it is, where it comes from, how it functions, and why it is perpetuated" (PISAB, 2006). The institute offers a two-and-a-half-day workshop that is designed to educate and empower participants to "undo" the structures of racism that hinder racial equality and to become effective organizers for change. The workshop, entitled *Undoing Racism,* was provided to state administrators and to administrators in the Houston and Arlington CPS regions as the foundation upon which efforts to address disproportionality would be built. *Undoing Racism* has since expanded throughout the state and to most administrators as well as to a significant number of frontline staff.

Values-Based Leadership Development

A key aspect of the Texas story has been the development of leaders throughout the state to facilitate the cultural change necessary to address disproportionality. The agency's approach to leadership development presumes that effective leadership is required to facilitate cultural change that is embraced by others. To facilitate this, the leadership team developed a vision and corresponding set of values that integrates the desired aspects of cultural change. The vision, "Children First: Protected and Connected," includes five core values: respect for culture; inclusiveness of families, youth, and community; integrity in decision making; compassion for all; and commitment to reducing disproportionality. In addition to supporting the values of *Undoing Racism* and community engagement, CPS administrators are charged with operationalizing these values in their daily management practices so that staff can see how these values are interconnected in their day-to-day work (Casey Family Programs, 2007; James, Green, Rodriguez, & Fong, 2008).

Community Engagement

A hallmark of the Texas story of addressing disproportionality has been and continues to be recognition of the need to involve community stakeholders and those directly impacted by disproportionality in the system's efforts to address this problem in order to create sustainable change. These stakeholders include CPS clients, youth in care, foster and adoptive families, community-based agencies, local government, law enforcement, and multiple service-delivery systems, including education, juvenile justice, health, and mental health. In collaboration with Casey Family Programs and Texas Strategic Consulting, CPS developed a four-stage community change model to address disproportionality, with the cornerstone of this model being the formation of community partnerships using the HOPE model as the foundation. The four stages of the model involve: (1) creating community awareness by raising the issue of disproportionality and sharing related data, (2) expanding the leadership to include community members and representatives, (3) developing relationships with community residents to learn their needs and the strengths of the community, and (4) encouraging community leaders to take responsibility for changes that go beyond the work of CPS into the community (THHSC, 2006b).

Data-Driven Strategies

The data that inform policy decisions can come from varying sources and disciplines. Independent studies have shown that the most influential data is that which reflects an issue that policymakers care about. It is also beneficial when policymakers are invited to participate in the development of research questions and formulation of data collection methods (Huston, 2002). Continuous dialogue of policymakers and community members that serve on advisory committees and participate in evaluative activities offers continuous consultation and insight into the needs of the policymakers in terms of decision making (Jefferys, Troy, Slawik, & Lightfoot, 2007). This process helps to make the research relevant to policymakers' concerns and creates a desire for the results when they appear.

In essence, a data-driven systems change framework advocates for a more holistic consideration of the problem that starts with the needs of the micro- or macro-subsystems before placing the need within the larger societal context. The approach is often in direct opposition to the symptomatology and assumed rationality that permeates many legislative proposals that seek to curb specific behaviors rather than create structural change by shifting societal norms (Stewart & Ayres, 2001). Defining a problem for a legislative audience requires empirical contributions from a multitude of stakeholders and multidisciplinary researchers typically engaged in the policy process (e.g., congressional staff, think tank analysts, lobbyists). Incorporating a data-driven perspective into the problem definition allows for a natural transition to proposal formulation, where the problem is framed for legislators and an engaged general public. In the briefings, committee hearings, and periods of public engagement that occur before a legislative vote for passage, research and general observations have shown that a proposal can take on many shapes as it makes its way through the political process (Henry, 2009). When considering social forces, strategies may shift as the parameters of what is legislatively possible expands or contracts. Social policy proposals that do not result from major public support can be scaled back in scope during the legislative process to more specifically address a desired behavior in a cost effective manner or are repositioned to fit within a larger legislative "vehicle" expected to move during the period of consideration. Thus, through the process of continual community engagement and education on the problem of disproportionality, as well as the ongoing use of data to describe the problem to community members and policymakers, the Texas leadership began the process of gathering support for policy mandates that would support comprehensive and systemic change.

Promoting Legislative Mandates

The four widely accepted steps in the policymaking process are (1) defining the problem, (2) developing and presenting a legislative solution, (3) implementing the adopted policy, and (4) evaluating the policy's impact. The simplicity of this model often masks the incremental, noncasual, and unpredictable characteristics that are indicative of the actual policymaking process experienced within legislatures across the country (Sabatier, 2007). Before a social policy or policy reform is adopted, a societal impetus must arise that drives the problem identification and subsequent definition for broader audiences. The driving force may stem from a variety of sources including a single noteworthy event highlighting a long-standing problem, such as revisions to child protection laws due to a particular case that highlights a systemic gap, or by contractions in the economy that lead to a period of renewed fiscal austerity and cuts to social service programs. Legislative sessions, moreover, are typically time limited when considering the multitude of public issues to be considered. Thus, by creating systemically data-driven information for legislators, a societal problem, such as disproportionality, can be defined in ways that build upon existing services in the community while avoiding unintended consequences, such as those created by the nonidentification or delinking of subsystems in marginalized communities. The immediate need for systems changes in public social service agencies is more obvious when data-driven strategies can be associated with identifying the problem.

Once a legislative proposal has successfully been adopted by the legislature, work needs to be done to steer the policy toward implementation and later to evaluation—the third and fourth steps of the policy process. From the preliminary examination of early program findings through to the long-term impact assessments, the final evaluation phase of the policy process affords opportunities to connect the dots between intervention sub-systems and changes in targeted populations.

Remediation Plan and Implementation of System Reforms

Data-driven strategies that revealed disproportionality and disparities in the public child welfare system, combined with the promotion of legislative mandates, led to the passage of Senate Bill 6 in 2005, which was the starting place for systemic change resulting from legislative action. Following the passage of Senate Bill 6 and the subsequent research documenting the presence of disproportionality in the Texas CPS system, the state was required to develop a remediation plan to address this phenomenon. Subsequently, TDFPS conducted a comprehensive evaluation of its policies and developed its remediation plan based on this analysis. Although most policies were found to be sound, several areas in need of program improvement were identified to enhance positive outcomes for children and families and to mitigate disproportionality. These improvements were informed by the system's values and vision and included changes to casework practice, training, workforce recruitment efforts, and engagement with external systems (THHSC, 2006b). Specifically, the following system improvements were identified and implemented.

Family Group Decision-Making Practice Model

To address the findings that African American children in Texas spent a longer time in substitute care, were less likely to be reunified with their families, and waited longer for adoption than White or Hispanic children, several changes were instituted. Most significantly, the Family Group Decision-Making (FGDM) practice model was implemented throughout the state. FGDM engages families (including youth, extended family, and community supports) in the planning and decision-making processes that occur once a child becomes involved in the child welfare system. For children who have entered substitute care, families participate in a Family Group Conference (FGC), where family members participate in the development of the child's service plan to ensure the child's safety, and they agree upon the goals and tasks that are necessary to facilitate reunification. In this process, the "family group" is vested with a high level of authority and decision-making responsibility in the development of this plan.

Data from the state's preliminary evaluation of FGDM indicated that this practice model led to considerable benefits for children exiting care. For families who participated in FGCs in 2004–2005 during the first 30–45 days following a child's removal from the home, foster care placements were decreased from 54% to 38%, relative placements were increased from 29% to 45%, and 31% of children whose families participated in an FGC were reunified with their families—compared to only 14% of families who did not participate in a conference (THHSC, 2006b). Additionally, these preliminary evaluations showed that FGDM held considerable benefits for African American families. Specifically, 32% of African American children whose families participated in FGCs were reunified with their families, compared to only 14% who did not participate in a conference (THHSC, 2006b). Thus, what initially began as a pilot program in just five cities in 2003 was expanded throughout the state as part of the state's efforts to address disproportionality.

Another component of FGDM, Family Team Meetings, was instituted for families in which children were at risk of removal to bring family groups together to develop a plan to ensure a child's safety and to prevent the need for removal. These meetings operated in a similar manner by engaging family members and others in the decision-making process to identify ways of protecting children and providing necessary services to family members while hopefully avoiding foster care placement (TDFPS, 2010).

Kinship Care

Another area of significant expansion involved increased supports to kinship (i.e., relative or kin) providers, both as temporary placements while children cannot remain in their homes and as permanent placements when children are not able to be reunified with their parents. Although relatives are often willing to care for children to prevent them from entering foster care, taking on this responsibility can be an emotional and financial challenge for many extended family members, and little supportive services had previously been available to them. Beginning in 2006, services to kinship caregivers were significantly expanded. Designated positions were established throughout the state to work specifically with kinship caregivers to ensure their needs were being met, including referrals for counseling, daycare, and other supportive services. The passage of Senate Bill 6 also provided for financial assistance to caregivers to address the multiple start-up costs associated with a new placement, including bedding, clothing, school supplies, and others, as well as yearly maintenance payments. Additional enhancements to the Kinship Care program included statewide training to ensure all staff were aware of the benefits available to kin caregivers, as well as improvements to speed the approval process for potential kinship placements (TDFPS, 2010; THHSC, 2006b).

Adoption

Because African American children were found to be overrepresented among those waiting for adoption, several improvements to facilitate the adoption process were instituted. These included streamlining the application process for potential adoptive parents and significantly expanded recruitment efforts for African American adoptive parents. These recruitment strategies included a faith-based initiative entitled Congregations Helping in Love and Dedication (CHILD), as well as a marketing plan and community engagement and public awareness efforts in African American communities. Additional improvements were made to the reporting and monitoring processes within TDFPS to track children's progress through the system and to prevent delays (TDFPS, 2010; THHSC, 2006b).

Family-Based Safety Services

In addition to the findings concerning African American children's exits from foster care, data also indicated that African American families were less likely than White families to receive in-home services to prevent removal in certain parts of the state. Thus, enhancements were made in the provision of in-home services, referred to as family-based safety services, including training to ensure caseworkers understood the values and strengths-based approach used in this model of service delivery and to ensure caseworkers were familiar with and had access to community resources necessary to support families. The previously described implementation of Family Team Meetings to prevent removal was also a critical part of the enhancements to this stage of service delivery (THHSC, 2006b).

Cultural Competence and Diversity Training

In addition to the statewide implementation of *Undoing Racism* training for administrators and staff, another training program entitled *Knowing Who You Are* was integrated into the foundational training program for new caseworkers as well as provided to current caseworkers throughout the state. *Knowing Who You Are* was developed by Casey Family Programs to help case-workers explore their own racial and ethnic identity, while educating them of the importance of healthy racial and ethnic identity formation among children in substitute care (Casey Family Programs, 2013). In addition to training new and existing staff, several improvements were made to recruitment and retention efforts to facilitate a more diverse staff (TDFPS, 2010).

Disproportionality Specialists

Specific positions were created that were dedicated solely to addressing disproportionality in the CPS system to ensure these efforts remained at the forefront of activities occurring throughout the state. These positions, entitled disproportionality specialists, were created in each region of the state. A statewide disproportionality manager was also hired to oversee all aspects of the efforts to address disproportionality and to coordinate activities across the state. These specialists worked to train and educate staff on the multiple initiatives put in place to address disproportionality as well as to ensure staff understood the multiple factors contributing to this problem and the need for systems change. Finally, disproportionality specialists worked in collaboration with staff and community stakeholders to facilitate the development of community-based efforts to address disproportionality within their specific regions and communities.

Regional Efforts to Address Disproportionality

In addition to the statewide systems improvements, regional efforts to address disproportionality were intended to engage community stakeholders using the Texas community engagement model and to respond to local concerns that impacted disproportionality as identified by members of communities affected by disproportionality. The Texas child welfare system is led by an assistant commissioner for CPS, who is responsible for leading the development of policy and for managing the CPS program on a state-wide level. The state is then divided into 11 regions and each region is led by a regional director. The Arlington region of CPS is a 19-county region in northern Texas that includes the cities of Dallas and Fort Worth. The Arlington region has the largest child population in the state as well as the highest numbers of completed investigations, confirmed victims of maltreatment, families receiving services, and children in foster care. Because of these figures, as well as the high number of African American children in foster care, the Arlington region was selected as one of two pilot regions (along with Houston) that would begin efforts to address disproportionality, with plans to expand to other regions at later dates, using lessons learned from the pilot regions.

THE ARLINGTON REGION—AN EXAMPLE
OF COMMUNITY ENGAGEMENT

Work in the Arlington region began in early 2005 with the formation of a regional advisory committee that would provide leadership and direction for the planning and implementation of each region's disproportionality initiatives. The advisory committee consisted of broad stakeholder representation, including representatives from the community and child and family serving systems, service providers, parents, kinship providers, and other community stakeholders. CPS and Casey Family Programs assisted the work of the committees with technical aid and logistics support. Due to the size of the Arlington region, participants agreed that the regional committee would function as a Steering Committee with oversight over the regional effort, with advisory committees organized by service areas that would focus on county-level initiatives to address disproportionality. Subsequently, advisory committees were formed in Dallas, Tarrant, and Denton counties, with selected members of each advisory committee also serving on the regional steering committee to provide information on county initiatives.

With this structure in place, the advisory committees focused on developing plans for community engagement, following the community engagement model. Efforts to raise community awareness began with a series of town hall meetings that were designed to educate the community about disproportionality and to inform community members of the agency's commitment to addressing this issue. Following these town hall meetings, a series of focus groups was held in each of the communities as a means of gathering the information necessary to guide the development of regional initiatives. These focus groups provided the opportunity to gather in-depth data from community members on their perceptions of the causes of disproportionality in their communities as well as their recommendations for how to address disproportionality. Focus groups were conducted through a partnership with university researchers and resulted in a report to the regional and advisory committees that outlined community members' perceptions of the factors contributing to disproportionality and recommendations for addressing this issue. Advisory committee members were then charged with the task of developing initiatives to respond to these recommendations. A summary of the issues and recommendations identified through these focus groups can be found in Dettlaff and Rycraft (2008).

Since 2005, multiple initiatives have been implemented across the region that were designed to strengthen the workforce and enhance the service delivery system to reduce the disproportionality of African American children. These initiatives included: (1) staff and community partners participated in *Undoing Racism* training, (2) multiple town hall meetings and community events were held to inform the public and the workforce of the commitment to address disproportionality, and (3) external funding was secured from a local foundation to enhance services and provide additional supports to African American children and families, particularly those in kinship care. These services and supports included a culturally competent parenting program for African American parents, training of community representatives to facilitate FGCs, case management services and support groups for kinship caregivers provided by a faith-based community agency, financial assistance to kinship families to facilitate placements and to prevent placement disruption, and a dedicated position (community resource manager) to identify and connect families with supportive community services to strengthen parents' and kinship caregivers' abilities to provide for their children.

EXPANSION TO OTHER REGIONS AND THE STATEWIDE TASK FORCE

Work in the Houston region followed a similar process to that in Arlington, which was subsequently followed by a third region's implementation in Austin beginning in 2006. Each of these sites used administrative data on rates of overrepresentation within their communities to guide their efforts, followed by a process of community engagement and information gathering via town hall meetings and community focus groups. As initiatives were implemented, *Undoing Racism* training was provided not only to staff working with those communities but also to community stakeholders engaged in these local efforts. Following the lessons learned from these regional sites, initiatives have since been established in each of the 11 regions of the Texas CPS system, led by each region's disproportionality specialist.

In addition, a statewide disproportionality task force was established in 2008 to bring together stakeholders from each of the regions. Task force members represented a broad range of community constituents, and state-level systems leaders were charged with ensuring that each region's efforts to address disproportionality were faithful to the state's vision and values underlying this work. Task force members also participated in developing the statewide evaluation plan to ensure that community input was obtained on the methods and strategies used in this evaluation.

STRATEGIES USED IN REGIONAL SITES

In addition to the strategies and program changes implemented across the state to address disproportionality, many regional efforts were also developed and documented to support and enhance this work. Although regional initiatives varied by community, a number of strategies that initially developed at the local level have since been implemented across the state to support the system's efforts to address disproportionality. A summary of some of these efforts is provided here.

SPOTLIGHT: STRATEGIES USED TO ADDRESS DISPROPORTIONALITY IN THE TEXAS CHILD WELFARE SYSTEM

Disproportionality Book Club

Engages staff by selecting and reading a book related to racial disproportionality with regional disproportionality specialists and promotes discussion of how the concepts in the book relate to their daily practices.

Case Mining

This practice uses a tool to probe into case records, upon the request of CPS staff, to identify potential relationships, permanency options, and other positive outcomes that may have been overlooked in previous stages of a case. Case mining is done in collaboration with disproportionality specialists, CPS staff, volunteers, and others.

Case Staffings

Regional disproportionality specialists participate in various staffings concerning children's cases to ensure culture is honored and to encourage staff to think creatively when identifying permanency and other well-being outcomes.

Chin Up, Mix-It-Up, and Speak Up

This one-hour presentation is facilitated by regional disproportionality specialists for teens in foster care to explore the impact of prejudice, stereotypes, and discrimination. The workshop encourages youth to take pride in their identity and to learn how to combat the effects of negative stereotypes.

Communication to Connections

This forum is designed to take the concepts from *Undoing Racism* to the next level by encouraging and helping staff to integrate the principles from this training into their daily practice. Facilitated by regional disproportionality specialists, this forum encourages staff to challenge their beliefs and to better understand how institutions provide privilege to some and not to others.

Courageous Conversations

This is a three-hour facilitated session that engages the audience in "Courageous Conversations" on race and racism that challenge beliefs and stereotypes while advocating for children, families, and other vulnerable populations. The forum enhances the knowledge of community and systems leaders in understanding institutionalized racism as the underlying cause of disproportionality and disparities.

Cultural Presentations

Disproportionality specialists provide presentations that discuss the importance of culture to promote deeper understanding of everyone's unique American heritage. Presentations are often timed to particular cultural events or holidays.

Diversity in Our Lives

This activity encourages staff to examine their own circle of influence and encourages discussion of how this shapes their worldviews. Discussion allows for courageous conversations and cross-cultural sharing.

Liberated Zone

This forum is open to participants who have gone through the *Undoing Racism* workshop and want to further discuss the concepts of the training or feelings that may have arisen in a confidential and safe environment. The "Liberated Zone" provides a supportive place for those committed to addressing institutional racism within systems.

Presentations to Local, State, and National Audiences

Disproportionality specialists and other administrators provide presentations for community audiences to inform them of the problem of disproportionality and the agency's commitment to addressing it in the child welfare system. These presentations provide a context for understanding disproportionality and encourage external stakeholder involvement.

Program and Unit Presentations

Disproportionality specialists often present to staff and management in all aspects of service delivery to review data, progress made, and challenges in the work to reduce disproportionality.

Talkback Forums

These forums encourage staff to further explore the concepts presented in *Undoing Racism* and *Knowing Who You Are*. They are designed to improve cultural awareness and sensitivity and encourage staff to consider the next steps in changing systems. Facilitation engages two individuals of different racial backgrounds to model respectful discussion. Participants often include individuals from other systems that impact child welfare outcomes.

Think Tanks

Groups of 10–15 regional staff members from all levels of service delivery meet monthly to think creatively about tools and strategies that can be used to reduce disproportionality. Membership in Think Tanks rotates periodically to allow a continuous input of new ideas and energy.

Values Miniseries

Disproportionality specialists facilitate discussions with staff over lunch. The content of these discussions is designed by the participants and addresses racial or cultural issues that have arisen in their work with families. The series focuses on staff self-awareness in order to reduce the potential impact of bias and stereotypes (adapted from Casey Family Programs, 2010).

STATEWIDE EVALUATION

In 2010, the Texas CPS system conducted a statewide evaluation of its efforts to address racial disproportionality and disparities (TDPFS, 2010). The study period focused on fiscal year 2005, when efforts to address disproportionality began, through fiscal year 2008. As indicated previously, because preliminary research conducted by the evaluation team at the beginning of these efforts identified that disproportionality in the Texas CPS system results from racial disparities in entries into substitute care and exits from care, the evaluation focused on changes at these points of entry into and exit from the system.

Findings indicated that the rate of entries into substitute care for White children statewide went from 6.1% in 2005 to 5.1% in 2008, a decrease of one percentage point. In comparison, the rate of entries into substitute care for African American children went from 8.7% in 2005 to 6.2% in 2008, a 2.5 percentage point decrease. Similar results were found at the county level; the disproportionality between White and African American children was reduced in four of the five largest counties in the state, including the regional sites where efforts to address disproportionality were initiated—Harris County (Houston), Tarrant County (Fort Worth), Bexar County (San Antonio), and Travis County (Austin).

Findings also indicated that some progress had been made in reducing the disproportionate rates of African American children exiting substitute care. Although African American children were still more likely to remain in substitute care when compared to White children, the length of time African American children stayed in care prior to an exit to reunification was reduced. Similar findings were observed for exits to kinship care. Not enough time had elapsed at the point of this evaluation to examine exits to adoption.

Although these gains in reducing disproportionality were acknowledged as small, and disproportionality was still present in the state, these gains were seen as notable improvements and as considerable progress in the state's overall vision to reduce and eliminate disproportionality. Rather than being viewed as a short-term initiative, efforts to address disproportionality had been institutionalized throughout the state by 2010, and the commitment to continue this work into the future remained throughout the agency. Major achievements identified by the evaluation team as contributing to these gains included:

- Institutionalization of *Knowing Who You Are* into the training academy for new caseworkers and continued implementation of *Undoing Racism* throughout the state
- Increased proportion of African American staff relative to White staff within the workforce
- Institutionalization of Family Group Decision Making throughout the state
- Implementation of the Kinship Caregiver Program to support relative caregivers
- Increased recruitment activities for African American adoptive parents
- Collaborative partnerships with community organizations in efforts to address disproportionality

TO THE FUTURE: THE CENTER FOR THE ELIMINATION OF DISPROPORTIONALITY AND DISPARITIES

Texas Senate Bill 758, endorsed by Senator Jane Nelson and Representative Patrick Rose, was passed by the 80th Texas legislature as a continuation of the child welfare reform efforts of Senate Bill 6. The goals of Texas SB 758 were keeping families together while ensuring child safety in the home, limiting the length of time that children remain in state care, and improving the quality of and accountability for care in the foster care system. Various provisions of the bill also facilitated adoption procedures, investigations conducted by CPS, and discharges from the child welfare system. The 80th legislature also provided funding for additional disproportionality specialists throughout the state. A growing number of efforts to address disproportionality and disparities spread to all CPS regions in Texas, and additional funding was allocated for continued training on *Undoing Racism*. This enabled communities and systems across Texas to begin to have a unifying analysis and common language from which to consider strategies to address disproportionality and disparities.

In September 2010, Health and Human Services Commissioner Tom Suehs created the Center for Elimination of Disproportionality and Disparities (CEDD) and appointed Joyce James to provide the leadership for expanding the Texas Model to all HHSC agencies. In addition, the Office for Elimination of Health Disparities was moved to the CEDD. The creation of the CEDD developed as a result of the significant gains that were made in reducing disproportionality within the Texas child welfare system and as an acknowledgement that the experiences and knowledge gained from these efforts could be used as the foundation for expansion and continued improvement across other health and human service systems.

In 2011, the 82nd Texas legislature passed Senate Bill 501, which replaced an earlier Health Disparities Task Force with the newly established CEDD. This senate bill provided the legislative mandate for CEDD requiring Texas HHSC to maintain the CEDD to address disproportionality and disparities across the Texas health and human service systems. SB 501 also mandated the creation and establishment of an interagency council for addressing disproportionality. SB 501 aimed to promote more comprehensive approaches across state agency boundaries to resolve disproportionality and disparities for the same populations. Such interagency collaboration was expected to increase the efficiency and effectiveness of the state's various, but previously uncoordinated, efforts.

The Interagency Council for Addressing Disproportionality drew representatives from relevant agencies and the public to "examine best practices and training, review the availability of funding, consider both entry into the juvenile justice, child welfare, education, mental health systems, and ultimate outcomes and make recommendations to the legislature to address disproportionality over the long term" (CEDD, 2011). The head of the CEDD serves as the presiding officer of the interagency council, along with the following representatives:

- Department of Family and Protective Services
- Department of Aging and Disability Services
- Department of Assistive and Rehabilitative Services
- Department of State Health Services
- Health and Human Services Commission
- Juvenile Justice
- Texas Education Agency
- Office of Attorney General
- Texas Supreme Court Judicial Commission on Children, Youth, Families
- Office of Court Administration
- Governor's Office on Criminal Justice
- Medical community
- Faith-based community
- Community-based organizations
- Foster care alumni

The legislation also closed the Office for Elimination of Health Disparities and transferred all of the former duties of this office to the CEDD, expanding the CEDD role to include serving as the State Office of Minority Health. This legislation and the creation of the CEDD provided a comprehensive statewide approach to the reduction of disproportionality across HHSC and other systems, elevating the level of accountability for systems serving vulnerable populations to develop strategies that cut across all systems in order to produce improved results for reducing disproportionality (CEDD, 2011). The state task force was eliminated once the interagency council was created, with most of the state agency representatives transitioning to the council.

The work of the CEDD is built upon a cross-systems approach that acknowledges that many families who receive services from one agency or system may also be receiving services from other systems. Thus, eliminating disproportionality and disparities requires cross-systems reforms that examine and address the factors that contribute to disproportionality across these systems. These include health, mental health, child welfare, juvenile justice, education, housing, and other systems that serve children, families, and vulnerable populations. Specific goals of the CEDD are:

1. To eliminate disproportionality and disparities in the health and human service systems
2. To raise the bar for those least likely to achieve positive outcomes so that the outcomes for all children, their families, and other vulnerable citizens served by health and human services are improved
3. To develop leaders who will be committed to understanding institutional racism and serve as role models while giving their staff permission to do the same
4. To enhance the health and well-being of all children, their families, and other vulnerable citizens served by health and human services system
5. To expand the knowledge and cultural competence of practitioners who work with children, families, and vulnerable citizens of color using antiracist principles
6. To preserve the fidelity and integrity of disproportionality and disparities work
7. To house relevant data and serve as the home for research, data analysis, and dissemination of data and reports by race and ethnicity
8. To expand the availability of resources offered to increase the awareness of disproportionality and disparities in the health and human services systems and to develop their best practices and methods to improve outcomes
9. To create tools and models that can be used where any racial disparities exist
10. To use data and the Texas Model for addressing disproportionality and disparities to drive systems improvement and accountability internally and across systems
11. To ensure the voices of youth, parents, and vulnerable citizens are heard and incorporated in a community engagement model
12. To ensure that the community engagement model is sustainable throughout systems and time

CEDD provides expertise in training and technical assistance, leadership development, shaping leadership policy, innovation, media, and marketing. The center is involved in several initiatives that relate to its mission to eliminate disproportionality. These initiatives include the Texas State

Partnership to Address and Eliminate Health Disparities; Learning Lunch Series; Nutrition, Physical Activity, Obesity Prevention and Tobacco Prevention; and African American Medicaid Managed Care Study. CEDD also has a Disproportionality and Disparities Resource Center, which provides educational and training resources.

OUTCOMES OF LEGISLATIVE AND SYSTEMS CHANGES: THE TEXAS IMPACT

Because Texas began its process of addressing racial disproportionality and disparities, first in the child welfare system and then broadening to a multisystemic effort to address disparities across systems, the state has been recognized as a leader in implementing and sustaining systems change. These efforts have led to a number of positive outcomes, within the state and across the country. These outcomes include:

- Legislative staff, judges, health and human services commissioners, and executive leaders of juvenile justice and education systems in Texas have attended *Undoing Racism* workshops to educate themselves about the issues and inequities seen in health and human service systems.
- Policymakers across Texas have expressed interest in replicating the one-stop service center as conceptualized by Project HOPE in their own legislative districts to ensure better access for families to services in their communities.
- Policymakers have become more informed about disproportionality and disparities and have begun speaking out about these concerns at conferences and in less formal venues, having recognized the importance of addressing these concerns.
- At least 11 other states have used SB6 legislation in Texas to craft legislation for advancing their own efforts to address disproportionality and disparities in child welfare and across systems.

CONCLUSION

Since 2005, Texas has become a model for other states, not only for its efforts to address disproportionality within the child welfare system but also for the way in which state leaders used their experiences in addressing disproportionality within the CPS system to inform this statewide multi-systemic effort. By uniting these efforts and coordinating them through a multisystemic approach, agency leaders share a common vision and common strategies to address the racial inequities that have affected children, families, and all vulnerable populations of color throughout the state, many of whom are involved in multiple systems. Today, the Center for the Elimination of Disproportionality and Disparities leads a multisystem, coordinated approach to the reduction and elimination of racial disproportionality and inequities for vulnerable populations in all systems.

REFERENCES

Belanger, K. (2002). Examination of racial imbalance for children in foster care: Implications for training. *Journal of Health and Social Policy, 15,* 163–176.

Casey Family Programs. (2007). *Engaging communities and taking a stand for children and families: Leadership development and strategic planning in the Texas child welfare system.* Seattle, WA: Author.

Casey Family Programs. (2010). *Processes, activities, and methods to impact disproportionality in the Texas child welfare system.* Seattle, WA: Author.

Casey Family Programs (2013). *Knowing who you are.* Available at http://www.casey.org/resources/initiatives/KnowingWhoYouAre/default.htm

Center for the Elimination of Disproportionality and Disparities. (2011). *About the Center.* Available at http://www.hhsc.state.tx.us/hhsc_projects/cedd/

Dettlaff, A. J., & Rycraft, J. R. (2008). Deconstructing disproportionality: Views from multiple community stakeholders. *Child Welfare, 87*(2), 37–58.

Heckler, M. M. (1985). *Report of the Secretary's task force on Black and minority health.* Washington, DC: U.S. Department of Health and Human Services.

Henry, C. (2009). The political science of immigration policies. *Journal of Human Behavior in the Social Environment, 19,* 690–701.

Huston, A. (2002). From research to policy: Choosing questions and interpreting the answers. *New Directions for Child and Adolescent Development, 98,* 29–42.

James, J., Green, D., Rodriguez, C., & Fong, R. (2008). Addressing disproportionality through Undoing Racism, leadership development, and community engagement. *Child Welfare, 87,* 279–296.

Jefferys, M., Troy, K., Slawik, N., & Lightfoot, E. (2007). *Issues in bridging the divide between policymakers and researchers.* Minneapolis, MN: University of Minnesota.

People's Institute for Survival and Beyond. (2006). *Our principles.* Retrieved from http://www.pisab.org/our-principles#undoing-racism

Sabatier, P. A. (2007). *Theories of the policy process* (2nd ed.). Boulder, CO: Westview.

Stewart, J., & Ayres, R. (2001). Systems theory and policy practice: An exploration. *Policy Sciences, 34,* 79–94.

Texas Department of Family and Protective Services. (2004). *Addressing disproportionality: 2004 end-of-year report and 2005 work plan.* Austin, TX: Author.

Texas Department of Family and Protective Services. (2010). *Disproportionality in child protective services: The preliminary results of statewide reform efforts.* Austin, TX: Author.

Texas Health and Human Services Commission, Texas Department of Family and Protective Services. (2006a). *Disproportionality in child protective services: Statewide reform effort begins with examination of the problem.* Austin, TX: Author.

Texas Health and Human Services Commission, Texas Department of Family and Protective Services. (2006b). *Disproportionality in child protective services: Policy evaluation and remediation plan.* Austin, TX: Author.

13

Future Directions for Eliminating Racial Disproportionality and Disparities

▸ *ROWENA FONG AND ALAN DETTLAFF*

FUTURE DIRECTIONS FOR ELIMINATING DISPROPORTIONALITY AND DISPARITIES

ETHNICALLY DIVERSE POPULATIONS ARE GROWING, and it is important to understand within and between group diversity in order to meet the needs of the changing demographics in the United States. The Latino population is the fastest-growing and largest U.S. minority group. By 2050, the Latino population is expected to double, reaching 30% of the total population. Within the Latino population, foreign-born immigrants make up 52% of Latino adults (Pew Hispanic Center, 2010). Thus, the Latino population has needs relevant to the native born and foreign born populations of adults, children, and families.

African Americans are the second largest minority group in the United States (U.S. Census Bureau, 2012). Although there are within and between group differences between Africans and African Americans, there is a tendency to uphold the stereotypic belief that "all Blacks are alike." As explained by McRoy and Runnels in Chapter 3, there is a distinction between the terms *Black* and *African American*; the term *Black* may or may not be inclusive of all persons of African descent. Race, as a socially constructed concept, has consequences for the experiences of and life opportunities for Africans and African Americans.

Although American Indian/Alaska Native children and families represent the smallest population among the four major ethnic minority groups, there are more than 566 federally recognized tribes living on 334 federal lands and state recognized American Indian reservations. According to Deserly in Chapter 6, 15 states have more than 100,000 American Indian and Alaska Native residents, with Alaska having the highest rate (19.5%) of any state for this racial group. To refer to American Indians/Alaska Natives as "Native Americans" does not acknowledge the diversity that exists by referring to their tribal name. As Deserly explains in Chapter 6, "Each Indian nation sets its own criteria for membership. . . . Criteria for citizenship in Indian nations may or may not be directly linked to biological heritage or to cultural identification. Only the nations themselves are capable of setting standards for citizenship. . . ."

Great diversity within and between groups exists among the Asians and Pacific Islanders. The traditional groupings of East Asians, South Asians, and Southeast Asians generally categorize the populations by geographic locations of home countries. Among the Asian American populations, immigrants and refugees still impact the diverse needs of each group. The traditional East Asian American populations of Chinese, Japanese, Filipino, and Korean have American-born and immigrant issues because family reunification is permitted through immigration laws. The fastest growing immigrant group is the South Asians from India. They have outnumbered the Southeast Asians—the Vietnamese, Cambodians, and Laotians. The purpose of pointing out the differences among the East Asian, South Asian, and Southeast Asian populations is to emphasize the great diversity within the populations, which may be associated with their differing representation levels in child welfare, health, mental health, educational, or juvenile justice systems.

For example, Godinet, Arnsberger, Li, and Kreif (2010) explain that among the Pacific Islander population in the state of Hawaii, "the children and families of Hawai'ian ancestry as well as the Pacific Island racial group that includes Samoans, Tongans, and Micronesians and others are shown to be consistently overrepresented in the child welfare system" (p. 388). Scholars continue to caution that although population groups such as American Indians and Asians/Pacific Islanders are underrepresented at the national level, further analyses at the state level indicate otherwise (Dougherty, 2003).

Disaggregating ethnic populations within racial groups because of marked cultural and historical differences (Godinet et al., 2010) is important in acknowledging the great diversity that exists and the complexity of the needs of people within the same racial group. Needs related to disproportionality and disparities ought to be addressed through culturally competent services offered in the various systems of care in child welfare, juvenile justice, education, mental health, and health. As part of the services offered, assessments and interventions need to be evidence-based and culturally competent to fit the ethnic population.

EVIDENCE-BASED CULTURALLY COMPETENT SERVICES

As the population of the United States has changed over the last several decades, so has the population of children who come to the attention of health and social service systems, resulting in increasing calls for cultural competence in all aspects of assessment, intervention, and evaluation. Historically, these activities have been designed and conducted from the perspective of the dominant culture, with a pervasive White standard often used in the development and implementation of health and social services. Yet over the past several decades, there has been increasing awareness that the specific social, cultural, and historical contexts of service recipients need to be embedded within the services provided by health and social service systems. As a result, it is important to provide services that address these contexts and that are meaningful and relevant to the population being served. Services that are embedded with ideas from the majority culture can be limited by a number of factors—conceptual mismatches, language barriers, differing values, or differences in the meaning and manifestation of emotions—each of which can lead to poor outcomes.

Even in systems that have made efforts to improve cultural competence in recent years, these efforts have often been limited in scope. Within many systems, efforts to improve cultural competence have primarily focused on U.S.-born populations, and discussions of cultural aspects have primarily focused on U.S.-born ethnic groups (e.g., African American, Asian American). Similarly, the evaluation of outcomes has primarily been approached from a nationalistic perspective, with the achievement of positive outcomes guided by predominant U.S. values and norms of health and well-being. Yet given the rapid growth of the immigrant population in the United States, it is important to understand the complexity of issues faced by immigrant children and families and to consider those issues when planning for services and evaluating outcomes. Indigenous interventions of immigrant populations should be considered and a biculturalization of intervention approaches to treatment may be necessary to assure culturally competent practices.

Thus, effective assessment, intervention, and evaluation of services designed for diverse cultures requires not only cultural competence but also an increased awareness and understanding of the populations being served. Providers need to understand how groups of individuals perceive the services being provided, communicate their views and experiences, and then respond to interventions. Further, providers working with diverse cultures need to understand a number of different variables within those cultures, including differences resulting from country of origin, level of acculturation, and socioeconomic status. As a result, cultural competency is not only an essential component of service systems but also a necessary skill for service providers.

Yet the notion of cultural competence is sometimes misinterpreted to imply that service providers must know everything there is to know about a particular culture in order to be competent in that culture. This interpretation of cultural competence may not be practical because it is not possible to be perfectly competent in every culture for which one might provide services. Rather, service providers need to have cross-cultural skills that allow them to have an open mind, to avoid making assumptions, and to gather the appropriate information to make accurate assessments and intervention plans. To do this, providers need to invest time learning about the history and culture of the population in order to understand what questions need to be asked and what interventions are culturally appropriate. For the service system, this will involve significant input from and collaboration with community-based stakeholders and others with expertise in the social, cultural, and historical contexts in which the system is based.

Although it is clear that there is a need for cultural competence in all aspects of service delivery, it is also essential that assessment and intervention activities be grounded in evidence-based practices. Yet the integration of cultural competence and evidence-based practice is often limited by the lack of data on the effectiveness of interventions designed to be culturally competent. Although there is a large body of literature on interventions that are designed to be culturally competent as well as existing interventions that were adapted to improve cultural competence, much of this literature lacks accompanying evaluations that could demonstrate the effectiveness of these interventions. Even in studies that include some form of evaluation, the outcomes are considerably limited by evaluation designs that failed to use appropriate comparison groups or that failed to isolate the cultural components of the interventions in order to demonstrate their effectiveness. For example, a recent systematic review of the effectiveness of interventions designed to improve the cultural competence of health and mental health services identified only 30 studies for inclusion in the review of more than 8,000 that were screened due to design limitations (Healey et al., 2012). Thus, the available evidence base on the use of culturally competent interventions is extremely limited. Considerable improvements to this evidence base need to be made in order for service systems to be able to successfully integrate cultural competence and evidence-based practice.

DISPROPORTIONALITY AND DISPARITIES IN CROSS SYSTEMS

Despite the limitations that exist in the current body of research on culturally competent interventions, the chapters in this text have addressed the current state of empirical knowledge across service systems and have provided recommendations for improving culturally competent service delivery in order to reduce disproportionality and disparities. Although these recommendations are expanded upon within their respective chapters, three primary issues identified within each of these systems are summarized here.

THE CHILD WELFARE SYSTEM

1. Research on the factors contributing to disproportionality in the child welfare system, as well as on strategies to reduce disproportionality, have largely focused on the African American population, although concerns are increasing regarding disparities affecting other children of color. Much additional research is needed to understand how disparities and disproportionality manifest themselves for Native American and Latino children, and strategies that address these disparities need to be implemented and evaluated.

2. Although there is a large body of research on disproportionality of African American children in the child welfare system, much of this research focuses on understanding these phenomena rather than on how to address or reduce them. The evidence base of strategies designed to address and reduce

disparities and disproportionality needs to be strengthened and improved, not only through additional research but also by ensuring that rigorous evaluation methods are employed.

3. Increased collaboration is needed across systems to more effectively meet the needs of youth involved in the child welfare system that intersect with the juvenile justice, health, mental health, and education systems. This collaboration is necessary to increase the understanding of the complex needs of crossover youth, as well as to improve service delivery.

THE JUVENILE JUSTICE SYSTEM

1. Similar to the child welfare system, efforts are needed to increase collaboration with other systems that children and families of color intersect. Youth involved in the juvenile justice system often have cross-system involvement with both the child welfare and mental health systems. Further, enhanced efforts need to be made to better understand and address the school-to-prison pipeline, whereby large disparities among youth of color in suspensions, expulsions, and school-based arrests contribute to the disparities that exist in the juvenile justice system.

2. In addition to collaboration among systems, increased collaboration and involvement is necessary with youth and the families involved in the juvenile justice system to ensure that their voices are heard and integrated into system improvement efforts.

3. Efforts are needed to improve the evidence base of interventions designed to reduce disproportionality in this system. Although promising practices have been identified, further research is needed to strengthen the evidence base of these interventions. Further, more attention needs to be given to the evaluation of cross-systems efforts to reduce disproportionality and disparities, such as those that involve collaborations with the child welfare, mental health, and educational systems.

THE EDUCATION SYSTEM

1. Efforts are needed to transform the culture within schools to one that is responsive to changing demographics. Although the populations of schools reflect these changing demographics, the practices, procedures, protocols, and structures have remained the same. As part of these efforts, attention

should be given to workforce development that ensures that educators are not only reflective of the populations whom they serve but also that educators understand the historical foundations of race and racism in the United States and how the existing structures within schools may perpetuate the inequalities that exist.

2. Educational systems need to be equipped with culturally relevant curricular materials and resources as part of the overall process of system improvement. This is necessary not only to engage diverse students but also to ensure that educational systems respect and value the histories, experiences, and value systems of culturally diverse groups.

3. Increased efforts need to be made to address the disparities that result from zero tolerance policies within educational systems. These disparities contribute not only to poor educational outcomes for youth of color but also contribute to their involvement in other systems, particularly to their involvement in the juvenile justice system. As part of these efforts, increased collaboration with the juvenile justice system is needed to better understand and address the school-to-prison pipeline.

THE MENTAL HEALTH SYSTEM

1. Efforts are needed that emphasize the development of a workforce of racial and ethnic minority professionals that are well-trained in evidence-based behavioral health treatments that address the diverse needs of youth and families of color. These efforts are necessary to not only facilitate culturally competent service provision but also facilitate engagement of children and families of color in the mental health system.

2. At the systems level, efforts are needed to address the institutional issues that contribute to bias and inequities. These include examining and addressing the ways in which funding streams, payment methods, insurance coverage, and other institutional policies limit access to services or otherwise perpetuate existing inequities.

3. Efforts are needed to ensure that the voices of children and families of color are included and valued in the development and delivery of mental health services. This can be addressed through multiple methods, including enhanced community engagement with communities of color, increased use of community-based paraprofessionals, and increased involvement of service recipients in policy development and service decisions.

THE HEALTH CARE SYSTEM

1. Because disparities in health are closely tied to the factors that affect health care for all, such as limited income and lack of health care benefits, addressing the financial and structural barriers to health care is essential because children and families of color are disproportionately represented among the poor and the near poor and among those with insufficient health benefits.

2. Efforts are needed to improve cultural competency and linguistic appropriateness within health-care systems to enhance and increase engagement of people of color in preventative services. These efforts need to be extended to the engagement of communities of color through direct interaction and access to services within those communities.

3. Efforts are needed to improve public awareness of health disparities and to improve health literacy among racial and ethnic minorities in order to increase engagement in health services. These efforts need to include considerable outreach and engagement to communities of color that are most vulnerable to these disparities.

CROSS-SYSTEMS THEMES

Although each system has unique issues that have emerged as priorities to address disproportionality and disparities, there are a number of common themes that provide future directions for eliminating disproportionality and disparities across systems.

1. Further research is needed that identifies culturally competent practices that demonstrate effectiveness in achieving positive outcomes for youth and families of color within and across systems. Systems need to ensure that culturally competent, evidence-based practices are integrated throughout all aspects of service delivery.

2. Improvements are necessary among service providers to ensure that the workforce is not only reflective of the populations whom they serve but also knowledgeable of the factors that contribute to disproportionality and disparities, as well as culturally competent strategies to reduce them.

3. Efforts are needed to improve access and equity of service delivery and to address the structural and institutional barriers that perpetuate inequalities in the access to and receipt of health and social services.

4. Children and families of color need to be involved in the development and delivery of services. This requires service systems to not only ensure that the individual voices of service recipients are heard and valued but also that service systems engage communities of color in system improvement efforts.

5. Much additional research is needed to better inform systems of strategies that can address and reduce disproportionality and disparities. Although practices have been identified within systems that have shown promising results, the evidence base of these practices is still in its infancy.

6. Increased efforts need to be made to facilitate cross-systems collaboration to address the multiple and complex needs of children and youth of color that intersect with multiple systems. Meaningful and comprehensive cross-systems efforts are needed to address these needs and to reduce the involvement of youth of color in these systems.

7. In addition to addressing the needs of crossover youth, increased efforts are needed to understand and address the complex pipelines that contribute to multiple system involvement. Systems need to collaborate across systems and with the communities they serve to address these pipelines and to reduce co-occurring system involvement.

Finally, future directions to address disproportionality and disparities for each of the ethnic minority populations addressed in this text are reproduced here:

AFRICAN AMERICAN CHILDREN AND FAMILIES

1. States must prioritize identifying factors leading to disproportionate outcomes across systems and must develop strategies to track and eliminate the disproportionality and disparate outcomes of individuals who move from one system to another.

2. Culturally based model programs need to be developed and evaluated for effectiveness in providing prevention, family support, resources for educational attainment, job skills training, and other services that will improve overall outcomes for African American families.

3. Programs utilizing the strengths of African American families to cope, to survive, as well as to thrive through strong religious beliefs should be developed to provide ongoing support for families to remain together and to prevent child removals.

4. Staff in various service systems must be required to receive training on service delivery to African American families and communities and to be regularly evaluated to assess effectiveness.

5. Family group or team decision-making practice models need to be widely implemented in order to enhance service delivery to African American families.

6. Service systems (mental health, education, child welfare, etc.) that are demonstrating differential outcomes for specific populations groups must be held accountable for inequitable outcomes, and funding should be tied to equitable and successful outcomes for all populations.

7. States should be given financial rewards for providing evidence of an increase in the number of family reunifications and of improved educational outcomes for children.

8. States should be rewarded for improvement in the number of African American children passing achievement tests, for reducing the number of African American men in prison, for reducing the number of child removals, for shortening the time African American children remain in out-of-home care, and for increasing the number of African Americans graduating from college.

LATINO CHILDREN AND FAMILIES

1. Further research is needed that addresses differences within the Latino population according to generation and citizenship status. Issues of country of origin and citizenship contribute to the diversity of the Latino population but also may considerably impact Latinos' access to and receipt of health and social services. Although some data is available concerning the differential involvement of Latinos in certain systems based on these factors, much additional data is needed to fully understand issues of over- and/or underrepresentation in service systems and how generation and citizenship status affect this.

2. Further research is needed that examines the effectiveness of culturally competent interventions with Latino children and families. Although there is a body of literature on interventions that may be effective with Latinos, much of this literature is limited by designs that fail to use appropriate comparison groups or that fail to isolate the cultural components of the intervention to determine their effectiveness. As a result, little is known

about how to adapt or develop interventions to improve cultural competence with Latino children and families.

3. Cross-systems collaborations are needed that address the pipelines that exist among systems that negatively impact Latino children, youth, and families. These collaborations should engage in efforts that enhance our understanding of the factors that contribute to cross-systems involvement and in the development of policies and programs designed to address the needs of cross-system youth to reduce their representation across systems.

4. Strategies to address disproportionality and disparities lie not only within systems but also within Latino communities affected by those phenomena. Systems need to engage with community partners to understand the factors that contribute to disproportionality and disparities and to develop programs that provide support for families in need. This includes community members, community service providers, law enforcement, the courts, schools, local government, and other community stakeholders. To be successful, a strategic plan for community engagement must be developed through a coalition of service providers and community stakeholders that emphasizes developing and utilizing support systems within the community to ensure access to needed services. Where resources do not exist, service systems need to work with community leaders to develop them. In doing so, systems need to recognize the barriers that may exist to community engagement. Within many communities of color, these barriers include fear, distrust, and a perception of some systems as harmful. Overcoming these barriers will require a longstanding commitment that begins with efforts to promote healing and a change in those perceptions.

ASIAN AMERICAN AND PACIFIC ISLANDER CHILDREN AND FAMILIES

1. The discussion on cultural ways of knowing and doing, indigenous knowledge, and cultural practices is a discourse that needs to continue. Asian and Pacific Islanders focus on cultural values as a means of knowing and behaving, which cannot be ignored in culturally competent practices. The traditional value of "saving face" needs to be respected when serving this population but not used as a justification for not providing the necessary social services needed.

2. Like the Lōkahi Wheel and Family Group Conferencing, indigenous knowledge can contribute to the understanding and improvement of the human condition. Indigenous knowledge requires a biculturalization of interventions, blending Western and indigenous approaches to addressing disproportionality and disparities.

3. Promising practices such as Family Group Conferencing facilitate opportunities for cross-systems work because the family system and the helping systems are able to dialogue in a conference setting that honors various perspectives and contributions to the solution.

4. The model minority myth is detrimental for Asians and Pacific Islanders who experience disproportionality and disparities in child welfare, mental health, and in health systems of care. The stereotype undermines the welfare, mental health, and health needs of this population.

5. Community involvement is important in cross-systems treatment to show respect for traditional cultural values and norms, to facilitate language interpretation for immigrant family members, and to monitor overgeneralizations that could be made leading to inaccurate assessments, inappropriate interventions, and to social services that are not culturally competent.

6. Particularly for Pacific Islanders, historical factors (i.e., colonization and loss of land, culture, and/or language), cultural dissonance, intergenerational disconnect, and context of migration are important factors to be cognizant of when assessing and engaging Native Hawaiians and Pacific Islander (NHPI) families in various cross systems because they will guide the practitioner toward more culturally relevant services for clients.

AMERICAN INDIAN AND ALASKA NATIVE CHILDREN AND FAMILIES

1. Increase awareness of disparities because systemic problems represent some of the most pressing challenges for American Indians/Alaska Natives. Community awareness must begin at many levels—from the tribal leadership level to the tribal (reservation) community level, at the urban Native organizational level, as well as among Native and non-Native agencies at the local, state, and federal levels. Attention must include accurate and current data related to the issue.

2. Engage tribal leaders and off-reservation Native leaders as well as community advocates and community members in a common mission to reduce disproportionality of American Indian/Alaska Native (AI/AN) across all systems, with an initial national focus on child welfare systems nationally.

3. Form community partnerships that include Native and non-Native agency leaders who are committed to the long and difficult challenges of systems change. Include mechanisms to gather data and track the effectiveness of the work.

4. Conduct culturally appropriate agency and community assessments followed by community-driven and multisystems strategic planning.

5. Conduct research to learn tribal, state, and national efforts to reduce the overrepresentation of AI/AN people, always documenting lessons learned in order to share successful prevention and intervention strategies.

6. Increase funding for off-reservation and on-reservation services that are designed to address community needs and to prevent the flow of American Indian/Alaska Native people into public systems, such as the criminal justice system, child welfare system, and so on.

CONCLUSION

Racial disproportionality and disparities are not caused by a single factor. Rather, as the chapters in this text have demonstrated, disproportionality and disparities are complex phenomena that have persisted for decades within and across health and social service systems. As a result, efforts to address disproportionality and disparities need to address the complexity of these factors across system levels, including those that exist within individuals, families, communities, and the health and social service agencies within which they manifest.

As stated in the introduction to this text, there currently exists some debate regarding the relative contribution of factors such as poverty, racial bias, risk, and need that result in disproportionality and disparities in each of these systems. Yet this debate largely serves to distract from engaging in efforts designed to address these phenomena. There is no question that disproportionality and disparities exist, and there is no question that they result in harmful outcomes for ethnic minority populations. Thus, it is imperative that researchers, practitioners, policymakers, and advocates unite in efforts to address and ultimately eliminate the disproportionality and disparities that exist within and across systems. These efforts should address the underlying social conditions that contribute to their existence and the agency and systemic problems that perpetuate them.

REFERENCES

Dougherty, S. (2003). *Mitigating the effects of racial/ethnic disproportionality.* Seattle, WA: Casey Family Programs.

Godinet, M.T., Arnsberger, P., Li, F., & Kreif, T. (2010). Disproportionality, Ohana conferencing, and the Hawai'i child welfare system. *Journal of Public Child Welfare, 4*, 387–405.

Healey, P., Dettlaff, A. J., Vergara, A., Janke, R., Jantz, I., Caplan, D., ... Wells, S. J. (2012). *Effectiveness of adaptations to enhance cultural competence, appropriateness, and safety of health and mental health services.* Kelowna, BC: Centre for the Study of Services to Children and Families, University of British Columbia.

Pew Hispanic Center. (2010). *Statistical profiles of the Hispanic and foreign-born populations in the U.S.* Washington, DC: Author.

U. S. Census Bureau. (2012). *The black population: 2010, 2010 census briefs.* Census Bureau Reports. Washington, DC: U.S. Census Bureau. Retrieved from http://www.census.gov/prod/cen2010/briefs/c2010br-06.pdf

EDITORS

DR. ROWENA FONG is the Ruby Lee Piester Centennial Professor in Services to Children and Families in the School of Social Work at the University of Texas at Austin and a Fellow of the American Academy of Social Work and Social Welfare. She is the past president of the Society for Society Work and Research. Dr. Fong received her BA in Chinese studies and psychology from Wellesley College, her MSW in children and families from UC Berkeley, and her EdD in human development from Harvard University. Her areas of research are focused on adoptions and child welfare, transracial adoptions and ethnic identify formation of Chinese adoptive children and families, domestic and international victims of human trafficking, and racial disproportionality in public child welfare. She has numerous publications, including seven books: A. J. Dettlaff and R. Fong (Eds.) (2012), *Child welfare practice with immigrant children and families*; C. Franklin and R. Fong (Eds.) (2011), *The church leader's counseling resource book: A guide to mental health and social problems*; R. Fong, R. McRoy, and C. Ortiz Hendricks (Eds.) (2006), *Intersecting child welfare, substance abuse, and family violence: Culturally competent approaches*; R. Fong, (Ed.) (2004), *Culturally competent practice with immigrant and refugee children and families*; M. Smith and R. Fong (2004), *Children of neglect: When no one cares*; R. Fong and S. Furuto (Eds.) (2001) *Culturally competent social work practice: Skills, interventions and evaluation*; and E. Freeman, C. Franklin, R. Fong, G. Shaffer, and E. Timberlake (Eds.) (1998), *Multisystem skills and interventions in school social work practice*. Dr. Fong received the 2008 Distinguished Recent Contributions in Social Work Education Award of the Council on Social Work Education; the 2007 Texas Exes Teaching Award of the University of Texas at Austin; the 2001 Regent's Teaching Award of the University of Hawaii at Manoa; and the 2001 Social Worker of the Year in Education and Training of the National Association of Social Work, Honolulu Chapter. She has served on the editorial boards of *Social Work, Journal of Social Work Education, Research and Social Work Practice, Journal of Ethnic and Cultural Diversity in Social Work* and is currently serving on *Child Welfare, Journal of Public Child Welfare,* and *Journal of Social Work Education.*

ALAN DETTLAFF, PHD, MSW, is an associate professor in the Jane Addams College of Social Work at the University of Illinois at Chicago. Dr. Dettlaff received his PhD in social work from the University of Texas at Arlington in 2004. His practice background includes several years in public child welfare as a practitioner and administrator, where he specialized in investigations of child maltreatment. Dr. Dettlaff's research focuses on understanding and addressing racial disparities in the child welfare system, with a particular emphasis on understanding and addressing the unique needs of Latino and immigrant children involved in this system. He has published numerous articles in peer-reviewed journals addressing these topics. Dr. Dettlaff is cochair of the Migration and Child Welfare National Network, a coalition of individuals and organizations focused on the needs of immigrant families involved in the child welfare system. Through this network, Dr. Dettlaff conducts research and develops and disseminates resources to improve service delivery to immigrant children and families. Along with Rowena Fong, he is editor of *Child Welfare Practice with Immigrant Children and Families* (2012). He also sits on the editorial boards of *Child Welfare, Child Abuse & Neglect,* and *Journal of Public Child Welfare.*

JOYCE JAMES has established an impressive 34-year history in the field of child welfare. Her voice has been influential in Texas and nationally in raising and increasing awareness about disproportionality and disparities that affect African American children and other vulnerable populations. Ms. James served as the assistant commissioner for Texas Child Protective Services (CPS) from 2004–2009, leading successful renewal efforts resulting in reduction in disproportionality for African American and Native American children and overall improved outcomes for all children, youth, and families. Her testimony during the 2005 legislative session contributed to Texas becoming the first state in the country to implement legislation to address disproportionality. Ms. James served as the associate deputy executive commissioner of the Center for Elimination of Disproportionality and Disparities (the Center) and the State Office of Minority Health at the Texas Health and Human Services Commission (HHSC) from September 2010–September 2013. The Center was created out of recognition that the Texas Model, created under

Ms. James' leadership that resulted in significant and unprecedented improvements in CPS, should be applied in addressing disproportionality and disparities in all HHSC agencies. Senate Bill 501, enacted during the 82nd Texas legislative session, statutorily established the Center and expanded its role by creating an 18-member interagency council of which Ms. James was chair. The role of the council was to identify, examine, and make recommendations to the Texas legislature for reducing and ultimately eliminating racial disparities in child welfare, juvenile justice, education, and mental health services for children. Ms. James is coauthor of several articles, has presented at congressional briefings, and has received numerous awards for her leadership, advocacy, and willingness to speak out on issues impacting the most vulnerable of populations. Ms. James is currently a private racial equity consultant bringing her years of experience and expertise to multiple states and systems in Texas and across the country, assisting through recommendations on practice models for improving outcomes for children, youth, and families, leadership development, data-driven strategies, community engagement, cross systems collaborations and the importance of addressing disproportionality and disparities using antiracist principles and practices.

CAROLYNE RODRIGUEZ, LCSW, ACSW, has worked in the child welfare field since 1970, with her most recent work focusing on broad, systemic changes in all stages of child protective services; on kinship and transition services; and on impacting disproportionality and disparate outcomes of children of color in child welfare system and other related systems. She directed the systems improvement work in Texas for Casey Family Programs from 2002 through 2013. The Texas Strategic Consulting involved a collaborative effort between Casey Family Programs and the state child welfare system as well as numerous stakeholders and other systems. Ms. Rodriguez retired from Casey Family Programs on May 31, 2013, after more than 28 years of service to the organization. She earned her BA from the University of Texas at Austin in May 1969 and her MSW from Our Lady of the Lake University, Worden School of Social Service, in San Antonio in 1983. Ms. Rodriguez has received various awards, including Casey Family Programs' 2008 Linda Wilson Diversity and Anti-Racism Award; the 2007 Bill Underwood Award, presented by the Family Preservation Institute; the 2005 Commissioner's Award for Outstanding Leadership and Service in the Prevention of Child Abuse and Neglect, presented by the Department of Health and Human Services, Administration of Children and Families; and recognition awards in 2006 and 2009 from the Texas Department of Family and Protective Services and in 2011 from the Health and Human Services Center for the Elimination of Disproportionality and Disparities for collaborative partnering to eliminate disproportionality and disparities in child welfare and related systems. She was recently recognized for her six years of service as an appointed commissioner on the Texas Supreme Court Commission on Children, Youth and Families. Ms. Rodriguez now privately consults and provides technical assistance and project support for various topics in the human services field. Her most recent assignment involves collaborative support, technical assistance, and consultation for statewide faith-based initiatives of the Texas child welfare system. She will also be assisting the Texas Health and Human Services Center for the Elimination of Disproportionality and Disparities in the final development and statewide rollout of the center's developing cultural competency curriculum.

CONTRIBUTORS

MARGARITA ALEGRÍA, PHD, is the director of the Center for Multicultural Mental Health Research at the Cambridge Health Alliance and is a professor in the department of psychiatry at Harvard Medical School. She currently serves as principal or coprincipal investigator of three National Institutes of Health (NIH)-funded research studies. Dr. Alegría's published work focuses on the improvement of health care services' delivery for diverse racial and ethnic populations, conceptual and methodological issues with multicultural populations, and ways to bring the community's perspective into the design and implementation of health services. She has actively mentored numerous students and junior investigators. Dr. Alegría has received numerous awards including the 2003 Mental Health Section Award of the American Public Health Association (APHA), the 2008 Health Disparities Innovation Award from the National Center on Minority Health and Health Disparities (NCMHD), the 2008 Carl Taube Award from APHA, the 2009 Simon Bolivar Award from the American Psychological Association, the 2011 Harold Amos Diversity Award from the Harvard Medical School, and the Award of Excellence in Mentorship from the National Hispanic Science Network on Drug Abuse. In October 2011, she was elected to be a member of the Institute of Medicine.

ELIZABETH BOWEN, AM, LCSW, is a doctoral candidate in the Jane Addams College of Social Work at the University of Illinois at Chicago. She earned her master's degree from the University of Chicago School of Social Service

Administration and has several years of practice experience working with homeless people affected by HIV/AIDS, substance use, and other health and mental health conditions. Her research interests include place-based health disparities, the social determinants of health and risk behaviors, and homelessness, drug use, and HIV/AIDS as intersecting epidemics. In addition, Elizabeth is interested in international social work education and served as a Fulbright English Teaching Assistant in rural Malaysia in 2009.

TIANCA CROCKER, MSW, is a doctoral student at the University of Texas at Austin School of Social Work and is project manager at the Center for Budget and Policy Priorities. She was a health disparities specialist for the Department of Health and Chronic Disease Prevention and Control in Richmond, Virginia.

KATHY DESERLY, a graduate of the San Diego State University Native Teacher Training Project, has worked in the field of child and family services in Native communities since 1974. She spent 12 years serving tribal communities in Southern California, as assistant director of a Native American foster and adoption agency, before joining the National Indian Child Welfare Association in 1993 as a community development specialist. Kathy later spent five years as Indian Child Welfare Specialist for the State of Montana, Child and Family Services. In 2004, she cofounded the Indian Child and Family Resource Center (ICFRC), a training and technical assistance center for Tribal social service programs. ICFRC is a partner in the new National Resource Center for Tribes where Kathy also serves as associate director. Kathy continues to provide extensive training and technical assistance to Native and non-Native programs related to tribal child welfare and Native disproportionality issues. She and her husband Lannie, a member of the Assiniboine Tribe, reside in Helena, Montana.

SARAH GIRLING is a research assistant at the Centre for the Study of Services to Children and Families based at the University of British Columbia, Canada. Sarah is from the United Kingdom, where she worked as a registered nurse before further qualifying as a lawyer. Upon qualification, Sarah gained significant experience as a lawyer specializing in child welfare and protection.

DR. MERIPA GODINET is an associate professor with the Myron B. Thompson School of Social Work at the University of Hawaii. She has been a principal investigator of numerous research projects that focused on the impact of various systems and institutions on Pacific Islander adolescents and their families. Her scholarship include issues of disproportionality and overrepresentation of Pacific Islanders in the juvenile justice and child welfare systems, risk and

protective factors involving juvenile delinquency among Pacific Islander adolescents, and advancement of cross-cultural resonance in social work practice.

DEENA HAYES is a racial equity consultant, trainer, and community/institutional
organizer whose work focuses on the impacts of race and racism on systems,
institutions, organizations, and individuals. She seeks to instigate a national
examination on the impact of race in systemic outcomes to include the broader
environmental and social determinants of well-being and opportunity. She
has presented keynote speeches, workshops, and seminars across the nation to
organizations interested in addressing and eliminating racial and ethnic inequities. Ms. Hayes is a former human relations commissioner for the city of
Greensboro, North Carolina. She has served on the Guilford County Board
of Education since she was elected in 2002. She chairs the Achievement Gap
Committee, the Historically Underutilized Business (HUB) Advisory Committee, and the School Safety/Gang Education Committee. As a member of
the Guilford County Board of Education, her advocacy has challenged the district to investigate the structural causes of the disparate outcomes of African
Americans and other students of color. As chair of the HUB Advisory Committee, she has illuminated the disparities in school construction and goods
and services data and initiated efforts focused on examining institutional practices and systemic barriers. Ms. Hayes currently serves as chair of the board of
the International Civil Rights Center and Museum, the Guilford Gang Commission, and the Ole Asheboro Street Neighborhood Association. She received
her BA in African American studies, psychology, and justice and policy studies
from Guilford College. She lives with her family in Greensboro.

MICHELLE JOHNSON-MOTOYAMA, PHD, MSW, is associate professor at the University of Kansas, School of Social Welfare. Dr. Johnson-Motoyama's research
focuses on community-based approaches to child maltreatment prevention and
on the elimination of disparities in child health and child welfare. She completed her PhD at the University of California, Berkeley, where she received
several awards for her dissertation regarding the role of neighborhood dynamics in the Hispanic infant health paradox. Her subsequent research on the
health and development of vulnerable Latino children and families has been
supported by the National Institutes of Health; the University of California,
Los Angeles (UCLA); the University of Kansas; and the Silberman Fund in
the New York Community Trust. She received her BS and MSW from the
University of Illinois at Urbana-Champaign. Prior to joining the faculty of the

University of Kansas, Dr. Johnson-Motoyama was an assistant professor at the UCLA Department of Social Welfare, Luskin School of Public Affairs.

DR. LAWANNA LANCASTER is an associate professor of social work at Northwest Nazarene University (NNU) in Nampa, Idaho. Prior to moving into full-time teaching at NNU, Lawanna spent several years working in the child welfare arena, including the Title IV-E program at NNU, partnering with the state of Idaho to conduct foster parent training. Lawanna has primarily taught research for undergraduate and graduate students, supervising more than 25 MSW theses. She administered the MSW field program for five years and is now the chair of the social work department and the MSW program director at NNU. During the course of her PhD program at the University of Texas at Austin, Lawanna focused on child welfare issues and racial/ethnic disproportionality in foster care, writing her dissertation on disproportionality for Latinos and Native Americans in the Idaho foster care system. Lawanna enjoys teaching and research, particularly data analysis, and hopes to continue to study the area of child welfare.

TOM LIDOT is an enrolled member of Chilkat Indian Village (where his grandmother was born). He is actively involved with local, regional, and national Tribal issues related to health, child welfare, and self-determination. His work experience is built on direct service expansion for health-care and education programs since 1989. His experience in mediation/alternative dispute resolution serves as the foundation for his approach to cross-cultural training and facilitation. He has served as the curriculum coordinator for Tribal STAR (Successful Transitions for Adult Readiness) since 2003. He also leads Pacific Mountain Philanthropy, a team of executives with experience providing local, regional, and national training and technical assistance that has been improving outcomes for American Indian/Alaska Native communities since 2000. He walks in two worlds—as a Tribal member who strives to maintain culture and tradition and as an active advocate for the advancement of science and education.

HENRIKA McCOY, MSW, MJ, PHD, is an assistant professor at the Jane Addams College of Social Work at the University of Illinois at Chicago. She has been previously funded as a principal investigator by the Robert Wood Johnson Foundation New Connections program, Boston College, and the Institute for Research on Race and Policy for a project focused on identifying strategies to change the negative trajectories for youth of color with mental health disorders in the juvenile justice system. Her research interests include the intersection between mental health disorders and juvenile delinquency for youth of color; addressing the broader issues that create and sustain the race and ethnic disproportionality and disparities in the juvenile justice system; and identifying strategies for increasing measurement equivalence on mental health screening tools for youth of color in the juvenile justice system. She currently serves as a member of the Illinois Juvenile Justice Commission, Disproportionate Minority Confinement Committee.

RUTH G. MCROY, became the first holder of the Donahue and DiFelice Endowed Professorship at Boston College Graduate School of Social Work in September 2009. From 2005 to 2009, she served as a visiting research professor and consultant at Boston College. Prior to joining the Boston College faculty, McRoy was a faculty member at the University of Texas (UT) at Austin School of Social Work for 25 years. While at UT, she served for 12 years as the director of the Center for Social Work Research, director of the Diversity Institute, and in 2002, became the associate dean for research. Dr. McRoy has published numerous articles, book chapters, and ten books, including: *Transracial and Inracial Adoptees: The Adolescent Years* (with L. Zurcher, 1983); *Social Work Practice with Black Families* (with S. Logan and E. Freeman, 1990); *Openness in Adoption: Family Connections* (with H. Grotevant, 1998); *Special Needs Adoptions: Practice Issues* (1999); *Challenging Racial Disproportionality in Child Welfare* (with D. Green, K. Belanger, and L. Bullard, 2011); *Intersecting Child Welfare, Substance Abuse and Family Violence: Culturally Competent Approaches* (with R. Fong and C. Ortiz-Hendricks, 2006); and *Building Research Culture and Infrastructure* (with J. Flanzer and J. Zlotnik, 2012).

E. SUSANA MARISCAL, MSW, is a doctoral candidate at the University of Kansas, School of Social Welfare. She has a *Licenciatura* from the Catholic University of Bolivia and an MSW from the University of Kansas, where she is currently a research assistant in the Office of Child Welfare and Children's Mental Health. Her career has focused on family violence prevention and resilience. She has developed programs to prevent child sexual abuse, child maltreatment, and to enhance youth resilience for diverse nongovernmental organizations in Bolivia, such as UNICEF, Foundation La Paz, and S.O.S. Villages. Susana has made several invited and refereed presentations of her research at national and international conferences. As a Fulbright Scholar, she is interested in international social work as well as violence prevention, resilience, and the strengths perspective, particularly among Latinos.

ORA NAKASH, PHD, is an assistant professor at the School of Psychology at the Interdisciplinary Center in Herzliya, Israel. She earned her doctorate in clinical psychology at Boston University and completed post-doctoral training at the Cambridge Health Alliance/Harvard Medical School. Her research focuses on the study of the effects of social and cultural factors on mental health with a specific interest in mental health disparities, with the goal of improving the access, equity, and quality of these services for disadvantaged and minority populations. She has a private practice in Modiin, Israel.

DANIEL C. ROSEN, PHD, is an associate professor at Bastyr University in the Department of Counseling and Health Psychology. He earned a PhD in counseling psychology from Arizona State University after completing his predoctoral internship at the Center for Multicultural Training in Psychology at Boston Medical Center/Boston University School of Medicine. He completed his postdoctoral fellowship at Cambridge Health Alliance/Harvard Medical School. Dr. Rosen's scholarship is focused in multicultural psychology, and he has explored issues of ethnic identity, social justice in mental health—addressing disparities in access to and quality of mental health services—and the experiences of persons with disabilities. He has a private practice in Seattle, Washington.

RATONIA C. RUNNELS, PHD, is a licensed master social worker and is on the faculty at Texas Woman's University in Denton, Texas. Her research focuses on the intersection of spirituality and culture and its impact on social work practice and public health. Dr. Runnels has extensive training and experience in community outreach, counseling, training, and advocacy in the fields of HIV/AIDS services and substance abuse prevention. Her contributions include publications on topics such as church-based mental health services, spirituality among trauma survivors and women with chronic illness, disproportionality and health disparities among minority populations, and presenting at national and international conferences.

BRITT URBAN is a licensed clinical social worker in Austin, Texas, who is currently serving in Peace Corps Latin American in the Youth in Development sector. Ms. Urban graduated with an MSW from the University of Texas at Austin (UT Austin) in 2008 and began working in inpatient and outpatient mental health settings, where she developed her clinical skills through work with individuals, groups, and families. She then worked for several years as a victim counselor with survivors of family violence and sexual assault. In addition to her role as a clinician, Ms. Urban worked as a research associate at the UT Austin

School of Social Work for three years, examining human trafficking, international adoption, and disparities within the child welfare system. She has been active in the social work community, acting as a field instructor for BSW and MSSW students and serving as a board member of the Social Work Alumni Network. Ms. Urban graduated from the University of Oregon in 2001 with a BA in political science.

ANDREW VERGARA is currently pursuing his MA in child and youth care at the University of Victoria. He previously completed a BS at the University of Manitoba (focus in zoology and microbiology) and a BS at the University of British Columbia (honours psychology). His research has included developing treatments for concurrent disorders in Aboriginal populations; evaluating cultural appropriateness in health, mental health, and juvenile justice disciplines; and evaluating social work practice models. Andrew has gained much experience working with children and families through his employment with Aboriginal social work and bail support agencies. During his free time, he enjoys playing and coaching various sports.

ANGELA M. WARD manages the Austin Independent School District (AISD) focus on Cultural Proficiency and Inclusiveness and is motivated to study local implications of the multiple relationships of education to culture, power, and society. Prior to leading this effort as a district administrator, she served as campus administrator, teacher leader, and classroom teacher. As an expert on differentiation of curriculum, she led her district in writing the first curriculum documents. In collaboration with partners from the University of Texas (Austin), Angela presented AISD Central Office Cultural Proficiency work at the 2012 Critical Race Studies in Education Conference, Columbia University, and was invited to present at the 2014 Hawaii International Conference on Education, Honolulu. A doctoral student at the University of Texas at Austin in the Department of Curriculum and Instruction, Angela is focused on cultural studies in education. Currently, she serves on the board of directors of Learning Forward Texas (LFTX), an affiliate of the international organization the purpose of which is engaging adult learners in the field of education in meaningful, effective, professional learning.

SUSAN J. WELLS is professor at the University of British Columbia where she holds a joint appointment in psychology and social work. Dr. Wells is principal investigator of the Canadian Institutes of Health Research funded project, "Interventions to enhance cultural competence of service systems and reduce health inequities: A multidisciplinary perspective," in which her research team conducted a systematic review of interventions in the health and mental health disciplines to reduce health disparities. In 2007, Dr. Wells brought together community representatives, researchers, practitioners, and policymakers to formulate an approach to ensuring that evidence-based practice in child welfare is culturally competent. A special issue of *Children and Youth Services Review*, on the intersection of evidence-based practice and cultural competence, followed in 2009. She recently received funding from the Canadian Foundation for Innovation to establish a Centre for the Study of Services to Children and Families to focus on the development of research to better identify and test effectiveness of interventions with an emphasis on serving diverse populations.

CPSIA information can be obtained
at www.ICGtesting.com
Printed in the USA
JSHW052053170122
22064JS00001B/17